# A HISTORY OF BRITISH INDUSTRIAL RELATIONS
## 1914 – 1939

# MODERN REVIVALS IN ECONOMIC AND SOCIAL HISTORY
*Series Editor: Professor Chris Wrigley*

# A HISTORY OF BRITISH INDUSTRIAL RELATIONS 1914–1939

Edited by
Chris Wrigley

*Professor of Modern British History,
University of Nottingham*

*Gregg Revivals*

First published in Great Britain in 1987 by
The Harvester Press Limited

Reprinted in 1993 by
Gregg Revivals
Gower House
Croft Road
Aldershot
Hampshire GU11 3HR
England

Gregg Revivals
Distributed in the United States by
Ashgate Publishing Company
Old Post Road
Brookfield
Vermont 05036
USA

British Library Cataloguing in Publication Data

History of British Industrial Relations. -
1914-1939. - New ed
  I. Wrigley, Chris
  331.0941

  ISBN 0-7512-0181-2

Printed by The Ipswich Book Co.

# Contents

# List of Tables

vi

# List of Contributors

**Dr Howard F Gospel** is Senior Lecturer in Industrial Relations at the University of Kent, and Research Fellow of the Business History Unit at the London School of Economics.

**Dr Richard Hyman** is Professor of Industrial Relations at the University of Warwick.

**Dr Rodney Lowe** is Lecturer in Economic and Social History at the University of Bristol.

**Dr Joseph Melling** is Lecturer in Economic History at the University of Exeter.

**Dr Steven Tolliday** is Professor in Economic and Social History at the University of Leeds.

**Dr Noel Whiteside** is Senior Lecturer in Social Policy at the University of Bristol.

**Chris Wrigley** is Professor of Modern British History at the University of Nottingham.

# Introduction

The First World War was a turning-point in British industrial relations just as it was for so many other aspects of British history. Whilst it is possible to exaggerate the novelty of developments during the war, nevertheless the changes were very considerable. Perhaps a good analogy is with science and technology in Britain during the war in which there were striking innovations but relatively few inventions. Labour's position in the economy was greatly strengthened, and this and the requirements of the state led to a great extension of collective bargaining and many more national negotiations.

The period 1911–14 was marked by increased trade union membership, heightened industrial unrest and more government intervention. However, in terms of trade union history, the developments of these years were a continuation of the struggles of the late 1880s and early 1890s. The conditions and the groups involved were largely different from those of 1915–18. As for government intervention in 1911–14, it was very much *ad hoc*, whereas in 1915–18 it rested on legislation and widespread 'physical controls' in the economy.[1] Though, as with all periods of history, change and continuity were both present, and there is inevitably much arbitrariness in selecting a starting-point for a book of this kind.

Indeed one can argue that the post-war unrest of 1919 and 1920 marks some kind of continuation with the pre-war unrest.[2] James Cronin, in his statistical study of British strikes, has observed:

> the relationship between the pre- and post-war strike waves is complex. The post-war militancy was in many ways the last act of the 'Labour Unrest', yet it was also conditioned by the political and economic transformation stimulated by the war. . . . The pattern of participating closely paralleled that of 1910–1913, except for the fact that the engineers and builders took a greater part, the dockers a lesser one. Miners, textile workers and railwaymen again played leading roles.[3]

This is reasonable enough. In terms of industrial unrest there was a continuity between 1910 and 1921; though there is a case for seeing much of the 1919–20 unrest as an attempt to consolidate and build on labour's gains during the First World War, and there being a certain qualitative difference between then and the pre-war period with its expressions of previously repressed anger at being deprived of decent pay and working conditions. However what is clear is that the First World War, in terms of industrial relations generally, was very distinctive.

The urgent needs of the state in 'a war of production' ensured that the government affected trade union functions, shopfloor practices and managerial prerogatives. The trade unions found their voluntarist principles severely curtailed by the Defence of the Realm Act (DORA), the Munitions of War Acts and the Military Service Acts, even if they escaped outright industrial conscription.[4] In engineering and various other industries the volume and standardised nature of war work combined with a shortage of skilled labour made it especially worthwhile for employers to extend dilution of labour (the using of unskilled or semi-skilled labour on part of the work previously done by skilled workers) and various piecework payment systems in their workplaces. The Munitions of War Acts gave state support for such developments, as well as bringing in industrial tribunals to enforce workplace discipline. Management found its 'freedom to manage' also curtailed in a wide range of ways; from strict limitations on the supply of raw materials to wage levels being settled by national awards made through national negotiations or by government arbitration (through the Committee on Production and other means).

Management also found its prerogatives under pressure at the workplace. Carter Goodrich in his classic study of 'the frontier of control', written in 1919, observed,

> At what point does the employer say—beyond this there shall be no discussion, the rest is my business alone? The line is a hard one to draw; the issues are rarely thought out in the abstract and rarely presented dramatically. The real frontier, like most lines in industry, is more a matter of accepted custom than of precisely stated principle.[5]

The extent of the workers' say in workplace practices varied (and varies) from industry to industry according to the nature of the work and the strength of labour. During the First World War and the immediate post-war period the lines shifted markedly in favour of labour across a wide range of industries. Though later, with the severe recession of 1921–22, employers took the offensive and vigorously reasserted their 'rights' to discipline and manage.[6] The reassertion of managerial prerogatives in the 1920s was something of a rerun of what had taken place in coal, cotton and engineering in the 1890s, also in the face of tough competition in export markets.

During the First World War labour was in a strong position. Those on the Right in British politics complained that the workers 'had only to threaten to strike and immediately wages were raised'.[7] Yet it can be forgotten that employers did well during the First World War, as is suggested by successive governments bringing in excess profits taxes and legislation after the war to deal with profiteering that had taken place during it. Some wartime changes were very much to the advantage of management. Thus, for example, the war gave the employers in engineering and several other sectors an excellent opportunity to spread premium bonus and other payment systems that the unions had been opposing before the war. On some issues the employers succeeded in keeping the unions at bay even in the post-war boom. Thus the Metal-workers' Minority Movement in 1928 could note how the engin-eering unions had failed over 40 years to change various clauses of the agreement imposed by the employers after the 1897–98 lock-out. In particular, with regard to 'the machine question' ('the question of the employers' right to determine what labour shall be employed on the new machines and processes which are continually being introduced into the engineering industry') they noted: 'The employers postponed coming to a decision on this question, playing the unskilled unions off against the skilled until the trade boom of 1920 had given way to the trade depression of subsequent years.'[8]

What actually happened in industrial relations at the workplace is often obscured by the rhetoric of trade union activists and of management. Shop stewards' activities during the First World War were not understated at the time or later by the Left, as is well displayed by Willie Gallagher's *Revolt on the Clyde* (1956).[9] Simi-larly, management has often had its reasons to overstate the impact of shopfloor problems. Alleged trade union obduracy and the workforce's addiction to strike have been ready excuses for all manner of managerial failures. Thus recently, in 1985, one finds the labour relations director of Ford being reported as saying, 'If the trade unions have been significantly weakened by economic pressures or by industrial legislation, it has whipped away the crutch which managers have been using for the past 30 years.' He added, 'The competitive pressure is bringing about a change in management. I'm not a supporter of the myth that says the British worker is a decent chap and if it wasn't for politically-motivated shop stewards he would work his whatsits off for life.'[10]

Also, Parliament may legislate to achieve certain ends in industry but whether the desired changes come about at the workplace is another matter.[11] During the First World War, for example, the Ministry of Munitions often found that employers were reticent to take advantage of powers given to them under the Munitions of War Acts, often fearing that their taking action would sour industrial relations in their workplaces. Edward Heath's government was later to find similar reluctance on the part of employers. Workers' attachment to customary practices can also frustrate state action, even when that action has been intended to improve their lot. The case of the dockers and decasualisation is a good example of this. When they were in a strong position in the labour market the dockers preferred to maintain traditional working practices than to bring about decasualisation.[12]

During the First World War government intervention throughout much of the economy required the cooperation of the trade unions on labour matters and of businessmen in providing technical advice and in running industries. At the top this meant getting individual unions, or the TUC, involved and also 'someone from industry'—a need which stimulated the growth of employers' associations and the emergence of the Federation of British Industries.[13] During the First World War, to use Professor Middlemas's words, 'what had been merely interest groups crossed the political threshold and became part of the extended state'. That is clear enough. What is more doubtful is whether this 'corporate bias' lasted through the interwar period.[14]

In the immediate aftermath of the First World War, faced with the large number of industrial disputes, and with some Ministers even fearing the disintegration of the existing social order, the government still turned anxiously to these organisations for help. The National Industrial Conference, which met on 27 February 1919, with its representatives from employers' organisations, trade unions and joint industrial councils, was very much an expression of this. It formed a Provisional Joint Committee, which first met in March and which set about making proposals, among other things, concerning 'The methods of negotiations between employers and trade unions, including the establishment of a permanent Industrial Council to advise the government on industrial and economic questions, with a view to maintaining industrial peace'. In due course its recommendations were unequivocal on collective bargaining: 'Basis of negotiation between employers and workpeople should be the full and frank acceptance of employers' organisations and trade unions as the recognised organisations to speak and act on behalf of their members.'[15]

The months immediately after the setting-up of the National Industrial Conference in early 1919 very much mark the interwar high tide of 'corporate bias' in Britain. After that those arguing for 'Home Rule for Industry', for the government to leave industries alone to resolve their own difficulties, were increasingly in the ascendant. This was very much the case with the coming of the severe economic recession of 1921–22, when trade union moderates found that the talk of industrial harmony and 'pulling together' did not apply whem employers had the whip hand.[16] During the 1920s, apart from taking a tough line with the miners in 1926, the Conservative governments preferred to leave industry to resolve its own problems. In the 1930s, while the predominantly Conservative governments abandoned Free Trade and made some positive responsives to the problems of the old staple industries as well as of agriculture, they did not desire or need to intervene often in industrial relations; the major exception being the threatened collapse of collective bargaining in the cotton industry. Against this background, Whitehall did not involve employers' organisations or the TUC closely in the machinery of state. While Whitehall might find it convenient to consult the TUC or employers' organisations about industrial legislation or industrial issues, it is rare to find them having much of an input. The TUC, in the person of Walter Citrine, was more established in the corridors of Whitehall in the 1930s than the pre-First World War Parliamentary Committee of the TUC had ever been. But whatever the quantitative numbers of Whitehall–TUC consultations in the 1930s may have been (and they were not that great), qualitatively the impact of the TUC was very minor compared to what it had been during the First World War or was to be during the Second World War.

Some of the changes which had come about in the First World War survived the post-war depression. In several hitherto weakly organised industries the joint industrial councils (associated with the Whitley Report of 1917) survived long after the war, receiving support notably from unskilled or white-collar unions. The Ministry of Munitions left its mark on many of the firms which it had controlled. Such control had encouraged not only the adoption of the latest machinery but also the adoption of newer, often tougher, managerial practices.

The First World War stimulated the greater spread of welfare provision in British industry. The Ministry of Munitions' Health and Welfare section set about 'to convince employers that it is both good business and good management, as well as a duty, to regard with sympathetic consideration the health and comfort of their employees'.[17] These considerations, plus the facts that such provision might lessen labour unrest and that the cost could be offset against excess profits tax, combined to boost the spread of welfare. As Alan Fox has commented, ' "Welfare", as a term, was something of a ragbag. It included profit-sharing, co-partnership, joint consultation committees, provident funds, canteens, recreational and sports clubs, medical services, and the attempts to create a pleasant and healthy working environment through attention to such factors as heating, lighting, ventilation and machine design.'[18]

Industrial welfare fitted in well with such strands of management thought as paternalism and tough efficiency. Hence such developments could flourish in the 1920s and 1930s, and could be a major element in trying to attach the workforce's loyalty to the firm and not to the union, as well as being a way of attracting and holding skilled labour while paying standard national or local wage rates. William Morris, the Oxford car manufacturer, was not unusual in combining a firm anti-union stance with a vigorous fostering of participation in sport, bands and social events among his workforce in this period.[19] The employment of welfare supervisors had spread during and after the First World War. The early supervisors had been people (mostly women) with a strong feeling of vocation to improve conditions in industry, early twentieth-century equivalents of the Victorian philanthropists working in the slums. During the First World War some welfare supervisors became much more explicitly identified with management and with maintaining output, even if this undermined health (as in the case of TNT workers). With the tougher economic climate and the weaker bargaining position of labour, where firms kept on welfare supervisors the emphasis very often was on their helping to maximise production. This was reflected in the change in 1931 of the name of the professional organisation to which these people belonged from the Institute of Industrial Welfare Workers to the Institute of Labour Management.[20]

While there was a spread of 'welfarism' during the interwar period, there was still a casual attitude to injuries and even deaths in many parts of British industry. Workers at Pressed Steel, at Cowley, Oxford have recalled, 'Loss of fingers, thumbs and hands was commonplace in the factory', and safety precautions for those using lead and other dangerous processes were near or actually non-existent.[21] In coal mining in the 1920s on average 1044 miners were killed each year, coal miners accounting for 34.1 per cent of the industrial deaths of the decade (a percentage which increased a little to 35.2 per cent in the 1930s when overall fatalities dropped). Though the totals of industrial fatalities were lower in the interwar period than the decade before the First World War, the slaughter remained grim enough.[22] In coal mining the fatalities and accidents were a significant element in the bitterness in industrial relations. In many industries in the interwar period trade union officials pressed for more frequent inspections by the factory inspectorate and more powers for them, even if many of their membership took a fatalistic attitude to workplace injuries and even deaths.[23]

Even by the Second World War, notwithstanding the Factory Act 1937 which brought about some improvements in standards as well as consolidating earlier legislation, many workers were still outside the scope of the Factory Acts. Shopworkers were still subjected to extremely arbitrary discipline, bad working conditions, very low pay and long working hours, even if the practice of forcing staff to live in was fading out in the 1920s.[24] Much the same can be said of other service sector work, including such areas as garages. Office staff also remained in very bad working conditions; an attempt by the Labour MP Ellen Wilkinson to get Parliament to pass an Office Regulations Bill in 1928 having failed.[25]

In many respects the history of British industrial relations is still in its infancy. There have been notable contributions in the past by writers such as Sidney and Beatrice Webb, G. D. H. Cole and Carter Goodrich. Though for a long time few historians tried to emulate the Webbs in their *Industrial Democracy* (1898) in going beyond institutional studies. Even now the number of wide-ranging historical studies of British industrial relations that attempt to interpret the subject within the framework of economic, social, cultural and political change is not that great.[26]

Historians have rightly been nervous about generalising across the whole of Britain. They have been faced with the sheer diversity of experience not only from industry to industry but within industries. There has also been an awareness that 'industrial relations' covers a wide range of issues and relationships.

The interwar period in Britain was marked by considerable differences in the fortunes of industries and of parts of the country. This was a situation which used to be depicted as a contrast between rapidly growing 'new' consumer-oriented industries and declining export-oriented staple industries. This simplification has some truth in it, notably with regard to the 'old' industries, though it has to be qualified by emphasising that the experience of neither group was uniform. It conceals the opportunities that were available for some sectors of the 'old' industries to benefit from rising domestic consumer demand and, especially in the 1930s, from tariffs. Thus steel suffered from declining demand from old customers such as railways, shipbuilding and heavy engineering but gained from the motor car and aircraft manufacturing, electrical engineering and, eventually, from the rearmament programme. It also overlooks, as Professor Alford has observed, the fact that several 'new' industries grew out of 'old' ones, notably in textiles and chemicals.[27]

In some of the growth areas, such as motor cars and the new sectors of chemicals, employers tried, often with success, to keep the unions out. Where they failed it is notably that the patterns of different unions for the different trades and levels of skill were much the same as in long-established industries. In the older industries employers *generally* lived with the unions and did not try to exterminate them even in the depths of the economic depressions—though, of course, they often succeeded in moving 'the frontier of control' considerably in the direction of 'managerial rights'. The clashes between employers and unions in the declining staple industries are major features of trade union history in the period and are discussed in Chapter 2. In this book the industrial case studies are of two of the consumer-oriented rapidly growing sectors: electrical contracting and motor cars (Chapters 8 and 9).

Another feature of the period was the growth of concentration in British industry in the 1920s. An increasing number of firms went to the stockmarket or even to the banks for finance. Alongside these changes there was a marked move away from family ownership, though family directors remained on the boards of more than half the 200 biggest firms throughout the interwar period. More large firms had boards of directors made up of people who held only relatively small financial stakes in the firms.[28] Professional managements often took a different line in labour relations than the paternalistic approach of some of the old family firms, especially when faced with the harsh economic circumstances of the 1920s and 1930s. Much work needs to be done on the effect on industrial relations of concentration and of changing managerial patterns in this period. Joseph Melling, however, has been engaged in pioneering work in the neglected area of supervisory workers, and he provides the third case study in this book (Chapter 7).

If generalising across a range of industries has its hazards, so, in the current state of research, has writing much on several aspects of industrial relations which still await detailed examination. Even the most dramatic area, strikes and lock-outs, has not received, since K. G. J. Knowles' classic study, *Strikes* (1952), the detailed attention that the post-1945 period has been given.[29] Knowles discussed in some detail industrial and regional strike-proneness. However the pattern of strikes according to size and ownership of workplace deserves more attention, as does the effect of state policies on giving or withholding welfare, tax rebates etc. to strikers and their families. With regard to the latter area, some employers' organisations, at least, were keen to see that their members took up the 1900 Merthyr Tydfil judgment which refused Poor Law relief to an able bodied man in an industrial dispute whilst he was physically able to work. Thus in 1922 during the engineering lock-out a letter was sent by the Engineering Employers' Federation advising its members:

> I am desired to suggest that your association should watch carefully the action of the Boards of Guardians in your district, and that in the event

of any Board proposing to give relief contrary to the principles of the Merthyr Tydfil case, an arrangement be made for a number of the ratepayers intimating to the Board that they object to the course which they are taking.

If thought advisable they might also state at the next half-yearly audit they will object to any items in the accounts which represent relief to able-bodied men who have refused to avail themselves of the opportunity afforded by the opening of the works.[30]

There are also large groups of workers of whom insufficient has been written. These include many in the service and white-collar sectors of the economy. Unionisation was growing among white-collar workers in this period, but union density remained fairly low before the Second World War. Recent estimates suggest densities of 11.6 per cent in 1911, 24.2 per cent in 1921 and 21.2 per cent in 1931.[31] These sectors included large numbers of women workers. Whilst there are several institutional studies of women's trade unions, there have not been detailed adequate discussions of women workers and their responses to work (other than those which judge them as being in some way deviant for not fitting the patterns which suited male workers). That women did not join trade unions in some sectors of the economy may relate to the failure of trade unions to take up the issues immediately affecting women.[32] It may also relate to the fact that outside of textiles sex discrimination has pushed women into less unionised (and hard-to-unionise), low-paid jobs, rather than it being a sign of women being more anti-union as such.[33]

One area where there has been much work done in recent years is that of the government and industrial relations. For the First World War considerable solid work was published soon after it, much under the auspices of the Carnegie Endowment for International Peace. The opening in the mid-1960s of the private papers of several leading politicians and civil servants as well as the release of government papers has led to the First World War being reviewed and detailed examination getting underway for the interwar period. Such work has considered the role not only of the politicians but also of the civil servants.[34]

This book, like its companion volume on the 1875–1914 period, is intended to offer a basic survey of what has been done so far, and also to provide a starting base for future research. Hence it is not intended to be a book of essays on new territories. However it is possible to suggest some areas needing attention, above and beyond the gaps already mentioned.

There is a need for more local studies of industrial relations in an industry and the effects of that industry on the local community. For the interwar period there have been some excellent studies of coalfields, notably of South Wales and part of Nottinghamshire, and one on the motor car industry in Oxford; but there is a very real need for studies of this kind for the textile industry in this period as well as for many other newer industries.[35] One also needs more than studies of an industry; there is a need also for studies of a local labour market, with its options of alternative employment within it or migration to another centre.[36] Most places are not dominated by a single industry. For the unskilled and some of the skilled the options go wider than just one industry.

This leads to the point that changes in industrial relations usually take place over many industries within a fairly short timespan. Managements across a range of industries are often faced by similar market pressures. Hence it can be very revealing to see the different managerial strategies and labour responses to such changes in several industries. Hence there is a need for more thematic studies which cover numerous industries, and, indeed, go beyond national borders.[37]

Indeed some key issues in the history of British industrial relations are highlighted by international comparisons as well as by careful, detailed examination of British industrial practices. In the interwar period in many industries there appears a persistent failure by employers to invest in new machinery and to rely on working labour harder in an attempt to be competitive; a good example being the cotton industry and the 'more looms' controversy. A comparative analysis should be part of an explanation for this. Similarly, comparative studies can point to alternative responses to international economic recessions. A good example is a study of motor car manufacturing in recession in recent years, which shows employers in Britain and Italy responding with large-scale redundancies and tougher managerial attitudes whilst in West Germany and the USA the response has included attempts to extend guaranteed working and to involve the unions more in decision making at plant level.[38]

Memories seem to be especially long in industrial relations. The tough anti-union policies in much of the interwar British motor car industry, with the long lay-offs and the arbitrary managerial decisions, were major contributors to the bitter relations of the 1950s and 1960s. Similarly in the coal industry the experiences of 1921 and 1926 lived on, and were remembered in the Second World War and even in 1972 and 1974, just as the experiences of 1984–85 will not be quickly forgotten. Moreover the great job insecurity for much of the labour force in so many industries, with the workforce treated as 'hands' and employment depending on the immediate needs of the marketplace, was inimical to creating loyalty to the firm or enthusiasm to increase output. Such treatment, perhaps best epitomised by the launching of great ships in the lean years, where the workforce would collect their last pay and leave but high society people would arrive and partake of the champagne and ceremonials, reinforced class divisions and had implications well beyond the workplace.

To study the history of British industrial relations is to study a major aspect of modern British history. It explains much in English, Welsh and Scottish society and politics today just as a study of history is crucial to understanding current events in Ireland.

Table 0.1: Strikes and lock-outs, 1913–39: Number of disputes beginning in each year (UK)

| Years | Building | Mining and quarrying | Metal, engineering shipbuilding | Textiles | Clothing | Transport | Other industries and services | Total |
|---|---|---|---|---|---|---|---|---|
| 1913 | 192 | 192 | 391 | 240 | 73 | 115 | 256 | 1459 |
| 1914 | 177 | 176 | 232 | 97 | 50 | 53 | 187 | 972 |
| 1915 | 63 | 85 | 189 | 67 | 40 | 75 | 153 | 672 |
| 1916 | 73 | 75 | 105 | 74 | 44 | 44 | 117 | 532 |
| 1917 | 51 | 148 | 225 | 70 | 55 | 32 | 149 | 730 |
| 1918 | 107 | 173 | 420 | 75 | 37 | 48 | 275 | 1165 |
| 1919 | 134 | 250 | 335 | 65 | 77 | 113 | 378 | 1352 |
| 1920 | 242 | 248 | 339 | 126 | 68 | 129 | 455 | 1607 |
| 1921 | 135 | 170 | 151 | 28 | 29 | 42 | 208 | 763 |
| 1922 | 62 | 169 | 114 | 21 | 23 | 53 | 134 | 576 |
| 1923 | 54 | 196 | 102 | 35 | 24 | 58 | 159 | 628 |
| 1924 | 58 | 204 | 136 | 50 | 31 | 78 | 153 | 710 |
| 1925 | 54 | 176 | 93 | 59 | 31 | 46 | 145 | 604 |
| 1920a | 268 | 250 | 340 | 126 | 68 | 150 | 405 | 1607 |
| 1921 | 158 | 173 | 151 | 28 | 29 | 42 | 182 | 763 |
| 1922 | 77 | 169 | 115 | 21 | 23 | 56 | 115 | 576 |
| 1923 | 65 | 197 | 103 | 35 | 24 | 61 | 143 | 628 |
| 1924 | 66 | 204 | 136 | 50 | 31 | 81 | 142 | 710 |
| 1925 | 58 | 175 | 94 | 59 | 31 | 54 | 132 | 603 |
| 1926 | 43 | 69 | 62 | 33 | 12 | 42 | 61 | 323b |
| 1927 | 34 | 115 | 69 | 27 | 10 | 16 | 37 | 308 |
| 1928 | 38 | 100 | 51 | 33 | 9 | 16 | 55 | 302 |
| 1929 | 40 | 162 | 80 | 58 | 17 | 21 | 53 | 431 |
| 1930 | 47 | 158 | 70 | 44 | 21 | 22 | 60 | 422 |
| 1931 | 57 | 155 | 61 | 38 | 21 | 17 | 71 | 420 |
| 1932 | 29 | 115 | 46 | 105 | 24 | 25 | 45 | 389 |
| 1933 | 20 | 117 | 68 | 43 | 20 | 30 | 59 | 357 |
| 1934 | 44 | 150 | 81 | 57 | 25 | 31 | 83 | 471 |
| 1935 | 46 | 233 | 73 | 64 | 28 | 36 | 73 | 553 |
| 1936 | 77 | 290 | 148 | 79 | 27 | 66 | 131 | 818 |
| 1937 | 98 | 470 | 220 | 84 | 33 | 50 | 174 | 1129 |
| 1938 | 110 | 374 | 138 | 42 | 36 | 49 | 126 | 875 |
| 1939 | 122 | 417 | 181 | 73 | 25 | 34 | 88 | 940 |

Notes: a. The classification of industries was slightly revised in 1920 to come into line with that used for the 1921 Census.

b. General Strike included in totals but not in groups of industries.

Source: *Abstracts of Labour Statistics*, 1926, 1931, 1934 and 1937; and *Ministry of Labour Gazette*, 1936–40.

Table 0.2: Strikes and lock-outs, 1913–39: Total number (in thousands) of work people directly and indirectly involved in disputes beginning in each year (UK)

| Years | Building | Mining and quarrying | Metal, engineering shipbuilding | Textiles | Clothing | Transport | Other industries and services | Total |
|---|---|---|---|---|---|---|---|---|
| 1913 | 40 | 214 | 153 | 93 | 15 | 84 | 65 | 664 |
| 1914 | 38 | 273 | 51 | 22 | 7 | 13 | 43 | 447 |
| 1915 | 16 | 298 | 46 | 33 | 6 | 25 | 24 | 448 |
| 1916 | 6 | 64 | 75 | 61 | 16 | 28 | 26 | 276 |
| 1917 | 7 | 281 | 429 | 65 | 12 | 26 | 52 | 872 |
| 1918 | 36 | 383 | 242 | 268 | 25 | 59 | 103 | 1116 |
| 1919 | 22 | 925 | 403 | 488 | 28 | 571 | 154 | 2591 |
| 1920 | 42 | 1411 | 179 | 80 | 34 | 34 | 65 | 1932 |
| 1921 | 26 | 1256 | 63 | 380 | 5 | 5 | 25 | 1801 |
| 1922 | 8 | 124 | 369 | 5 | 3 | 3 | 8 | 552 |
| 1923 | 20 | 189 | 61 | 36 | 4 | 4 | 58 | 405 |
| 1924 | 114 | 137 | 71 | 11 | 5 | 5 | 244 | 613 |
| 1925 | 5 | 136 | 24 | 172 | 5 | 5 | 29 | 442 |
| | | | | | | | | |
| 1920[a] | 49 | 1411 | 183 | 80 | 34 | 70 | 105 | 1932 |
| 1921 | 29 | 1256 | 63 | 380 | 5 | 27 | 41 | 1801 |
| 1922 | 10 | 124 | 369 | 5 | 3 | 10 | 31 | 552 |
| 1923 | 21 | 189 | 61 | 37 | 4 | 58 | 35 | 405 |
| 1924 | 115 | 137 | 71 | 11 | 5 | 245 | 29 | 613 |
| 1925 | 6 | 136 | 24 | 172 | 5 | 29 | 69 | 441 |
| 1926 | 3 | 1091 | 14 | 17 | 1 | 20 | 8 | 2734[b] |
| 1927 | 8 | 67 | 16 | 5 | 9 | 2 | 1 | 108 |
| 1928 | 3 | 82 | 8 | 25 | 1 | 2 | 3 | 124 |
| 1929 | 3 | 80 | 39 | 400 | 1 | 7 | 3 | 533 |
| 1930 | 4 | 149 | 10 | 127 | 1 | 5 | 11 | 307 |
| 1931 | 12 | 281 | 12 | 163 | 1 | 5 | 16 | 490 |
| 1932 | 3 | 53 | 4 | 300 | 2 | 12 | 5 | 379 |
| 1933 | 1 | 72 | 15 | 7 | 2 | 27 | 12 | 136 |
| 1934 | 8 | 74 | 15 | 16 | 4 | 11 | 6 | 134 |
| 1935 | 3 | 194 | 17 | 14 | 3 | 24 | 16 | 271 |
| 1936 | 8 | 181 | 47 | 13 | 12 | 26 | 29 | 316 |
| 1937 | 8 | 382 | 107 | 23 | 10 | 52 | 15 | 597 |
| 1938 | 14 | 174 | 44 | 7 | 7 | 15 | 14 | 275 |
| 1939 | 35 | 206 | 56 | 9 | 6 | 12 | 13 | 337 |

Notes: a. The classification of industries was slightly revised in 1920 to come into line with that used for the 1921 Census.

b. General Strike included in totals but not in groups of industries.

Source: Abstracts of Labour Statistics, 1926, 1931, 1934 and 1937; and Ministry of Labour Gazette, 1936–40.

*Table 0.3: Strikes and lock-outs, 1913–39: Aggregate duration in working days of all disputes in progress in each year (in thousands) (UK)*

| Years | Building | Mining and quarrying | Metal, engineering shipbuilding | Textiles | Clothing | Transport | Other industries and services | Total |
|---|---|---|---|---|---|---|---|---|
| 1913 | 814 | 1656 | 2985 | 2019 | 173 | 1184 | 973 | 9804 |
| 1914 | 3184 | 3777 | 1308 | 765 | 79 | 87 | 678 | 9878 |
| 1915 | 130 | 1657 | 357 | 369 | 28 | 152 | 260 | 2953 |
| 1916 | 103 | 326 | 305 | 1161 | 156 | 103 | 292 | 2446 |
| 1917 | 68 | 1183 | 3063 | 710 | 142 | 184 | 297 | 5647 |
| 1918 | 186 | 1263 | 1499 | 1704 | 298 | 277 | 648 | 5875 |
| 1919 | 391 | 7713 | 12,248 | 8160 | 239 | 4200 | 2018 | 34,969 |
| 1920 | 696 | 17,508 | 3402 | 1443 | 727 | 509 | 2283 | 26,568 |
| 1921 | 538 | 72,961 | 4420 | 6939 | 81 | 291 | 642 | 85,872 |
| 1922 | 169 | 1387 | 17,484 | 68 | 46 | 80 | 616 | 19,850 |
| 1923 | 386 | 1200 | 5995 | 1228 | 28 | 1031 | 804 | 10,672 |
| 1924 | 3134 | 1628 | 1400 | 200 | 45 | 1539 | 478 | 8424 |
| 1925 | 79 | 3754 | 183 | 3173 | 38 | 68 | 671 | 7966 |
| | | | | | | | | |
| 1920[a] | 789 | 17,508 | 3414 | 1443 | 727 | 549 | 2138 | 26,568 |
| 1921 | 557 | 72,962 | 4420 | 6939 | 81 | 296 | 617 | 85,872 |
| 1922 | 179 | 1387 | 17,484 | 68 | 46 | 107 | 579 | 19,850 |
| 1923 | 394 | 1212 | 5997 | 1228 | 28 | 1031 | 782 | 10,672 |
| 1924 | 3145 | 1628 | 1400 | 200 | 45 | 1543 | 463 | 8424 |
| 1925 | 85 | 3740 | 184 | 3173 | 38 | 73 | 659 | 7952 |
| 1926 | 38 | 146,456 | 221 | 188 | 8 | 167 | 155 | 162,233[b] |
| 1927 | 129 | 695 | 81 | 36 | 199 | 7 | 27 | 1174 |
| 1928 | 84 | 461 | 60 | 695 | 25 | 11 | 52 | 1388 |
| 1929 | 28 | 666 | 768 | 6752 | 11 | 13 | 49 | 8287 |
| 1930 | 46 | 671 | 92 | 3392 | 10 | 25 | 163 | 4399 |
| 1931 | 145 | 2859 | 99 | 3717 | 16 | 13 | 134 | 6983 |
| 1932 | 36 | 292 | 48 | 5811 | 32 | 194 | 75 | 6488 |
| 1933 | 9 | 455 | 112 | 85 | 6 | 272 | 133 | 1072 |
| 1934 | 172 | 373 | 160 | 88 | 36 | 44 | 86 | 959 |
| 1935 | 37 | 1385 | 93 | 106 | 44 | 82 | 208 | 1955 |
| 1936 | 44 | 969 | 206 | 97 | 155 | 86 | 272 | 1829 |
| 1937 | 39 | 1501 | 778 | 156 | 72 | 748 | 119 | 3413 |
| 1938 | 115 | 701 | 243 | 84 | 33 | 40 | 118 | 1334 |
| 1939 | 131 | 612 | 332 | 100 | 13 | 57 | 111 | 1356 |

*Notes:* a. The classification of industries was slightly revised in 1920 to come into line with that used for the 1921 Census.

b. General Strike included in totals but not in groups of industries.

*Source: Abstracts of Labour Statistics*, 1926, 1931, 1934 and 1937; and *Ministry of Labour Gazette*, 1936–1940.

Table 0.4: Number and percentage of stoppages over pay and over all other issues, 1913–39 (UK)

| Year | Number of stoppages over pay | Number of stoppages over all other issues | Total number of stoppages | % Over pay | % Over all other issues |
|------|------|------|------|------|------|
| 1913 | 956   | 503 | 1,459 | 65.5 | 34.5 |
| 1914 | 603   | 369 | 972   | 62.0 | 38.0 |
| 1915 | 489   | 183 | 672   | 72.8 | 27.2 |
| 1916 | 398   | 134 | 532   | 74.8 | 25.2 |
| 1917 | 521   | 209 | 730   | 71.4 | 28.6 |
| 1918 | 770   | 395 | 1,165 | 66.1 | 33.9 |
| 1919 | 857   | 495 | 1,352 | 63.4 | 36.6 |
| 1920 | 1,079 | 528 | 1,607 | 67.1 | 32.9 |
| 1921 | 560   | 203 | 763   | 73.4 | 26.6 |
| 1922 | 385   | 191 | 576   | 66.8 | 33.2 |
| 1923 | 353   | 275 | 628   | 56.2 | 43.8 |
| 1924 | 436   | 274 | 710   | 61.4 | 38.6 |
| 1925 | 305   | 298 | 603   | 50.6 | 49.4 |
| 1926 | 148   | 175 | 323   | 45.8 | 54.2 |
| 1927 | 165   | 143 | 308   | 53.6 | 46.4 |
| 1928 | 169   | 133 | 302   | 56.0 | 44.0 |
| 1929 | 224   | 207 | 431   | 52.0 | 48.0 |
| 1930 | 249   | 173 | 422   | 59.0 | 41.0 |
| 1931 | 232   | 188 | 420   | 55.2 | 44.8 |
| 1932 | 230   | 159 | 389   | 59.1 | 40.9 |
| 1933 | 180   | 169 | 357   | 52.7 | 47.3 |
| 1934 | 228   | 243 | 471   | 48.4 | 51.6 |
| 1935 | 255   | 298 | 553   | 46.1 | 53.9 |
| 1936 | 369   | 449 | 818   | 45.1 | 54.9 |
| 1937 | 588   | 541 | 1,129 | 52.1 | 47.9 |
| 1938 | 339   | 536 | 875   | 38.7 | 61.3 |
| 1939 | 482   | 458 | 940   | 51.3 | 48.7 |

Source: C. T. B. Smith, R. Clifton, P. Makeham, S. W. Creigh and R. V. Burn, Strikes in Britain (1978), p. 127.

Table 0.5: *Number of persons killed in industrial accidents in UK,*
*1913–39*
(A) *Processes covered by the Factory Acts*

| Year | Factory processes | Construction processes | Docks, wharves, quays and inland warehouses |
|------|-----|-----|-----|
| 1913 | 996 | 129 | 184 |
| 1914 | 969 | 149 | 169 |
| 1915 | 1109 | 110 | 185 |
| 1916 | 1194 | 145 | 168 |
| 1917 | 1346 | 78 | 161 |
| 1918 | 1357 | 78 | 144 |
| 1919 | 1153 | 85 | 147 |
| 1920 | 1175 | 94 | 135 |
| 1921 | 751 | 108 | 92 |
| 1922 | 697 | 70 | 97 |
| 1923 | 701 | 90 | 93 |
| 1924 | 757 | 106 | 108 |
| 1925 | 688 | 149 | 113 |
| 1926 | 573 | 124 | 120 |
| 1927 | 743 | 143 | 107 |
| 1928 | 695 | 154 | 125 |
| 1929 | 759 | 135 | 110 |
| 1930 | 684 | 139 | 94 |
| 1931 | 573 | 124 | 71 |
| 1932 | 417 | 116 | 80 |
| 1933 | 535 | 96 | 77 |
| 1934 | 589 | 109 | 96 |
| 1935 | 641 | 137 | 93 |
| 1936 | 683 | 152 | 103 |
| 1937 | 729 | 187 | 110 |
| 1938 | 643 | 226 | 93 |
| 1939 | 724[a] | 303[a] | 77[a] |

Note: *a.* This includes figures for Northern Ireland
Source: Department of Employment and Productivity: *British Labour Statistics:*
*Historical Abstract 1886–1968* (1971), p. 399.

Table 0.5 (B) Industries covered by other acts

| Year | Notification of Accidents Act | Explosives Act | Coal Mines | Metaliferous Mines Regulation Act | Quarries Acts | Railways | Shipping | Commercial aviation | Total persons killed (A+B lists) |
|---|---|---|---|---|---|---|---|---|---|
| 1913 | 32 | 13 | 1753 | 32 | 85 | 463 | 1164a | | 4851 |
| 1914 | 35 | 21 | 1219 | 24 | 95 | 477 | 1371a | | 4529 |
| 1915 | 24 | 21 | 1297 | 21 | 74 | 471 | 1304 | | 4616 |
| 1916 | 31 | 195 | 1313 | 23 | 58 | 453 | 942 | | 4522 |
| 1917 | 23 | 54 | 1370 | 25 | 56 | 382 | 1059 | | 4554 |
| 1918 | 16 | 44 | 1401 | 19 | 67 | 337 | 1023 | | 4486 |
| 1919 | 20 | 8 | 1118 | 65 | 46 | 377 | 745 | | 3764 |
| 1920 | 16 | 2 | 1103 | 27 | 54 | 420 | 663 | | 3689 |
| 1921 | 18 | 5 | 756 | 12 | 47 | 262 | 695 | | 2746 |
| 1922 | 9 | — | 1105 | 9 | 47 | 244 | 828 | | 3106 |
| 1923 | 9 | 5 | 1297 | 11 | 81 | 252 | 763 | | 3302 |
| 1924 | 24 | 3 | 1201 | 17 | 79 | 264 | 617 | 1 | 3177 |
| 1925 | 20 | 6 | 1136 | 23 | 76 | 301 | 708 | — | 3220 |
| 1926 | 18 | 2 | 649 | 13 | 68 | 201 | 636 | — | 2404 |
| 1927 | 16 | 6 | 1129 | 13 | 70 | 250 | 547 | — | 3024 |
| 1928 | 11 | 10 | 989 | 25 | 69 | 261 | 603 | — | 2942 |
| 1929 | 10 | — | 1076 | 19 | 70 | 269 | 560 | 1 | 3009 |
| 1930 | 15 | 1 | 1013 | 12 | 73 | 242 | 439 | 2 | 2714 |
| 1931 | 18 | 2 | 859 | 10 | 53 | 199 | 382 | — | 2291 |
| 1932 | 13 | 4 | 881 | 12 | 54 | 214 | 306 | 1 | 2098 |
| 1933 | 15 | 2 | 820 | 11 | 49 | 201 | 392 | 2 | 2200 |
| 1934 | 12 | — | 1073 | 16 | 65 | 244 | 445 | 2 | 2651 |
| 1935 | 5 | 5 | 861 | 25 | 53 | 212 | 464 | 6 | 2502 |
| 1936 | 4 | 3 | 790 | 12 | 80 | 246 | 398 | 16 | 2487 |
| 1937 | 9 | 11 | 859 | 18 | 89 | 238 | 457 | 10 | 2717 |
| 1938 | 4 | 7 | 858 | 14 | 69 | 240 | 501 | 8 | 2663 |
| 1939 | 3 | 31 | 783 | 17 | 87 | 259 | 373 | 7 | 2683 |

## Notes

1 For recent surveys of the pre-1914 period, see the essays in both C. Wrigley (ed.), *A History of British Industrial Relations 1875–1914* (1982), and W. J. Mommsen and H. Husung (eds), *The Development of Trade Unionism in Great Britain and Germany 1880–1914* (1985).

2 For the government figures on strikes 1913–39 see Tables 0.1–4. I have provided both sets of figures for the early 1920s so that pre-1920 and post-1926 comparisons can be made with figures derived from the same classifications.

3 J. E. Cronin, *Industrial Conflict in Modern Britain* (1979), p. 52.

4 For a lengthy essay on trade union attitudes, see R. Currie, *Industrial Politics* (1979) generally, and in particular pp. 91–2.

5 C. L. Goodrich, *The Frontier of Control* (1920), p. 56.

6 See p. 96 for the engineering employers' terms of 1922.

7 As Henry Page Croft later recalled. For the National Party on this, see '"In the Excess of their Patriotism": the National Party and Threats of Subversion', in C. Wrigley (ed.), *Warfare, Diplomacy and Politics* (1986), pp. 93–119. See also J. Turner, 'The Politics of "Organised Business" during the First World War', in J. Turner (ed.), *Businessmen and Politics* (1984), pp. 33–49.

8 The Metalworkers' Minority Movement, *Our Reply to Sir Allan Smith* (1928), pp. 6–7.

9 See J. Hinton, 'The Clyde Workers' Committee and the Dilution Struggle', in A. Briggs and J. Saville (eds), *Essays in Labour History 1886–1923* (1971), and *The First Shop Stewards' Movement* (1973), I. McLean, *The Legend of Red Clydeside* (1983), and A. Reid, 'Dilution, Trade Unionism and the State in Britain During the First World War', in S. Tolliday and J. Zeitlin, (eds), *Shop Floor Bargaining and the State* (1985) pp. 46–74, for reassessments and further reassessments.

10 *The Times*, 20 August 1985.

11 For a recent view of theories concerning state action, see J. Zeitlin, 'Shop Floor Bargaining and the State: A Contradictory Relationship', in Tolliday and Zeitlin, *op. cit.*, pp. 1–45.

12 On this see N. Whiteside, 'Public Policy and Port Labour Reform: The Dock Decasualisation Issue 1910–1950', in ibid., pp. 75–107, and G. A. Phillips and N. Whiteside, *Casual Labour: The Unemployment Question in the Port Transport Industry 1880–1970* (1985).

13 Whilst there has been no shortage of histories of individual trade unions, employers' organisations and managerial strategies generally have received less attention. See Chapter 4 of this book. For other surveys see H. Gospel, 'The Development of Management Organisation in Industrial Relations: A Historical Perspective', in K. Thurley and S. Wood (eds), *Industrial Relations and Management Strategy* (1983), pp. 91–110; the essays by Gospel, Zeitlin and Lewchuk, in H. F. Gospel and C. Littler (eds), *Management Strategies and Industrial*

*Relations* (1983); and W. R. Garside, 'Management and Men: Aspects of British Industrial Relations in the Inter-war Periods', in B. Supple (ed.), *Essays in British Business History* (1977), pp. 244–67. The most detailed studies of the interwar period include the unpublished theses of H. Gospel, 'Employers' Organisations: Their Growth and Function in the British System of Industrial Relations' (London University PhD, 1974), which studies engineering, building and electrical contracting, and A. J. McIvor, 'Employers' Associations and Industrial Relations in Lancashire 1890–1939: A Comparative Study of the Development, Organisation and Labour Relations Strategies of Employers' Combinations in the Cotton, Building and Engineering Industries' (Manchester University PhD, 1983). Various employers' organisations papers, including the predecessors of the Confederation of British Industry, will soon be made available on microform by the Harvester Press Microform in its series 'British Industrial Relations and Social Change, *c.*1850–1939'.

14  K. Middlemas, *Politics in Industrial Society* (1979), p. 373, and for 'corporate bias' Chapter 13 in particular. For comments on his broad thesis that it is 'clear that corporate bias in the British stage ensured a uniquely low level of class conflict' see, for example, R. Lowe, in *The Bulletin of the Society for the Study of Labour History*, 41 (1980) and *Economic History Review*, 35 (1982).

15  *Report on Conciliation and Arbitration: 1919* (1920), pp. 35–43.

16  It is interesting to find similar disillusion with the belief in 'accommodation and cooperative attitude between labor and management' among some American union officials in June 1983 after the experience of some elements of Reaganomics. T. A. Kochan (ed.), *Challenges and Choices Facing American Labor* (1985), p. 258 (and also p. 266).

17  Report on the Welfare and Health Section, 23 April 1917; cited in C. Wrigley 'The Ministry of Munitions: An Innovatory Department', in K. Burk (ed.), *War and the State* (1982), p. 48.

18  A. Fox, *History and Heritage* (1985), p. 299.

19  For the recollections of some of his car workers, see Television History Workshop, *Making Cars* (1985), especially pp. 47–51, 59–61.

20  A. Ineson and D. Thom, 'TNT Poisoning and the Employment of Women Workers in the First World War', in P. Weindling (ed.), *The Social History of Occupational Health* (1985), pp. 89–107. M. M. Niven, *Personnel Management 1913–1963* (1967), pp. 80–5. In recent years there has been increasing attention paid to the significance of both industrial welfare and state welfare in British industrial relations. On the latter see Chapter 6 of this book. See also, for example, J. R. Hay, 'Employers' Attitudes to Social Policy and the Concept of Social Control 1900–1920', in P. Thane (ed.) *The Origins of British Social Policy* (1978), pp. 107–25; N. Whiteside, 'Welfare Legislation and the Unions during the First World War', *Historical Journal*, 23, 4 (1980), pp. 857–74; J. Melling, 'Employers, Industrial

Welfare and the Struggle for Workplace Control in British Industry 1880–1920', in Gospel and Littler, *op. cit.*, pp. 55–81; and H. Jones, 'Employers' Welfare Schemes and Industrial Relations in Inter-war Britain', *Business History*, 25, 1 (1983), pp. 61–75.

21 Television History Workshop, *op. cit.*, pp. 26–9.

22 See Table 0.5 for industrial deaths, 1913–39. In the decade 1904–13 there were 44,449 such deaths recorded of which 13,431 were coal-miners (30.2%).

23 H. Jones, 'An Inspector Calls: Health and Safety at Work in Interwar Britain', in Weindling, *op. cit.*, pp. 223–39.

24 P. Pagnamenta and R. Overy, *All Our Working Lives* (1984), pp. 106–9. P. C. Hoffman, *They Also Serve* (1949), pp. 205–34.

25 Niven, *op. cit.*, p. 75.

26 Some of the more notable studies which go some way to doing this include E. H. Phelps Brown's study of the 1906–14 period, *The Growth of British Industrial Relations* (1959); K. Burgess, *The Origins of Industrial Relations* (1975); Middlemas, *op. cit.*; and Fox, *op. cit.*.

27 For reassessments of British industry in the interwar period and whether there is value in the notion of 'new' and 'old' industries, see B. W. Alford, *Depression and Recovery?* (1972) and 'New Industries for Old? British Industry Between the Wars', in R. Floud and D. McLoskey (eds), *The Economic History of Britain Since 1700*, vol. 2 (1981), pp. 308–31.

28 For surveys of such changes, see L. Hannah, *The Rise of the Corporate Economy* (1976), and 'Visible and Invisible Hands in Great Britain', in A. D. Chandler and H. Daems (eds), *Managerial Hierarchies* (1980), pp. 41–76. Also W. A. Thomas, *The Financing of British Industry* (1978), Part 1. There is also the dimension, most notably after 1945, of foreign-owned firms in Britain. For a study of the 1960s, see M. Steuer and J. Gennard, 'Industrial relations, labour disputes and labour utilisation in foreign-owned firms in the United Kingdom', in J. H. Dunning (ed.), *The Multinational Enterprise* (1971), pp. 81–144.

29 The most valuable recent book is Cronin, *op. cit.*, which surveys nearly a century. However for the period after 1945 one has J. W. Durcan, W. E. J. McCarthy and G. P. Redman, *Strikes in Post-War Britain* (1983) and a much more sizeable literature on aspects of strikes. For a recent survey of some of the literature, see S. W. Creigh, 'Strikes in Britain: A Selective Annotated Bibliography', *Quality of Working Life Journal*, 1, 5 (1984), pp. 3–12.

30 Letter of 16 May 1922. Cited in Metal Workers' Minority Movement, *op. cit.*, p. 11. For the policy during the mining dispute of 1926, see P. Ryan, 'The Poor Law in 1926', in M. Morris (ed.), *The General Strike* (1976), pp. 358–78. For the fullest discussion of these issues, with some treatment of the interwar period, see J. Gennard, *Financing Strikers* (1977). For the broad issue of the state and social welfare see Chapter 6 of this book.

31   G. S. Bain and R. Price, *Profiles of Union Growth* (1980), p. 41.
32   Eleanor Gordon has discussed this and the nature of women's collective protests for Scottish women workers before the First World War in her Glasgow University PhD thesis (1986), 'Women and the Labour Movement in Scotland, *c.*1850–1914'.
33   There is some suggestion that this is the case, at least in recent times, in the USA, see Kochan, *op. cit.*, pp. 32–3.
34   See Chapters 1 and 5. See also the essays in Burk, *op. cit.*; J. Harris, *William Beveridge* (1977), and Rodney Lowe's forthcoming study of the Ministry of Labour 1916–39, *Adjusting to Democracy*. Dr Lowe has also edited a microform collection of government records, mostly from the Ministry of Labour, entitled 'Conflict and Consensus in British Industrial Relations 1916–1948' (Harvester Microform, 1985).
35   The recent coalfield studies are H. Francis and D. Smith, *The Fed* (1980), and R. Waller, *The Dukeries Transformed* (1983), earlier ones of particular value for this period are those by W. R. Garside and A. R. Griffin (see Chapter 2). On Oxford, see R. C. Whiting, *The View from Cowley* (1983). For valuable studies of textiles for earlier periods see P. Joyce, *Work, Society and Politics* (1980), and J. White, *The Limits of Trade Union Militancy* (1978).
36   One does have such valuable works as S. Pollard, *A History of Labour in Sheffield* (1959), and P. Waller's wide-ranging study of Liverpool, *Democracy and Sectarianism* (1981).
37   For recent examples of sets of essays with such dimensions for this period see Gospel and Littler, *op. cit.*, and Tolliday and Zeitlin, *op. cit.*. H. Phelps Brown's enquiry into *The Origins of Trade Union Power* (1983) also includes comparative studies of the USA, Canada and Australia. For an important comparison with Japan, see R. Dore, *British Factory–Japanese Factory* (1973).
38   This example is drawn from J. Zeitlin, 'Shop Floor Bargaining and the State', in Tolliday and Zeitlin, *op. cit.*, p. 13.

# 1

# The First World War and State Intervention in Industrial Relations, 1914–18

*Chris Wrigley*

The First World War really did mark a drastic change in economic notions and economic behaviour, even if there was a considerable (but not total) reversion to pre-war ways after 1918. In terms of *industrial relations* as a whole, the changes of 1915, 1916 and 1917 were more marked than any comparable period outside of the Second World War.

The key feature of this was the strong position of labour in much of the labour market. During the First World War 4,970,000 men were enlisted in the Army, 407,000 in the Navy, and 293,000 in the Air Force out of a total male labour force of some 15 million.[1] This left the remaining labour, especially skilled labour in essential war work, in a very strong bargaining position.

But this was not all. This and other dislocations of ordinary economic activity ensured that the state intervened. As well as shortages of labour, industry faced shortages of imported raw materials, disruption of internal transport, various financial restrictions and much else. War shortages heightened the need for establishing priorities. Businessmen who swore by *laissez-faire* in peacetime were quick to grasp that in wartime their interests often were best served by government intervention. In key war work this involved recognition of, and working with, the trade unions from early on. More generally, even in industries which were less well organised by the unions and which were less crucial for the war effort, the extent of the state's involvement in the economy ensured that wage and other agreements would be settled nationally. This encouraged the growth of both employers' organisations and trade unions and, of course, widened the area of British industry covered by collective bargaining.

The way in which labour was withdrawn for the Armed Forces in Britain between 1914 and 1918 had a considerable impact on British industry. In the first six or seven months of the war voluntary recruiting was close to being unbridled (the exceptions being some employees of the railway companies and the Admiralty), and as a result some volunteers left what was to prove to be very high priority war work. Whilst there were growing checks on recruiting during the later period of voluntary recruiting, it was not until conscription was introduced (in two stages in January and May 1916) that the government really began to determine who could be spared from war work and who could not.

Voluntary recruiting succeeded in getting large numbers of men into the Army very rapidly in the last five months of 1914. The strength of the Armed Forces on mobilisation was 691,000 (including 100,000 in India and elsewhere abroad). In August and September 1914 761,824 men enlisted, and during October, November and December a further 424,533 joined the Armed Forces. By the end of July 1915, after one year of the war, 2,008,892 men had enlisted.[2]

The effect of such large-scale voluntary recruitment was a sizeable drop of labour in essential war production. By July 1915 the estimated drop in the total occupied male population employed in coal and other mining was 21.8 per cent, iron and steel 18.8 per cent, engineering 19.5 per cent, electrical engineering 23.7 per cent and shipbuilding 16.5 per cent. The loss of manpower in the areas directly involved in equipping the huge volunteer armies was just as bad: in small arms 16 per cent, chemicals and explosives 23.8 per cent, wagon-building, cycle and motor carriage 22.3 per cent, and wiredrawing, anchor-chain manufacturing, etc. 19.7 per cent.[3] The loss of numbers was made up partly—and in a few industries entirely—by drawing labour in from other occupations. However usually such replacement labour did not match the skill of that which had gone.

In the case of coal mining, the serious loss of labour in the opening months of the war led in February 1915 to the government setting up a committee, the Coal Mine Organisation Committee, to ensure that coal production met the needs of the country. It found that during the first seven months of the war 191,170 men, nearly 19 per cent of all labour employed at collieries in the United Kingdom, had joined the Armed Forces. In terms of men of military age (19–38) some 40 per cent gave military service during the war, a very high proportion of these going in 1914. The effect of this early enlistment was little offset by some 50,473 people going into the mines from elsewhere. Overall in this period there was a drop of 14 per cent in mining labour and a fall in output of 13½ per cent. After 1915 the enlistment rate in mining was below average.[4]

The shortage of skilled engineers and the rapidly growing demand for output from munitions factories and shipyards ensured that the government could not leave the supply of labour to market forces. After negotiations between employers' associations and trade unions had failed to reach an agreement, the government arranged the Shell Conference on 21 December 1914. This was the first of several moves by the government to increase output from the reduced skilled labour force. It was followed by the setting-up on 4 February 1915 of the Committee on Production, which was given the task of advising 'as to the best steps to be taken to ensure that the productive powers of the employees in the engineering and shipbuilding establishments shall be made fully available', and by the Treasury Conference of 17–19 March 1915. At the Treasury Lloyd George, Chancellor of the Exchequer, and Runciman, President of the Board of Trade, reached a voluntary agreement with the trade unions that disputes should be settled by arbitration, not by strikes or lock-outs, and that, in order to increase production, the unions should suspend restrictions on output, including the existing limits to the numbers of machines a person could operate and the exclusion of semi-skilled and female labour from various work. This agreement followed on from one which Runciman had made immediately before with the employers which involved a far from tough level of profit limitation in munitions establishments controlled by the Defence of the Realm Acts.[5]

However voluntary agreements did not actually limit profits or remove the workers' belief that any concessions they made boosted private profits, so legislation was deemed necessary to achieve increased output. By the time that the Ministry of Munitions was formed in June 1915 the number of engineers at work were 48,000 less than in July 1914, while the government factories and sixteen private firms carrying out munitions work were some 14,000 workers short of the numbers they required.[6] Parliament gave legislative force to the Treasury Agreement and to some further measures in the Munitions of War Act of 2 July 1915, 'An Act to make provision for furthering the efficient manufacture, transport and supply of munitions'. This Act, in trying to bring about increased industrial output, was also an attempt by the British state to legislate good industrial relations.

Whilst various controls were exercised over war work by regulations under the Defence of the Realm Act, the Munitions of War Act was the most important legislation during the First World War in industrial relations.

One of its central elements was compulsory arbitration to avoid strikes and lock-outs in munitions work. The definition of 'munitions work' was fairly wide in the 1915 Act, it was considerably extended in the Munitions of War (Amendment) Act 1916, and it was further widened by the courts. Moreover compulsory arbitration could be applied to work of any kind by Proclamation by the King. This was done not only to striking South Wales miners in July 1915 but two other notable groups who tried to stay outside of the Act; textile workers (Lancashire card and blowing-room operatives) and dockers (in Glasgow, Liverpool and London).

In fact, the Munitions of War Act 1915 did permit the Board of Trade to try to settle disputes by means other than compulsory arbitration. However very few cases were handled by other means. As is observed in the official report on conciliation during the war, 'in practice differences when referred to the Board had in most cases already been through the procedure arranged by the parties and had not been adjusted; in some cases, too, procedure which had worked satisfactorily before the war proved to be unsuitable under war conditions'.

In war conditions compulsory arbitration often suited both unions and employers. This also is put well in the official report:

> Most of the references arose out of reports or differences made by the unions on behalf of their members arising from advances of wages or improved working conditions, the unions finding arbitration an expeditious means of getting disputes settled. The ordinary Conciliation Board procedure in many cases proved too slow, and the unions, instead of spending a considerable time in negotiating, with the possibility ultimately of not reaching a settlement, found it quicker to report the difference under the Munitions of War Acts at an early stage. If the difference was a *bona fide* one, the Board of Trade, under the Amended Act, was required to refer the case to arbitration within 21 days, and, moreover, the advantage of a reference under the Acts was that the

award was legally enforceable through a Munitions Tribunal. In this way, too, the unions were frequently able to force arbitration on employers who had not previously negotiated with them. On the employers' side arbitration was often found to be the most satisfactory procedure; at a time when so much work was being done for Government purposes, the employers sometimes had not the same financial interest in the result of the negotiations as when reimbursement of increased wages by the consumer was not possible.[7]

The Committee on Production had been acting as an arbitration tribunal since its terms of reference had been extended on 21 February 1915. With the Munitions of War Act the Committee became a statutory arbitration tribunal and was to be central to government activities in resolving industrial differences by the end of the war. The number of cases it settled rose from 141 in 1915 to 500 in 1916, 815 in 1917 and 2298 in 1918. (Until 1918 most matters referred to arbitration had been referred to single arbitrators; the numbers being 81 in 1914, 256 in 1915, 877 in 1916, 1,552 in 1917 and 898 in 1918.)[8] The Committee on Production's first award had been to review wages in shipbuilding, and in making it the Committee had observed that it was 'to be regarded as war advances and recognised as due to and dependent on the existence of abnormal conditions prevailing in consequence of the war'. Once arbitration had taken place on wages or other matters the government resisted efforts to vary the matter for at least four months. It also resisted attempts by Arthur Henderson (on behalf of the Parliamentary Labour Party) to get worker representatives on the Committee. In fact Asquith's government used the Committee as part of its policy of economising on finance, a policy which included resisting wage increases with little regard to the soaring cost of living. By late 1915 the Committee was acting under government instructions to respect the need for economy and to see that any wage advances granted 'should be strictly confined to the adjustment of local conditions'.[9] That there was not more unrest than there was in engineering due to this policy and to the relaxation of working practices in some sectors was due not just to patriotism but also to high money earnings. As A. L. Bowley has written,

> In many cases it became easy to make high earnings on piece work both because the work was well systematized and repetitive on a large scale and because the same rate being ensured whatever the output, there

was no fear of any cutting of prices. At the same time night work and overtime at enhanced rates were common. The earnings of piece workers consequently increased greatly, independently of any increase in rates, time workers received more in return for more work, and a very large number of persons passed from unskilled to skilled rates of pay. These processes were specially marked in 1917 and 1918.[10]

The Committee on Production came to determine national wage rates in engineering and many other sectors of industry. In engineering, in the first part of the war, the employers and unions discussed wage claims locally and then nationally before going for arbitration. In February 1917 the Amalgamated Society of Engineers (ASE) and other engineering unions agreed with the Engineering Employers' Federation (EEF) to short circuit this process, to suspend district wage negotiations and for national wage claims to be considered by the Committee on Production in February, June and October each year during the war. Both sides also pressed the government to arrange that 'all employers in the trade or trades affected should be subject to the awards'. Agreements on similar lines were made by shipbuilders on Merseyside, domestic engineers, both the industrial chemical trade and the drug manufacturers, soap and candlemakers and the building trade. Elsewhere—in shipbuilding generally, the docks, the clay industry, railway workshops and the Scottish Iron and Steel Trades—the principle of four-monthly revision of wages at the national level (without other aspects of the engineering agreement) was also adopted.[11]

One problem arising from this method of settling wage awards nationally was that grave problems arose over differentials. Semi-skilled persons on piecework could earn more than skilled workers on time rates. The erosion of differentials was a major grievance among skilled workers. The Ministry of Munitions was given powers under the August 1917 Munitions Amendment Act to deal with wages, both to allay unrest and to prevent skilled men from moving into less skilled work. In October 1917 it gave a 12½ per cent bonus to skilled workers in engineering and foundries. However this succeeded in sparking off a long series of strikes from November until Spring 1918 among others suffering from the same problem (including semi- and unskilled time workers). The government was forced to grant the 12½ per cent to more and more time workers. Moreover as the government and employers were keen to extend piecework, the government was forced to respond to the complaints of pieceworkers (some of whom were on low wages anyway). One government official observed, 'the 12½ per cent increase had done more to kill the premium bonus principle than anything else in the last ten years. ... [The men] considered the refusal to extend the 12½ per cent to piece workers and premium bonus workers a penalty on higher wages due to increased effort.' Eventually the War Cabinet in January 1918 agreed to a 7½ per cent increase for them.[12]

This episode, like so much else in the war, illustrated that it was one thing to legislate against strikes and another to achieve no stoppages of work. In fact, as Table 0.1 shows, there were considerable numbers of strikes during the First World War.

The Munitions of War Act 1915, as well as trying to secure a continuous output from the labour force also aimed at securing maximum output from it (through the relaxation of trade union restrictions, etc.). It was also designed to facilitate the supply of skilled labour for government war work.

When the Munitions of War Bill was being drawn up it is quite clear that Lloyd George intended to bring in provision for compulsory transfers of labour to where it was most needed. A precedent for industrial compulsion had been set in the Liverpool docks. There the military authorities had been concerned about congestion in the port, irregular working by dockers and an unofficial strike. Lord Derby raised a volunteer body, the Liverpool Dockers' Battalion, who worked under military law and received guaranteed pay of six shillings a day. Those in it had to be trade unionists (members of the National Union of Dock Labourers). They worked primarily on government work, but could be employed by private employers (who paid fees for their use). The Dock Battalion's significance was in the nature of its organisation, rather than its scale in the Mersey docks; at most it comprised 1750 out of a total labour force of 28,000. Lloyd George chose to visit it on 4 June 1915, and observed, 'I have heard a good deal about your battalion, and everything that I have heard had encouraged me to have a good opinion of the possibilities which you have disclosed.'[13]

The ASE made very clear its opposition to compulsory transfer of work people from commercial to munitions work. Lloyd George backed away from industrial conscription or extending elsewhere the Liverpool Dock Battalion formula. Instead the Munitions of War Act made provision for a voluntary scheme without military discipline—the War Munition Volunteers. Lloyd George said of it that it was 'purely an attempt to avoid compulsion. . . . It is an experiment, which if it fails, will bring us face to face with compulsion. I think it would be a very good thing if the workmen knew that. . . . If we cannot get workmen . . . then there is only one way of doing it, and that is by laying it down as a principle that every man during the war must render the service the state thinks he can render. But we will try this experiment first.' As Dr Grieves has observed, 'While shortages of skilled labour could be met by the Munitions Volunteers, industrial conscription could not be introduced on the pretext of a failed voluntary system. This was a political situation similar, in principle, to Lord Derby's voluntary scheme for military recruiting in the autumn of 1915.'[14] However whilst the Derby scheme for recruiting was followed by military conscription (for single men under the Military Service Act, 27 January 1916 and for all men between 18 and 41 under a second Act, 25 May 1916), direct industrial conscription was not introduced during the First World War in Britain.

Another highly controversial part of the Munitions of War Act was the leaving certificate. This was intended to prevent the drift of skilled labour to higher paid but unskilled or private engineering work. There had been an attempt to do this indirectly in April 1915 by Regulation 8B under the Defence of the Realm Act, which had prohibited employers from inducing men to leave government work. In practice it had been hard to prove that employers had offered inducements in order to poach skilled labour. Under section 7 of the Munitions of War Act severe constraints were put on the workman. The first clause laid down:

A person shall not give employment to a workman who has within the last previous six weeks, or such period as may be provided by Order of the Minister of Munitions as respects any class of establishment, been employed on or in connection with munitions work in any establishment of a class to which the provisions of this section are applied by Order of the Minister of Munitions, unless he holds a certificate from the employer by whom he was last so employed that he left work with the consent of his employer or a certificate from the munitions tribunal that the consent has been unreasonably withheld.

In practice this gave employers great power over their labour forces. A man who was unfairly dismissed would have to prove his case before a tribunal and in the interim be out of work. Also, under it, as one Liberal MP observed, 'there is no competition for labour, the only commodity which the worker has to sell, whereas there is open competition for every commodity which he has to buy'.[15] Moreover the leaving certificates could be turned into 'character notes', which could hinder the departing worker securing other work. Resentment over leaving certificates led to strikes, most notably at Messrs Fairfield on the Clyde in August 1915 which started over the dismissal of two shipwrights and the belief that management intended to make adverse remarks on their leaving certificates.

Leaving certificates became a major grievance in industrial relations under the Munitions of War Act. This is shown by the sheer number of cases before munitions tribunals. By December 1915 89 employers had been brought before tribunals and 61 convicted. Local tribunals had heard 3913 applications for certificates, of which 990 were successful.[16] Among trade union activists the leaving certificate section led to the Act being dubbed 'the Slavery Act'. In the face of great hostility the government first amended the leaving certificates regulations in the Munitions of War (Amendment) Act of January 1916, and, after the May 1917 engineering strikes, abandoned them altogether as causing more trouble than they were worth.

Much of the Munitions Act was concerned with giving legal sanction to the Treasury Agreement. This involved declaring workplaces 'controlled establishments' so that profit limitation and the suspension of restrictive rules, practices or customs would apply. The squeeze on profits was far from tight. Profits were to be limited to 20 per cent above the average of the two pre-war years. In retrospect some civil servants felt that the failure to take early action against excess profits was a mistake. U. Wolff observed in 1917 that 'compulsion in dealing with private profits is the fundamental method of grappling with all labour difficulties at the outset.'[17]

Trade union practices were recognised by government departments as a sensitive area. H. Llewellyn Smith observed in January 1915 that they were 'the most difficult and delicate of all the matters with which the Board of Trade have undertaken to deal'; and added, 'The men are full of suspicion as to the real motives of the employers and the ultimate result of any concessions that they may make'.[18] One especially difficult matter was dilution—the use of semi- or unskilled labour (including female) on part of the work usually done by skilled labour. This caused serious unrest in some engineering works, though the impact in shipbuilding was much less. On the Clyde, where most of the unrest over dilution took place, only 1000 of 14,000 female dilutees went into shipbuilding, and only Beardmore's and Fairfields took on large numbers of women. Outside of the Clyde, as Dr Reid argues, the importance of dilution as a cause of unrest has been exaggerated.[19]

Nevertheless the wartime manpower shortages had a major impact on the shopfloor in engineering, challenging craft traditions. The ensuing changes, involving not only work practices but often new rates of pay for changed jobs, new payment systems, and minimum rates for women, were often negotiated workshop by workshop. This gave new importance to the shop stewards and in several engineering centres they became the spokesmen of the workers.[20] In the latter part of the war, especially with the widespread engineering strikes of May 1917, many in the government saw the combination of revolutionary shop stewards with the accumulated causes of discontent during the war as a serious threat to the war effort and even to the social stability of the country.

Another aspect of the Munitions of War Act which led to resentment among many working in controlled establishments was the munitions tribunal system. Ten general munitions tribunals were set up across the British Isles to deal with major offences, and 55 local munitions tribunals to deal with lesser matters. The tribunals consisted of a chairman and assessors, the latter being representatives of the employers and workmen. Both kinds of tribunal could hear all types of offences, but in practice the general tribunals dealt with strikers and prosecutions over leaving certificates. The consideration of granting leaving certificates was undertaken by the local tribunals, a complex and controversial task given the wide scope for differing interpretations of the meaning of the Act. The tribunals could impose fines. Until the Munitions of War Amendment Act of 1916 general tribunals had the power of imprisonment.[21]

The taking of employees to these tribunals was not likely to enhance good feelings in the workplace. While all aspects of the tribunals' work were likely to cause resentment, the aspect of enforcing works rules was especially likely to do so. By a regulation under the Munitions Act, the Minister of Munitions laid down that 'The owner of any controlled establishment shall as soon as practicable post rules relating to order, discipline, time keeping, and efficiency conspicuously in his establishment so as to bring them effectively to the knowledge of workmen employed therein.' Some employers took the view that such rules would be best designed by the Ministry, and from 18 August 1915 it supplied model rules (dealing with regular and punctual attendance and diligent work, suspension of restrictive practices, sobriety and good order) which employers could use. Most controlled establishments did post rules acceptable to the Ministry by the end of 1915. The Ministry of Munitions pressed them to do so, but another element in encouraging them was that the failure to do so excluded the possibility of the employer initiating prosecutions before munitions tribunals.

The Engineering Employers' Federation took a tougher line on rules. They drew up a detailed code of rules for their members, rules which enforced various regulations employers had been trying to introduce in normal times. These included:

All persons employed shall work on piecework or the premium bonus system as and when required by the company, time rates in the case of piece work being guaranteed.

Deductions will be made from wages for all bad, negligent, uncompleted or untested work or injury to any material or property.

All time lost shall be made up before overtime is reckoned.

Persons losing 2½ hours or less shall be liable to a fine not exceeding 6d per hour. Persons employed losing more than 2½ hours but not exceeding 5 hours per week shall be liable to a fine not exceeding 1s. per hour for each hour or part of an hour so lost. Persons employed losing more than 5 hours per week shall be liable to a prosecution under the Munitions of War Act 1915.[22]

Such rules led to unrest in several areas, leading to strikes in Halifax and coming close to strike action in Sheffield. As a result the EEF withdrew its code and adopted the Ministry of Munitions' model rules.

In the interests of good industrial relations the Ministry sometimes itself took on prosecutions, especially of bad time-keepers. However, whoever undertook prosecutions, such action did cause resentment in many workplaces. In the last five months of 1915

4166 persons were taken to tribunals for alleged breaches of controlled establishment rules. Of these 2771 were convicted and £2273 0s 6d in fines were imposed, 624 defendants were found not guilty and 771 cases with withdrawn.[23] The munitions tribunals were continued after the end of the war to adjudicate on problems arising under the Restoration of Pre-War Practices Act 1919, and they finally ended in October 1920.

Initially the number of firms made controlled establishments was 134. However soon the places which were controlled extended beyond the principal armament and shipbuilding firms. By the 1 January 1916, 2422 establishments had been declared controlled. In mid-November 1915 the numbers of people working in controlled establishments were 1,077,800 men and 103,300 women.[24]

The reverberations of state control in coal mining lasted long after the First World War ended. The TUC and the Miners' Federation of Great Britain (MFGB) had passed motions in favour of national-isation of the coal mines from 1892 and 1894 respectively, and these were given increasingly serious support from about 1906 onwards.[25] The experience of state control in the war transformed the issue into one of practical politics, making it seem a much more realisable end. While the coal-owners later could try to depict state control during the First World War as an argument against nationalisation. W. A. Lee, who was to be chairman of the Mining Association of Great Britain, could claim: 'The Government took control of the industry in the early part of 1917 with results little short of disastrous to efficiency', and present as proof figures for falling output per shift and rising cost per ton of coal from the middle of the war (with no reference to manpower or other wartime problems).[26]

State control in coal mining mainly came about as a response to the decline in coal production, part of this problem being seen as a deterioration in industrial relations in the industry in the early part of the war. There was also a problem of securing a satisfactory distribution of coal between various domestic priorities and also between Britain's Allies and the neutral states. The South Wales coalfield was taken over on 1 December 1916 'in order to eliminate war profits, to avoid industrial disputes during the war, and to secure the best results from the labour of the mines'.[27] When

Lloyd George became Prime Minister on 7 December, he promised Labour that the state would undertake control of all the coalfields. This was done under the Defence of the Realm Act and came into force as of 1 March 1917, with a Coal Controller in charge of a new department of the Board of Trade.

The miners were initially suspicious of state control, fearing that its prime purpose was to control them. The MFGB executive insisted on seeing Lloyd George and gained reassurances that it was not intended to extend munitions tribunals or other aspects of the Munitions of War Act to them.[28] The coal-owners pressed hard to ensure that they got sizeable profits during the war. After some had challenged the legality of profit-limitation under the Defence of the Realm Act, the government brought in in October 1917 the Coal Mines Agreement Bill. In the committee stage the coal interest succeeded in excluding subsidiary undertakings (blast furnaces, coke ovens and various by-product works) from the government's financial controls. As G. D. H. Cole has observed, 'This had an important effect on the financial results of the measure; for very high profits were made during the remainder of the control period on the working of these subsidiary enterprises, and these profits were retained by the coal-owners in addition to the standard profits under the Act.'[29]

Up to the time of control the miners had received district wage awards. When, in response to the rising cost of living, the miners demanded a 20 per cent national wage increase in March 1915, Asquith as Prime Minister arranged and chaired a national joint meeting in late April. When this reached deadlock Asquith got both parties to refer the matter to him for a settlement. Asquith's award, issued on 5 May 1915, took the employers' view that circumstances varied so much from district to district that a uniform national award was impossible. The resulting district awards, however, were higher than the owners' offers at Asquith's joint meetings.[30]

Under state control there were national wage agreements. The existence of a national profits pool, whereby profits were equalised to compensate for the considerable variations in selling price according to whether coal was for domestic use or for export, demolished the argument that there could not be national wage settlements. The fact that all districts were subject to the rapidly rising cost of living, which was the main basis for adjusting wage rates, reinforced the case for national not district agreements. This case was pressed on the government by the MFGB and, after initial opposition by the War Cabinet, the miners were granted flat-rate wage increases of 1s 6d for adults and 9d per day for juniors on a national basis in September 1917. In July 1918 the government conceded a further 1s 6d per day flat-rate increase. On both occasions the government was forced to make sizeable concessions because of the overwhelming need for coal for the war effort.[31]

The MFGB did not greatly influence the administration of coal, which was firmly in the hands of Guy Calthrop, the General Manager of the London and North-Western Railway. Richard Redmayne, Chief Inspector of the Mines, took the view that 'the introduction of systems of controllership by single individuals was a mistake' and felt instead that coal should have been controlled by a board of experts under an independent chairman.[32] The miners were on the Coal Controller's Advisory Board, which was initially made up of five representatives of the owners and five of the MFGB. Though they refused to appoint one of their members to be in constant attendance on Calthrop to advise him when the Board was not in session. Smillie recalled, 'The miners declined to do this, mainly on the ground that their prospective adviser might be held responsible, by the outside public, for any action that might arise when the Board was not sitting.'[33] However the most significant feature of the Advisory Board was that the miners were having a say in the management of the industry and this experience, as well as that on some of the pit committees, whetted many appetites for real control of a nationalised coal industry after the end of the war.

The government was keen on the establishment of pit committees to police absenteeism. During 1916 they were pressed on the MFGB as an alternative to conscripting men who were absent from work without good cause. In 1918 the government made MFGB support for them a condition of granting the second national wage advance. The National Conference of the MFGB approved suggested rules for them in December 1916. These laid down a system of district and local committees, always evenly made up of owners' and workers' representatives. The rules included:

The Local Committee shall be empowered to impose fines, and the persons so fined shall have the option of signing a book for such fine to be deducted or to be dealt with by the management, or appear before the magistrates.

(a) If the first method is selected by the workman and he attends the works full time for one month after the fine is inflicted, the fine to be returned to him.

(b) All fines not so redeemed to be paid over to some charitable institution to be selected by the Local Committee.[34]

In short, such joint committees and the punishment they could impose were a somewhat milder version of the munitions tribunals. It is not surprising that such committees met resistance from some miners, even when the MFGB supported them. Hence a leading MFGB figure in November 1916 could report that in South Wales, 'at a large number of collieries there are no committees set up, the argument being used by the workmen that this is the thin end of the wedge to bring in industrial conscription; and they have turned a blind side to all we have urged upon them'. Later, in some places, according to G. D. H. Cole, the pit committees were turned into a forum where labour could press against managerial prerogatives and widen discussion beyond absenteeism to broader issues affecting coal output.[35]

The war also gave the miners an opportunity to try to extinguish non-unionism in the coalfields. For the MFGB the problem was exacerbated by the influx of replacement labour into the mines. In South Wales there was pressure for 'Show Card days', and a series of strikes against working with non-unionists began from March 1915. These became more serious in 1916 and led to an agreement, after intervention by Sir George Askwith in March 1916, whereby the owners made membership of a trade union a condition of employment during the war, albeit with the stipulation that this was 'without prejudice to their position after the war'.[36]

One effect of control elsewhere was also to strengthen trade unions' bargaining positions. Just before the outbreak of the First World War new conciliation machinery had been agreed for the railways but this was suspended in favour of the 1911 Scheme of Conciliation. The 'Truce Agreement' included 'that all existing contracts and conditions of service shall remain in operation, and that no new agreements shall be made by the companies with either deputations or Conciliation Boards during this suspensory period'. E. A. Pratt, in his monumental history of the railways in the First World War, gives the verdict:

Whatever may have been the intention at the time, there is no doubt that the 'Truce Agreement' in stereotyping conditions of service and in taking from the railway companies and the Conciliation Boards all power to vary the conditions of service, had the effect of enormously strengthening the development of trade union principles among railwaymen, the unions becoming the negotiating parties in all subsequent labour questions.[37]

During the war the National Union of Railwaymen (NUR) and the Associated Society of Locomotive Engineers and Fireman (ASLEF) negotiated various war bonuses for railway operating staff. The negotiations until March 1917 were with the General Managers' Committee representing the railway companies; from then on they negotiated with the Railway Executive Committee which acted on behalf of the government. Their wage claims were based usually on the soaring cost of living. Eventually, in September 1918, the government called for a joint committee to be set up to arrange for a sliding-scale to bring about automatic wage adjustments in response to cost of living changes. This came into operation on 1 November 1918, just before the war ended. Like the miners, these wage settlements were on a national basis and not negotiated through separate conciliation boards for each company; but unlike the coal industry, on the railways there was no abandonment of national wage bargaining after the war ended. Also like the miners, the negotiation of flat-rate increases during the war years benefited the poorest-paid grades of railway workers most.[38]

There were other areas of the economy where state intervention was substantial from early on, but there was not outright 'control' as with munitions, coal and the railways. The docks were a case where the trade unions were closely involved with such government intervention. The war led to serious dislocation of the ports, with, on the one hand, serious congestion early on in Liverpool, and, on the other, some east coast ports, notably Goole, Grangemouth and Bo'ness, nearly being closed down. In Liverpool, as C. R. Fayle has written,

The experience of the first nine months of war showed that the demands of the various importing Departments and of the various branches of the fighting services tended to come into conflict not only with commercial interests but with each other and in May 1915, as the result of strong representations by the Liverpool Steam Ship Owners' Association, the Government agreed to the creation of a small committee representative of the chief interests concerned, and empowered to supervise the general working of the port and decide between competing demands on its facilities.[39]

This, the Liverpool Coordination Committee, did not include union representation, but the national body which followed in November 1915, the Port and Transit Executive Committee, did include Harry Gosling, President of the National Transport Workers' Federation, from that December when its terms of reference were widened. However union representation on that, even when three further labour representatives were added in August 1917, was slight compared with that accorded to the employers. At local level the unions were involved in the port labour committees, most of the 32 set up in 1916 were formed after the introduction of conscription and had the prime purpose of issuing exemption certificates.

As with the coal mines and elsewhere, one problem in the docks for the unions was the influx of non-union replacement labour. Mitigating the need for this was a high priority for them. In Liverpool the National Union of Dock Labourers (NUDL) was deeply involved in Lord Derby's Liverpool Dock Workers' Battalion. The union also supported the establishment of Transport Workers' Battalions from March 1916, another scheme whereby some dock labour could be used more regularly and adaptably. Of this scheme, Harry Gosling later observed,

> One of the things we had to steer clear of was the military coming in and doing civilian work while civilian labour was available. These transport workers' battalions were paid civilian rates by the employers for all the work they did, were only brought in during an emergency, and were sent away again as soon as it was over.[40]

As in the rest of the economy there was a drive to economise on the use of labour. As one of the Port and Transit Executive Committee policy statements put it, 'No custom of a port, or trade practice, must be allowed to interfere with obtaining the utmost possible dispatch . . . [and] a *speeding-up* of work at all ports'.[41] The wartime pressures on the docks, most notably the volume of work to be done and the loss of men to the Armed Forces, did lead to a temporary reduction in casualism. In a period of overall labour shortage, it was not hard for such a cooperative union as the NUDL to ensure that union members continued to be given preference for work. The union also claimed that only union members should be given reserved status, thereby avoiding enlistment. James Sexton recalled, 'Many who had been bitterly antagonistic to our union clamoured for admission to it when all the men registered at the clearing house were ruled to be ineligible for military or naval service because they were already serving the country by handling its supplies of food and its war materials.[42]

As well as a shortage of labour, especially skilled labour, some sectors of British industry were seriously affected by a shortage of raw materials. As the war developed, restrictions on shipping space and of finance limited imports, and the government allowed or encouraged the running down of industries which were seen as less essential for the war. As a result some industries lost sizeable parts of their overseas trade.

Cotton was to be the archetypal industry of this kind in 1917. Earlier, before the USA entered the war on 6 April 1917, the maintenance of cotton exports was especially important in order to earn foreign exchange. By mid-1917, with heavy losses of ships through the German U-boat campaign and the severe restrictions on shipping space, the importation of cotton from the USA was being more and more restricted. The timing of control of cotton was determined by rampant speculation on the Liverpool futures market, resulting in its temporary closure on the 20 June 1917. The Cotton Control Board was set up on 28 June.

It was created not only to deal with the immediate problem of speculation but also to regulate consumption of cotton and to maintain the morale of the large Lancashire population dependent on the cotton industry. With the appointment of the Board, the Board of Trade issued the Raw Cotton Order, whereby all purchases of cotton within Britain had to be made under licence from the new Board. Under the Cotton (Restriction of Output) Order, brought into operation on 10 September 1917, consumption of cotton was regulated by restricting the percentage of machinery which could be used at any spinning or weaving mill. As there was no shortage of Egyptian cotton, the restrictions on spinning or weaving cotton from this source were less severe than for those using American cotton. Initially in spinning, mills could use 60 per cent of their machinery, but above that—up to 70 per cent for those using American cotton and 100 per cent for those using Egyptian—the employers had to pay a levy on additional machines. The funds resulting from such levies were applied across the trade to pay those who were laid off work as a result of the restrictions brought in by the Cotton Control Board. Thus some of the prosperity of the Egyptian sector of the trade was pooled for the benefit of the American sector, just as in coal mining, the export sector contributed to the profits pool for the benefit of the less profitable domestic sector. There were similar restrictions on use of machinery in weaving (with initially a maximum of 70 per cent allowed, with a levy on those working more than 60 per cent of their machinery).[43]

As with the Port and Transit Executive, the Cotton Control Board (after the first few weeks) gave greater representation to the employers than to the unions. Like other such bodies, the person in the chair was very acceptable to the employers. Indeed Hubert Henderson, who was Secretary of the Board, later wrote,

> Sir Herbert Dixon was an employer, with an employer's outlook and ideas. . . . He never pretended to be anything else than an employer, who, indeed, owed it to the remarkable offices which he filled to be scrupulously fair and to do his best to understand and allow for opposing points of view; but whose bias was none the less that of an employer, and as between spinners and manufacturers, of a spinner. Inevitably he responded more readily to the views of the employer members of the Board, to their suggestions and criticisms, to their objections and their fears than to those of the Labour members, who always represented to him 'the other side'. His unquestioned assumption of the initiative thus meant in effect that the initiative rested with the employers. The operatives' leaders fulfilled essentially the role of a friendly opposition, now pleading for concessions, now issuing warnings, but at no time playing an equal part in the determination of policy.[44]

Yet the cotton unions could find benefits from working with this system of control. Those who were out of work received payment from the levies, and these were paid out by their union branch official. Henderson, somewhat patronisingly observed,

> Without any encroachment upon their own carefully accumulated funds, they had all the pleasure of paying out to their members benefits upon an unprecedentedly generous scale, with a satisfying sense that it was in a large measure their scheme and that credit was due to them. When it came to paying a non-unionist, the pleasure was heightened for most by the excellent opportunity afforded for a little homily. For their

trouble they received certain small but welcome allowances from the Control Board, proportioned to the number of workpeople whom they paid.[45]

The Amalgamated Association of Weavers paid out £1,174,659 5s 9d between the start of the out-of-work payment on 15 September 1917 and June 1919.[46] The unions also gained greater centralisation of collective bargaining.

The employers benefited much more. Samuel Hurwitz has observed, when writing of shipping, 'As in coal, in munitions and in various lesser commodities, government "control", sometimes equated to "nationalization", meant simply that the industries were practically (and in many cases this qualifying adverb may be omitted) guaranteed a minimum profit far exceeding their pre-war profits'.[47] This is especially true of cotton where, especially in spinning, immense profits were made. Moreover, as Henderson observed, 'The levies which they were called upon to pay were of no great moment in those days of an Excess Profits Duty of 80 per cent; but in return for them . . . they received a *quid pro quo*, in the form of the acceptance by the workpeople of lower wages than would otherwise have been inevitable.' The levies vanished with the end of the war and post-war wage negotiations began from a lower base.[48]

Trouble first came to this system when the employers were too greedy. The operatives gave in strike notices over a wage claim in November 1917. At this time the cotton workers had only had 20 per cent rises over the pre-war rates, yet it was well known that the employers were making huge profits. The employers tried to negotiate a low wage settlement as a condition of the continuance of the unemployment payments (thereby making it transparent that it was the operatives who were funding these by taking low wages). A strike was narrowly averted by an agreement on 6 December 1917 to a six-month settlement giving the cotton workers a 15 per cent rise on the Standard Lists.

The terms of the next settlement did lead to a national spinners' strike in September 1918, after the membership rejected it by 10,998 votes to 2526. After the German offensive of March 1918 the Shipping Controller had suspended all supplies of American cotton for two months. As a result, mills dependent on that cotton closed on Saturdays and Mondays (and eventually in October a shortage of American yarn led to a close-down for a week of all weaving). The Cotton Control Board then raised levies on all machinery worked. However it also ended the rota system. Under this, lay-offs were shared by nearly all the workforce, with them not working one week every few weeks. The ending of the rota enraged many millworkers and boosted a shop stewards' movement. The indignant could point to the hypocrisy of the employers in ending sharing of the consequences of the war for the workers yet themselves insisting that all employers should share in the wartime profits, resisting successfully suggestions that fuel would be saved if some mills were closed entirely rather than keeping all open but with some machinery idle. At the same time the wage settlement of 25 per cent on the Standard Lists was meagre and gave cause for discontent. It gave those still on a 55½ hour week a wage level 57 per cent up on pre-war rates yet prices had roughly doubled, and those on a 40-hour week a drop in earnings.

The combination of the ending of the rota system and the wage settlement caused the most serious unrest in textiles during the war. The point of the spinners' strike was somewhat undercut by the government announcing an increase in cotton imports. The government used the Defence of the Realm Act to prevent strike pay. The strike was called off when Lloyd George offered an inquiry. This highlighted the unreasonably low pay being given to the operatives, but nothing was done about that before the war ended.[49]

In the cases of wool and worsted, the industries were under the control of the War Office until the autumn of 1917. The wool trade, like cotton, was adversely affected by Britain's worsening shipping situation. As a result, the Central Wool Advisory Committee, made up of employers and union representatives, agreed in April 1917 a priority scheme for manufacturers and the following month agreed a reduction in working hours per week from 55½ to 45. The various restrictions led to considerable discontent among manufacturers and they pressed hard for an equivalent of the Cotton Control Board for the woollen and worsted industries. A Board of Control was set up in September 1917, though with more limited functions and on a tripartite basis (War Office, employers and trade union representatives). The needs of the Armed Forces did lead to extensive intervention in the wool trade but Ben Turner was going too far when he wrote, 'It was the socialist productive experiment of the war. Soldiers and sailors needed cloth and clothing and private enterprise could not do it.' Perhaps the most notable change that the Labour representatives on the Board of Control got was the introduction of a standard clothing scheme. As E. M. H. Lloyd has written, 'The plan was to apply the system of costing and price fixing to the manufacture of goods for civilian consumption in the same way as it was already applied to goods for military purposes.'[50]

Overall, state control was very varied in its operation from industry to industry. As Lloyd wrote in his study of War Office and Ministry of Food control over a range of industries:

> The development of war time control was ... due almost entirely to the overwhelming force of circumstances and hardly at all to a deliberate policy of State intervention consciously thought out and consistently applied. The conflict between the private interests of individual traders and the general interest of the nation considered as a fighting unit was never resolved by a clear enunciation of general principles, but only gradually in part, by piecemeal adaptations and convenient compromises.[51]

However the interests of private enterprise almost always came before those of labour, even with labour's enhanced bargaining power. This is most vividly illustrated by employers' profits and workers' wages in the cotton industry. Of course a large part of the reason was labour's usual reluctance to exercise its extra power to the full during the national crisis.

Throughout the war the withdrawal of men for the Armed Forces remained highly contentious. The government tried to involve organised labour in this at local and national level. Labour Movement figures were involved in recruiting meetings from the start of the war. After the coming of conscription, trade unionists were involved in the Manpower Distribution Board in 1916, the National Service Department under Neville Chamberlain in the first part of 1917, and in the Recruiting Advisory Board of the Ministry of National Service under Sir Auckland Geddes. Both Asquith and Lloyd George paid court to organised labour to win its cooperation to get men out of industry and into the Armed Forces.[52]

The operation of all industries were affected by recruiting. Some sectors of the economy, such as food and drink, paper and printing, furniture and clothing, clerical and retailing, were tapped heavily for manpower. Even key war industries, especially after the German offensive of March 1918, were seriously disrupted. The actual administration of conscription led to considerable friction. In due course this led to recruiting being taken from the War Office and carried out under civil control.[53]

One particular cause of unrest was where skilled workers had agreed to dilution to make up the shortage of skilled labour and then found that the army was still taking skilled men. A deputation from the Amalgamated Society of Engineers saw the Minister of Munitions on 27 September 1916 with a list of some 600 members who had been taken into the army in spite of repeated pledges from the government and in spite of the Minister of Munitions repeatedly complaining of the absolute shortage of skilled engineers. The next day they received further assurances from Asquith. The ASE returned on 3 November 1916 to complain to the Manpower Board that in spite of the Prime Minister's pledge skilled men were still being taken, in some cases even men badged and certificated for exemption had been arrested. They offered to issue cards to their members certifying that they were skilled and to find such skilled men for skilled work in the Army as were needed (after the Army had exhausted supplies of skilled men already serving in non-mechanical corps).[54]

Before new proposals on exemptions from military service could be agreed, serious unrest broke out in Sheffield over the Army taking a fitter named Leonard Hargreaves. Arthur Henderson warned his Cabinet colleagues that they were facing the gravest crisis since the start of the war. He told them that the unrest in Sheffield was symptomatic of the widespread complete lack of confidence in the fairness and efficiency of the existing manpower policies. He warned that there was widespread concern about victimisation, when skilled men had their protection removed because they had offended the employer in some way, preferential treatment, when an employer improperly sheltered a friend, and improper enlistment, when skilled men were taken in defiance of all pledges and in spite of all badges and certificates of exemption. In Sheffield engineers went on strike on 16 November 1916, disregarding advice from the ASE leadership, and the stoppage spread to Barrow. It only ended when Hargreaves actually appeared before them. The official *History of the Ministry of Munitions* observed, 'Sheffield was noted for its steadfast devotion to war work and its freedom from industrial trouble. Yet in the annals of the war no strike showed so few signs of indecision or half-heartedness.'[55]

Whilst the Sheffield strike was taking place, the national conference of the ASE considered new proposals from the government. After negotiations with government Ministers, the ASE concluded the Trade Card Agreement on 18 November 1916 whereby it would issue exemption cards. The government soon extended this privilege to the Boilermakers, the Shipwrights, the Sheet Metal Workers, the Ironfounders, the Scottish Moulders and the British Steel Smelters.[56] The giving of such powers to skilled unions, at a time when exemptions were being removed from semi- and unskilled men, did nothing to enhance inter-union feelings. In addition, the boundaries of membership of skilled unions did not match precisely the skilled needs of wartime production. Moreover, there were many cases where skilled and semi-skilled workers were crucial. Thus a Ministry of Munitions official warned in February 1917:

> It had yet to be realised that in some industries basic to Britain's role as the arsenal of the Allied war effort semi-skilled and unskilled labour, by their very familiarity with the work process, were actually engaged in essential war work. The trade card scheme protected skilled men in the foundries, but, with the removal of 1005 semi-skilled men under twenty-three years of age, the dislocation of skilled work in the industry was severe. Similarly, in gas works most stokers were fit for general service, but the work had not been undertaken by the Army Reserve Munition Workers. Consequently munitions output had been affected by growing inefficiency in neighbouring gas works. In the engineering trades the same problem had quickly become apparent because the cancellation of exemptions was carried out on a far larger scale.[57]

It is not surprising, therefore, that the government soon abolished the Trade Card Scheme. In November the Man Power Board had stated that of 314,000 men needed for the Army by mid-March 1917, 200,000 would be found from among those hitherto exempted. By early 1917 the government was moving away from the loose Trade Card Scheme towards a rigorous Schedule of Protected Occupations. The announcement of this, plus the proposals for the extension of dilution to private engineering work, were the prime causes of the May 1917 engineering strikes, though the strikes reflected a wide range of accumulated grievances and the mix of grievances varied from area to area. By the end of the strikes, 1,500,000 working days were lost and 200,000 men had been involved in them.[58]

Coal mining is another example where there was serious unrest over the incidence of recruiting. Among the miners there was an expectation that the men who had entered the mines after the outbreak of war would be taken first. In the mines dilution was less of an issue than in engineering, as the skills of underground workers, especially those at the coal face, could not easily be substituted.

Coal miners were among the occupations which had been categorised in late 1915 as vitally important for the war effort. Whether or not men could be allowed to join the Armed Forces, and other manpower matters, were decided by Colliery Recruiting Courts (made up of an inspector of mines aided by a representative of both the employers and mines) with the right of appeal to a Central Colliery Recruiting Court. As with the engineers, some miners were needed by the Army for specialised work; and the Central Court in January 1916 laid down that 10,000 skilled miners a year should be recruited for tunnelling. From April 1916 there was a comb-out of some of the single men who had entered the mines after the first year of the war.

The increasing demand for men from the mines in 1917 led to unrest in some areas. In February the government agreed to the withdrawal of 20,000 men by 9 May and a further 20,000 by the end of July. As the surface workers had already been depleted, most had to come from underground workers.[59] Guy Calthrop, the Coal Controller, repeatedly urged the War Cabinet to be cautious in securing the miners for the Armed Forces. In early July he urged, 'The greatest tact is necessary in dealing with a body like the Miners' Federation, and any attempt to force the pace unduly will merely play into the hands of the section less keen on recruiting.' Later in the month, he pressed again on Milner and Barnes the view 'that the miners can be led but not driven'; and added, 'At the present time I believe it to be a fact that, although it is not entirely absent, there is less unrest among the miners than among other classes of workmen and I believe this to be due to the fact that we have never broken a bargain with them and have always taken them into our confidence . . .'[60]

In fact, the government succeeded in gaining the support of the Miners' Federation as a whole to new recruiting proposals. As only 19,256 of the 40,000 men required by the War Cabinet had been raised by means already accepted by the MFGB, the MFGB agreed to the raising of the remainder by withdrawing exemptions from some of the men aged between 18 and 25. This led to a strike from 6 to 11 August of 27,000 Yorkshire miners who objected to young pre-war miners being taken whilst older men who had entered mines after the start of the war remained. The scheme was postponed on 8 August, and the Miners' Federation in September agreed that it be 'not put into operation until all persons of military age who have entered the mines since August 1914 have been combed out'.[61]

In South Wales there had been repeated opposition during 1917 to aiding a comb-out of men from the coal mines. The Special Conference of the South Wales Miners' Federation on 8 October agreed to take a strike ballot, putting before the members the resolution,

> That the South Wales Miners' Federation take no part in assisting the recruitment of colliery workers for the army and navy. Are you in favour of a Down Tools Policy in South Wales in the event of the government proceeding with their comb-out scheme in the mines?

That there was already a lengthy strike going on in part of the Rhondda when this ballot was called clearly worried Lloyd George, who pressed Albert Stanley, the President of the Board of Trade, to settle it quickly. This was done in a way favourable to the miners.[62] In the event, when the ballot result was declared on 15 November, there were 94,946 votes against a strike over the comb-out proposals and only 28,903 for such action.

By the end of 1917 the overall manpower situation was grave, with the Bolshevik Revolution in Russia having 'shut the Allies off from what was formerly their largest reserve of manpower' and American resources not yet fully available. As a result, a Cabinet Committee Report noted that to meet Britain's manpower priorities would involve 'a gigantic shuffle of the industrial man-power of the country'. It suggested,

> Among these . . . methods may be . . . the stimulation and fostering of drifts of population from one industry to another. For example, where

coal mines are not working full time, as on the East Coast, a drift would perhaps be caused by working short time in the neighbourhood of ports while keeping the more distant areas working at full pressure. Another method is to introduce war industries into a district where the war has caused normal occupations to work short time. For example, an attempt is being made to establish an aeroplane industry in Lancashire, where the cotton factories are working short time.

By late 1917 shipbuilding was a top priority and the government was eager to take more men for the Army from coal mining and elsewhere.[63]

This led to the government holding a general conference on 3 January 1918 with the unions who, when the Schedule of Protected Occupations was set up, had been promised further consultations should it be revised. After further meetings with various industrial groups the government introduced a new Military Service Bill on 14 January which, when it became law on 6 February, gave the government powers to cancel certificates of exemption, and a revised Schedule of Protected Occupations which came into force on 1 February and which brought in the 'clean cut' for recruiting up to the age of 23 (except for certain shipbuilding and shale oil mining work).[64]

Faced with demands for 50,000 men to be withdrawn from the mines in late February 1918, the MFGB decided to take a ballot on whether it should agree to this and, if so, whether the MFGB machinery should be used to find them. Before this took place, the War Cabinet agreed on 5 March to the Minister of National Service getting the required numbers by withdrawing all certificates of exemption issued to miners between the ages of 18 years 8 months and 25. The ballot resulted in a majority against (248,067 to 219,311) but a small majority for the latter proposition. Given the smallness of the majority and after a deputation had heard from Lloyd George and the Director of Military Operations the gravity of the military situation, the MFGB accepted the comb-out on 22 March, the day after the great German offensive on the Western Front began.[65]

There was also further industrial unrest in engineering as a result of the tougher manpower policies. In December 1917 the government decided to take 108,000 men from munitions (of which 12,500 would even be taken from shipbuilding). The ASE were refused separate consultations over the new manpower proposals in January; their demand for these led to some other unions declaring that they would only support the government's proposals if the government rejected such preferential treatment for the ASE. There was unrest in some munitions centres, including the threat of a strike in Coventry and Sir Auckland Geddes getting a rough reception when explaining the proposals in Glasgow and Liverpool; and the union took a ballot as to whether their members were in favour of accepting the new manpower proposals or were prepared to resist them until the government had consulted with the ASE. The result of the ballot was 120,675 for resistance until consultation took place and only 27,416 for acceptance. As a result Lloyd George and Geddes did see a deputation from the ASE separately, though they offered no extra concessions. After this a second ballot gave a majority in favour of accepting the manpower scheme.[66]

With the German offensive of 21 March 1918 the government was forced to take an even harder line on manpower. Lloyd George told his Ministers, 'It looks as if we should have to make up in two or three weeks losses which under previous conditions would have allowed us two or three months.'[67] The government rapidly got through the House of Commons what became on 18 April 1918 the Military Service (No. 2) Act 1918, which set age limits for military service at 18 and 50, gave the government powers to extend conscription to Ireland, and to extend the 'clean cut' to all but those engaged on crucial work. The government also took the opportunity to try to increase labour mobility by proposing a measure of compulsory enrolment of War Munition Volunteers and also, under the Defence of the Realm Regulations, brought in a policy of embargo on the engagement of skilled labour at certain firms in order (as a press notice put it) 'to ensure not only a more equitable distribution of labour throughout the war industries but a better economy of man power remaining in the country'. The embargo policy was applied to nearly 70 firms in late June and early July 1918 and led to a serious strike beginning in Coventry on 23 July by engineers who saw the two schemes as tantamount to industrial conscription. The strike spread to Birmingham, and a national conference of local officials in engineering threatened a national strike from 30 July. The government refused to negotiate other than with national trade union officials and threatened to withdraw protection from military service from strikers; but it did make it clear that the notice put up by the firm in Coventry, which had sparked off the dispute, was unauthorised and the Ministry instructed the firm to withdraw it. These actions settled the strike.[68]

The withdrawal of large numbers of men for the Army had serious effects on industrial output. In munitions output of even important items such as tanks and aero-engines fell seriously below the levels planned, and by the autumn there was plant and machinery standing idle and even unskilled labour unemployed through lack of skilled supervisors. In agriculture the removal of further men ensured no increase in food production. In coal mining, after the German offensive, there was a demand for the withdrawal of a further 50,000 men and, although the number was later halved, the result was the major cause of a reduction in coal production and supplies to both industrial and domestic users. Coal shortages were made worse by strikes in South Wales in May and in Yorkshire in August and by the influenza epidemic which in July alone cut output by nearly 3 million tons. Eventually the War Cabinet had to agree to miners being brought back from the Army.[69]

By the time of the final Allied offensive in late summer 1918, Britain had fully exhausted her manpower reserves. Even the military were becoming aware of this. Thus the Chief of the Imperial General Staff wrote to the British representative with Marshal Foch,

> The more we look into the question of our manpower the uglier it seems to be. Agriculture, Vital industries for ourselves and our Allies, Coal, Shipbuilding, Aeroplane and Tank Construction—and personnel—and so on and so forth all show such formidable demands that little remains for the fighting services. The Cabinet therefore are anxious about the future. They do not want to end the war in an absolutely exhausted condition, if this can be avoided.[70]

Ten days before the Armistice the President of the Board of Trade warned Lloyd George, 'I need not remind you of the extreme gravity of the coal situation. Our stocks are rapidly declining and unless men of the required categories are obtained immediately it will be impossible to carry on many of the essential industries . . .'[71] At the end of the war parts of British industry were indeed close to grinding to a halt.

The relationship between the government and employers was somewhat mixed. On the one hand, in organising a war economy the government frequently turned to businessmen for expertise. The War Office and then the Ministry of Munitions brought them into the government administration to help organise munitions supply. Men such as Eric Geddes of the North-Eastern Railway and Allan Smith of the EEF were to be influential in production and labour policies. Also, at the local level, employers were the key figures in organising engineering capacity through the District Armaments Committees. However, on the other hand, for many employers the First World War was a frustrating, if not humiliating time, in regard to their relations with the government. The government was the largest purchaser of goods and services, and the Ministry of Munitions became the largest employer of labour in the country. In the face of urgent needs of war materials and the strong position of labour, government departments often paid scant respect to the views of the business community, especially in the first half of the war.

Many businessmen felt that their industrial experience was too readily disregarded by the wartime administrators. Sir Charles Macara, for example, who had long been the leading figure in the Federation of Master Cotton Spinners' Association, from early on in the war campaigned for cotton to be listed as contraband of war as it was used in the manufacture of explosives. It took a year for the government to act on this; thereby assisting the immodest Macara to observe later, 'that the government in control at that day were not prepared to take the advice of the people who had spent their lives in dealing with practical affairs'.[72]

Businessmen also felt unduly restrained by the wartime regulations. This feeling is well expressed by the comments of the Huddersfield engineering employers in early 1918:

> Employers have had imposed upon them conditions and restrictions which in normal times would be unthinkable. They have been deprived of almost all freedom of action. Their profits have been largely acquired by the government. Their own personal income from their business has been controlled. Their men have to a large extent been spoiled not only by wages awards which have been expedient rather than just, but also by marked weakness on the part of the government. In many other ways the just rights of the employer have been ruthlessly put aside for the purpose of maintaining industrial peace.[73]

In some cases the government was more realistic than the

employers' organisations. This was so with the leaving certificate issue of which, with the notable exception of Allan Smith, the employers on the Ministry of Munitions Advisory Committee repeatedly asserted that no significant problem existed.[74] They felt, at the time of the revision of the Munitions Acts in 1917, that 'the Advisory Committee were being absolutely ignored by the Government' and, when Addison did not inform them of what he had agreed with the trade unions, their chairman indignantly wrote to Addison,

> My committee, as you understand, are all men actually engaged in important munitions businesses, some of them have to travel consider-able distances to attend the meetings and they have separated today with a feeling that much valuable time has been wasted.[75]

During the war employers were frequently shocked by the way in which their views were not heeded when pay claims were settled. They had cause for concern. Winston Churchill's award of a 12½ per cent increase in some groups of skilled time workers in engineering in October 1917 was as good example of a Minister blundering in where angels feared to tread.

However the exigencies of war did press employers into having to accept national wage bargaining in more industries, as is shown in Chapter 4. With the National Wages Agreement of early 1917, as we have seen, the employers agreed with the ASE that wage levels would be considered every four months by the Committee on Production and that the resulting awards would be accepted nationally. National wage settlements were also agreed for the first time in other areas, such as gas supply in 1917 and in flour milling, chemicals, soap and tramways in 1918.[76]

Employers felt they were being left behind by the trade unions. Sir William Peat, when chairing the inaugural meeting of the Federation of British Industries (FBI), received warm assent when he told those present 'we have much to learn from labour'.[77] Increased union power and national pay awards by the Committee on Production made employers more ready to band together in national organisations. In the context of the war, employer divisions over protection or free trade became less important.

There had been attempts in the past to form an employers' equivalent of the TUC; but such organisations had not lasted long.

In 1911 some businessmen, enraged by the Liberal government's failure to take much notice of their views on the National Insurance Bill, set up the Employers' Parliamentary Association. Sir Charles Macara, its President, observed later, 'the trend of legislation made it highly desirable that businessmen should be able collectively to take action and to insist upon being consulted on all matters affecting industry and commerce'. This association attracted 40 federations and numerous large firms and was largely Free Trade in outlook.[78] Macara was also a leading figure in 1915 in creating the Central Association of Employers' Organisations, also launched from Manchester. That year also saw another group form the British Manufacturers' Association. This body was centred on Birmingham but had support in Sheffield, Manchester and elsewhere. It campaigned for 'a reciprocal customs tariff within the Empire', and also called for the 'adoption of a minimum wage or of some system of profit sharing whereby labour would receive a fair share of the rewards of labour'.[79] There were also moves towards encouraging political activity by business men by the Associated British Chambers of Commerce and by the British Engineers' Association.[80]

A measure of the FBI's success was that it absorbed the Employers' Parliamentary Association and brought the British Manufacturers' Association into close cooperation with it, thereby, as Stephen Blank has put it, 'joining for the first time the industries of Birmingham and Manchester in a single organisation'.[81] The minutes of the latter body recorded, in May 1917: 'The chairman gave it as his opinion that the Federation of British Industries was now becoming such a powerful body that it was necessary to fall into line with them.'[82] The FBI grew rapidly. In 1917 its membership was made up of 494 firms and 73 associations. In 1918 it rose to 793 firms, 152 firms and 15 controlled establishments.[83]

Whilst the FBI's growth gave employers more leverage with government, it is clear that a strong employers' organisation to counterbalance the trade unions was not unwelcome to the government. As the government had become increasingly involved in organising industry it had become insistent that it should deal, at as high a level as possible, with both sides of industry. This was also the case later, as the government planned reconstruction after the war. Whether or not employers' organisations had existed before in individual industries, during the war the government made clear it needed them for its various committees. In many cases where organisations did not exist, government arranged their creation.

Once the FBI had got off the ground, it was welcomed by the government. At its Annual General Meeting in October 1918, the membership could be assured, 'There is every wish now, from the Prime Minister downwards, for everyone to consult your Federation upon all questions which are appertaining to trade, and I think our advice is generally acceptable and has considerable force in the decisions of the Government.' Another leading figure could report,

> It was in the early part of the present year that many of us waited upon the Prime Minister to discuss certain matters which were then coming, and he said to us then: 'The reason why we, the Government, have not consulted manufacturers in the past is because there was nobody that we could consult. If we consulted one trade association, other trade associations said that that association had no right or qualification to speak for them.' He said, 'We want to consult you. Labour comes to us and speaks more or less with one voice, but hitherto manufacturers have utterly failed to realise their duty and the position they ought to occupy.' He said, 'Go away and organise, and if you will come to us and give us your opinion as manufacturers speaking for industry as a whole, we will not only listen to you, but we will welcome your assistance on every possible occasion.' Since that time the recognition that the Federation is fulfilling that qualification has rapidly grown with the members of the Government.[84]

Employers wanted state controls to be removed as soon as practicable at the end of the war. Yet they had hopes of state help. As the President of the FBI observed in October 1918, 'we feel that the ideal should be state assistance and not state interference.'[85] Many also had faith in their new employers' organisations. Thus Sir Vincent Caillard wrote in July 1919, 'In the sphere of manufacture and production the day of unadulterated individualism is over, and a new spirit of cooperation is being born to meet the new problems of the future. . . . It is now scarcely an exaggeration to say that there is no trade which is not represented by a body to protect its corporate interests and to express its corporate opinions.'[86]

The government needed to gain the cooperation of the unions in organising the economy for war. This involved increasing reliance on the leadership of the main trade unions and, by the end of the war, it increased the influence of the TUC.

Whilst the introduction of industrial or manpower changes involved negotiations with those unions affected most and protesting most, on broad labour matters the Parliamentary Committee of the TUC was consulted more than before the war and it also helped to provide the Labour nominees on various government bodies. Its significance as the forum for the trade union movement was recognised by Lloyd George when, in the midst of his drive for increased munitions production, he asked to speak to the annual Congress in September 1915. Yet it was not the sole or dominant voice of the Labour Movement. When Arthur Henderson was in the Cabinet, between 1915 and 1917, he and the Labour Party were more conspicuous than the TUC in representing the views of the Labour Movement to the government. Also throughout the war urgent working-class issues arising from it were dealt with by the War Emergency Workers National Committee. Whilst earlier in the war the TUC was outshone by these, its chief rival for the role of speaking for the trade unions collectively, the General Federation of Trade Unions, was finally eclipsed after 1915. In the last year or so of the war the TUC's role became more significant. Henderson's replacement in the War Cabinet, from August 1917, was George Barnes, a much less significant figure in the Labour Movement. The TUC also emerged more into the limelight as it was the appropriate forum for the trade union movement's debates about post-war industrial and social policies.[87]

The government was more eager to involve the leadership of the unions covering key war work in helping to organise war production. With regard to munitions, leading trade unionists were drawn into the government apparatus by participating in the National Advisory Committee (NAC), a body which stemmed from those attending the Treasury Conference in March 1915. Using the threat of industrial conscription, Lloyd George was skilful in pressing the trade union leaders to agree to further means of increasing output, measures which usually substantially changed the working conditions of their members. In the autumn of 1915 Lloyd George successfully pressed the NAC to take it on themselves to organise dilution. Members of the NAC joined with the staff of the Ministry of Munitions to form the Central Munitions Labour Supply Committee to carry out measures which would clearly cause serious unrest in engineering workshops. Thus skilled trade union leaders were transformed from men who represented their men's grievances to employers and the government, to men who quite literally saw to the organisation of the government's policies on removing restrictive practices and bringing in unskilled and semi-skilled labour to do work normally done by their members, often, as on the Clyde in 1915 and 1916, in the face of the violent opposition of their members.

The government gained much from the active cooperation of trade union leaders. Moreover, as time went by, such trade union leaders who closely cooperated with the government in support of the war effort came to depend on government support in return. Some, indeed, wanted government support in controlling their own members from early on; some being quite explicit on this as early as the discussions on what was to become the Munitions of War Act, 1915. Many soon found that their active help in facilitating government policy made them as much the target of rank-and-file hostility as the government itself. This was true in engineering over dilution and 'combing-out' of men for the Armed Forces, as well as in other industries. Lloyd George and other Ministers soon found it very important to buttress the position of such trade union leaders and carefully tried to follow a policy of only negotiating with 'official' trade union leaders, not with shop stewards or other local leaders. After the near national wave of engineering strikes in May 1917 the government, in search of ways to defuse the unrest, pressed often reluctant trade union leaders to absorb into their union structure, and thereby control, shop stewards.[88]

Many trade unionists were delighted to be involved in the various government committees set up, both nationally and locally, in the war.[89] Such involvement enhanced their own status (certainly in their own eyes, as the memoirs of men such as Ben Turner and Harry Gosling clearly reveal) and gave an outlet for their desire to 'serve' in the war.

They were also involved in the multiplicity of joint committees set up in industry, ranging from such bodies as the Cotton and Wool Control Boards down to committees at factory level. The setting-up of joint committees was a regular proposal in the period 1910–21 when employers found industrial relations particularly menacing. In April 1915 when dilution was to be introduced, Allan Smith, normally the Secretary of the Engineering Employers' Federation but then working for the Ministry of Munitions, put the matter bluntly to some employers: 'if we are to . . . rush through this thing [dilution] at top speed, the rate at which we will have to progress, and the breaking down of trade union restrictions, will be so great that you will require a safety valve, and the only safety valve we can think of as such is a small joint committee to deal with the question where the two interests bump up against each other.'[90] At factory level the enhanced position of labour pushed management this way well before the Whitley Report. Thus in the case of the firm Hans Renold Ltd, a Manchester engineering firm, Sir Charles Renold has written:

> It was towards the end of 1916 that the Directors of the Company felt the need for closer contact with their workpeople. Conditions were in a state of flux. Products and processes were changing; departments were being reorganised; unskilled labour was replacing skilled; numbers were increasing, bringing in many strangers and there was a growing flood of wage awards and government directions to be applied. All the old familiar landmarks were going and if a general break-down of works morale was to be avoided some means of talking things over between management and workers was essential . . .
> About this time the Ministry of Munitions was active in getting employers to establish Accident Prevention Committees jointly with their employees. This gave a pretext and an occasion to raise with the departmental superintendents the novel idea of a joint committee of management and workers and they were persuaded to help in getting together an *ad hoc* committee of workers to discuss it. The scope was, however, to be wider than accident prevention.[91]

After the May 1917 engineering strikes, the government sent Special Commissioners to each area of the country to inquire into the causes of industrial unrest. Earlier the Whitley Committee had recommended that the government 'should propose without delay to the various associations of employers and employed the formation of Joint Standing Industrial Councils in the several industries, where they do not already exist, consisting of representatives of employers and employed . . .'. The Special Commissioners for several areas called for the Whitley proposals to be implemented, especially at the lowest of the suggested three tiers (works, district and national councils). The North West Commissioners observed that they would be:

a message of hope to those who are rightly dissatisfied with their conditions. Many a sensible young man who now thinks that the only hope of betterment for himself and his class lies in the spreading of advanced doctrines would understand how far more useful he would be to himself and his fellow-men by taking a seat on the Shop Committee and doing direct work in improving the condition of the shop.[92]

The unskilled unions and those in industries where collective bargaining was not well established welcomed the Whitley Report and were eager for these joint councils to be set up. The government made moves in these areas but was less keen to act in the public sector, only coming out in favour of implementing the Whitley Report in its own establishments 'where the conditions are sufficiently analogous to those existing in outside industries' in July 1918.[93]

The creation of joint councils in the less strongly unionised areas was one among many developments in the war which encouraged trade union growth. In the case of the pottery the initiative came before the Whitley Report was published. W. H. Warburton has written of the Joint Industrial Council for the Pottery Industry,

> With the view of getting all operative potters organised in a trade union, posters were displayed on factories advising all workers to join the National Society of Pottery Workers. The Council also requested manufacturers to grant facilities to trade union officials to enter factories at meal times for propaganda purposes, or at such other time as were convenient. This request was fairly generally granted, with the provision that there was to be no undue interference with the carrying on of the operatives' work.[94]

In that case the joint council was set up by private initiative. Elsewhere many were due, in part at least, to government encouragement. Union growth was also helped by the government through it requiring some employers to recognise unions for collective bargaining as well as by such developments as the involving of the unions in a range of committees affecting working class life (from relieving distress to conscription), thereby enhancing their prestige at local and national level.

Government wartime pressure towards national collective bargaining was not unwelcome to many employers by the later part of the war, who were becoming concerned about leapfrogging local settlements. Thus in printing, the employers were alarmed by this in late 1917 and 1918, and moved towards national agreements, which were negotiated in detail in 1919. With boots and shoes, much of the industry came under government control. Government departments insisted on working through the unions. As a result of the centralised control of the industry both the union and the employers moved their organisations to London in 1918 to be close to government.[95]

Another marked feature of trade union development in the war was the considerable number of amalgamations and federations which took place. Federations were easier to organise and most union mergers in the war came about this way. However amalgamations were made more easy by the Trade Union Amalgamation Act of 10 July 1917, which required half the members entitled to vote to do so and the majority in favour being at least 20 per cent (as opposed to requiring two-thirds of the membership approving it before). The Amalgamated Society of Carpenters and Joiners and the Amalgamated Union of Cabinetmakers had long wanted to merge, thereby removing, as the official history puts it, 'difficulties which inevitably occurred when equally skilled men capable of doing the same class of work were enrolled in distinct and separate unions enforcing dissimilar rules'. This was achieved as of 1 April 1918.[96]

The drastic wartime changes in the labour market encouraged amalgamations. In lace the trade had shrunk by half by 1918, and this encouraged amalgamations or federations among Scottish textile unions and with the English ones. In printing dilution upset many of the traditional demarcation lines. As John Child has written,

> One method of resolving the clash between the separate interests was to enrol all workers in each branch of the industry in one union. Thus the Lithographic Printers amalgamated with the Stone and Plate Preparers; the Stereotypers' craft union opened its ranks to the Stereotypers' Assistants; the Bookbinders abandoned their traditional hostility to women unionists and started a Women's Section; The S.T.A. [Scottish Typographical Association] amended its constitution to provide for an Auxiliary Section of assistants and women.[97]

Necessity forced the male trade unionists to try to enrol women into the existing unions. Many areas where women usually worked were cut back by the war, from cotton and flax to jam-making and herring preparing. Large numbers of women moved into areas which had previously been male preserves and joined a union. Whilst overall trade union membership went up rapidly, that of women went up faster, with the general unions benefiting especially. The Workers' Union, which grew from just over 140,000 members to 379,000 during the war, employed 20 women organisers by the end of the war. At the end of the war, it had more than 80,000 female members. Similarly women replaced most of the large numbers of male shopworkers who had enrolled in the Armed Forces and, by the end of the war, women accounted for 42 per cent of the membership of the shopworkers' union as opposed to 20 per cent at the outset of the war. Recent work suggests that overall trade union density among female workers went up from 8 per cent in 1913 and 1914 to 21.7 per cent in 1918.[98]

Lloyd George, writing to Ben Tillett in late August 1914, observed, 'It is very difficult to gauge what the actual effect of war under modern conditions will be upon either capital or labour but one thing is already perfectly obvious—it must effect a revolutionary change in the relations of the state to both.'[99] However the government's administrative response was for much of the war very *ad hoc* and even fumbling.

In a 'war of production' the government became the employer of a large proportion of the labour force. It became directly involved in wage negotiations covering large numbers of people. Departments competed with each other for scarce resources, including skilled labour. Moreover numerous departments became involved in labour disputes. As an official report put it,

> Thus, the Ministry of Munitions and the War Office were concerned with the settlement of disputes on munitions work; the Admiralty, as regards war vessels and other Admiralty contract work; the Board of Trade as regards the coal-mining industry and the railways; the Ministry of Shipping with merchant vessels; the Air Ministry with the building of aeroplanes, the construction of aerodromes etc. All this had a tendency to result in lack of uniformity and absence of co-ordination.[100]

With Lloyd George's accession to the premiership in December 1916, new Ministries were created, including a Ministry of Labour. But this owed more to Lloyd George's need to win the support of

Table 1.1: Employment in the United Kingdom, 1914–20 (In thousands)

| Industry | July 1914 M | July 1914 F | July 1915 M | July 1915 F | July 1916 M | July 1916 F | July 1917 M | July 1917 F | July 1918 M | July 1918 F | July 1919 M | July 1919 F | July 1920 M | July 1920 F |
|---|---|---|---|---|---|---|---|---|---|---|---|---|---|---|
| Building | 920 | 7 | 703 | 7.5 | 559 | 10 | 465 | 20 | 440 | 29 | 655 | 13 | 796 | 10 |
| Mines & Quarries | 1,266 | 7 | 1,058 | 6.5 | 1,061 | 11 | 1,086 | 12 | 1,017 | 13 | 1,243 | 11 | 1,323 | 9.6 |
| Coal mines | 1,121 | 6.1 | 945 | 6.1 | 964 | 1 | 997 | 11 | 928 | 12 | 1,139 | 10 | 1,205 | 9.1 |
| Metal Trades | 1,634 | 170 | 1,573 | 203 | 1,707 | 370 | 1,768 | 523 | 1,824 | 594 | 1,953 | 303 | 2,104 | 303 |
| Iron & steel | 287 | 3.4 | 276 | 4 | 301 | 9 | 318 | 24 | 320 | 39 | 359 | 13 | 404 | 10 |
| Engineering (except marine & electrical and ordinance) | 437 | 15 | 408 | 29 | 450 | 104 | 457 | 156 | 457 | 173 | 470 | 42 | 507 | 40 |
| Electrical engineering | 80 | 17 | 76 | 21 | 84 | 37 | 86 | 51 | 89 | 55 | 100 | 38 | 114 | 39 |
| Shipbuilding & marine engineering | 289 | 2.3 | 336 | 11 | 344 | 20 | 370 | 29 | 411 | 32 | 447 | 3.6 | 433 | 6.8 |
| Cycles, motors & aircraft | 122 | 11 | 110 | 13 | 162 | 45 | 171 | 74 | 184 | 89 | 182 | 34 | 202 | 31 |
| Chemical Trades | 159 | 39.9 | 161 | 48 | 176 | 87 | 176 | 108.9 | 162 | 103.6 | 174 | 72.8 | 195 | 69.8 |
| Textile Trades | 625 | 863 | 562 | 888 | 497 | 908 | 453 | 884 | 411 | 827 | 483 | 823 | 560 | 884 |
| Cotton | 274 | 415 | 242 | 413 | 196 | 419 | 168 | 398 | 146 | 359 | 180 | 365 | 219 | 396 |
| Woollen & worsted | 134 | 170 | 131 | 178 | 119 | 181 | 110 | 178 | 103 | 169 | 124 | 182 | 135 | 188 |
| Clothing Trades | 287 | 612 | 263 | 634 | 226 | 603 | 196 | 574 | 183 | 568 | 226 | 582 | 238 | 569 |
| Clothing trades (tailoring, shirt-making, dressmaking, millinery, corset-making) | 109 | 368 | 102 | 394 | 81 | 365 | 70 | 335 | 68 | 341 | 85 | 356 | 87 | 349 |
| Boots & shoes | 110 | 56 | 107 | 56 | 96 | 65 | 84 | 71 | 76 | 70 | 93 | 68 | 99 | 63 |
| Food, Drink & Tobacco Trades | 360 | 196 | 326 | 209 | 294 | 227 | 255 | 226 | 243 | 235 | 328 | 258 | 359 | 242 |
| Paper & Printing Trades | 261 | 148 | 212 | 139 | 187 | 146 | 162 | 144 | 156 | 142 | 209 | 144 | 253 | 166 |

| | | | | | | | |
|---|---|---|---|---|---|---|---|
| Wood Trades | 258 44 | 209 48 | 195 56 | 173 68 | 168 79 | 213 66 | 245 65 |
| Other Trades | 456 90 | 388 106 | 343 124 | 317 143 | 305 155 | 394 142 | 447 137 |
| Total private & municipal establishments | 6,226 2,177 | 5,455 2,289 | 5,245 2,542 | 5,051 2,703 | 4,909 2,746 | 5,878 2,415 | 6,520 2,456 |
| Total government establishments | 76 2 | 151 6 | 201 72 | 243 206 | 257 225 | 161 27 | 113 6.3 |
| Total industries including municipal & government depts | 6,302 2,179 | 5,606 2,295 | 5,446 2,614 | 5,294 2,909 | 5,166 2,971 | 6,039 2,442 | 6,633 2,462 |
| Municipal services (including tramways & teachers but excluding gas, electricity, & water) | 433 197 | 378 205 | 317 222 | 294 238 | 288 245 | 405 226 | 466 226 |
| Civil Service | 243 66 | 209 86 | 203 149 | 194 191 | 192 234 | 249 201 | 276 121 |
| Other occupations covered by the Z8 inquiry including commerce, transport, under private ownership etc. | 2,831 755 | 2,503 997 | 2,206 1,135 | 1,944 1,291 | 1,846 1,392 | 2,466 1,276 | 2,716 1,210 |
| Total | 9,809 3,197 | 8,686 3,583 | 8,172 4,120 | 7,726 4,629 | 7,492 4,822 | 9,159 4,145 | 10,091 4,019 |

*Source:* The data are drawn from the Z8 inquiry compiled first by the Board of Trade and then the Ministry of Labour. This table is drawn from N. K. Buxton and D. I. MacKay, *British Employment Statistics* (1977), pp. 78–80. For a discussion of the drawbacks of these data see ibid., pp. 76–81.

Labour for his taking the premiership than to a determination to rationalise the administration of labour matters. In spite of Lloyd George's explicit promise to amalgamate the labour sections of the Board of Trade and the Ministry of Munitions and incorporate them in the Ministry of Labour, this was not done. Moreover, 1917 saw the creation of two new government bodies which cut across the Ministry of Labour's area: the Department of National Service and the Ministry of Reconstruction.[101]

The shortcomings of labour administration were deplored by employers and were highlighted in the reports of the Commissioners investigating industrial unrest in the summer of 1917. Later that year the government set up the War Cabinet Labour Committee, with George Barnes in the chair, which was 'to coordinate the action of Government Departments on matters connected with industrial wages and disputes by laying down general principles for their guidance, and settling questions of policy affecting more than one Department'. However this Committee did not prove to be very effective, and in January 1918 the War Cabinet again made the Ministry of Labour responsible for co-ordinating labour policy.[102]

The overriding priority of government policy towards labour matters was to achieve maximum output for the war effort, preferably at as cheap as price as possible. In carrying out the proposals of the Treasury Conference of March 1915 this led to a tough line, especially on the Clyde.[103] Though, given the chaotic coordination of labour policy, it would be a mistake to interpret overall labour strategy as a larger version of what was done on the Clyde in bringing in dilution or persecuting John MacLean. What happened overall was more subtle than that.

The *ad hoc* nature of state intervention enabled there to be 'state control' yet burgeoning private profits. Control went far enough to maintain morale for the war effort, yet avoided the more drastic changes to the running of British industry and the structure of society which could have occurred if market forces had been left free. If the war and state control encouraged thoughts that nationalisation of the coal mines and railways were both feasible and desirable, the war also helped to spread the values of social imperialism, held by men such as Milner. 'Rationalisation' and 'efficiency' were reasons enough in wartime for the state to bring into industries premium bonus systems and the like, which employers had long been trying to introduce before the war. In short, the political pattern revealed in the mosaic of *ad hoc* state controls and interventions was what was to be expected given the make-ups of Asquith's two governments and Lloyd George's coalition of some Liberals, Labour and Unionists, with men such as Milner, Carson, Bonar Law and Curzon prominent.

## Notes

1   H. Wolfe in *Labour Supply and Regulation* (1923), p. 2 offers the figures of 5.5 million out of 'an estimated total male population of 14,350,000 in July 1914'. The 1911 Census figures suggest a total male labour force (occupied and unoccupied) of 15,093,000; B. R. Mitchell and R. Deane, *Abstract of British Statistics* (1962), p. 60. For valuable reviews of the figures see P. E. Dewey, 'Military Recruiting and the British Labour Force during the First World War', *The Historical Journal*, 27 (1984), pp. 199–223, also his 'Agricultural Labour Supply in England and Wales During the First World War', *Economic History Review*, 2, 28, (1975), pp. 100–12; and N. K. Buxton and D. I. MacKay, *British Employment Statistics* (1977), pp. 76–81. For some of the figures see Table 1.1.

2   H.M.G. *History of the Ministry of Munitions* (hereafter *HMM*), 1, 1, pp. 9–10.

3   Board of Trade figures, cited in Wolfe, *op. cit.*, p. 14. For a caution in using such figures, see Dewey, 'Military Recruiting', pp. 200–5.

4   Sir R. A. S. Redmayne, *The British Coal Mining Industry During the War* (1923), pp. 12–15. Dewey, 'Military Recruiting', p. 204.

5   The full proceedings of the Treasury Conference are at the Public Record Office (PRO), MUN 5–10–18017. The most detailed account of it and the preceding government measures are in *HMM*, 1, 2. For a more recent discussion, see C. Wrigley, *David Lloyd George and the British Labour Movement* (1976), Chapter 5.

6   *HMM*, 1, 2, p. 3.

7   *Twelfth Report of Proceedings Under the Conciliation Act 1896: 1914–1918* (hereafter *Conciliation Act*) (1919), pp. 14–15.

8   Ibid., pp. 46–7.

9   Wrigley, *Lloyd George*, pp. 103–4, 149.

10   A. L. Bowley, *Prices and Wages in the United Kingdom 1914–1920* (1921), p. 125.

11   *Conciliation Act*, pp. 37–9.

12   *HMM*, 5, 1, 6; Wrigley, *Lloyd George*, pp. 219–22.

13   Ibid., pp. 115–16. K. R. Grieves, 'The Liverpool Dock Battalion: Military Intervention in the Mersey Docks 1915–1918', *Transactions of the Historical Society of Lancashire and Cheshire*, 131 (1982), pp. 139–58.

14   Ibid., p. 147; *HMM*, 1, 4, 6; Wrigley, *Lloyd George*, pp. 115–19.

15   W. Pringle, quoted in *HMM*, 1, 4, 6, p. 41. On leaving certificates, see also Wolfe, *op. cit.*, pp. 217–34.
16   Ibid., pp. 222–3.
17   He later changed his name to H. Wolfe. *HMM*, 1, 4, 6, p. 22.
18   *HMM*, 1, 2, 2, p. 37.
19   A. Reid, 'Dilution, Trade Unionism and the State in Britain during the First World War', in S. Tolliday and J. Zeitlin (eds), *Shop Floor Bargaining and the State* (1985), pp. 46–74. For another revisionist assessment of revolutionary shop stewards, see I. McLean, *The Legend of Red Clydeside* (1983).
20   G. D. H. Cole, *Workshop Organization* (1923); J. Hinton, *The First Shop Stewards' Movement* (1973).
21   *HMM*, 4, 2, 1, pp. 11–34; G. Rubin, 'The Origins of Industrial Tribunals: Munitions Tribunals during the First World War', *The Industrial Law Journal*, 6, 3 (1977), pp. 149–64, and 'The Munitions Appeal Reports 1916–1920: A Neglected Episode in Modern Legal History', *Juridical Review* (December 1977), pp. 221–37; G. D. H. Cole, *Trade Unionism and Munitions* (1923).
22   *HMM*, 4, 2, p. 30 (6d = 2½p; 1 shilling = 5p).
23   Ibid., p. 31.
24   Ibid., p. 24.
25   R. Page Arnot, *The Miners: Years of Struggle* (1953), pp. 127–33.
26   This was a contrast to the owners' portrayals of a golden age before 1914. W. A. Lee, *Thirty Years in Coal* (1954), pp. 13–14. For an assessment of wartime working of the mines, see N. K. Buxton, *The Economic Development of the British Coal Industry* (1978), pp. 159–64.
27   Redmayne, *op. cit.*, p. 63.
28   R. Page Arnot, *The South Wales Miners*, vol. 2 (1975), pp. 127–8.
29   G. D. H. Cole, *Labour in the Coal Mining Industry 1914–1921* (1923), p. 53.
30   Ibid., pp. 22–3.
31   Redmayne, *op. cit.*, pp. 153–7, 180–1. See also on this and other aspects of the coal industry in the war, M. W. Kirby, *The British Coalmining Industry 1870–1946* (1977), pp. 24–35.
32   Sir R. Redmayne, *Men, Mines and Memories* (1942), pp. 193–4.
33   R. Smillie, *My Life for Labour* (1924), p. 249.
34   Cole, *op. cit.*, pp. 40–1, 68.
35   Page Arnot, *South Wales*, p. 125; Cole, *op. cit.*, pp. 69–70.
36   Page Arnot, *South Wales*, pp. 22, 112–15.
37   E. A. Pratt, *British Railways and the Great War* (1921), p. 766.
38   The clerical and salaried railway staff generally received wage increases in line with those of the operating staff. Ibid., pp. 766–70, 781–2; P. Bagwell, *The Railwaymen* (1963), pp. 347–56.
39   C. R. Fayle, *History of the Great War: Seaborne Trade*, vol. 2 (1923), p. 193.
40   Ibid., pp. 284–5; H. Gosling, *Up and Down Stream* (1927), p. 216; E. Taplin, *The Dockers' Union* (1986), Chapter 9.

41  Cited in G. Phillips and N. Whiteside, *Casual Labour* (1985), p. 116.
42  Ibid., pp. 112–45; J. Sexton, *Sir James Sexton, Agitator* (1936), p. 239.
43  H. D. Henderson, *The Cotton Control Board* (1922), pp. 1–23. In both spinning and weaving the percentage of machinery in mills which could be run fluctuated. For details see the table in Henderson, p. 72.
44  Ibid., p. 11.
45  Ibid., p. 33.
46  E. Hopwood, *The Lancashire Weavers' Story* (1969), p. 82.
47  S. J. Hurwitz, *State Intervention in Great Britain* (1949), p. 195.
48  Henderson, *op. cit.*, p. 27.
49  Ibid., pp. 37–64.
50  E. M. H. Lloyd, *Experiments in State Control* (1924), pp. 151–4. B. Turner, *About Myself* (1930), p. 263.
51  Lloyd, *op. cit.*, p. 260.
52  Thus, for example, on 26 April 1916, before the second measure of conscription, Asquith, Bonar Law and Kitchener addressed a conference of trade unionists, presided over by Henderson, on the military situation; a secret session like that accorded to the House of Commons. Bodleian Library, Asquith Papers, vol. 90, 192–216ff.
53  On this see K. R. Grieves, 'The British Government's Political and Administrative Response to the Man-power Problem in the First World War', (Manchester University PhD, 1984), esp. pp. 525–7.
54  *HMM*, 6, 1, pp. 14–17; Wrigley, *Lloyd George*, pp. 170–4.
55  *HMM*, 6, 1, pp. 34–8.
56  Ibid., pp. 38–41.
57  Minute of 8 February 1917. Bodleian Library, Addison Papers, Box 25. Dr Grieves, attributes in his thesis, p. 191, the minute to Stephenson Kent.
58  Wrigley, *Lloyd George*, pp. 184–204.
59  Redmayne, *Coal Mining Industry*, pp. 49–55, 146–8.
60  Memorandum, 3 July 1917, GT 1318. Public Record Office, Cabinet Papers CAB 24-19. Calthrop to Barnes' Private Secretary, 20 July 1917, GT 1498; CAB 24–20, 440–2 ff.
61  N. B. Dearle, *An Economic Chronicle of the Great War for Great Britain and Ireland 1914–1919* (1929), p. 152. Page Arnot, *South Wales*, pp. 133–4.
62  For Lloyd George's letters of 8 and 9 October 1917 to Stanley, see House of Lords Record Office, Lloyd George Papers F/2/5/12 and 13.
63  Cabinet Committee Report on Manpower, forwarded to Lloyd George by Hankey, 13 December 1917; Lloyd George Papers F/23/1/30. As for aircraft factories in Lancashire, this was done in Oldham only and the factory completed after the Armistice.
64  *HMM*, 6, 2, pp. 39–43.
65  War Cabinet minutes (359) and (370), 5 and 22 March 1918; PRO CAB 23–5–141 and 23–5–177. Page Arnot, *South Wales*,

pp. 147–8. Redmayne is misleading in his chronology on this (and also on the South Wales unrest of the previous autumn); see *Coal Mining Industry*, pp. 193–4, 148.

66 *HMM*, 6, 2, pp. 45–66. J. B. Jefferys, *The Story of the Engineers* (1945), p. 186. The second ballot was arranged before the German offensive but declared after it.

67 At a meeting with Ministers normally in the Cabinet. War Cabinet (385), 6 April 1918; CAB 23–5–16.

68 *HMM*, 6, 2, pp. 48–67; Wrigley, *Lloyd George*, pp. 226–30.

69 On government alarm at the strikes, see Stanley to Lloyd George, 28 May and 22 August 1918, and Maclay to Lloyd George 29 May 1918; Lloyd George Papers F/2/5/18 and 23 and F/35/2/ 60. For the impact of the influenza, see Maclay to Lloyd George, 29 May 1918, F/35/2/60 and Redmayne, *Coal Mining Industry*, pp. 188–9.

70 Wilson to Du Cane, 1 August 1918. K. Jeffery (ed.), *The Military Correspondence of Field Marshal Sir Henry Wilson 1918–1922* (1985), p. 47. Lloyd George informed Clemenceau of Britain's manpower position in a lengthy letter, 30 August 1918; copy, Bodleian Library, Milner Papers, vol. 117, 114–31ff.

71 Stanley to Lloyd George, 1 November 1918; Lloyd George Papers F/2/5/29.

72 Sir C. Macara, *Recollections* (1921), pp. 235–7. See also W. H. Mills, *Sir Charles Macara, Bart.* (1917), pp. 163–7, and the entry by A. J. McIvor in D. J. Jeremy (ed.), *Dictionary of Business Biography*, vol. 4 (1985), pp. 7–14.

73 E. Wigham, *The Power to Manage* (1973), pp. 86–7.

74 Ministry of Munitions Advisory Committee minutes, 4 May, 6 and 7 June 1917; University of Warwick, Modern Records Centre Manuscripts (hereafter MRC) 200/F/1/1/177 ff. 13, 21 and 25.

75 Meeting of 15 June 1917; ibid., 28f.

76 R. Charles, *The Development of Industrial Relations in Britain 1911–1939* (1973), pp. 132–4.

77 *Proceedings of the Inaugural Meeting*, 20 July 1916; Archives of the FBI, MRC 200/F/3/D1/1/6.

78 Macara, *op. cit.*, pp. 219–26.

79 Minutes of the Governing Council of the British Manufacturers' Association, 22 October 1916; MRC 200/N/1/1/1.

80 For more on such moves, see J. Turner, 'The Politics of "Organised Business" in the First World War', in J. Turner (ed.), *Businessmen and Politics* (1984), pp. 33–49.

81 S. Blank, *Industry and Government in Britain* (1973), p. 14.

82 Minutes of the British Manufacturers' Association, 14 May 1917; MRC 200/N/1/1/1.

83 Labour Research Department, *The Federation of British Industries* (1923), p. 9.

84    Sir R. Vassar-Smith and W. P. Rylands, *Proceedings of the AGM*, 30 October 1918; Archives of the FBI, MRC 200/F/3/D1/1/9.
85    Ibid.
86    'Trade Organization', in E. Salmon and J. Worsfold (eds), *The British Dominions Year Book* (1920), pp. 218–22.
87    The best assessment of the TUC's role is in R. M. Martin, *TUC: The Growth of A Pressure Group 1868–1976* (1980), pp. 132–63. However he overstates his case in writing that the TUC was 'virtually swept aside' during the war, and underestimates the significance of the Committee on Production, pp. 132, 162. H. A. Clegg, *A History of British Trade Unions Since 1889*, vol. 2 (1985), pp. 208–11.
88    Wrigley, *Lloyd George*, esp. pp. 131–74.
89    On some of the political implications, national and local, see C. Wrigley, 'Trade Unions and Politics in the First World War', in B. Pimlott and C. Cook, *Trade Unions in British Politics* (1982), pp. 79–97.
90    Wrigley, *Lloyd George*, p. 132.
91    However the shop stewards soon organised their own committee which eventually ousted this management one. C. G. Renold, *Joint Consultation Over Thirty Years* (1950), pp. 18–25.
92    North West Commissioners' Report, p. 36. These 1917 reports are printed as Parliamentary Papers, Cd. 8662–8669. The first Whitley Report was made in March but only published in June 1917.
93    Clegg, *op. cit.*, pp. 204–7. On later developments see Chapter 2.
94    W. H. Warburton, *The History of Trade Union Organisation in the North Staffordshire Potteries* (1931), pp. 225–6.
95    J. Child, *Industrial Relations in the British Printing Industry* (1967), pp. 224–6. A. Fox, *A History of the National Boot and Shoe Operatives* (1958), pp. 373–4.
96    Clegg, *op. cit.*, p. 201. S. Higenbottom, *Our Society's History* (1939), pp. 212–13.
97    N. H. Cuthbert, *The Lacemakers' Society* (1960), pp. 118–22. Child, *op. cit.*, p. 229.
98    R. Hyman, *The Workers' Union* (1971), pp. 79–87; Sir W. Richardson, *A Union of Many Trades* (1979), pp. 69–71; Bain and Price, *op. cit.*, p. 37.
99    Letter of 25 August 1914; quoted in Schneer, *op. cit.*, p. 101.
100   *Conciliation Act*, p. 29.
101   R. Lowe, 'The Ministry of Labour, 1916–1919: A Still, Small Voice?', in K. Burk (ed.), *War and The State* (1982), pp. 108–34. See also his 'The Ministry of Labour 1916–1924: A Graveyard of Social Reform?', *Public Administration* (1974), pp. 415–38, and 'Industrial Problems and Bureaucratic Disputes', Society for the Study of Labour History, *Bulletin*, 30 (1975), pp. 67–71.
102   *Conciliation Act*, pp. 30–1; Clegg, *op. cit.*, p. 185.
103   J. Hinton, 'The Clyde Workers' Committee and the Dilution Struggle', in A. Briggs and J. Saville (eds), *Essays in Labour History 1886–1923* (1971), pp. 152–84. R. Davidson, 'War-time Labour

Policy 1914–1916: A Re-Appraisal', *The Journal of the Scottish Labour History Society*, 8 (1974), pp. 3–20, and 'The Myth of the "Servile State"', Society for the Study of Labour History, *Bulletin*, 29 (1974), pp. 62–7.

# 2

# The Trade Unions Between The Wars

*Chris Wrigley*

The role of the trade unions in British society between the wars was much more prosaic than many had hoped at the time of the Armistice in 1918. Direct Action did not achieve nationalisation of the mines or railways, or workers' control of any industry, let alone a workers' state as had emerged in Russia in 1917. Nor had the notions of consensus in industry which had been much heralded by 'men of goodwill' on both sides of industry during and immediately after the war, survived the economic setbacks of 1921 and after. The collapse of the joint committees in the wool industry in the late 1920s and the breakdown of collective bargaining in the cotton industry in the early 1930s were as symbolic of the collapse of one set of hopes as was the abandonment of the miners in May 1926—a sad comment on the realities facing other aspirations.

After the end of the post-war boom, the fortunes of the different trade unions varied considerably. Like the economy, whilst the mini-booms and the slumps give its overall history a pattern, there were wide variations of experience from industry to industry and, indeed, from area to area. Overall trade union membership dropped from a high of 8,348,000 in 1920 to a low of 4,392,000 in 1933, with the membership falling below the 5 million mark after the General Strike and emerging above it again in the late 1930s (see Table 2.1 for details).

The period was also marked by many amalgamations, creating giant unions such as the Transport and General Workers' Union (TGWU), constructed in 1921 and formally coming into existence on 1 January 1922, and the National Union of General and Municipal Workers (NUGMW), formed in 1924. Both were general unions, the former stemming from the dockers' and road transport unions, and the latter from Will Thorne's Gasworkers' Union of the late nineteenth century. The NUGMW was an amalgamation of the National Union of General Workers, the National

Amalgamated Union of Labour and the Municipal Employees'
Association. By late 1926 the TGWU was an amalgamation of 27
unions. With the merger with the Workers' Union in 1929 it gained
semi-skilled members in building, engineering and in other trades.
In 1926 there were negotiations for an amalgamation of the TGWU
and GMWU and the two executives agreed to this, but the proposal
lapsed after the General Strike.[1]

Table 2.1: Membership of trade unions in the UK, 1913–39

| Number of trade unions at year end | | Membership at year end (000s) | | |
| | | Male | Female | Total |
|---|---|---|---|---|
| 1913 | 1269 | 3702 | 433 | 4135 |
| 1914 | 1260 | 3708 | 437 | 4145 |
| 1915 | 1229 | 3868 | 491 | 4359 |
| 1916 | 1225 | 4018 | 626 | 4644 |
| 1917 | 1241 | 4621 | 878 | 5499 |
| 1918 | 1264 | 5324 | 1209 | 6533 |
| 1919 | 1360 | 6600 | 1326 | 7926 |
| 1920 | 1384 | 7006 | 1342 | 8348 |
| 1921 | 1275 | 5628 | 1005 | 6633 |
| 1922 | 1232 | 4753 | 872 | 5625 |
| 1923 | 1192 | 4607 | 822 | 5429 |
| 1924 | 1194 | 4730 | 814 | 5544 |
| 1925 | 1176 | 4671 | 835 | 5506 |
| 1926 | 1164 | 4407 | 812 | 5219 |
| 1927 | 1159 | 4125 | 794 | 4919 |
| 1928 | 1142 | 4011 | 795 | 4806 |
| 1929 | 1133 | 4056 | 802 | 4858 |
| 1930 | 1121 | 4049 | 793 | 4842 |
| 1931 | 1108 | 3859 | 765 | 4624 |
| 1932 | 1081 | 3698 | 746 | 4444 |
| 1933 | 1081 | 3661 | 731 | 4392 |
| 1934 | 1063 | 3854 | 736 | 4590 |
| 1935 | 1049 | 4106 | 761 | 4867 |
| 1936 | 1036 | 4495 | 800 | 5295 |
| 1937 | 1032 | 4947 | 895 | 5842 |
| 1938 | 1024 | 5127 | 926 | 6053 |
| 1939 | 1019 | 5288 | 1010 | 6298 |

Source: Department of Employment , British Labour Statistics: Historical
Abstract 1886–1968 (1971)., p.395.

In the interwar years these more amorphous unions grew in
importance in the trade union movement as the more distinctive
unions, as in coal, iron and steel, shipbuilding and cotton, dimin-

ished in relative importance with the decline of Britain's old staple industries. These large unions expanded on a broad front, across many industries and services. As a result, their impact in industrial relations could be less obvious than, say, the Miners' Federation, where action would be likely to be national and paralyse a sector of the economy.

The strength of the skilled unions was weakened also by the First World War. This had eroded differentials between the skilled worker and the semi- and unskilled workers, and, with dilution in the war and new technology, had diminished the preserve of the skilled worker. After the war the Amalgamated Society of Engineers (ASE) was active in trying to get a new amalgamated craft union in engineering, and in July 1920 the Amalgamated Engineering Union (AEU) was created. This was soon an amalgamation of the ASE and nine smaller trade societies.[2]

Trade unionism, whilst on the retreat for much of the 1920s and 1930s in the old staple industries, was slow to take a hold in the newer rapidly growing industries such as motor cars, chemicals and rubber. Amongst white-collar workers, a group increasing as a proportion of the national labour force, union membership continued to grow during the bad years of the 1920s and the early 1930s, when trade union membership overall fell. In 1920, the post-war euphoria affected the National Union of Clerks. It restructured its organisation on an industrial guild basis, thereby decentralising much power in the union, an experiment which was abolished in 1933.[3] This apart, the white-collar unions were cautious and far from radical in the interwar period.

By the 1930s the dominant tone of trade unionism was set by Ernest Bevin, Secretary of the TGWU, and Walter Citrine of the TUC. This was a tone of 'responsible moderation'. Bevin, in 1936, looking back to the 1920s and considering what the TUC was doing in the 1930s, observed, 'Most of these things were to them [the TUC in the 1920s] propaganda points. Those were the days of advocacy. Ours is the day of administration.'[4] In the turmoil of the postwar boom and slump, 1919–21, the tone was different.

The trade unions were in a strong position to press for improved pay and working conditions in 1919 and 1920. After the end of the war there was a backlog of unfulfilled demand from the war years, both from industry and consumers in general. British industry was offered not only orders to restock and to supply home demand, but also orders from overseas as many rival industrial areas had been devastated by the war or affected by the post-war political turmoil. In these circumstances the unions successfully pressed for both wage rises and substantial reductions in working hours. In some industries this took the form of a reduction in weekly hours with no loss in the weekly wage.[5]

The trade unions were also in a position to press for the reorganisation of some key sectors of the economy. Whilst state control of the mines, railways and much of engineering and shipbuilding had not transferred actual ownership from private hands (let alone transferred it to the workers in the controlled industries), it had given greater force to the case for nationalisation, a case argued by the miners and railwaymen since the early 1890s. In both industries there were strong economic arguments in favour. Thus, in the case of the railway companies before 1914, they had suffered from gross duplication of track, excess capacity of rolling stock, poor accounting methods and bad organisation generally. Wartime control had led to considerable rationalisation. The war had pointed to practical advantages that could be expected from nationalisation, and the experience of state control took notions of state planning in Britain out of the area of theory.

Labour's challenge in the 1918–20 period was on a wide front. Labour offered a different vision of society. In this nationalisation and a 40-hour week were not unrelated; redistribution of wealth and the reorganisation of society for the benefit of all and not for profit-maximisation would enable all to lead better lives. Thus J. H. Thomas writing in 1920, could observe,

A forty-hour week is in the realm of practical politics. This will be accomplished as soon as Labour comes into its own, as soon as the profits of industry do not accumulate in the pockets of the few, but are spread out into the possession of the whole.[6]

This, of course, was a widespread sentiment in the Labour Movement after the Armistice, and not restricted to the more advanced socialists such as Robert Smillie (who, in mid-January at the Miners' Federation conference, put the matter more succinctly: 'we can produce enough in less than a six-hour day if we were not producing to make millionaires').[7] The success of Lenin and the Bolsheviks in Russia in October 1917 had taken notions of a workers' state also beyond theory; it had offered an alternative way of organising society, and as such, like Robert Owen's notions some 90 years earlier, was an encouragement to greater assertiveness in industrial disputes.

Another element in the attitude of trade unionists after the Armistice was fear. Like the government, trade union leaders expected widespread unemployment after the end of the war, as had happened after the Napoleonic and Boer Wars. There was the prospect of some 5 million men being demobilised from the Armed Forces and some 3 million men and women being made redundant by the ending of the government's orders for war. As Sidney Webb and Arnold Freeman warned in an influential pamphlet, first published in September 1916, 'No industrial dislocation of such magnitude has ever been known'. They asked of the Miners' Federation, 'A quarter of a million colliers have enlisted; on the other hand, many thousands of new men have drifted into the mines. What will happen when the regular colliers come back?'[8]

On top of the fears about the state of the labour market at the end of the war, there was also concern about the changes the war had brought about in working practices. In engineering in particular there was considerable and justified anxiety as to whether the government would honour its repeatedly-made pledge to restore trade union conditions at the end of the war.[9] There was also concern as to whether the new technology and new working practices brought in during the war would benefit the workers or simply lead to intensification of work for those in employment and more people out of work. Thus John MacLean warned in a pamphlet published in the later part of the war,

Along with division of labour goes adaptation of tools and specialised automatic machines. One feature of the revolution inside the munition factories is the introduction of the American single-purpose automatic machines enabling unskilled male and female labour to turn out twice or thrice as much as was formerly done by skilled artisans using less efficient methods and machinery. Besides, continual improvements are being made with labour-time saving effects. A worker informs me that he was turning out 45 copper bands from 18-pounders per day, when, by the introduction of a 'forming tool' he turned out 80 per day. As an incentive to effort his wage was reduced from 15s. to 11s. per day![10]

Concern about the state of the post-war labour market was a

major element in the dramatic industrial disputes on the Clyde and in Belfast in early 1919.[11] Soon after the Armistice, the ASE and the federated engineering and shipbuilding craft unions reached an agreement with the Employers' Federation for a reduction in working hours, without a reduction in wages, from 54 or 53 to 47 hours per week. The ASE's journal proclaimed this to be 'one of the greatest triumphs of British trade unionism' and the agreement was endorsed by a ballot of members. This was not enough for engineers in Belfast, London and on the Clyde, and there were unofficial strikes. In Belfast there was a strike for the 44-hour week, which soon became a general strike in the city. The organisation of this strike developed features which were to be common in many local strike committees during the General Strike in 1926. Thus the Chief Secretary for Ireland informed the War Cabinet: 'The workmen had formed a "Soviet" Committee, and this committee had received forty-seven applications from small traders for permission to use light.'[12] In Glasgow shop stewards representing the views of many workshops wanted action to gain a 30-hour week. However, widespread support, including that from the ASE's district committee, could be gathered for a strike for the 40-hour week and on the Clyde this was what the strikers demanded. While a general strike was called, on the Clyde strike action was much less widespread than in Belfast; only the over-reaction of the authorities in using police, troops, tanks and the law courts ensured that it appeared a threat to the existing social order. Indeed, in 1919 the government made much of using troops and barbed wire to intimidate 'the enemy within'. They were even deployed at Paddington and Woking stations as well as in Glasgow in the September 1919 rail strike.

A major feature of the 1919–21 period was that the trade union movement came up against the government when pressing for improved conditions or trying to defend existing conditions. Against the background of international turmoil after the Armistice, the British government was concerned to re-establish order in the production system of the country. For a Conservative-dominated government this involved reasserting managerial control and restoring what was felt to be 'realism' in wage levels. In 1919–21 this could not be left to private enterprise, for the state still controlled key sectors of the economy. As Bonar Law observed, somewhat plaintively, when faced with a dispute over union recognition with the Railway Clerks' Association in February 1919, 'we cannot get out of it by any question of non-interference as the railways are under Government control'.[13]

The trade unions in mining and on the railways, those sectors still controlled by the state, pressed hard for advances for their members during the post-war boom. Even when economic conditions worsened they preferred bargaining nationally with the government rather than taking their chances area by area with private employers. In the case of the National Union of Railwaymen (NUR) in 1921, just three days before the railways were returned to private ownership, they pressed through an agreement for signalmen which was poor compared with that achieved for other railway workers. That way their members were covered by a national agreement not by a series of varying district ones.[14]

Moreover, during 1915–21, unions in sectors of the economy which were not directly controlled by the government could press their claims hard in the expectation that the government would become involved and would provide a national settlement. Thus after the Clyde dispute had begun early in 1919, Austen Chamberlain complained in the War Cabinet that,

> in recent years there had been an increasing reliance placed on the government as the ultimate arbiter in labour disputes, with the result that strikes were prolonged by the fact that neither side would say the last word as to what they were prepared to concede, as they expected the government to be called in.[15]

Both the miners and the railwaymen achieved many of their post-war demands during the year after the Armistice. The miners demanded a six-hour day and an advance of 30 per cent on total earnings exclusive of the war bonuses as well as nationalisation of the mines and safeguards for miners demobilised from the Armed Forces. After the Sankey Commission's interim report in March (dealing with hours and wages), the government agreed to a two shilling advance in wages (roughly 20 per cent) as well as a cut in hours from eight to seven in 1919, and to six in 1921, 'subject to the economic position of the industry'.[16]

After the Armistice the railwaymen pressed for a range of improved conditions as well as for nationalisation and some measure of workers' participation in the running of the railways.

By March 1919 the executive of the NUR could congratulate itself on achieving

> the eight-hour day, a guaranteed week, a guaranteed day, each day to stand by itself, extra remuneration for night duty, twelve hours rest with nine hours minimum, a week's holiday with one year's service, time-and-a-quarter for overtime and time-and-a-half for Sunday duty, the principle of standardisation and the principle of sharing in the control'.[17]

However, securing a reasonable interpretation of the eight-hour day and the principle of 'standardisation upwards' took considerable pressure, including the national rail strike in the autumn of 1919; whilst 'the principle of sharing in the control' was abandoned and, as in the case of the miners, nationalisation was not achieved.

Whilst under state control these unions could deal with the government directly as the employer. They were to find that the government was no push-over. Indeed the government, dependent on Conservative backbench support, was anxious, both early in the year and in facing the railwaymen in the autumn, to find good ground on which to take a stand against wage rises and trade union demands generally. In February, faced with unrest on the railways and the London Underground, Ministers were arguing that 'we should go ahead and use all means in our power to break the strike' and that they should 'take a strong line and see it through'. With regard to the miners there was much feeling that there should be a showdown. Bonar Law observed that 'possibly the present would be a favourable time for the Government to meet a strike' and added that the

> essence of the present problem was . . . the case the Government would be able to present to the country. The miners were claiming to fix their own rates of pay, irrespective of the effect that this might have on other trades.[18]

Similarly in the September, Lloyd George told J. H. Thomas,

> Whatever we lay down with regard to the railwaymen, you may depend upon it, it is going to be claimed throughout the country; and therefore we have to consider not merely your case but the cases of all the other trades in the Kingdom.[19]

While in 1919 and 1920 there was much huffing and puffing about Direct Action in the Labour Movement, the government in fact practised very direct action against strong challenges from the trade unions. In facing strikes amongst power workers and the London Underground workers in early 1919, the Cabinet turned away from depending on naval and military men and started to enrol civilian volunteers to break strikes.[20] The government then set about creating an emergency transport organisation, which could be used to break strikes.[21] It also turned out much propaganda. During the war propaganda had been aimed at the enemy and later at dissidents within the country; now it was turned against the trade unions. In February the government placed advertisements in the national press in an attempt to get miners to vote against a miners' special conference recommendation to reject the government's offer.

In September, with the national rail strike, the government went in for unrestrained propaganda. Lloyd George set the dominant tone of government propaganda in a statement he issued on the 27 September. In this he denied that the strike was over wages and conditions. He asserted,

> The Government have reason to believe that it has been engineered for some time by a small but active body of men who wrought tirelessly and insidiously to exploit the labour organisations of this country for subversive ends. I am convinced that the vast majority of the trade unionists of the land are opposed to this anarchist conspiracy.[22]

The government spent considerable sums in placing advertisements in the press to get this message over. Thus in one Lloyd George reassured 'workers',

> The Government is NOT fighting Trades Unionism. Trades Unionism is a recognised factor in the industrial life of the Country. What the Government is fighting for is to prevent the extremists of any industrial body from attempting to gain their ends by attacking the life of the community, and so bringing untold misery upon thousands of innocent people.[23]

This message, plus a picture of Lloyd George, was also projected on all the cinema screens in the country.

As usual the trade union movement was also up against a campaign run by the national press to stir up hatred of strikers.

The *Daily Express* headed its front page on 29 September with a strident denunciation of the strike:

> The little band of conspirators who forced their duped followers into a strike against the whole nation did not reckon with a power that will crush them. The People will not submit to tyranny. They never have and never will. It has been tried before. No King, no peer, no commoner can succeed in trampling on British Liberty. This nation, by God's will, has become great because it deserved to be great; and its greatness is due wholly to its love of Liberty, its sense of Justice, its detestation of Tyranny. The conspiracy hatched against the People by a handful of hare-brained agitators, has the word FAILURE written across it. It is unthinkable that at the very moment when the nation, struggling to free itself from the entanglement of five years of terror and disruption, with the first gleam of daylight, the first flickering hopes of recovery, should, at the behest of a group of conspirators, be plunged into Anarchy from which there can be no recovery. This is not a struggle between trade unionism and employers. It is not a fight between masters and men. It is a challenge by a few conspirators to the liberties, the rights, and the honour of Great Britain. If it were to succeed—as it cannot—this great nation would go under. It would be turned into a land of darkness and the shadow of death. But there are already clear, distinct signs that RIGHT and HONOUR and SANITY will prevail. The railways workers, led they know not where, are wavering. They begin to see that they have been duped into a false step, into a path which leads to their own destruction if followed to the end.
>
> *'Whoso diggeth a pit shall fall therein!'*

This heading to the front page was followed by 'news stories' in a similar vein ('Defeat of the Conspirators Ensured by National Effort' and such like). Similar views were expressed in The *Daily Mail*, *The Times*, The *Morning Post* and other newspapers. Virulent attacks of this kind in national and local newspapers have been one element in the difficulties facing trade unions in this and other periods and deserve mention in any consideration of trade union development. In this case press and ministerial misrepresentations were especially gross as J. H. Thomas had repeatedly stressed that the dispute was purely over wages and conditions, indeed over safeguarding them, and he and the NUR executive were emphatic in declining offers of sympathetic action by trade unionists in other industries; indeed it would be hard to think of many trade union leaders of the period keener to appease Lloyd George and the government.

In the case of the 1919 rail strike the misrepresentation was so bizarre that the railwaymen were able to counter it by their own advertisements in the press and on the cinema screen. Thus in one the NUR printed Lloyd George's remarks on railwaymen's wages not being treated in isolation (see above, p. 78) under a heading 'Lloyd George speaks the Truth', and followed it with:

> The Government proposals mean a reduction of thirteen shillings a week to the worst paid. Mr Lloyd George has told you he means to treat all other workers in the same way. YOUR TURN NEXT IF THE RAILWAYMEN LOSE. *THEIR* FIGHT IS *YOUR* FIGHT. SEE TO IT THAT THEY WIN.

After a week of such publicity as to what the strike was really about, public opinion moved towards the railwaymen, the press moderated its line (even the *Daily Express* admitted on its front page on 3 October that 'The railwaymen have a case'), and the government settled the dispute.

However, the government propaganda machinery, like the government's strike-breaking organisation, was only put aside for future use. Whilst the trade union movement countered such propaganda again in 1926 during the General Strike, there were other occasions when it failed to match the government and the press. Indeed the image of industrial disputes being brought about by some 'little band of conspirators who forced their duped followers into a strike' became a recurring theme of government, press and popular mythology. At the popular level it was propagated in a mix of anti-Bolshevik, anti-Jewish and anti-trade union activist literature. It was an element in some of the 'rattling good yarns' of the post-war period, by authors such as John Buchan, Dornford Yates (William Mercer) and 'Sapper' (Lieutenant-Colonel Herman Cyril McNeile); and also in some of the wilder writers of conspiracy theory history, such as Nesta H. Webster and her *World Revolution: The Plot Against Civilisation* (1921). In the case of Sapper some books are almost didactic in dealing with 'the Red element' in society who 'are prepared to utterly destroy sound labour'. Thus in Sapper's *The Black Gang* (1922) one has a vigilante group which dealt with 'undesirables' ('Whenever a man appeared preaching Bolshevism, after a few days he simply disappeared') and a moral explicitly put that subversive ideas will have to be stamped out ('the time is coming when freedom as we understood it in the past will have to cease') and in their place 'we want sound teaching, with the best representatives of the employers and the best representatives of the employed as the teachers'.[24]

The long-running dispute between the Miners' Federation of Great Britain and the government over wage increases and coal prices in 1920 was in large part a propaganda war between the two. After the first Sankey recommendations were received in June 1919, the Cabinet discussed whether the cost should be paid by the Exchequer or by consumers directly. As one Cabinet Minister put it, when arguing that the whole additional cost per ton should be borne by the community, 'By administering such drastic medicine we might bring the community to a state of sanity.'[25] In early 1920 the miners produced their 'indivisible demand' of a wage rise combined with a cut in coal prices in the interests of the consumer. In this the miners were out to win public support for their policies and, by cutting the very high profits being made, to make it very hard for the government to decontrol the mines, as well as aiming to gain a wage increase at a time of soaring prices. As their President, Robert Smillie, put it at their annual conference in July 1920, 'that if we ultimately have to fight, that we should fight with a far stronger backing if part of our claim was for a reduction in the cost of living'. Smillie went on to warn,

> Sometimes we say that public opinion is neither here nor there, that we are sufficiently strong to ignore public opinion. I believe as soon as our campaign, whatever form it takes, for this advance in wages is set on foot, you will perhaps have 99 per cent of the capitalist press ranged against you, lying like troopers, and no troopers lie like some parts of the press. There will be a campaign, particularly in the Sunday press, as there already is, to mislead the public.
>
> Now we do want ranged with us, if possible, the rank and file of the workers in this country, if we are ultimately faced with a fight.[26]

Cabinet Ministers had been in a state of near panic in February.[27] As time went on and coal stocks grew during the summer they became less anxious and more ready to take on the miners. By mid-June the Cabinet had the draconian Emergency Power Bill drafted and ready to rush through Parliament if necessary, and had reviewed its strike-breaking organisation. Lloyd George personally undertook to arrange for people to conduct propaganda against the miners. Soon he could report to Bonar Law that propaganda 'has clearly put public opinion very emphatically on our side'.[28]

Lloyd George succeeded for some time in dividing the other Triple Alliance unions from the miners and in exploiting divisions within the miners as to the use of arbitration (a sensitive subject for many miners after their experience with the Sankey Commission). However, after the miners came out on strike on 16 October and the NUR pledged support, Lloyd George did compromise on wage advances (but not on cuts in coal prices), and the 'Datum Line strike' ended on 4 November.[29]

Lloyd George and the government were usually very skilful in the post-war period in dividing moderate trade unionists from the more militant. 'Direct Action' had been propagated within the trade union movement before the First World War. Thus *The Syndicalist* in September 1912 had proclaimed,

> Even with a separate Labour Party, compromise reigns supreme; there are conferences, committees, bargainings, and what not, with the political parties of our employers . . . *Down* with parliamentary politics that divide the workers, and *Up* with Direct Action that unites them.

The large Parliamentary majority of the Lloyd George Coalition Government after 1918 and its persistent intervention in industrial disputes to thwart trade unionists' demands gave 'Direct Action' considerable appeal amongst trade union activists in the post-war boom. One major way this expressed itself was in demands that the Triple Alliance unions (miners, railwaymen and transport workers) should strike to alter government policies. The railwaymen, at a special General and EC meeting in July 1919, recommended that the Triple Alliance should take strike action if the government did not quickly withdraw armies from Russia and Ireland and end conscription. In May 1920, following on from the 'Hands Off Russia' campaign, East London dockers refused to load with ammunition and supplies a ship which was bound for Poland to help that country's campaign against Russia. Thereafter a joint conference of the TUC Parliamentary Committee, the Labour Party Executive and the Parliamentary Labour Party set up a Council of Action and stated that 'The whole industrial power of the organised workers will be used to defeat this war'. At the local level councils of action proliferated, some 350 being set up, and for some months this movement exerted considerable pressure on the government.[30]

On issues other than Russia in the summer of 1920 'Direct

Action' did not gain the support across the trade union movement that activists hoped for. Trade union solidarity in the shape of the Triple Alliance, however, was successful in putting pressure on the government early in 1919. This was a challenge that the government took seriously and one that the government tried to thwart by trying to divide the unions by giving concessions to some groups in the Alliance. Thus in March 1919, when the Cabinet agreed to concessions to the railwaymen, a strong argument for these was that they would reinforce the moderate railway leadership and split the Triple Alliance. Sir Robert Horne was explicit:

> it was worthwhile to pay the extra cost of the railwaymen's demands in order to secure their support at the present time. If the miners came out on strike, the railwaymen might come out too, but with this difference, that if the above concessions were now granted, they would be striking without a grievance.[31]

At that time the Triple Alliance was not put to the test as the miners accepted the setting up of the Sankey Commission. However it is interesting to note that in the summer of 1919 the government made concessions to drivers and firemen but not to other grades of the railwaymen; but when the strike came in September, nevertheless the ASLEF men came out on strike in support of the poorer paid railway workers.

However, as has already been noted, J. H. Thomas did not ask for non-railway union support in the autumn 1919 rail strike. After the strike Robert Williams, the Secretary of the Transport Workers' Federation, publicly said that Thomas's failure to turn to the Triple Alliance had been an 'error in tactics'.[32] Lloyd George, throughout his post-war government, was adroit in the way he handled trade union leaders such as Thomas and Frank Hodges of the miners. During the tension over the railwaymen's claims in March 1919, Thomas flew over to Paris to see Lloyd George. In her diary, Frances Stevenson noted of Thomas on this visit, 'he is an amusing creature, not very reliable and very open to flattery and coaxing. However he is playing our game at the moment'.[33] Of the September 1919 rail strike Maurice Hankey, the Cabinet Secretary, noted that there was 'continuous liaison between the Prime Minister and Thomas throughout the whole strike'. After that strike Lloyd George could tell his friend Lord Riddell, the newspaper proprietor, 'The railwaymen have agreed not to strike until

September 1920. That breaks up the Triple Alliance.'[34] Similarly, before 'Black Friday' in 1921, Lloyd George was confident that Thomas would be against taking action on behalf of the miners. He observed, 'J. H. Thomas . . . wants no revolution. He wants to be Prime Minister', and 'He does not want a row to please Hodges. I have complete confidence in Thomas's selfishness.'[35]

In fact Thomas was representative of many leading trade union leaders after the First World War who were fearful of 'Direct Action' and of the Bolsheviks in Russia. While Thomas did support the Council of Action in the summer of 1920, otherwise he spoke out against Direct Action. Thus on 9 February 1919 he told the London Underground men who were on strike that they 'should not be led away by mere claptrap sentiment or appeals to passion' and that they should avoid attempting to do 'by industrial action what your intelligence should have told you to do at the ballot box'. He went on to tell them:

> People may tell you, or assume, that there is an unlimited amount of wealth locked up somewhere, of which some people have the key. They say that if the key can be obtained all will be well. But they are leading you in a false path. The real facts are that the only wealth is that which we all produce. If we do not keep that in mind we are going headlong for disaster.
>
> Our union is the strongest in the country. We can demand that unless such and such a thing is done, we can paralyse the community. . . . I want to examine what is our duty in relation to that power. However strong and powerful we may be, the State is more powerful and more important. Citizenship has a stronger claim than any sectional interest. We as trade unionists have got to keep clearly in mind that we have to make our sectional claims consistent with and part of our duty as citizens of the State. The unfortunate tendency today is to assume that we can hold the State up to ransom at any time. We may succeed and achieve our object, but if we did it at the expense of the State, then as citizens we would have destroyed all our claim to citizenship.[36]

This emphasis on constitutional paths and on sharing out wealth stemming from increased production was another theme very much present in trade unionism in the years after the First World War. It was very much present in 'the spirit of Whitleyism', arbitration under the Industrial Courts Act 1919 and the National Industrial Conference.

The National Industrial Conference, supported by the government at a time of acute industrial unrest in February 1919 (just as the National Industrial Council in 1911 had been), succeeded in gathering together much centre opinion in British industry. The setting up of this grand national body with over 800 delegates was greeted by commentators at home and abroad as a British alternative to Bolshevism. Many of the trade unionists who supported it had been involved in the 1911 experiment and were prominent in the Whitley committees in their own industries. As with the prewar National Industrial Council, once the acute pressure on the existing social structure had lessened in 1919, so the government's interest in the National Industrial Conference evaporated and it was left to be an ineffective talking shop.[37]

The Industrial Courts Act, which became law in November 1919, set up a standing industrial court and enabled the appointment of *ad hoc* courts of inquiry into industrial disputes. In this it was following the suggestions of the fourth report of the Whitley Committee. In so doing it was, in effect, continuing the wartime Committee on Production, but under this Act arbitration was voluntary. The most notable use of this Act in the immediate postwar period was by the National Transport Workers' Federation over a wage claim for dockers. Negotiations with employers had not got far on the Central Joint Committee on Port Labour, so the Federation agreed to the employers' suggestion of a public court of inquiry. At this, before Lord Shaw of Dunfermline, Ernest Bevin made a powerful indictment of the conditions which dockers endured: the dockers achieved a national award without strike action.[38] After this success, following on from the exposé of appalling conditions in the mines during the Sankey Commission, trade unionists in cotton and some other sectors not unnaturally wished that they could focus public attention on conditions in their industry in a similar manner.

Whilst disputes in cotton, coal mining, iron and steel and on the railways were rarely referred to the industrial court, in other sectors the unions were more ready to agree to this procedure. This even included the engineers until the court refused a pay rise in June 1920. The unions were in a stronger position in 1919–20, and so employers were more willing to go to arbitration where a compromise was likely. 539 cases were taken to it in the first year and, after the severe recession of 1921–22, over 100 cases a year went to it until after 1926; thereafter the number of disputes referred to it dropped. According to Dr Sharp, between 1919 and 1939 approximately 42–43 per cent of the court's decisions were a compromise, about 35 per cent were favourable to the employers' views, and about 22–23 per cent were favourable to the unions' views.[39]

The setting-up of a court of inquiry was a more exceptional measure. This was no doubt partly due to the cost, and partly due to Conservative or Conservative-dominated governments not wanting repetitions of Ernest Bevin's success on behalf of the dockers in 1920. There were twenty appointed between the wars, all but four of them before 1926. (It is interesting to note that when labour was in a strong position again during 1939–46 24 courts were appointed.) The courts were usually appointed to avoid disputes in major industries, hence nine of the twenty courts were in transport, three in engineering, two in coal mining and three in building; in at least four cases, the engineers in 1922, the dockers and builders in 1924 and the woollen workers in 1925, disputes were already in progress.

In the case of the engineers, the Engineering Employers' Federation was out to crush the engineering unions under the wide-ranging notion of managerial prerogatives. The court of inquiry's verdict, which largely supported the employers' views, and included such observations as 'The managing of a business is a responsible and difficult task, and no individual workman or Trade Union official should unnecessarily or without good cause add to its anxieties', did not settle the dispute.[40] The Amalgamated Engineering Union, at that time, would not agree to a return to work on the employers' terms, and the employers rightly felt that it was an opportune time to confront the unions and to go for complete victory.

The weaker trade unions found collective bargaining under the Whitley Committees attractive—at least outside of booms or slumps. In some cases effective collective bargaining in an industry arrived with the adoption of Whitley councils. This was the case entirely, or to a considerable extent, for those in employment in the electricity and water supply utilities, local authorities, paper-making, silk, quarrying and cement. Even so, the employers could often keep the unions at bay on key issues. In the case of silk they even succeeded in excluding wages and conditions of employment from the remit of the joint industrial council. The silk workers were one of the last groups to gain from the post-war boom, yet were an early group to face demands for a reduction in wages.[41]

In some cases the unions achieved temporary successes through the joint industrial councils in rearguard action against wage reductions in the 1920s. One of the most striking of these was in 1924 in pottery, when the union got the industry's joint industrial committee to set up a special committee to consider the employers' demand for a 10 per cent wage reduction (on top of earlier ones). As the result of a lengthy enquiry the union gained a 2½ per cent wage increase on the official rates, not a reduction. However, the problem in pottery, as in other areas where the unions were relatively weak, was whether or not such agreements were honoured by individual employers. When the union got another such committee appointed in the very unfavourable economic circumstances of 1931 the decision went against the union; thereafter they did not turn to such methods again.[42]

Whilst some of the unions involved in joint industrial councils (mostly the unskilled unions) could claim some such minor successes in the 1920s, it is probable that the Whitley councils lessened or delayed gains in good times, in much the same way as sliding-scale agreements and conciliation boards had affected the unions in the second half of the nineteenth century.[43] Ben Turner of the woollen workers noted in May 1924 that 'the regrettable five per cent basic reduction in 1921' had been accepted by the wool unions 'with the object of helping the Trade to better times', but he found when conditions improved that the employers' attitude was 'not in conformity with the spirit in which the trade unions met the employers' three years before.[44]

Yet in the 1920s several unions found negotiating through Whitley councils attractive. Thus even after the 1925 strike in the woollen industry Ben Turner could observe that: 'when the settlement came the relationships were not as evil as could have been expected in the days gone by and showed that the movement for joint action was certainly a good one'.[45] Given that surveys of trade union development tend to concentrate unduly on strikes, it is interesting to look in more detail at the experiences of the trade unions in the woollen industry as an example of an industry which operated under Whitley councils for some years.

The National Wool and Allied Textile Joint Industrial Council was set up on 15 January 1919. During the First World War the unions had become used to resolving problems in the industry through a tripartite committee, consisting of eleven trade unionists, eleven employers and eleven representatives of the War Office. This was the Board of Control of Wool Textile Industries set up in September 1917. In addition, the trade unions had joined with employers in participating in Manpower and Production Committees which helped to deploy people on essential war work and to release hundreds of men to the Armed Forces without impairing production. After the war the trade unions were represented on the Joint Industrial Council through a federal body, the National Association of Unions in the Textile Trade (NAUTT), which had been formed in 1917.[46]

The Yorkshire woollen industry was covered by a sliding-scale agreement based on the Ministry of Labour's cost of living index. This was negotiated in the West Riding during the autumn of 1919 and ratified by the Joint Industrial Council. The sliding-scale was based on the cost of living index for August 1919. Increases or decreases were adjusted so as to maintain proportionate differentials between wages of time-workers and others; this being 100 per cent for time-workers, 85 per cent for female pieceworkers, 80 per cent for male pieceworkers, and 60 per cent for pressers and blanket raisers.[47]

The Northern District Joint Industrial Council for wool was also much involved in conciliation. After every effort had been made to settle a dispute at local level, it was then referred to the Council's Emergency Committee. From the committee minutes it is clear that numerous problems were settled before a stoppage of work took place or, where work had stopped, the dispute was resolved before it spread to other areas. If this and the full district council failed to solve the matter, then the dispute was referred to a court of arbitration. The unions and employers nominated people to a panel of chairmen and a panel of members of arbitration court and when a dispute was referred to this, the parties concerned each selected two members and a chairman for it. If this failed to agree upon an award, then the matter went to an outside umpire, drawn from a panel nominated by the Joint Industrial Council. Most disputes were settled by the Emergency Committee and did not go to the arbitration court. Thus the report for the national woollen joint council for the 15 months from October 1922 to December 1923 noted,

The settlement of differences has called for a considerable amount of attention by the Council, in several instances the complex character of the disputes having required very delicate handling and the expenditure of much time and patience. The method of procedure laid down in the constitution of the Council has, however, invariably proved effective in composing differences without any serious development of the trouble, and in cases of dispute which have reached the arbitration courts of the Council the awards of the courts have been honourably observed by both sides.[48]

The wool trade did find advantages in this system. It did bring into line maverick employers who would respond to the employers' association and this avoided the union calling strikes in individual factories on several occasions. Thus in June 1922 the Emergency Committee resolved for the unions a dispute with a firm in Morley, stopping it working the 48-hour week in just five days, and also resolved, in the same month, a dispute with another Morley firm, which had received the council's agreement to work extra hours but which until then had not been paying overtime rates for these hours. The unions even got the employers to agree to publicise in their mills the desirability of their employees being members of trade unions, whilst they in turn put pressure on employers not in the employers' associations to respect conditions of work agreed by the joint councils.[49] As economic conditions worsened, the woollen unions may have benefited from their Whitley councils in so far as the system slowed down the introduction of longer hours, 'one-break' systems, and the like.

However, there appears to be some feeling amongst trade unionists in the woollen industry that the joint councils were undermining trade union members' feelings that there was a need to be in a trade union. In this context the employers' agreement to publicise the desirability of trade union membership among their workforce can be seen as strong evidence that the employers, in good times, felt that they had much to gain from the Whitley council system. Thus the West of England District Council minutes record,

With regard to the employment of non-unionists in factories and the continuance of the Joint Industrial Councils, Mr Shaw stated that this was now an urgent question—that the unions had lent their aid to get employers into the various associations but the trade union officials felt that the Joint Industrial Councils are retarding the progress of trades unions rather than otherwise: that if the Industrial Council was to function the employers would have to give trade union officials an opportunity to state their case. On behalf of the employers, Mr Fox stated that they quite appreciated the importance of the points raised. It was difficult to deal with outside firms as well as non-unionists, but the employers felt that no compulsion could be brought to bear. On the side of the employers there was no antagonism to trade unions as a whole.

After lengthy discussion they all agreed to the resolution,

> That this council is of the opinion that the interests of the industry will be best served by strong organisation on the sides of both the employers and trade unions.[50]

For all this, the woollen trade unions were subjected to wage cuts and unsatisfactory overtime when economic conditions worsened. The unions struggled hard to maintain the 48-hour week and to avoid firms working overtime. In December 1921 they succeeded in getting the joint industrial councils to reaffirm the 48-hour week and to see that overtime was treated as an exceptional matter, requiring prior approval by the Emergency Committee. However, by the latter half of 1922, it was clear that many firms were working overtime as a norm and not because of exceptional circumstances, and by early 1924 many firms were ignoring the joint industrial councils' policy on overtime.[51] With the formation of the first Labour government in 1924, the unions hoped—without fulfilment—that there would be statutory enactment of the 48-hour week.

The Whitley councils in wool were also put under strain in the 1920s with regard to wages, with the employers pressing hard to cut costs, by which they basically meant wages. All along unions had expressed doubts about the sliding-scales linked to the cost of living index. During the rapid post-war inflation they felt that the full impact of price rises was not reflected in the Ministry of Labour's index. Even more doubts were expressed when wages were pushed down in advance of the index. By July 1923 there were calls for the government to set up a public inquiry into how the index was constructed.[52] In 1922 the unions and employers were able to agree on wages, with a Ministry of Labour official, A. J. Broom, helping to achieve a settlement. In 1925, a further stalemate on wages was reached. This time the employers initially rebuffed government mediation and simply put up notices of the new wage rates that they proposed. A lock-out ensued, starting on the 27 July 1925. The unions noted on the 18 July,

> That we learn with regret that firms have already posted up notices that wages will be reduced, without official intimation being given to the workers' side of the industrial council. We consider that this is a distinct violation of the industrial council's constitution and appears to be a dissolution of the council.

They went on to set up a central council of action and local ones in woollen centres across the West Riding.[53]

The 1925 woollen dispute was settled with wages not being cut. It lasted until 14 August, with considerable public support for the trade unions. They were led by Ben Turner who, as Jowett and Laybourn have commented in their study of the dispute, 'talked the language of firm moderation, not class conflict'.[54] Sir Arthur Steel-Maitland, the Minister of Labour, induced the employers to agree to the setting-up of a court of inquiry under the Industrial Courts Act 1919, which in due course recommended that the old wage rates should continue to be paid.

When this agreement ran out in 1927, there was deadlock again. This time the employers would not agree to the dispute being referred to another independent tribunal. Thereafter there were localised disputes until the summer of 1929 when the employers called for a general wage cut in the West Riding. When no agreement was reached the Labour government set up a court of inquiry. When the Macmillan Report was published in February 1930, the wool workers overwhelmingly voted against accepting its recommendation of cuts in the region of 9 per cent. Thereafter there was a lock-out, starting in April, affecting 70,000 workers at one stage. The unions suggested to their members that they settle with any employers who would accept wage cuts of less than 5.8 per cent.

The different unions in wool settled separately, thus breaking their common front and ending industry-wide collective bargaining. Over the next three months most operatives returned to work under local settlements. Even after this, Ben Turner still hoped for a revival of the north of England joint industrial council. However the employers' organisation no longer could or would control its side, and the unions were left to pursue a policy of exploiting disunity among the employers as wage rates deteriorated.[55]

The trade unions in the early 1920s were faced with severe economic conditions and a heavy loss of membership. By the middle of 1921 the post-war recession was having serious effects on the unions. Industrial production was down by over 18 per cent, exports by 30 per cent, and some 2.4 million workers were unemployed. British industries heavily reliant on exporting, including coal, cotton, shipbuilding, iron and steel, were hard hit then and later, as there was a slowing-down in the rate of growth of world demand for such commodities and as other countries produced for their own markets and competed in world markets.

In 1921 wage rates dropped sharply from their post-war high points. Part of this came about through the operation of sliding-scale agreements as prices fell. In many cases these drops were more severe than the fall in the cost of living. According to the official index the fall during 1921 and 1922 was (July 1914 = 100) from 265 to 178.[56] Thus during 1921 and 1922 in engineering, fitters' and turners' wage rates dropped by 37 per cent and labourers by 43 per cent. In shipbuilding, shipwrights' wage levels dropped by 43 per cent and labourers' by nearly 45 per cent. In agriculture, farmworkers' wages went down by nearly 41 per cent while in other trades, such as boot and shoe manufacturing and printing and bookbinding, the drops were less severe (in the former 12 per cent for men, 19 per cent for women; in the latter 18 per cent), they did put the trade union movement as a whole on the defensive.

Between 1920 and 1923 trade union membership dropped by 35 per cent. There were very notable drops in agriculture, horticulture and forestry (68.9 per cent), bricks and building materials (54 per cent), pottery (49.4 per cent), clothing (47.3 per cent), metals and engineering (47.1 per cent), chemicals and allied trades (44 per cent), and construction (43.6 per cent). Industrial workers whose unions suffered least losses in these years included those in coal mining (22.5 per cent), cotton, flax and man-made fibres (19.8 per cent; or if one takes the Ministry of Labour figures for cotton alone, 18.1 per cent) and footwear manufacturing (14.6 per cent). In a few cases these drops in size took the union memberships back to roughly their 1913 level (as in the case of coal mining), but in most cases membership levels were still markedly higher than in 1913.[57]

In 1921 the sudden decisions of the Lloyd George Coalition Government to pull out of its commitments to the coal mining industry and agriculture exacerbated difficult economic situations which would have made for bad industrial relations anyway. The dramatic fall in coal prices at the start of 1921 led the government to decontrol the mines at the end of March (instead of the end of August). The miners expected wage reductions but were not prepared for the savage cuts which the mine-owners demanded—cuts of as much as 40–53 per cent in the less competitive mines. The miners appealed to their Triple Alliance allies, the railwaymen and the transport workers, but after much sympathetic talk the other unions failed to support them. This failure, on 'Black Friday', ended the Triple Alliance and effectively finished off the Transport Workers' Federation. The miners went on strike for three months, a strike which was as bitter as the disputes of 1893, 1912, 1926 and 1984–85. At the end of it the settlement was somewhat more generous than the owners' original proposals. It included a government subsidy but was a settlement made on a district not a national basis. The miners had exhausted their union funds, their personal savings, and their credit with the Cooperatives and other shopkeepers. As a result they were in a much weakened state when they faced the employers and the government in 1926.

In agriculture, as in coal mining, the early retreat of the Lloyd George coalition government from intervention created major problems for the farmworkers. Agriculture had been covered by wages boards under the Corn Production Act 1917. The Act had established a national minimum wage, albeit at an unsatisfactory level for the higher paid areas. The government's 'Great Betrayal' of British agriculture, which scrapped the 'guarantees' which had been renewed some eight months before in the Agriculture Act 1920, included the abolition of the minimum wage. Wages fell from 46 shillings in 1920 to under 28 shillings by 1923. These reductions led to sporadic strikes. By early 1923 farmers in Norfolk were talking of increasing hours from 50 to 54 per week, paying by the hour and not by the week, and reducing wages still further. The farmers may well have been trying to force government intervention by causing a crisis, having seen the coal mining industry receive a subsidy after the 1921 dispute. If so they failed, as they gained neither a subsidy nor tariffs from the government. Their actions did however lead to the last big agricultural strike, involving some 6000–10,000 men in Norfolk. The strike was marked by effective mass picketing which, when successful, was followed by the police arresting all and sundry in an attempt to intimidate the strikers. The strike did stop further wage cuts until the early 1930s. However, as with the General Strike in 1926, the settlement (in this case negotiated by Ramsay MacDonald) failed to protect the activists from victimisation after the strike.[58]

The sharp rise in unemployment and the subsequent falls in membership were serious blows to the trade union movement generally in 1921 and subsequent years. The pervading mood is captured well in one of Beatrice Webb's diary entries after the June 1921 Labour Party conference:

> The conference was a gloomy gathering with the imminence of the miners' defeat, with the funds of every trade union fast disappearing, some of the wealthiest unions, e.g. the steel smelters, being bankrupt, not through any strike or lockout, but merely because of unemployment benefit; whilst other unions are not only denuded of money but are engaged in or on the eve of a strike or lock-out. But though the delegates were depressed, they were not exasperated or revolutionary. Quite the contrary: the trend of opinion was towards the right, the pendulum was once more swinging to political action.[59]

Even before the 1922 lock-out, the AEU's financial position had been seriously weakened. During 1921 the union paid out £2,136,579 in unemployment benefit, and the union's resources which had amounted to £3,250,000 when the new union had been formed in July 1920 had fallen to £2,382,240 by January 1922. A. H. Smethurst, the General Secretary of the union, observed of the 1921 financial situation,

> Just as an epidemic destroys all actuarial calculations (as to the cost of health or life insurance) so in the same manner did this unprecedented slump in the engineering industry cast to the air the carefully prepared basis regarding the amount required per member per week to meet the obligations of the union respecting payment of unemployment or donation benefit.[60]

Thus the unions were in a poor state to resist the early 1920s wave of lock-outs. Threats of lock-outs had been made by the

Engineering Employers' Federation against mid-Lancashire sheet metalworkers in late 1919 and against electricians nationally over a dispute at Cammell Laird's Penistone factory in the summer of 1920. With the deepening of the recession, the employers in engineering pressed for national wage cuts. As the economic situation worsened in 1921 the Engineering Employers' Federation widened the issue of confrontation with the unions from the union's embargo on overtime to the general issue of managerial prerogatives. On 18 November 1921 the AEU officials reluctantly agreed to the following memorandum on this subject:

### I.   General

1. The trade union shall not interfere with the right of the employers to exercise managerial functions in their establishments and the Federation shall not interfere with the proper functions of the trade union.
2. In the exercise of these functions, the parties shall have regard to the provisions for avoiding disputes of April 17, 1914, which are amplified by the Shop Stewards and Works Committee Agreements of May 20, 1919, and to the terms of other national and local agreements between the parties.
3. Instructions of the management shall be observed pending any question in connection therewith being discussed in accordance with the provisions referred to.

### II.   Overtime

It is agreed that in terms of the Overtime and Night Shift Agreement of 29 and 30 September, 1920, the employers have the right to decide when overtime is necessary, the workpeople or their representatives being entitled to bring forward under the provisions referred to any cases of overtime they desire discussed. Meantime, the overtime required shall be proceeded with.[61]

When the AEU members rejected this in a ballot (by proportions of nearly 3:2), the Engineering Employers' Federation then gave notice of a national lock-out. They went further. They issued demands to the other unions in the industry, who until then had not been parties to dispute, to agree to the general points in the memorandum. Eric Wigham, in his official history of the Engineering Employers' Federation, has referred to this widening of the dispute as 'what must surely be among the most high-handed operations in the history of industrial relations'. One of the National Union of Foundry Workers' organisers observed of the tough take-it-or-else attitude of this time, 'The club was used in a fashion that it may be well to imitate when occasion arises. One wonders where the spirit of co-operation has got to.'[62] At the end of it the employers were victorious, and the unions' funds were in dire straits. In the case of the foundry workers, in June 1922 their union had assets of £33,000 and a bank overdraft of £29,000 and had to suspend benefits, thereby losing more members.[63]

The recession hit the labour movement hard in various ways. The laying-off of large numbers of workers gave employers good opportunities to remove activists. In engineering the shop stewards' movement was weakened with many leading figures made redundant and then blacklisted. In November 1922 J. T. Murphy observed,

> In England we have had a powerful Shop Stewards' Movement. But it can and only does exist in given objective conditions. These necessary conditions at the moment . . . do not exist. . . . You cannot build factory organisations in empty and depleted workshops while you have a great reservoir of unemployed workers.[64]

Guild socialism was another victim of the recession. The Building Guilds movement had achieved a fair measure of success in 1920. As with radical moves amongst builders some 90 years earlier, this movement raised high hopes. As one man put it:

> By an organisation such as this we again become master craftsmen. We are the oldest organised craft in the country, and if these proposals can be carried through, we shall lay more bricks than private enterprise dreams of.[65]

The recession hit the building trade hard and this, combined with the Guilds' weak finances plus poor organisation and the campaign against them by private employers, ensured their collapse by late 1922.

At grassroots level trade union activists responded to the recession by trying to increase trade union membership. In Huddersfield the trades council organised a campaign in the town. In its annual report it recorded,

> The most interesting feature of our year's work has been the Back to the Union Campaign.
> The Trade Union Congress General Council definitely informed us that they had abandoned their intention of conducting a campaign in

the summer, but urged us to take the matter up on our own responsibility. They forwarded us a large quantity of suitable literature for distribution, and after an encouraging response from our affiliated societies, arrangements were accordingly made and the campaign entered upon.

Forty-nine meetings were held at the workshop gates and in the districts in the evening. On the whole the meetings were well attended and the case for trade unionism was well presented by the national organisers from the various societies, assisted by local comrades.[66]

In many industries the lead in such recruiting campaigns was taken by the Communist Party. This was done in '100 per cent trade unionism' campaigns amongst some areas of the miners in 1921, and later as one aspect of the Minority Movement.

The Minority Movement was strongest in coal mining, engineering, the railways, the docks and the building industry, and achieved strong support from many trades councils. At its inaugural conferences its aims included 'to carry on a wide agitation and propaganda for the principles of the revolutionary class struggle, and work within existing organisations for the National Minority programme and against the present tendency towards social peace and class collaboration and the delusion of the peaceful transition from capitalism to socialism'. The programme itself included a minimum wage, a 44-hour week, the abolition of overtime, workers' control of industry, wider representation on the General Council of the TUC and wider powers for it within the trade union movement.[67]

The General Council, with its existing composition, was to prove a grave disappointment to militant trade unionists in 1926. The TUC had been reorganised during the First World War and the post-war boom, largely in response to the greater role offered to it by the government during a period of wide ranging state intervention in the economy. In 1921 it was restructured, with the more powerful General Council replacing the Parliamentary Committee. The General Council's powers were considerable when formed. At the 1924 Congress they were enhanced further when a motion was passed which permitted the General Council to try to resolve an impending major dispute and, if conciliation failed, to mobilise the resources of the trade union movement in support of the unions involved.[68] In May 1926 the General Strike was a magnificent display of solidarity with the miners made by very large numbers of working people; but the objective of the action, beyond being that, was not thought through by the General Council or many others. The calling-off of the strike and the failure to prevent victimisation or to save the miners from being starved back to work caused bitterness, recriminations and much disillusionment with both the TUC leadership and with direct action.[69]

It provided Baldwin's government with the occasion on which to bring in anti-trade union legislation which had long been desired by much of the Conservative Party and its supporters. Three of the eight clauses of the Trades Disputes Act 1927 directly dealt with banning general strikes and in so doing imposed a maximum prison sentence of two years for those disregarding the legislation. The government also covered other issues saying that their approach 'should be such as will command the support of the great mass of public opinion, including the moderate trade unionist'. These issues included making picketing more difficult, forbidding civil service and local government workers to join unions which could affiliate to the TUC, banning strikes by local government workers, and changing the mechanics of the political levy to the Labour Party from contracting out to contracting in.[70] This was not all. The Eight Hours Act 1926 allowed the lengthening of the miners' working day and the Board of Guardians (Default) Act 1926 prevented Poor Law Guardians providing what the government deemed to be over-generous levels of poor relief.

Following on from the General Strike and the coal lock-out of 1926 there was a further dip in trade union membership. Between 1925 and 1928 membership overall in Britain went down by 12.5 per cent. The coal miners' unions were hardest hit with a drop of 32.9 per cent. Whilst they had suffered less badly than many unions in the early 1920s, over 1920–28 they lost more members (48.6 per cent) than the trade unions as a whole (42.4 per cent). This was not just due to a contraction of employment. It represented a serious reduction in union density. This has been estimated at 74.1 per cent in 1911, 76.7 per cent in 1921, dropping to 61.9 per cent in 1926 and 51.8 per cent in 1928. The other main groups to lose sizeable union membership between 1925 and 1928 were the agricultural, horticultural and forestry workers (35.2 per cent), those working in paper and board industries (25.8 per cent) and the railwaymen (21.8 per cent).[71]

As well as hostile legislation from the government and falling membership, the trade union movement was faced with breakaway trade unions. This problem was most marked in mining, with the most serious case being George Spencer's Nottinghamshire Miners' Industrial Union being set up and being a separate union in that area until fused with the Nottinghamshire Miners Association in September 1937. There were campaigns to set up 'non-political' trade unions in other mining areas, spreading from Nottinghamshire and Derbyshire to South Wales and Durham.[72] Attempts by J. Havelock Wilson, the leader of the Seamen's Union and who earlier had been a leading figure in the British Workers' League (an imperial and 'patriotic workers' organisation backed by Lord Milner), to create a 'non-political' trade union movement to rival that affiliated to the TUC did not get far. Appeals for money got a ready response from the shipping and coal-owners and some other businessmen, and individual subscribers included twelve peers, eight knights or baronets and one relative by marriage to the royal family. Some of these businessmen were associated directly or through their companies with the Mond–Turner talks.[73]

The Mond–Turner talks, between a group of employers and the TUC, represented continuity with one prominent strand of thinking in the trade union movement which (as has already been discussed) was present even in 1919 and 1920. Given Ben Turner's warm support of joint councils in the woollen industry, it was very appropriate that he should have been President of the TUC when the talks started. The employers' invitation in December 1927 called for joint discussions on 'the entire field of reorganisation and industrial relations'.[74] The trade union movement was faced with these issues for most of the next decade: whether to negotiate rationalisation and job losses or whether to be confronted with wage cuts and job losses as British industries readjusted to new patterns of demand and to periods of falling demand in the international economy.

The actual Mond–Turner talks only lasted until March 1929. From these stemmed four reports: on the Gold Standard, on trade union recognition, on victimisation, and on the creation of a national joint industrial council.[75] Whilst the Mond–Turner talks went no further because of hostility from employers, the overall notion of finding areas of agreement with representatives of the employers remained in favour with many of the leading figures of the TUC for the next few years. As a result, between 1929 and

1932, there were discussions between the Federation of British Industries (FBI) and the TUC on evidence to be put to the MacMillan Committee on Finance and Industry, on the 1930 Imperial Conference, on the state of the British film industry on Anglo-Russian Trade and on the 1932 Ottawa Conference. The TUC also had abortive talks on rationalisation with the National Confederation of Employers' Organisations (NCEO), which was generally much tougher in its attitudes to the trade unions than the FBI.

All this, it has been argued by Martin Jacques, constituted major features in a change of policy in the trade union movement. Thus he has written:

> The 'new direction' marked a sharp break with the 1918–1926 ideology. It assumed the continued existence and viability of capitalism rather than its imminent demise: the emphasis on class conflict was at least partly superseded by the concept of an 'industrial interest'; the perspective of socialism was blurred and the idea of gradual evolutionary change—which was seen as already well advanced—largely substituted.[76]

Whilst, as this chapter has suggested, the break with the earlier period was not sharp, it is nevertheless important to emphasise the wider belief in a community of interest between employers and unions in industries held by trade union leaders in this period—a belief which was to be shaken by tough action by many employers in the industries worst affected by the world recession of 1931–33.

One aspect of this belief in an 'industrial interest' was belief that mergers and rationalisation would benefit labour as well as capital. Sir Alfred Mond himself was prone to hold forth on the theme that 'amalgamations mean progress, economy, strength and prosperity'. In early 1927 he reassured one audience, 'Modern mergers are not created for the purposes of creating monopolies or for inflating prices. They are created for realising the best economic results which both capital and labour will share to the best advantage.'[77] The TUC leadership at first shared Mond's optimistic view that rationalisation would benefit labour as well as capital. However by 1930 its Economic Committee was expressing reservations; and by June 1931 the TUC was forced to recognise the adverse impact rationalisation had on employment.[78] The economic crisis undermined trade union leaders' talk of 'industrial interests' or 'producers' alliances'.

Those on the shopfloor were often much quicker to realise what rationalisation meant for labour. People who had worked for years in a firm and who had paid their union dues year in and year out were not pleased to find their unions agreeing to 'rationalise' their jobs out of existence. Similarly, the various governments' proposals to assist rationalisation in the old staple industries, which usually involved compensation to mill-owners whose plant and machinery were to be scrapped but no compensation, only redundancy, for much of the workforce, were not popular solutions with those who were to lose their jobs as a result.

This was a rich area for rank-and-file opposition in the unions. The National Minority Movement, proscribed by the TUC in 1928 and the Labour Party in 1929, campaigned vigorously against 'capitalist rationalisation'. The effects of such rationalisation were defined as 'lower wages, longer hours, speeding up, rate cutting, increased accidents, physical exhaustion and deterioration, increased unemployment, increasing use of women and youth in industry, at low rates of pay, and little attention to factory safeguards to protect the health conditions and compensation rights arising out of accidents'.[79] The second Labour government could be condemned as being united with the employers to enhance profits. Thus one letter to South Wales miners in October 1929 complained, 'This is the government that has pledged itself to carry out "capitalist rationalisation", that is capitalist attacks upon the hours and wages of the workers. It has already shown its hand in the attack on the cotton workers where, under the screen of "arbitration" it assisted the textile bosses to impose a wage cut of 6¼ per cent upon the textile workers.'[80] The attacks on Labour Party and trade union leaders became increasingly strident during the Communist Party's 'Class against Class' period (1928–32). Thus, for example, in South Wales the Cymmer Movement Group in urging the miners at the Cymmer Colliery to support Will Paynter, observed, 'trade union and Labour Party leaders have become *social fascists*—men making use of their position and influence among the workers [to] aid the capitalists in carrying out their plan of rationalising industry at the expense of the workers by lowering wages, by speeding up, and generally intensifying the exploitation of the worker'.[81]

While the Communist Party was moving to its new line in 1928–29, it did resist pressure from the Red International of Trade Unions to set up independent revolutionary trade unions. The main exception to this was among the Scottish miners. In Fife, in 1922, there had been a breakaway union, the Fife, Kinross and Clackmannan Miners' Reform Union, which had reunited with the Fife Association in 1926. When the left-wing candidates won a landslide victory in the reunited body, the old right-wing leaders refused to accept the result of the vote and formed a breakaway union which was then recognised by the National Union of Scottish Mine Workers. In these circumstances the Communist Party and the Minority Movement backed the democratically elected but thwarted left-wing miners and the setting-up of a separate union, the United Mineworkers of Scotland. This was largely confined to Fife and Lanark, and, after organising strikes against the eight-hour day and wage cuts in 1931 and 1932, it became weaker.[82] The other notable breakaway union backed by the Communist Party was the London-based United Clothing Workers' Union. This split from the Leeds-based National Union of Tailors and Garment Workers in March 1929, but was in a weak state by 1931 and, like the United Mineworkers of Scotland, it was formally dissolved in 1935.[83]

Cotton, like coal, was a major industry in serious economic trouble after 1920. It became a centre of industrial strife in the late 1920s and early 1930s. The industry was very hard hit by a sharp fall in exports. In 1913 cotton yarn exports had amounted to 210.1 million lb and cotton cloth exports to 1291.4 million lb; these volumes dropped to 145.9 and 554.5 million lb respectively in 1921, and averaged 176.2 and 760.5 million lb respectively between 1924 and 1929. Cotton yarn exports dropped further in the world recession, to 130.4 million lb in 1934, as did cotton cloth exports, to 390.2 million lb in 1934.[84] As a Board of Trade report later noted, 'Roughly speaking, two-thirds of her export losses were due to the development by her former customers of their own industries, and one-third was captured by Japan.'[85]

The trade unions in the cotton industry were faced with a series of industrial relations crises as the industry made a painful series of responses to this situation. The employers saw the problem as being that Lancashire's prices were 10 per cent too high. In this, like other export-oriented industries, the government's return to the Gold Standard in 1925 at the pre-First World War parity between the pound and the dollar of 4.86 had not helped—though given the nature of the problem it is unlikely that any parity for the pound would have led countries developing their own textile industries behind tariff barriers to buy cotton goods from Lancashire.[86] The employers' response generally was to go for longer working hours and wage cuts or for increasing output from the existing out-dated machinery, by getting the workers to mind more looms. The employers had not invested in new automatic machinery in the good years. Thereafter, as one recalled,

> We were struggling desperately, financially and commercially. . . . There just wasn't the sort of money around, or at any rate the mill masters conceived that there wasn't the sort of money around, to indulge in massive capital expenditure.[87]

During the disputes in the cotton industry from 1928 to 1935 the rank-and-file trade union members were much more militant in resisting such changes than the trade union leadership. For one thing the more intensive use of labour (either longer hours or more looms or, more rarely, automatic machinery) all added weavers to the already lengthy dole queues. As well as this the various changes affected those still at work, adversely affecting mill floor work practices. Thus, for example, the system of fining was one way of cutting back on wages and pressuring the workers to increase the quality of output. As was observed in a Minority Movement pamphlet, fining was 'a method of getting first-class cloth out of third-class material'. The employers relied on further exploiting their labour force rather than investing in new machinery. As one later official report observed of Lancashire:

> For the success of this system it is essential that there should be a large and cheap, but nevertheless highly skilled, labour force available. It is a system based on the allocation of a relatively large part of the work of weaving to the operative and a relatively small part to the machine.[88]

The arbitrary sacking of a distinguished trade unionist over a fining dispute in a Nelson firm in 1928 led to a lock-out of the town mills plus support from the county employers' organisation. The dispute raised the issue of managerial prerogatives and it gave the employers a chance to try to cut-back trade union strength in that town.[89]

The workforce in weaving generally was more reluctant than the trade union leadership to accept, without a fight, longer hours, wage reductions or working with more looms. This was true in the summer of 1929 when the employers declared a lock-out to try to enforce a 25 per cent reduction in piece rates, involving a 12½ per cent reduction in wages. The union leaders, supported by the Labour government, took the issue to arbitration, where half the reduction was awarded to the employers. The rank-and-file members were enraged and demanded that an application should be made to the employers for a 25 per cent increase in list prices, and when this was refused, voted in a ballot by 94,142 to 43,531 in favour of strike action. The Amalgamated Weavers' Association (AWA) did not carry out this policy. The 1929 lock-out also highlighted the division between the spinners and the weavers; the former making clear that they preferred to accept wage cuts rather than face a lock-out. Thereafter the weavers acted on their own.[90]

The AWA leadership was much more willing to negotiate the working of more looms by weavers than were its members. To the employers more looms systems, increasing the workers' number of looms from four to six, eight or even ten, was an alternative to investing in new machinery and it was a way to undermine the Uniform List of payments which had been accepted since the 1840s. Thus, the adoption of such a system could give some employers advantages against their British competitors, and it became an industrial relations equivalent of the competitive currency devaluations and other beggar-thy-neighbour policies operated in the international economy in the early 1930s.

In 1929 the AWA had agreed to a more looms system being tried as an experiment in ten mills in Burnley for a year as part of a process of reorganising the industry. In March 1930 the weavers voted by 21,109 to 1113 against permitting the experiment to continue. However, the union leaders allowed the experiment to continue longer whilst they awaited the outcome of the Labour government's enquiry into the industry. The Clynes Report offered little positive support for the weavers as it called for reorganisation of the industry but provided no state action to bring it about. During 1930 rank-and-file groups sprang up opposed to the continuation of the more looms experiments, and in November the AWA rejected the employers' proposals for extending the more looms system to other mills and for a new price list for the system. The employers declared that they would go ahead with their proposals. This led in January 1931 to strikes in the Burnley mills experimenting with the more looms system and was followed by the employers applying a lock-out to the whole county. The AWA balloted its members as to whether negotiations should take place with the employers. This resulted in 90,770 voting against and 44,990 in favour. In spite of this the AWA leadership did try (unsuccessfully) to negotiate a settlement via Ramsay MacDonald and some other Ministers. This led to a 'rebel delegation' of activists based on Nelson going to the House of Commons to publicise the AWA ballot decision, to press for state money to reorganise the industry and to gain relief for the locked-out weavers. After four weeks the employers called off their lock-out and abandoned the more looms experiment.

One reason why the AWA leaders were more cautious than their members was that many of them felt that the working of more looms was inevitable in the existing economic situation and that it was best to negotiate the conditions for this to take place rather than leave it to individual employers. Ironically the weavers' position was made more difficult by the serious weakening of the employers' organisations. The economic crises weakened them as well as the unions. As economic circumstances deteriorated more and more employers went their own way, taking any means at hand to cut wage costs. The employers' lock-out in early 1931 collapsed partly because of this, and partly because the dispute was about an issue, the introduction of more looms systems, which did not interest them all.

As a result of the weakening of the employers' organisations collective bargaining was soon near to collapse in the cotton industry, with maverick employers undercutting employers who kept to the agreed rates and conditions of work. In 1931 there were several strikes aimed at such employers, and mass picketing against blackleg labour. When the AWA leadership negotiated terms for introducing more loom working with a Burnley employer, these terms were repudiated by the Burnley weavers and by an AWA Special General Council meeting in October 1931. With more firms ignoring agreements, the weavers in Burnley took strike action in February 1932 against mills which disregarded the collective agreements and succeeded in stopping this. Elsewhere the unions were less successful against employers using blackleg labour. As for the employers' organisations, the Federation of Master Cotton Spinners Associations decided, after a ballot of its membership in November 1931, to abrogate all agreements, and the Cotton Spinners and Manufacturers Association followed suit in April 1932.

Against a background of the employers pressing for wage cuts, and the employers' organisations having given notice to terminate all agreements on wages and hours, the weaving unions held ballots of their members in May 1932. However, the ballot resulted in a confused result, with 55 per cent for strike action and 13.5 per cent against, yet on the other question 35 per cent favouring negotiations on wage reductions with 19.3 per cent against. A second ballot secured a clearcut 55 per cent vote in favour of strike action among the AWA membership. The employers made definite proposals of a 30 per cent reduction in the Uniform List and other changes in it. At the local level employers put up notices of wage reductions and in Burnley this led to a strongly supported strike beginning in late July. Central negotiations between the employers and unions broke down in late August over the failure of the employers to guarantee the reinstatement of the Burnley strikers or to reassure the unions that collective agreements would be observed in the future, and the weavers called out all their members on strike. The result was a strongly supported four-week strike, which reduced the wage cuts and reasserted the need for collective agreements in the industry.

The 1932 weavers' strike forced the Ministry of Labour to intervene. After lengthy negotiations at the Midland Hotel an agreement was made which covered a 15.5 per cent wage reduction, the honouring of collective agreements, the reinstatement of strikers, the establishment of a joint committee to avoid stoppages of work, and arrangements to consider terms for the introduction of more looms systems. The AWA did negotiate terms for the introduction of more looms systems. However, the Midland Agreement was breached wholesale by employers, including many within the employers' organisations. By 1934 the anarchy in the industry convinced the employers that legislation was needed to underpin collective agreements in the cotton industry. The government obliged with the Cotton Manufacturing (Temporary Provisions) Act 1934, which legalised wage agreements in weaving made by representatives of the employers and unions, in order to outlaw a minority of employers and workers working at rates below those agreed through collective bargaining. However, it took protracted negotiations for the employers' organisations and unions to agree a new Uniform List; this was brought in after a Board of Inquiry had heard objections, in July 1935. Later, in 1937, the unions secured the first increases in weavers' rates since 1921 and the temporary legislation became thereafter, in effect, permanent by repeated renewal.[91]

The 1932 cotton strike was notable for being the last national strike in Britain until after the Second World War. The problems in cotton in 1929 to 1932 were also notable for highlighting again the willingness of the unions in an economic crisis to sacrifice women trade unionists first. Hitherto much emphasis had been put on 'the family wage' and the unions had resisted two-shift systems as disrupting family life. With the considerable unemployment after 1929, and with more looms systems likely to displace 40 per cent of the operatives, the employers promised to keep on heads of households (i.e. mostly males), but with married women without dependants being the first to go and single men and women working part-time. However, the fall in the proportion of female trade unionists to male in cotton between 1928 and the mid-1930s was less than for all trade unionists, so perhaps in practice employers in cotton were not especially drastic in discriminating against women when making people redundant.[92]

Of course, a major problem for the trade union movement was the lower density of unionisation amongst female workers. According to Bain and Price's figures, from 1922 to 1932 female union density ran at an average of 13.8 per cent (fluctuating between high points of 16.2 and 16 per cent in 1922 and 1939 respectively, and lows of 12.1 per cent in 1933 and 1934), in contrast to male union density which ran at an average of 33.8 per cent (fluctuating between high points of 39.1 and 39.3 per cent in 1922 and 1939 respectively, and a low of 27.9 per cent in 1933). In 1920 the cotton industry had employed about 22 per cent of all female trade unionists, a proportion which probably rose to about 28 per cent in 1928. The contraction of the cotton industry in the 1930s, with its large female workforce and its tradition of unionisation, was a major reason why the recovery of female trade union membership from 1933 to 1939 (a 37.7 per cent increase) was less than male.[93]

The problem was that attitudes to women workers after the First World War remained much as they had been before. They were second-class workers, whose real work was to be housewives and mothers. In many areas women's work was deemed almost by definition to be unskilled. This was reinforced by the fact that many women workers were employed in the service sector and in small businesses generally, areas where labour was in a weak bargaining position anyway. Women were paid less, even for doing the same work. Given such points as these and that male-dominated trade unions had reinforced discrimination against women in the labour market, it is hardly surprising that less women workers were in unions. With the recessions of 1921–22 and 1929–33 male trade unionists gave explicit or tacit support to women being pushed out of jobs first when industry contracted. Women had had a taste of this after the Armistice when up to 1½ million had lost their jobs with the ending of most war production and the return of the men from the Armed Forces. However, until 1920 there was a buoyant demand for female labour. It was then that the post-war campaigns, led by the press, against 'limpets'—married women holding on to jobs whilst men were unemployed—became even more effective.[94] Between 1920 and 1923 the fall in female trade union membership (38.5 per cent) was higher than the fall of male membership (34.1 per cent), and this figure was cushioned by the comparatively light drop in union membership in the cotton industry in those years.

The lack of success of the General Strike and of the miners on their own in 1926, followed by the world economic slump, led to the trade union movement, outside of cotton, generally avoiding setpiece battles from 1927 onwards.[95] In cotton the weavers did fight, and government legislation maintained collective bargaining. In wool centralised collective bargaining in the northern counties collapsed in 1930. In coal mining industrial relations remained bitter and the stoppages were many, but they were localised not national confrontations.

With the world recession employers were especially eager to cut production costs. In cotton the working of more looms was seen by many employers as an easier and cheaper option than large-scale investment in automatic machinery and new plant or better marketing. Management elsewhere turned to various methods to intensify the exploitation of labour. Taylorism, which had spread in munitions factories during the First World War and elsewhere in the 1920s as factories introduced new production lines with greater opportunity for subdividing jobs and making labour more easily substitutable, was especially attractive in the depressed economic conditions after 1929. As one publiciser of payment of results systems wrote in 1924, such methods could be put forward as a means of reconciling the almost irreconcilable. 'The consumer seeks low prices, quick delivery. The manufacturer seeks large profit, repeat orders. The worker seeks high wages, continuous employment'. However, as the writer emphasised, 'When a system of payment by results is introduced the existing rate of output is almost bound to be reflected in the job rates fixed, and as this rate is unsatisfactory *so will the approach to true efficiency be barred excepting by cutting job rates.*'[96]

The introduction of Taylorism and, in particular, the Bedaux form of it, was easiest where unions were weak and where the labour force was unskilled or semi-skilled. In some cases, such as food processing, hosiery and textiles, female labour was predominant, and the male-dominated unions failed to organise adequate resistance to the imposition of such systems. Once brought in, Bedaux systems led to the workers policing themselves in maintaining a speeded-up output. The slow worker did not survive long. As a result there were high labour turnovers, labour being reduced, as Craig Littler has put it, to 'a sea of unknown faces attending to the wants of continuous running machines'. This was often a stark contrast to the old paternalism of family firms. The introduction of Bedaux systems was the cause of, or an element in causing, many strikes in the early 1930s. These included disputes in motor car components at Lucas in Birmingham in 1932, in hosiery at the Wolsey Works in Leicester in 1932, in the Venesta Plywood Factory in the East End of London in 1933, in window manufacturing at Henry Hope of Smethwick in 1933, and in the Manchester metalworking firm of Richard Johnson and Nephew between 1933 and 1935. In the last case, in spite of mass picketing, the 600 male strikers were replaced by outside non-union labour.[97]

With the coming of mass unemployment the unions were weakened by loss of members and of finances. The loss of membership was not just due to members losing their jobs. In many industries there was also a fall in the proportion of union members among those still in work. This was very marked, even before the recession, in the coal mining unions after the 1926 coal lock-out. In the Yorkshire area membership expressed as a percentage of those employed dropped from 85.2 per cent in 1925 (roughly the level at which it had been from 1922 onwards) to 63 per cent in 1927 and down to 58.5 per cent in 1931.[98] In South Wales the average membership of the South Wales Miners Federation was about half of those employed until about 1935.[99] Such figures gave rise to union 'Show Cards' and '100 per cent union membership' campaigns. Whilst these had an impact at the pits at which they were carried out, overall union density amongst the miners, as amongst other groups of workers, went up as unemployment dropped in the mid-1930s.

During the world recession the unions had to concentrate much of their energy on trying to lessen the wage cuts that employers were proposing. In some cases these cuts did not arise from the needs of the firms. This was so in the case of the lead manufacturing industry where, even though profits had remained stable, a 10 per cent wage cut was brought in after the National Government had cut the salaries of state employees by an average of 10 per cent in 1931.[100] Where unionisation was weak or non-existent, employers could make the most of market forces. This is well illustrated by the recollections of Matt Hardy:

When I was in the painting trade I got a job working at Stannington, working on some new houses, and he [his employer] came to me one day and said he had got someone who would work for 4d or 5d an hour less than me. I said, 'Ah, good. Well find him some work.' But he said, 'If you don't work for that money he's going to work instead of you.' I let him take the job. I was single and he had two kiddies. He was so desperate for a job. He did apologise. He couldn't carry on any longer. He knew what he was doing was wrong. He just had no option.[101]

While trade union leaders such as Bevin negotiated lesser cuts with employers, in many sectors rank-and-file movements sprang up in 1932 and 1933 to oppose cuts or to demand the restoration of the rates cut. The inaugural conference of the Railwaymen's

Vigilance Movement, held in the autumn of 1932, put their case briefly when it declared that:

> as in the case of the London busmen . . . a movement, organised in the local depots and branches, and embracing all workers irrespective of Grade or Union division, can be a most powerful means of defeating . . . the wage cuts demands of the companies.[102]

The London busmen were to gain the reputation of being among the most militant trade unionists between 1932 and 1937. In 1932, after Bevin had negotiated with the London General Omnibus Company, the busmen were faced with terms still involving 800 redundancies and cuts in wages. These proposals were denounced at a series of unofficial mass meetings and a ballot by the Central Bus Committee rejected them by 16,000 to 4000 votes. Faced with a strike, the company agreed, in negotiations with Bevin, to better terms, including no wage cuts and no dismissals when new and faster schedules were introduced. After this there were further successes for the Rank and File Committee in opposing changes in working conditions, disciplinary injustices and such like; successes which involved small scale immediate unofficial strikes, action which attracted widespread publicity. In 1936 there were sizeable but short strikes by busmen in Northampton, Scotland, East Anglia, Liverpool, Oxford, Hull, Kent and elsewhere.

The London Busmen's Rank and File Movement was the most successful of such activists' groups in the mid-1930s. The Communist Party had abandoned the Minority Movement in 1932. Their new approach was outlined by J. R. Campbell in a much-quoted speech made to the Communist International in 1935:

> From the beginning of 1932 we have in a number of unions developed rank-and-file movements and there are important differences between these and the old Minority Movements which we were trying to develop previously. The Minority Movement was constructed in such a way that it appeared as a body outside the trade unions, dictating to the unions what they should do. . . . This enabled the officials to raise the question of loyalty and discipline. . . . It is not easy with the rank-and-file movements because they grew up from within the unions and cannot be open to the same charge and can defend themselves against expulsion tactics in a way that rallies a greater amount of support than the old form of opposition movement could do.

The Communist Party did play a major role in the London

busmen's campaigns, but they were, as Hugh Clegg has written, more of an ally than a dominant body. In helping to organise the movement the Communist Party did gain support; their membership on the London buses going up from 12 to 98 between 1932 and 1937. However, whether communist-dominated or not, the rank-and-file movement in its actions—forming an organisation within the union, which had its own constitution, officers and journal (*Busman's Punch*) and its persistent attacks on union officers and union policy—challenged the union leadership's authority.

Ernest Bevin, Arthur Deakin and the rest of the TGWU leadership crushed the Busman's Rank and File Movement after the Coronation Strike of May 1937, which involved nearly 25,000 London busmen. The strike was over the men's demands for a 7½-hour day, instead of an 8-hour day, on health grounds arising from the stress and strain of their work. Once the strike had begun the government set up a court of inquiry, at which Bevin put the men's case. When the court found that the busmen had 'a case for investigation', the TGWU executive recommended a return to work. The Rank and File Committee successfully opposed this but after four weeks the TGWU executive ordered the men back to work. The Finance and General Purposes Committee of the TGWU then conducted an inquiry into unofficial movements and on its recommendation the Biennial Delegate Conference agreed to ban rank-and-file and similar organisations within the union, to stop branches affiliating to unofficial bodies or propagating their literature, and to forbid branch machinery being used to distribute unauthorised literature. The TGWU also suspended the Central London Area Bus Committee as a body and expelled or suspended eight strike leaders. This tough action led to a breakaway union, the National Passenger Workers Union, which gained some support in London and the Midlands but which fizzled out shortly after the Second World War.[103]

By the mid-1930s the unions were no longer in retreat. Advances in wages were being pressed for, often with vigour. In 1934 the aggregate number of working days lost through strikes and lockouts had fallen below 1 million for the first time since the figures had been compiled in 1893. During 1935–39 the average number of days lost was just under 2 million per year. Of these, half the days lost took place in the coal mining industry.[104]

After the 1926 dispute the coal-owners had reimposed district rather than national negotiations. Baldwin's government had brought in the Eight Hours Act in 1926, which, for five years, permitted the eight-hour day to be worked and which resulted in a wide variety of working practices from area to area. In 1931 the number of hours was reduced to 7½ by the Coal Mines Act 1931, but the second Labour government failed to link this with a minimum wage for the miners. The 7½-hour day was continued under the Coal Mines Act 1932 in spite of the miners' protests. Ebby Edwards, the Secretary of the Miners' Federation, complained to Ramsay MacDonald that the legislation had 'taken away the bargaining power' of the mineworkers. Edwards threatened another national strike. Thus, when pressing again for guaranteed minimum wages, in March 1933 he warned Ramsay MacDonald that:

> another stoppage would be more than a national disaster. The last stoppage affected the balance of trade by not less than £600,000,000 and this stoppage, if it comes, will end the export trade in coal. It may also create an industrial psychology beside which the General Strike situation of 1926 may be insignificant. In these days a fire is easy to kindle, but may be extremely difficult to control.[105]

However, in the early 1930s, with unemployment amongst insured miners reaching a high of 41.8 per cent in August 1932, the Miners' Federation were in a weak position to carry out a national strike.

By 1935 the Federation felt strong enough to campaign for a national increase of two shillings per shift and to hold its first strike ballot for fifteen years. This was held in the three days before polling in the 1935 general election, and resulted in a massive 93 per cent vote for strike action to secure the 'miners' two bob'. Faced with such a clear statement of the miners' determination, ICI and other companies offered to revise upwards their current contracts for coal so that the miners could be paid more. In these circumstances the miners gained sizeable wage advances (one shilling per shift in the more profitable coalfields), although not uniform advances across the country, and a return to national negotiations through the setting-up of the Joint Standing Consultative Committee for the coal industry.[106] The 1935 wages campaign was the nearest the miners came to a national strike in the 1930s.

However, the defeat of 1926 and the employers' tough actions after it provided ample fuel to maintain smouldering resentment up to the Second World War and beyond. Stories are legion of vindictive action in the years that followed; action such as telling men that there was no work at times and places which ensured that they would miss signing on for unemployment pay or providing three days' work and deliberately making it difficult for the men to claim unemployment pay.[107] Whole lodge committees were victimised, and leading activists blacklisted.[108] With soaring unemployment, miners in some areas became fearful of complaining about safety hazards or anything else; a point tragically illustrated during the inquiry into the Gresford Colliery explosion of September 1934, a disaster which resulted in the loss of 265 lives.[109] In these economic circumstances the mining firms could, and did, speed up and intensify production, whilst pushing wages down.

In some areas employers' actions sparked off local strikes. Thus in South Wales there were strikes in 1927 at Maesteg (over non-unionism), in 1928–29 at Nine Mile Point Colliery (over wage cuts), and in 1929 in Ogmore Vale and in the Garw Valley (over non-unionists). In 1931, faced with unilateral action by the employers over hours and wages, the South Wales Miners' Federation called what was to be the only coalfield-wide strike of the 1930s; a strike which lasted two weeks but which failed to prevent sizeable wage cuts. In Scotland the United Mineworkers led a three-week strike in July 1931, also against employers' unilateral action on hours and wages. There were also more localised disputes in Scotland before this, including strikes over wage cuts in 1930 at Shotts and neighbouring pits.[110]

In the mid-1930s, as the economy recovered, the struggle with non-unionism and company unions intensified. In South Wales, starting with the Nine Mile Point Colliery in October 1935, there were successful 'stay-down' strikes, where union men refused to come out of the pits until industrial union men were taken away. In Nottinghamshire the Spencer union was a source of conflict on the coalfield. In 1936 this led to an extremely bitter dispute at Harworth, which, as in the cotton disputes, involved tough action by the police on behalf of the employers. The Miners' Federation balloted its membership in April 1937 as to strike action 'with the object of obtaining recognition of the MFGB in the Nottinghamshire coalfield and to secure adequate assurances to prevent any victimisation of the workmen in Harworth', and secured an 87.9 per cent vote in favour on a 98.9 per cent poll. The ensuing negotiations, however, led to negotiations which brought about fusion between Spencer's Nottinghamshire Miners' Industrial Union and the Nottinghamshire Miners' Association, with Spencer as President of the new body.[111]

The Ministry of Labour's annual report for 1937 included the comment,

> The question of recognition of trade unions and the refusal of unionists to work with non-unionists gave rise to a number of disputes and provided further evidence of increasing organisation and the desire to extend the field of voluntary collective bargaining.[112]

The miners' unions were not unique in this.

Overall union membership in Great Britain grew by 42.7 per cent between 1933 and 1939. Whilst the coal mining unions increased their membership from a low of 570,600 in 1933 to 741,300 in 1939, a lower than average rise (29.9 per cent), the significant thing about the miners was their increase in union density. This went up from a low of 51.3 per cent in 1932 to 81.1 per cent in 1939, which contrasts with estimates for overall union density of 23.3 per cent in 1932 and 31.9 per cent in 1939. Many of the unions whose membership grew faster than average in this period started from a low union density and were in sectors of high economic growth. Thus, for example, union membership in the area of bricks and building went up 150.3 per cent between 1933 and 1939 (from 14,500 to 36,300) but it was from a union density of 10.4 per cent (rising to 21.2 per cent). Much the same is true of chemicals and allied trades and also of electricity (though in the latter case density had been higher, 25.3 per cent in 1931) which experienced increases in membership of 115.8 per cent and 102.8 per cent respectively.

A key union in the 1930s was the AEU. In metals and engineering the long-term trend of employment was up, unlike in cotton and coal mining; union density at 24.3 per cent in 1933 had been a little above average (22.9 per cent) and rose to 35.5 per cent in 1939 (the average then being 31.9 per cent); and the increase in union membership over these years (from 551,300 to 993,700) was 80.2 per cent.[113] The AEU was the major union in this sector, and its membership rose by some 200,000 to 390,873 by the outbreak of war in September 1939. A large part of this increase came from the AEU enrolling more semi-skilled workers in the 1930s. Between 1920 and 1925 these had been recruited to Section III of the union, and that section covered about 10 per cent of the membership. From 1926 less skilled workers joined Section V or Va, and between 1936 and 1939 these sections covered 36.5 per cent of the membership (though some of these were skilled men who thereby avoided paying higher subscriptions).[114]

As elsewhere, the wage cuts in engineering in the depression sparked off a vigorous rank-and-file movement. This was further fostered by the apparent over-cautiousness of the AEU leadership. In 1931, to the dismay of the activists, the AEU leadership had accepted the employers' ultimation for further reductions in overtime rates, night-shift rates and piecework prices without holding a ballot of the membership. They were also unduly cautious in supporting action in the fast-growing motor car industry. Thus, in the case of the Pressed Steel strike at Cowley in 1934, the TGWU took on the organisation of the workforce whilst the AEU and the National Union of Vehicle Builders condemned the stoppage as unconstitutional.[115] The slowness of official negotiations over apprentices' wages and providing them with proper training led to spontaneous strikes by them in Scotland and later in England. The apprentices' actions forced the employers to negotiate seriously on these issues and to recognise the AEU's right to bargain on the apprentices' behalf in the future.[116]

Trade unionism in engineering grew in strength during the 1930s as the economy recovered and as the government spent more and more on armaments. The government boosted expenditure on aircraft from 1934 onwards. With the government paying them under favourable contract procedures and with guarantees of a continuing flow of orders, various subsidies and loans, the aircraft manufacturers were insulated from economic hardship. The resulting high level of profits became an issue in Parliament and on the shopfloor.[117] Sir Warren Fisher, the Permanent Secretary of the Treasury, caustically wrote at the start of 1939 that British society continued

to amble along in our old and well-tried and (for the small minority) very comfortable economic paths. Which means . . . business . . . profiteering out of the occasion of the country's need, and, with this patriotic example before him, the workman . . . stimulated to insistence on some improvement of his rather shabby lot in life.[118]

Lord Weir, the industrialist, who was an adviser to the Secretary of State for Air, was exasperated by the employers' high demands and threats of non cooperation during the bargaining with the government and wrote,

> A stupid letter with threats would at once provoke [a] grave polit[ical]-indust[rial] situation & open up the whole case of private munitions supply. To blackmail the State in emergency is a present to Socialism, Communism & all evil movements. More than that, no sector of Pr[ivate] Enterprise can do this by itself, risking all Pr[ivate] Enterprise.[119]

The huge profits and managerial efforts to undermine trade union standards gave the shop stewards' movement in the aircraft industry ample ammunition. With the growing demand from the government, trade unionists took effective strike action in many parts of the country between 1935 and 1939. There were strikes in aircraft factories over non-unionists and over youths doing fitters' work, over the introduction of Bedaux and other time-and-motion systems and over various attempts to cut payments.[120] The Government and the *Daily Mail* and *Daily Express* attempted to discredit the workers in the aircraft factories with allegations of sabotage. Given the huge profits being made, the shop stewards could easily respond in their paper, *New Propellor*:

> We would like the public to know that there is a great danger to our pilots and also a danger that the quality of aircraft in general will not be up to standard because of the greed for profit of the aircraft companies. The employment of boys upon work formerly done by skilled men and speeding up methods which make for bad work are only two of the recent manifestations of this determination to cut down costs for the sake of profit.[121]

Trade unionism spread quickly in this rapidly growing industry. Membership of 90 per cent and higher has been claimed for many of the aircraft factories in the period before the outbreak of the Second World War. From 1937 the engineering unions became markedly stronger outside of the aircraft industry as well as in it, as the shortage of skilled labour became more acute as the economy recovered. By 1939 strike action was at its greatest for the decade, with strikes in the aircraft industry accounting for about an eighth of all days lost in the metal, engineering and shipbuilding sector.[122]

The AEU was not the only union in engineering to grow markedly in the 1930s. Electrical engineering grew rapidly in the early twentieth century as factories and homes went over to electric power. In 1907 electrical engineering had employed 5 per cent of engineering workers; by 1935 it accounted for 20 per cent. The membership of the Electrical Trades Union (ETU) stood at 27,589 in 1924, rose slowly by 1000 by 1929 but shot up to about 70,000 members by the outbreak of war in 1939. As with the bus drivers, strikes by ETU members often resulted in widespread press attention. This was so with striking cinema projectionists in 1938. In London there was much militancy, and in 1937 the London Central Committee was expelled by the ETU's executive for supporting an unofficial strike at Earl's Court over extra pay for working in abnormal conditions.[123]

The trade union movement generally secured better pay and conditions in the late 1930s. One marked feature of this was many unions securing reductions in working hours. Another was the spread of holidays with pay. Before the First World War some white-collar workers and a few others had enjoyed these. After the war other workers gained them. In 1937 the Minister of Labour set up a committee under Lord Amulree to look into the extent of holidays with pay in British industry. The Ministry's Report for that year commented on these:

A noteworthy agreement was that reached in the engineering industry whereby the employer credits to the worker for each full week's work performed, a sum representing 1/50th of the appropriate day time rate plus time workers' bonuses for the time being, as an *ex gratia* allowance in respect of holidays. General agreements were also made, either nationally or by districts, affecting employees of various grades in a large number of undertakings. The effect of these new agreements was to increase the number of persons in receipt of holidays with pay under collective agreements by a million during the year, which represents an increase of about 60 per cent on the number covered by collective agreements at the end of 1936. There were also numerous arrangements of a varying character made by individual firms . . .[124]

Overall, both in boom and in slump between 1914 and 1939, the trend towards centralisation in Britain's trade unions appears to have continued. The First World War and the post-war boom gave a tremendous boost to national collective bargaining. Thereafter the unions generally (with the notable exception of the wool unions in 1930) continued to bargain centrally or tried to, including when attempting to lessen the cuts in the severe recessions of 1921–22 and 1929–33. National bargaining, appearances before courts of inquiry, arbitration tribunals and government commissions put greater emphasis on research. This might be provided by other bodies, notably the TUC, the Labour Research Department and, in the case of the smaller unions, the General Federation of Trade Unions; or it might be done by the unions themselves. Like the employers' organisations, the unions spent more on providing professional services for their members. Of course, the amalgamations after the First World War facilitated larger bureaucracies—and it seems that even in the 1929–33 recession the number of full-time officers did not fall anywhere near proportionately with the fall in membership.[125]

After the General Strike trade union officials appear more powerful within their organisations both in settling wage negotiations on their own authority and in dealing with militants within their unions. Thus the TGWU and the ETU both expelled London committee members in the mid-1930s, and earlier, in 1927, the General and Municipal Workers' Union banned communists outright from being elected to union posts. Under Bevin and Citrine the TUC also took an anti-communist and more 'statesman-like' line generally. This was recognised by the knighthoods offered to them—and accepted in the case of Citrine in 1935.

In the 1930s the TUC was consulted by the government on a wide range of topics.[126] Many of these topics were important in themselves; but until 1938 it is hard to argue that the government allowed the TUC an important say in matters central to the economy or to industrial strife.

The development of the TUC *vis-à-vis* the individual unions was more significant in the 1930s than with the government. The TUC's importance in the trade union movement grew. This was at least in part due to the diminished strength of some of the older unions, notably the coal miners and the textile unions, and perhaps due to the more varied interests of the giant general unions. As Keith

Middlemas has remarked, 'Gradually, hesitantly, the TUC assumed the role of rule-maker and arbitrator for the movement . . .'.[127] When the General Council had been formed in 1920 it had been instructed to 'endeavour to adjust disputes and differences between affiliated unions'. The TUC in 1927 and 1929 took a firm line against breakaway unions, and its Disputes Committee in the 1930s considered a wide range of 'improper' union behaviour and not just 'poaching'. The TUC's policies in these matters were codified at the 1939 Congress at Bridlington. One of the clauses stated:

> Each union shall not commence organising activities at any establishment or undertaking in respect of any grade or grades of workers in which another union has the majority of workers employed and negotiates wages and conditions, unless by arrangement with that union.[128]

In the year and a half before the outbreak of war in September 1939, the government did turn to the TUC. Because of the government's need for the Labour Movement's cooperation in the rapidly increasing armaments programme the Prime Minister consulted the TUC's General Council in March 1938. They saw Chamberlain again in May 1938, when they took the opportunity to express the Labour Movement's detestation of government policy towards the Spanish Civil War and the widespread fears as to its attitude to the Fascist dictators. In taking such action the TUC, as Citrine commented in the *TUC Report* for 1938, was exercising its responsibility for general policy. He observed, 'The Council have tried to discharge their obligations of leadership always remembering very prominently the limitations of their authority.' In March 1939, the Permanent Secretary of the Ministry of Labour consulted Bevin and other TUC representatives about a plan for industrial regulation should there be a war. In April the General Council agreed to a resolution proposed by Bevin that machinery be set up 'for dealing with the matters raised by the government'.[129] When war came, the TUC General Council was prepared to take the lead for the trade unions in negotiations with the government concerning Britain's economy and society in wartime.

### Notes

1 A. Bullock, *The Life and Times of Ernest Bevin*, vol. 1 (1960), pp. 183–222. H. A. Clegg, *General Union* (1954), pp. 1–22; J.

Hinton, *Labour and Socialism* (1983), pp. 119–130; TGWU, *The Story of the TGWU* (1975), p. 46.

2   J. B. Jefferys, *The Story of The Engineers* (1946), pp. 189–91.

3   B. Nield, 'Herbert Henry Elvin', in J. Saville and J. Bellamy (eds), *Dictionary of Labour Biography*, vol. 6 (1982), pp. 106–7.

4   Bullock, *op. cit.*, p. 600.

5   M. A. Bienefeld, *Working Hours In British Industry* (1972), p. 149.

6   *When Labour Rules* (1920), p. 52.

7   Quoted by John MacLean in *The Call*, 23 January 1919; reprinted in J. MacLean, *In The Rapids of the Revolution* (1978), p. 149.

8   *Great Britain After The War* (1916, reprinted 1917 and 1918), pp. 13–14.

9   In the Ministry of Munitions Papers there is a list of fifteen pledges given by the government for full restoration during the twelve months from March 1915; MUN 5–91–344/1. On the fears 'that the nation has given a solemn pledge to labour which it cannot possibly fulfil' see, for example, S. Webb, *The Restoration Of Trade Union Conditions* (1917).

10  Reprinted in MacLean, *op. cit.*, pp. 130–1.

11  On this see, amongst others, Jefferys, *op. cit.*, pp. 187–8 and I. McLean, *The Legend of Red Clydeside* (1983), pp. 112–38.

12  War Cabinet (523), 31 January 1919; CAB 23–9–36.

13  Bonar Law to Lloyd George, 1 February 1919; Lloyd George Papers (hereafter L.G.) F/30/3/20.

14  P. Bagwell, *The Railwaymen* (1963), pp. 429–32.

15  War Cabinet (521), 28 January 1919; CAB 23–9–30.

16  War Cabinet (548), 20 March 1919; CAB 23–9–116/8. R. Page Arnot, *The Miners: Years of Struggle* (1953), pp. 184–202. The government refused the demands concerning demobilisation.

17  P. Bagwell, 'The Triple Industrial Alliance 1913–1922', in A. Briggs and J. Saville (eds), *Essays in Labour History 1886–1923* (1971), p. 107.

18  War Cabinet (529), 7 February 1919; CAB 23–9–57/9.

19  G. W. Alcock, *Fifty Years of Railway Trade Unionism* (1922), p. 552.

20  War Cabinet (526 and 527), 4 and 5 February 1919; CAB 23–9–48/52.

21  War Cabinet (530), 10 February 1919; CAB 23–9–62. For accounts of this organisation, see G. Glasgow, *General Strikes and Road Transport* (1926); R. Desmarais, 'Lloyd George and the Development of the British Government's Strike breaking Organisation', *International Review of Social History* (1975); and 'The British government's strike-breaking organisation and Black Friday', *Journal of Contemporary History* (1971); and K. Jeffery and P. Hennessy, *States of Emergency* (1983).

22  Cited in Bagwell, *Railwaymen*, p. 393.

23  This example from *The Morning Post*, 3 October 1919.

24  *The Black Gang* (1922), pp. 300–1, 310.

25 War Cabinet (589), 8 July 1919; CAB 23–11–1.

26 Arnot, *op. cit.*, pp. 240–1.

27 Thomas Jones, *Whitehall Diary*, vol. 1 (1969), ed. K. Middlemas, pp. 99–103.

28 Cabinet Minutes, 12 August 1920; CAB 23–22–131/2. Letter to Bonar Law, 4 September 1920; LG F/31/1/44.

29 It was known as the 'Datum Line strike' because of the negotiations over output involved levels over which additional payments would be paid automatically. For details see Arnot, *op. cit.*, pp. 232–78; and G. D. H. Cole, *Labour In The Coal Mining Industry 1914–1921* (1923), pp. 140–61.

30 S. R. Graubard, *British Labour and the Russian Revolution 1917–1924* (1956), pp. 83–114; H. Pollitt, *Serving My Time* (1940), pp. 94–121; Bullock, *op. cit.*, pp. 133–40.

31 War Cabinet (547), 19 March 1919; CAB 23–9–114/6.

32 Bagwell, *Triple Alliance*, pp. 382–3, 387, 399–401.

33 A. J. P. Taylor (ed.), *Lloyd George: A Diary By Frances Stevenson* (1971), p. 173.

34 S. Roskill, *Hankey: Man of Secrets*, vol. 2 (1972), p. 123. *Lord Riddell's Intimate Diary of the Peace Conference And After* (1933), pp. 130–1.

35 Entries for 4 and 5 April 1921. Jones, *op. cit.*, pp. 133, 136.

36 Quoted in G. Blaxland, *J. H. Thomas: A Life For Unity* (1964), pp. 121–2.

37 R. Charles, *The Development of Industrial Relations in Britain 1911–1939* (1973), Part 3, especially pp. 234, 237–49. For a more sympathetic appraisal of government policy, see R. Lowe, Chapter 5 of this book.

38 Bullock, *op. cit.*, pp. 120–32. Lord Shaw of Dunfermline, *Letters to Isabel* (1921), pp. 298–303.

39 I. G. Sharp, *Industrial Conciliation and Arbitration in Great Britain* (1950), pp. 347–60, esp. 359–60.

40 Ibid., pp. 360–4. *Report By A Court Of Inquiry Concerning The Engineering Trades Dispute 1922* (1922), Cmd.1653, p. 21.

41 Charles, *op. cit.*, pp. 130–8, 194–5. National Association of Unions in the Textile Trade (hereafter NAUTT), Executive minutes, 20 March 1920 and 26 April 1921. Copies are in the West Yorkshire Archive Service, Kirklees District Archives in Huddersfield, NUDBTW 32.

42 W. H. Warburton, *The History of Trade Union Organisation in the North Staffordshire Potteries* (1931), pp. 228–33. Charles, *op. cit.*, p. 192.

43 On this see J. H. Porter, 'Wage Bargaining Under Conciliation Agreements 1860–1914', *Economic History Review*, 23 (1970), pp. 460–75, and 'The Iron Trade' in C. J. Wrigley (ed.), *A History of British Industrial Relations 1875–1914* (1982), Chapter 12.

44 Northern Counties District Council—of the National Wool (and Allied) Textile Industrial Council (hereafter NWTIC)—minutes, 16

May 1924. Copies in Kirklees District Archives, NUDBTW 42. NAUTT executive minutes, 20 May 1924.

45  *The Reporter*, 21 May 1927.

46  *Report On The Establishment And Progress Of Joint Industrial Councils 1917–1922* (by the Ministry of Labour) (1923), pp. 34–6. E. M. H. Lloyd, *Experiments In State Control* (1924), pp. 151–4, 272–5. See also Chapter 1, p. 43.

47  *Report On . . . Joint Industrial Councils*, pp. 89–90.

48  Report of NWTIC; NUDBTW 42.

49  NWTIC Emergency Committee minutes, 12 June 1922. West of England District Council, minutes, 27 April 1922; NUDBTW 42.

50  West of England District Council, 1 May 1924; NUDBTW 42.

51  Northern Counties District Council minutes, 12 December 1921; NWTIC Emergency Committee minutes, 17 July 1922, 24 November 1922 and 18 February 1924; NUDBTW 42.

52  NAUTT Executive minutes, 20 March 1920 and NAUTT full council meeting, 28 May 1921; NUDBTW 32. NWTIC, West of England District Council minutes, 27 April 1922 and 26 July 1923; NUDBTW 42.

53  NAUTT, full council minutes, 18 July 1925; NUDBTW 32.

54  For a detailed account of the lock-out and an assessment of its significance, see J. A. Jowett and K. Laybourn, 'The Wool Dispute of 1925', *Journal of Local Studies*, 2, 1 (1982), pp. 10–27.

55  NAUTT, full council minutes, 19 November 1927; NUDBTW 32. H. A. Clegg, *A History of British Trade Unions Since 1889, Vol. 2: 1911–1933* (1985), pp. 480–90. *Huddersfield Examiner*, 7 and 14 June 1930. *National Union of Textile Workers Record*, August 1930 and February 1932.

56  Department of Employment, *British Labour Statistics: Historical Abstract 1886–1968* (1971), p. 167. Fur further discussion of this see Chapter 6 of this book.

57  *Twentieth Abstract of Labour Statistics of the United Kingdom* (1931), pp. 94–5, 130–1. The overall drop of 35 per cent is true of both the UK and Great Britain (i.e. England, Scotland and Wales). The other figures for drops in membership are for Britain and are drawn from the tables in G. S. Bain and R. Price, *Profiles of Union Growth* (1980), pp. 40–78. For a valuable analysis of the drawbacks of the Ministry figures of union membership by industry see ibid., pp. 16–18.

58  R. Groves, *Sharpen The Sickle!* (1949), pp. 170–205. H. Newby, *The Deferential Worker* (1977), pp. 221–6. A. Howkins, *Poor Labouring Men* (1985), pp. 130–75.

59  N. and J. MacKenzie (eds) *The Diary of Beatrice Webb*, vol. 3 (1984), p. 380.

60  Jeffreys, *op. cit.*, pp. 224–5.

61  E. Wigham, *The Power To Manage* (1973), pp. 118–19. See also Chapter 4 of this book.

62  Ibid., p. 119. H. J. Fyrth and H. Collins, *The Foundry Workers*

(1959), p. 164. See also A. T. Kidd, *History of the Tin-Plate and Sheet Metal Workers and Braziers Societies* (1949), pp. 240–52.

63 Fyrth and Collins, *op. cit.*, p. 165.

64 At the Fourth Congress of the Communist International. R. Martin, *Communism And The British Trade Unions 1924–1933* (1969), p. 23.

65 Quoted p. 301 in F. Matthews, 'The Building Guilds', in Briggs and Saville (eds), *op. cit.*, pp. 284–331.

66 *Huddersfield and District Trades and Labour Council Year Book*, September 1924.

67 Martin, *op. cit.*, pp. 23–101. J. Hinton and R. Hyman, *Trade Unions And Revolution* (1975), pp. 23–41.

68 G. A. Phillips, *The General Strike* (1976), pp. 14–20.

69 See, among many others, M. Morris, *The General Strike* (1976); Phillips, *op. cit.*; P. Renshaw, *The General Strike* (1975); and Hinton and Hyman, *op. cit.*, pp. 42–6.

70 For a discussion of the Bill, 'this apple of discord', see R. Muir, *Trade Unionism and The Trade Union Bill* (1927), an offshoot of the Liberal Industrial Enquiry. For a different appraisal of this measure see Chapter 5 of this book.

71 Whilst most unions lost members in these years, some white-collar unions continued to grow, including those in local and national government and education (4.5–5 per cent). Bain and Price, *op. cit.*, pp. 39–78.

72 A. R. Griffin, *The Miners of Nottinghamshire 1914–1944* (1962), pp. 203–75. W. R. Garside, *The Durham Miners 1919–1960* (1971), pp. 232–4. H. Francis and D. Smith, *The Fed* (1980), pp. 113–38.

73 A. R. F. Griffin and C. P. Griffin, 'The Non-Political Trade Union Movement', in A. Briggs and J. Saville, *Essays In Labour History 1918–1939* (1977), pp. 133–62.

74 G. W. MacDonald and H. F. Gospel, 'The Mond–Turner Talks, 1927–1933: A Study In Industrial Cooperation', *The Historical Journal*, 16, 4 (1973), pp. 807–29. See also Chapter 4 of this book.

75 B. Turner, *About Myself* (1930), pp. 145–51.

76 M. Jacques, 'The Emergence of "Responsible" Trade Unionism: A Study of the "New Direction" in TUC Policy 1926–1935', (Cambridge University PhD, 1976), p. 282. I am grateful to the author for permission to quote this passage.

77 E. Eldon Barry, *Nationalisation in British Politics* (1965), pp. 277–8.

78 Jacques, *op. cit.*, pp. 128–31.

79 National Minority Movement, *Another Year of Rationalisation* (1929), p. 110.

80 Letter to the miners by Garfield Williams, South Wales district secretary of the National Miners' Minority Movement, 9 October 1929. R. H. Mainwaring Papers, National Library of Wales.

81 Cymmer Movement Group to workmen of the Cymmer Colliery

(late February 1930). W. H. Mainwaring Papers. On the background to the 'Class against Class' line, see N. Branson, *History of the Communist Party of Great Britain 1927–1941* (1985), pp. 1–43. See also Chapter 3 of this book.

82    R. Page Arnot, *A History Of The Scottish Miners* (1955), pp. 167–70, 182–92, 213–22. A. Moffat, *My Life With The Miners* (1965), pp. 36–64; Martin, *op. cit.*, pp. 90–3, 127–9.

83    S. W. Lerner, *Breakaway Unions And The Small Trade Union* (1961), pp. 85–143; Martin, *op. cit.*, pp. 136–41; N. Branson, *op. cit.*, p. 42.

84    Exports fell still further in 1938 and 1939. R. Robson, *The Cotton Industry In Britain* (1957), p. 333. For a recent survey of the problems facing the British cotton industry, see J. H. Porter, 'Cotton and Wool Textiles', in N. K. Buxton and D. Aldcroft (eds), *British Industry Between The Wars* (1979), pp. 25–47.

85    Board of Trade Working Party Reports, *Cotton* (1946) (hereafter cited as *Cotton*), p. 5.

86    B. W. Alford, 'New Industries for Old? British industry between the wars', in R. Floud and D. McLoskey, *The Economic History of Britain Since 1700*, vol. 2 (1981), p. 310.

87    Michael Grey, of a family spinning firm. R. Pagnamenta and R. Overy, *All Our Working Lives* (1984), p. 35.

88    Textile Workers' Minority Movement, *The Struggle of the Lancashire Textile Workers* (1929), p. 8. The official report was by the Platt Mission to the USA in 1944, cited in *Cotton*, p. 8.

89    A. and L. Fowler, *The History of the Nelson Weavers Association* (1984), pp. 41–51.

90    Ibid., pp. 55–6. H. A. Turner, *Trade Union Growth, Structure and Policy* (1962), pp. 327–8. E. Hopwood, *The Lancashire Weavers' Story* (1969), pp. 93–4.

91    For the preceding paragraphs see Fowler, *op. cit.*, pp. 56–86; Hopwood, *op. cit.*, pp. 95–8, 108–18; Turner, *op. cit.*, pp. 328–30; and J. H. Richardson, *Industrial Relations in Great Britain* (1938 edn), pp. 127–9. More detail is provided in two valuable theses: A. J. Bullen, 'The Cotton Spinners and Manufacturers Association and the breakdown of the collective bargaining system in the cotton manufacturing industry 1928–1935', (University of Warwick MA, 1980), pp. 28–55; and J. H. Riley, 'The More-looms system and industrial relations in the Lancashire cotton manufacturing industry 1928–1935', (University of Manchester MA, 1981), pp. 31–409.

92    Riley, *op. cit.*, pp. 63–4, 84. Fowler, *op. cit.*, p. 65.

93    The drop in male and female trade union membership was similar between 1928 and 1933 (8.5 per cent). On these and the other figures here see Bain and Price, *op. cit.*, pp. 39, 51–2; *Abstract of Labour Statistics 1931*, pp. 130–5; and B. R. Mitchell with P. Deane, *Abstract of British Historical Statistics* (1962), pp. 62–3.

94    S. Boston, *Women Workers and the Trade Union Movement* (1980), pp. 132–53. For the sorry story of discrimination against women in

the civil service, see M. Zimmeck, 'Strategies and Stratagems for the Employment of Women in the British Civil Service 1919–1939', *Historical Journal*, 27, 4 (1984), pp. 901–24.

95   For the quantitative evidence for suggesting a discontinuity in trade unions' strike activity after 1926, see J. Cronin, *Industrial Conflict in Modern Britain* (1979), pp. 132–8.

96   J. E. Powell, *Payment By Results* (1924), pp. 2, vi. See also C. R. Littler, *The Development of the Labour Process in Capitalist Societies* (1982), esp. pp. 48–63.

97   Littler, *op. cit.*, p. 133, and also pp. 98–145, 188–95; G. Brown, *Sabotage* (1977), pp. 231–49.

98   Table 1 of A. J. Taylor, '"The Pulse of One Fraternity". Non-Unionism in the Yorkshire Coalfield 1931–1938', in Society for the Study of Labour History, *Bulletin*, 49 (1984), pp. 46–53. Whilst presumably there were members amongst the unemployed and retired members, these figures give some idea of the problem of falling union density that faced the miners. There are also figures for British coal mining in Bain and Price, *op. cit.*, p. 45 which gives densities of 53.1 and 51.4 per cent for 1927 and 1931 respectively. Their definition of 'potential union membership' includes the unemployed.

99   Francis and Smith, *op. cit.*, pp. 96–7.

100  D. J. Rowe, *Lead Manufacturing In Britain* (1983), pp. 349–50.

101  On the Channel 4 television programme 'People to People. A Tale to Tell: Us and Them', transmitted on 1 August 1984.

102  Martin, *op. cit.*, p. 169; Bagwell, *Railwaymen*, pp. 522–3.

103  H. A. Clegg, *Labour Relations In London Transport* (1950), pp. 103–33; V. L. Allen, *Trade Union Leadership* (1957), pp. 63–73; Bullock, *op. cit.*, pp. 519–24, 607–14; Branson, *op. cit.*, pp. 93–4, 174–7.

104  *British Labour Statistics*, p. 396.

105  Letters of 4 and 9 March 1933. R. Page Arnot, *The Miners: In Crisis And War* (1961), pp. 111–15.

106  Ibid., pp. 149–79. See also W. H. Williams, 'The Miners' Case', in W. H. Williams (ed.) *The Miners' Two Bob* (1935), pp. 1–26.

107  R. Duncan and Shotts History Workshop, *Shotts Miners* (1982), p. 24. C. Liddle to C. Wrigley, 3 November 1984.

108  For victimisation see, for example, Francis and Smith, *op. cit.*, pp. 76–82, 505–7; and C. Wrigley, '1926: Social Costs of the Mining Dispute', *History Today*, 34 (November 1984), pp. 5–10.

109  Arnot, *In Crisis And War*, pp. 131–43. On trade unionism and mining disasters, see the biography of Herbert Smith by J. Lawson, *The Man In The Cap* (1941), pp. 163–6.

110  Francis and Smith, *op. cit.*, pp. 126–37, 175–7. Arnot, *Scottish Miners*, p. 214; Duncan, *op. cit.*, p. 22.

111  Francis and Smith, *op. cit.*, pp. 278–98. Griffin, *op. cit.*, pp. 255–82; Arnot, *In Crisis And War*, pp. 205–40.

112   *Ministry of Labour Report For The Year 1937*, Cmd. 5717 (1938), p. 64.
113   Bain and Price, *op. cit.*, pp. 37–78.
114   Jefferys, *op. cit.*, pp. 208, 241. See also, in this book, p. 313.
115   Ibid., pp. 240–1. R. Croucher, *Engineers At War* (1982), pp. 29–31. R. C. Whiting, *The View From Cowley* (1983), pp. 53–73. For the motor car industry see Chapter 9 of this book.
116   Croucher, *op. cit.*, pp. 45–56; Jeffreys, *op. cit.*, pp. 244–5.
117   W. J. Reader, *Architect of Air Power* (1968), pp. 180–293. R. Shay, *British Rearmaments In The Thirties* (1977), especially pp. 92–128. G. C. Peden, *British Rearmament And The Treasury* (1979), esp. pp. 81–4, 118–21, 133–4. K. Middlemas, *Politics In Industrial Society* (1979), pp. 244–60.
118   In a letter to Sir John Simon, 3 January 1939; cited in Peden, *op. cit.*, p. 105.
119   Undated notes; cited in Shay, *op. cit.*, p. 120.
120   For the details of these strikes, see E. and R. Frow, *Engineering Struggles* (1982), pp. 114–31.
121   Issue of April 1938; cited ibid., pp. 126–7.
122   Croucher, *op. cit.*, pp. 41, 62–5.
123   Electrical Trades Union, *The Story Of The ETU* (1952), pp. 143–4, 151–5. See also Chapter 8 of this book.
124   *Report For The Year 1937*, p. 64. On the lack of them earlier in major industries, see Ministry of Labour, *Report on Collective Agreements Between Employers and Workpeople* (1934). On welfare generally see Chapter 5.
125   Hinton and Hyman, *op. cit.*, pp. 18–22; Clegg, *History*, vol. 2, pp. 449–52, 535–6.
126   H. Pelling, *A History of British Trade Unionism* (1963), p. 208. Middlemas, *op. cit.*, pp. 217–43; R. M. Martin, *TUC: The Growth Of A Pressure Group 1868–1976* (1980), pp. 205–46.
127   Middlemas, *op. cit.*, p. 219.
128   Lerner, *op. cit.*, pp. 66–81.
129   R. M. Martin, *op. cit.*, pp. 256–62; Bullock, *op. cit.*, pp. 624–6, 634–8; Middlemas, *op. cit.*, pp. 256–8.

# 3

# Rank-and-File Movements and Workplace Organisation, 1914–39

*Richard Hyman*

'Rank and file' is one of the most popular yet problematic elements in the vocabulary of trade unionism. A loose military analogy (ranks and files were the vertical and horizontal rows in which infantrymen were traditionally arrayed), the term has always possessed more obvious emotive resonance than analytical illumination. Its imprecision has indeed often permitted the tendentious usage of the label 'rank and file' in order to imply that the programme and initiatives of particular groups of activists are representative of the broader mass of 'lay' union membership.[1]

The quarter-century after 1914 represented a crucial phase of development in both the rhetoric of 'rank-and-filism' and the reality to which it referred. In the nineteenth century, those who spoke of the trade union rank-and-file usually implied no more than a functional division between leaders and led; they identified the movement's 'common soldiery' whose duty and disposition was to follow loyally the directions of their appointed (or elected) officers. After the turn of the century, however, the term was increasingly employed to indicate an *opposition* of interests, functions or attitudes between leaders and led. The contrast between 'rank-and-file' and 'bureaucrats' became, of course, a major theme of pre-war syndicalism.

The 1914–18 war carried this process a stage further. The idea of a Rank-and-File Movement—proudly deploying initial capitals—came into its own. Those who employed such terms were typically committed socialists: initially connected with the Amalgamation Committee movement, which convened the first of a series of Rank-and-File Conferences in 1916; later associated with the industrial activities of the Communist Party. It was the latter which, in the two interwar decades, provided the basis for coordinated oppositional activity in British unions. The National Minority Movement in the 1920s, and the more variegated initiatives of the

1930s—most prominently, perhaps, the London Busmen's Rank-and-File Movement—exemplified the formalisation of internal oppositional initiatives inspired by rank-and-filist ideology to an extent inconceivable before 1914.

The rise of organised opposition movements and the oppositional mobilisation of the rhetoric of rank and file must be viewed as a response to transformations within trade unionism and industrial relations more generally. Those on the left who denounced 'trade union bureaucracy' had a genuine point—though one pregnant with irony. Since the revival of British socialism, trade union radicals had bemoaned the complacency of a movement which comprised a small minority of the working class, fragmented within a vast number of typically tiny sectional organisations. Their complaints were at first sight alleviated by subsequent developments. The growth in union membership which had occurred unevenly but consistently in the 1890s and 1900s accelerated dramatically in the decade 1910–20 (an increase from 2.6 to 8.3 million); and though interwar unemployment caused a decline, numbers never fell below the pre-war maximum. At the same time a major consolidation occurred in trade union structure, particularly after 1917 legislation eased the process of amalgamation.

One obvious consequence was a transformation in the sheer *size* of British unions. At the turn of the century, the largest organisation under unified control, the Amalgamated Society of Engineers, had less than 100,000 members. In 1920 its successor, the Amalgamated Engineering Union, claimed over 400,000. The National Union of Railwaymen, formed in 1913, recorded 458,000. While the Miners' Federation, with over 1 million members, scarcely counts as one union, its largest area components were giants in their own right. The two massive general workers' unions, both established in the early 1920s—the Transport and General and the General and Municipal—helped complete the trend.

Quantitative alteration had qualitative implications. Nineteenth-century forms of 'primitive democracy', as the Webbs patronisingly termed it, had their origins in the small, localised craft society; they were largely inapplicable in a large, national, multi-occupational (and often multi-industrial) union. British unions remained far less 'bureaucratised' than their German counterparts which gave Michels the model for his 'iron law of oligarchy'; there nevertheless occurred a substantial increase in the number of full-time officials in the field and also in head office staffing and sophistication: a trend which continued between the wars despite the fall in membership. Amalgamation itself usually necessitated changes in union rules, giving the national officials and executives scope to initiate alterations which consolidated their own position. Legislative developments, such as the pre- and post-war provisions on sickness and unemployment insurance, also provided an opportunity for systematic rules revision. Accordingly, union rulebooks were frequently transformed from the amateur endeavours of working members into more clinical and far more elaborate documents bearing on every page the imprint of the general secretary's legal advisers.

The centralisation of authority associated with larger unions with many full-time officials was further encouraged by trends in collective bargaining. Before 1914 the key arena of negotiation in most industries was the district, allowing local union activists a direct impact on the formulation and presentation of demands. The emergence around the turn of the century of national machinery typically involved attempts at centralised control of decentralised initiative, not the elimination of local determination of substantive conditions; and even this limited encroachment on local autonomy provoked violent conflicts, as in engineering and building.

The centralisation of substantive bargaining proceeded apace after 1914. District bargaining for a farthing an hour on rates of pay made sense when prices altered modestly and often in response to local economic forces. It was eclipsed after 1914 with rapid and largely uniform increases in living costs, and the consequent need for similar and simultaneous wage advances in every district. Thus wage determination became increasingly centralised; while in growth areas of unionism without the traditions of local autonomy associated with the craft societies, national negotiation was the target from the outset. The years of mass unemployment and depression, with their dampening effects on autonomous local activities, reinforced these centralising tendencies.

Socialists who took the working class as a whole as their point of reference had naturally argued for fewer, larger unions. Envisaging an offensive challenge to increasingly centralised capital, they called for greater centralisation of trade union policy; a common trend from the 'radicals' in the ASE in 1892 to the postwar BSP and later CP activists who called for a 'general staff of labour'. Yet increasingly, the 'bureaucratic' accompaniments of large centralised organisation were deplored and resisted. It was precisely the opposition to such characteristics which gave the notion of 'rank and file' its potency. And it was above all else in the shop stewards' movement of 1914–18 that a new model of responsive, representative and spontaneous union activism was forged.

### Shop Stewards and Workplace Bargaining

The office of shop delegate or shop steward was familiar in many unions—notably in building and shipbuilding—long before the turn of the century. In many cases such workplace union representatives had come to play, well before 1914, a central role in the processes of informal domestic collective bargaining which were of significance even in the mid-Victorian era.[2] Nevertheless, it is only in the most rudimentary sense that one can speak of workplace organisation as part of pre-war industrial relations. Shopfloor collective action was only ambivalently linked to formal trade unionism,[3] and primarily concerned with the defence of customary standards against managerial encroachments. Stewards were less often negotiators than communicators, reporting on workplace conditions to the district union organisation and (in some unions) collecting membership contributions.

The war transformed the role of the steward. If one consequence of war conditions was to force collective bargaining from the district up to national level, a converse effect was to drive the struggle for job control down to the workplace. The cost of living escalated; but the industrial truce declared at the outbreak of war prevented national, and to a large extent local, union officials from vigorous pressure for redress. Speed-up of work, systematic overtime, disregard of safety precautions generated new grievances which established bargaining procedures were unable to remedy. The spread of payment by results made the price of a myriad separate jobs a potential focus of conflict. Craft unionists had as a special explosive concern the protection of traditional job demarcations under the twin challenge of new techniques and machinery and new classes of labour (dismissively entitled 'dilutees'); as the war progressed, protection from military conscription became even more provocative an issue.

The inevitable outcome, as in every other belligerent nation, was a rapid upsurge of independent organisation and autonomous action at the point of production. For the first time, the term 'shop steward' became a familiar component of industrial vocabulary. Though most firmly based in engineering and other munitions trades, steward organisation spread much more widely among British unions, and was indeed not unknown even among non-union workers.

From the outset, steward activity was inherently ambivalent. Its least publicised aspect was to act as a safety-valve, peacefully relieving potentially explosive accumulations of grievances. G. D. H. Cole stressed this function in his post-war assessment:[4]

> most of the stewards and other workshop representatives were concerned with the countless difficulties which arose in the readjustment of conditions which had to be made in order to adapt the industries of Great Britain to the needs of war. ... Almost every one of these readjustments was a potential source of friction and dispute; and the fact that the vast majority of them were accomplished without trouble shows that the shop stewards played a big part in preventing and settling difficulties as well as in conducting disputes.

The number of strikes indeed fell sharply during the war (in marked contrast to 1939–45); in the words of the Donovan Commission half a century later, it is clear that the typical shop steward was 'more of a lubricant than an irritant'.

Yet the more popular image of the shop steward (*plus ça change* . . .) was of a militant left-wing agitator. *Industrial Peace*, a journal of 'progressive' employers and right-wing union leaders, was anxious to dispel this simplistic view:[5]

> An erroneous impression of a very misleading character has been made on the public mind owing to the Rank and File Movement, which is essentially syndicalistic in its origin and aims, being referred to in the Press as the Shop Stewards movement. This latter term would more properly be used to describe the demand for decentralisation in the Trade Union world which is so well defined a feature in current labour thought. That these two movements should have been confused is unfortunate but not to be wondered at because, whilst the points of contact are on the surface, the points of separation are latent. It is the fact that Shop Stewards in certain districts have taken a prominent part in the Rank and File agitation; true also that the Syndicalist policy depends

for its success upon the co-operation of the Shop Stewards, but this is the extent of connection. . . .

The rise of the wartime Rank-and-File Movement is discussed in detail below; but at this point it is worth noting that the identification of the two movements is not merely accidental.

First, the functions of the steward, the manner of his (or very rarely her) election or appointment, the mechanisms of accountability and responsibility, were extremely ill-defined. Those union rulebooks which mentioned shop stewards did not refer to their role as negotiators. Much steward activity was mundane and tedious; a 'scramble in the ash heaps of industrialism for piecework and bonuses';[6] time spent in negotiating often meant loss of earnings; the prominent steward could well risk victimisation by the employer. Then as now, political commitment was not infrequently a motive to take on what could be a thankless office; competition for the job was rarely intense.

Secondly, shop steward activity created a natural receptivity to radical conceptions of industrial relations. Independent workplace bargaining challenged the drift to more centralised union organisation and negotiating procedures. Cole was to make this point strongly:[7]

> There is, indeed, a fundamental antagonism between orthodox Trade Unionism, as it has developed in Great Britain, and workshop organisation. Official Trade Union policy aims at centralisation—at the making of collective agreements covering the widest possible area, and laying down standard rates and conditions applicable to all establishments in a given area, or even nationally. Workshop organisation, on the other hand, tends to emphasise the grievances which are most felt in particular establishments, and to be more immediately responsive to waves of feeling among the rank and file. It also tends to foster the desire for the 'control of industry', by putting it into a form in which it is directly related to the actual working conditions in each particular establishment.

Crucially, the idea of workers' control offered historic significance to the prosaic day-to-day activities of even cautious shop stewards; it gave deeper meaning to the conflicts which the exigencies of war production spawned continuously. To be an active shop steward—frequently in the face of hostility or incomprehension from the official union machine—was to be receptive to the idea of a shop stewards' *movement*; and to identify with such a movement was to be open to a critique of capitalist industrial organisation and the compromises reached with it by orthodox trade unionism.

The paradox of the wartime shop stewards' movement stems from this tendency. Workplace organisation was typically strongest among relatively privileged sections of the working class whose privileges were under threat. Their responses were defensive, even reactionary; yet they were often led by revolutionary socialists whose politics were the negation of craft sectionalism. In part this reflected the self-selection of steward activists, and in particular those who were involved in unofficial activities at district and national level; procedures of delegation and accountability barely operated outside the individual workplace. But the unity of seeming opposites was facilitated by the duality of notions of workers' control: appealing simultaneously to the pre-capitalist self-determination of the independent journeyman, and the post-capitalist collective direction of the totality of economic relations. The beauty of the slogan was its elision of these two meanings.[8] The links between conservative craftsmen and their socialist leaders were reinforced by a common opposition to the constraints of union officialdom, and to its complicity in the erosion of traditional craft protections.

> We will support the officials just as long as they rightly represent the workers, but we will act independently immediately they misrepresent them. Being composed of delegates from every shop and untrammelled by obsolete rule or law, we claim to represent the true feeling of the workers. We can act immediately according to the merits of the case and the desire of the rank and file.

This declaration of the Clyde Workers' Committee[9] simultaneously looks back to the pre-war turmoil in the ASE—'the clashing of two antagonistic principles; centralised authority and local autonomy'[10]—and forward to the more overtly political confrontations of the interwar years.

Not surprisingly many employers, and not a few union leaders, were anxious to curb the shop stewards if they could not be suppressed. In engineering, the national agreements of 1917 and 1919 which defined a narrow range of stewards' rights and responsibilities were an evident attempt at containment. An example of union endeavours to 'constitutionalise' steward authority was provided by the Amalgamated Society of Carpenters and Joiners, whose 1918 rules included detailed provisions for Shop, Job and Yard Stewards, concluding with the principle that 'the stewards shall cooperate with, and be under the jurisdiction of, the Management Committee of the district'. More generally the Works Committees proposed in the Whitley Reports, but rarely implemented, may be viewed as a strategy to bypass shop steward authority.

It is a familiar story that the shop stewards' movement was in any event uprooted even more rapidly than it had emerged, first by the disruption in production which followed the Armistice, then by the more severe and more sustained onset of depression. 'The unofficial shop stewards' movement is at an ebb tide, because of the percentage of unemployed in the metal trades,' declared an observer in 1920. 'The man at the gate determines the status of the man at the bench.'[11] It was soon a wry joke that the shop stewards' leaders of the war had become the unemployed leaders of the 1920s, as employers took the opportunity to rid their works of 'troublemakers'. And for more recent writers it is the accepted view that meaningful shopfloor action was impossible thereafter:

In 1920–35, there appears to have been little shop-steward activity beyond 'minimum' union administration, and no evidence is available either from union histories or published works on the General Strike. Firstly, with the onset of recession in 1921, and the Depression, union organization in the workshop was badly hit. Largely, representatives either ceased to exist as such, or were reduced to being watchdogs, merely ensuring that employers complied with minimum terms and conditions of employment. With labour markets favouring employers, stewards could attempt little but to maintain the *status quo*, and were presumably often victimized. Even in those industries which traditionally had stewards, such as printing, the fathers of the chapel, although still existing, had few opportunities to be other than defensive in their dealings with management. Also, the radical characteristics of the Shop Stewards' Movement probably alienated many union leaders, who may have countenanced even the disappearance of some stewards rather than fight employers on the issue. This attitude might have been buttressed by the opinion that the way to economic recovery was by cutting wages to reduce prices, thus making goods more competitive. Such an atmosphere was hardly conducive to strong workshop representation.[12]

Nevertheless there is remarkably little systematic evidence of the extent of the collapse of workplace organisation as opposed to unofficial movements of stewards outside the workplace. The monthly reports of Amalgamated Engineering Union officials are the richest published source, revealing a general decline—and after the 1922 lock-out often a rout—but also considerable unevenness between and within districts.

There is any case a danger of generalising too far from the evidence of the AEU alone. Even in the depths of the depression, workers with particularly strategic skills could maintain the shopfloor collective strength to sustain their traditional controls. Outside the printing chapels, the sheet metal workers probably offer the outstanding example of such continued effectiveness.[13] For quite opposite reasons, workplace representation could also remain viable as a recognised substructure of bargaining arrangements in industries where collaborative union–employer arrangements persisted. The footwear industry exemplifies this situation: official control of the union had never been seriously challenged from below, workplace organisation being integrated with and subordinated to the national machinery of industrial relations. Hence in the 1930s the union's secretary could write, as a matter of course, that 'departmental shop stewards exist in most factories and this not only ensures maximum membership but reduces violation of the industrial conditions to a minimum'.[14] 'Safe' workplace organisation could also persist in those industries where new bargaining structures established in the mood of post-war reconstruction survived the slump. Local departmental committees on the railways are an important instance; works councils formed under the auspices of Whitleyism another example, usually of far lesser significance. Richardson noted the collapse of many such bodies in the early 1920s, but also the continuity of others: 'a considerable number of works councils can now look back over a period of ten or twelve years of successful operation.'[15]

Such survivals were in any event eclipsed in the later 1930s, with the recovery of industrial production and trade union membership, particularly in the armaments sector. As employers—at least in the healthier sectors of the British economy—once more experienced expanding order books, and needed to recruit additional workers after the years of lay-offs and contraction, so union membership began to rise again and with it the confidence of workers on the shopfloor. Croucher identifies 'a real change in the nature and tone of industrial relations':[16]

> the effect of seeing old mates, even in ones and twos, coming back into the shops, was out of all proportion to the numbers involved. The iron workshop discipline of the previous few years, when it was not unheard of for men to be sacked for laughing at work, slowly began to dissipate. ... A resurgence of independent trade union activity was a feature of these years in many industries: in the miners' struggles against company unionism, in the revival of the rank and file movements amongst busmen which had clung on since the end of the First World War, as well as in the docks and building trades. In the engineering industry it took the form of a renaissance of the shop steward system.

But as with the previous rise and fall of shopfloor representation, again there is little systematic information on the extent and character of the 1930s revival.

If it is difficult to map the incidence of workplace organisation between the wars, it is even harder to assess its effects or even to discover its functions.[17] Those bodies which existed on the basis of the joint complaisance of management and the union hierarchy were no doubt often confined to trivia, or at least operated within narrowly defined limits. Even within such limits, though, issues could at times be of some importance: the determination of work rosters and overtime rotas on the railways or the buses, for example.

Conversely, shop stewards' committees whose origins lay in the militant struggles of 1915–20, could pursue strategies of judicious accommodation as the only prudent course under adverse circumstances. This might bespeak compliance in the face of a boss who held the whip hand, and a new dependence on (and hence cooperative orientation towards) the full-time official.[18]

In the more favourable conditions of the later 1930s, it is clear that independence and assertiveness recovered. In engineering, the spread of unionisation and shopfloor organisation among semiskilled production workers paid by results was accompanied by a rapid expansion of piecework bargaining. More generally, plant-level negotiation became both vehicle and reflection of unevenness in the labour and product markets. The institutional reforms of the immediate post-war years had consolidated industry-wide bargaining as the dominant form of wage determination in Britain.

Some employers—notably in engineering—fiercely resisted any return to district negotiation over pay, while tying national settlements to the circumstances of the least profitable companies. If the scope for concession in the more thriving firms and sectors was to be exploited, this had to be through workplace organisation and struggle. Yet this required information, coordination and strategic planning which union leaderships—typically suspicious of the revival of shopfloor initiative—were unwilling to provide. Again, 'unofficial' leadership was often a precondition of success within the individual workplace. But in the 1930s there now existed an organisational framework for such leadership, the Communist Party. The vicissitudes of its industrial policy were of key importance for the evolution of the revived shop stewards' movement.

### Revolutionary Politics and the Communist Party

Before 1910, British socialists had normally been involved only as *individuals* in trade union affairs. Socialism was concerned with state direction of industry, the more equitable distribution of its products, and the provision of various welfare services; but not with the day-to-day proceedings of industrial relations. Bernard Shaw's characterisation of unionism as 'the capitalism of the proletariat' articulated a widespread view of industrial action as embedded within existing society, which *political* action alone could transform. And political action itself was conceived in terms of public propaganda, individual conversion and electoral campaigning. Hence while it might be desirable for socialists to be members—indeed active members—of their appropriate union, and to take whatever opportunities arose to argue for the cause within its ranks, none of the main socialist organisations thought it necessary or proper to intervene collectively in day-to-day union activities.

Pre-war syndicalism offered a radically transformed vision. Collective struggle, not individual conversion, was the means to socialist consciousness; direct action at the point of production, not parliamentary posturing, was the weapon which would destroy capitalist domination; workers' own industrial organisation, not bureaucratic state machinery, was the basis for the democratic control of a socialist economy. As has been seen, this vision—often it is true somewhat clouded, and perhaps refracted through contradictory ideological prisms—was vitally important in linking wartime shop steward activity to revolutionary notions of workers' control.[19]

One of the forces giving overt political meaning to wartime workplace assertiveness was the Amalgamation Committee movement. Originating in London in 1910, and strongly influenced by the ideas of Tom Mann, it pursued the merger of existing sectional societies (particularly in engineering) as the means of establishing revolutionary unionism. Thrown into disarray by the outbreak of war, the movement regrouped during 1916 and 1917, publishing the paper *Solidarity* and convening a series of Rank-and-File conferences. 'The movement', comments Pribićević,[20] 'had no direct hold in the workshops. Its propaganda was conducted mainly through trade union branches and local Trades Councils.'

By contrast, the Shop Stewards' and Workers' Committee Movement (SSWCM) developed directly out of workplace struggles, though the more extensive its constituency, the more tenuous its links with the grassroots membership. Hence the most cohesive organisation was at district rather than national level. The two most notable bodies both developed out of major local conflicts: the wages campaign on the Clyde in 1915, the revolt in Sheffield at the end of 1916 against the conscription of a skilled fitter. In both centres the outcome was a district-wide workers' committee, independent of (if not explicitly in opposition to) the official trade union machinery. In aspiration the committees worked on the principle of delegation from each workshop; in practice the mechanisms of representation were often imperfect, and critics denounced the local activists as self-appointed militants. Certainly the movement's local leaders were disproportionately left-wing socialists, and in particular connected with the Socialist Labour Party (SLP): a body which until 1914 had urged the creation of brand new revolutionary unions, but in the course of the war perceived the 'unofficial' organisation of workers in factory-based shop steward movements as a more realistic means of revolutionary combination.

Such socialists played the major role in the formation of the National SSWCM, following the May strikes of 1917 against the extension of 'dilution' and the limitation of craftsmen's exemption from conscription. The idea of a national body had been propagated by J. T. Murphy, a leader of the Sheffield workers' committee and an SLP activist; his pamphlet *The Workers' Committee* outlined a strategy to transform shop steward activity into a weapon for the overthrow of capitalism. Thus the national movement was launched as a functional equivalent of the revolutionary industrial unionism advocated by the SLP, whose Clydeside leadership was spread around the country under the 'deportation' orders of 1916. At the end of 1917 the new body merged with—and in effect absorbed—the Amalgamation Committee movement, taking over its paper *Solidarity* as a southern counterpart of the Glasgow *Worker*. But its twin weaknesses were the lack of any real mandate for national decisions, and the tenuous connection between the socialist politics of the leadership and the craft conservatism of most members. Both problems were exposed in early 1918 with the government's extension of conscription: moves to launch a national strike against the war proved futile, the members in the districts preferring a more limited struggle for craft exemption from military service.

Socialist aspirations for class unity from below, emerging out of spontaneous resistance in the workshops to employers, union officials and the state, had seemed vindicated at key moments in the war but ultimately came to nothing. The SSWCM became increasingly detached from any effective base in the workshops,[21] ironically committed to the Russian example of Soviet power at the very moment when its lack of analogous revolutionary mandate from below was manifest. Attempts to generalise the formation of local workers' committees were enthusiastically pursued; 'much was achieved on paper, little in practice'.[22] The National Rank-and-File Convention called in March 1920 attracted an impressive array of participants from socialist organisations and unofficial movements in a number of industries; but the links with the broader rank and file were now tenuous. A year later the SSWCM became simply the National Workers' Committee Movement (NWCM): a belated recognition that the insurgent workplace activism which had launched the movement had long since been contained or dissipated.

The main inheritance of the wartime struggles was the formation of the Communist Party (CP) during 1920 and 1921. The SSWCM agreed in autumn 1920 to participate with various revolutionary political groups in moves towards communist unity, sending delegates to Moscow. Murphy, one of its leading activists, headed the British Bureau of the Red International of Labour Unions (RILU); and in 1922 the NWCM merged into the latter body.[23]

Initially the CP lacked a clear industrial strategy. Its founding conference was preoccupied with debates over parliamentarism and the Labour Party, and barely mentioned the trade unions. This orientation altered, particularly after the 'Bolshevisation' of its organisation during 1922–23. The formative experience of the leading wartime activists (many of whom were in Moscow during much of the phase of unity negotiations), and the principles emphasised by the Communist International, pointed to industry as a vital terrain of revolutionary intervention. Two early pamphlets produced for Party members[24] provided advice on 'Formation and Work of Factory Groups' and 'How a Trade Union Branch Nucleus Works'. The key themes were coordinated activity of Party members in order to mobilise shopfloor workers and win them over to communism; and organised intervention within unions' machinery at every level in order 'to transform them into mass organisation of revolutionary struggle under the leadership of the Party'.[25]

Commitment to organised intervention in trade union affairs was thus a distinguishing feature of the CP for which pre-war socialist activity offered no precedent. One consequence was that key strategic decisions could not be derived from prior experience but had to be determined empirically and pragmatically. What, for example, was the appropriate attitude to official union structures and institutions? The Party inherited radically divergent traditions, both expressed in the Glasgow *Worker* shortly before its foundation. The first was presented in an editorial entitled 'The Failure of the Triple Alliance', following the withdrawal of national strike threats in both mining and the railways:[26]

> The power of the Triple Alliance has been rendered null and void by its leaders, once more demonstrating the fact that only by the workers organising along the lines of unofficial committees, whether it be at the pit-head or in the railway shop, in the shipyard or in the factory—only by this method can you ever hope to achieve success. Leaders are unreliable, they are an unknown quantity, and when a decision has to be made they shirk it. Fellow workers, you must do it yourselves, get your committees formed, and when the time presents itself you yourselves will not shirk the issue, and capitalism will receive its death blow.

The alternative approach—though not explicitly counterposed to this argument—was offered a fortnight later by William Gallacher in an article on 'Class Organisation':[27]

> The Triple Alliance has done well, but the Triple Alliance, backed up by an industrial organisation representing the engineering trades, would do even better. Such a combination would be all-powerful, and like an evil spirit, capitalism with all its pitiful poverty and degeneracy, would pass from our land.

These rival visions persisted in uneasy juxtaposition—at times one or the other clearly ascendant—throughout the Party's history. On the one hand, organisation and agitation from below: a suspicion of official structures and leaders, an emphasis on the consciousness-raising power of autonomous struggle. On the other, an emphasis on the need for coordinated strategy and collective discipline to confront the concentrated might of capital and the state; hence a concern to advance further the centralisation of the trade union movement, and to work within the official machinery so as to win positions of influence and shape policy in the desired direction.

The tension between these contradictory prospectives underlies the whole history of the National Minority Movement (NMM), which took over from the British Bureau of RILU in 1924 the better to pursue the task 'to convert the revolutionary minority within each industry into a revolutionary majority'.[28] At one and the same time the NMM sought to act as an organised opposition; a medium of independent leadership; a ginger group pushing for more militant official policies; a vehicle for party propaganda; and a recruiting ground for party membership. That these objectives were not always readily compatible was evident in the period leading to the General Strike, when 'All Power to the General Council' and the fostering of grassroots fighting organisation were simultaneously embraced as goals.

The more overtly oppositional character of CP activity in the unions after the General Strike was reinforced by the doctrine of 'class against class', enunciated by the Comintern in 1928 and enforced upon the British Party in the following year. Though never applied wholeheartedly,[29] the sectarianism of this period served to isolate CP militants from their potential supporters and encouraged the leaders of many key unions to proscribe their activities. By the early 1930s Party membership had fallen well below the level at its foundation, and its influence at the period of the most acute political and economic crisis of the two interwar decades was minimal. Symptomatic of the decline in organised impact within the broader trade union movement was an explicit acceptance that the NMM had become ineffectual:[30] at the end of 1930 a campaign was launched for a 'Workers' Charter', its six points presumably designed to appeal to the historians among the working class. The stated aim of the new initiative was to create the 'broadest possible mass movement. ... Through this Campaign, the Minority Movement is able to make contacts, break through its isolation and build up mass industrial sections'[31]—precisely the mediating role that the NMM itself was originally created to perform! Even within the party little enthusiasm could be mustered for this exercise.

The period of 'class against class' did however have one valuable by-product. The determined insistence on fostering struggle from below encouraged Party activists, previously often preoccupied with propaganda around broad political issues, to concern themselves with more mundane questions within the individual workplace. A rich variety of factory, pit and depot papers was generated—usually a simple duplicated sheet—documenting day-to-day instances of unsafe conditions, oppressive foremen, speed-up of production and wages problems. Direct collective action was urged as a solution to such grievances, and occasional successful initiatives were proclaimed.

Piecemeal and unspectacularly, there can be little doubt that sustained activity of this character won many individual communists the trust and respect of their workmates, irrespective of politics. The reward was reaped as evidence of working-class assertiveness returned in the form of a new wave of rank-and-file movements.

Most prominent, and for a time most successful of such initiatives was the London Busmen's Rank-and-File Movement which emerged out of individual garage organisation. Its paper, *Busman's Punch*, developed into a printed magazine, and the Movement succeeded in winning control of the official Central Bus Committee of the Transport and General Workers' Union.[32] A major focus of activity was resistance to the employers' efforts—with which the union leadership was willing to compromise—to cut costs by speeding up schedules; a very successful pamphlet *London Busmen*

*Demand the Right to Live a Little Longer* encapsulated the argument that 'speed' endangered busmen's health and passengers' safety. Other important initiatives of the early 1930s were the Railwaymen's Vigilance Movement (RVM), the Builders' Forward Movement, and a range of organisations in engineering, shipbuilding and iron and steel.

While communists were prominent in all these movements, they were by no means 'front organisations' in the way that the NMM had been. They did not stem from any centralised CP strategy, and indeed there was initially considerable suspicion that such movements, arising outside Party control, could further weaken its own position in the unions. But from the beginning of 1932 attitudes changed significantly, following a similar shift in Comintern policy. 'Independent leadership' by the Party was no longer the overriding objective; the task was again to work within the official institutions of the labour movement. 'We must correct anti-trade union tendencies,' insisted Harry Pollitt, Secretary of the Party.[33]

In the mid-1930s, in the context of a slow improvement in economic conditions and revival of trade union membership, the CP gradually strengthened its influence in industry. Most notable was the progress achieved in the rapidly expanding sector of aircraft production where the Hawker strike of 1935 marked a decisive turning-point in the reconstruction of effective shop steward organisation: 'The Communists had been able to use their network of contacts nationally to coordinate joint action and organise support. The CP had carefully prepared the way for the dispute . . .'[34] By the end of 1935 an Aircraft Shop Stewards' National Council (ASSNC) had been established, dominated by CP activists; and the Hawker workers' strike sheet had developed into a printed monthly claiming a 20,000 circulation, the *New Propellor*. Far more broadly—though certainly far from universally—the Party was establishing an influence in industry and the unions which exceeded the high points of the 1920s. CP successes both in influencing union policies and in winning election to official positions exceeded the achievements of the previous decade. Understandably so, for previously union leaders had sought to minimise confrontation with employers in a period of weakness and decline; while workers' demoralisation obstructed any significant response to appeals for militant resistance. In the expanding sectors of the 1930s, by contrast, workers were readier to respond to a vigorous lead, particularly when expansion was partly the result of an unrewarded intensification of their own labour; and union officials could not easily oppose the efforts of shop-floor communists where these resulted in an upsurge of membership and income.

But independent assertiveness was once more contained as a result of external changes in Party policy. From 1937, Stalin pursued a diplomatic strategy of seeking alliances with capitalist states regardless of political orientation; while to national parties was allotted the task of constructing a 'popular front' with 'progressive' forces in their respective countries. Accordingly, the oppositional characteristics of rank-and-file activities were rapidly suppressed, in favour of a simple policy of building up the grassroots strength of the official unions. When the T&GWU leadership finally clamped down on the Busmen's Movement at the end of 1937, Party activists offered little resistance.[35] Though few union leaders were anxious to reciprocate the collaborative attitudes of the Party, criticism of official policies and personalities was switched off. By the eve of war, industrial activity as such—once the dominant feature of Party strategy—barely received a mention in its reports and conferences.

## Two Contrasting Cases

The quarter-century 1914–39 reveals a complex ebb and flow of autonomous workplace activity and unofficial resistance to leadership policies; across these years, the relationship between 'spontaneous' membership revolts and organised opposition groupings shifted significantly, in the process transmuting the meaning of 'rank and file' itself. At the commencement of the period, the term typically denoted localised and intermittent defiance of a centralised union leadership whose actions could be challenged with the traditional discourse of 'primitive democracy'. By the end of the 1930s, 'rank-and-filism' implied a *generalised* and organised opposition associated with a putative alternative leadership—a 'union within a union'. Such organisation was necessary for a sustained and effective challenge to union leaders whose power was bolstered by elaborate bureaucratic resources; but it gave these leaders obvious scope to denounce criticism as the product of external interference; and it also made 'internal' militants highly vulnerable to unexpected shifts in outside Party policy.

Some features of this trajectory may be illuminated by considering, very briefly, experience in two industries: engineering and the railways.

The former industry was the context of the most prominent of the rank-and-file movements of the 1914–18 war, discussed previously. The conditions of the Industrial Truce created a vacuum of official leadership, while engineering craftsmen were faced with unprecedented problems. The upsurge in shop steward activity was an inevitable outcome; and left-wing activists were well placed *both* to draw on the traditional ASE principles of decentralised initiative, *and* to argue for a reconstruction and consolidation of a more effective fighting machine at national level.

The impact of such arguments was demonstrated in the election of Tom Mann in 1919 as General Secretary (a post no longer of key importance in the Society); and in the formation of the Amalgamated Engineering Union (AEU) in the following year. But the paradox of the amalgamation was that, while reflecting the pressure of wartime militants, it consolidated an officialdom anxious to develop 'modern' industrial relations in the industry. The AEU—which was to lose a large proportion of its members in the adverse circumstances of the early 1920s—inherited a considerable body of full-time officials whose positions were guaranteed for eight years, during which the traditional electoral machinery ceased to operate. The new rulebook enhanced the powers of the Executive Committee, and integrated shop stewards more firmly within the official structure. J. T. Brownlie, the Independent Chairman of the EC since the creation of the position in 1912, came as AEU President to exercise far more effective authority than any previous leader of engineering trade unionism had ever enjoyed.

From 1920 to 1926, old and new in internal politics were uneasily combined. Compromise with the employers was resisted by a combination of left-wing militants and craft traditionalists, who together dominated key district committees and through these the new policy-making National Committee (NC). The coordinated activities of CP members, latterly working through the Metal Workers' Minority Movement (MWMM), helped stiffen resolve. Membership ballots supported resistance to the employers' demands for swingeing wage reductions and a reassertion of managerial prerogatives, culminating in the protracted 1922 lock-out. From 1924 the MWMM was instrumental in sustaining a demand for £1 wage increase as the union's official target, blocking leadership aspirations to settle for a far lower figure.

Yet the militant left exerted no more than a nominal control over policy; and after 1926 even this token influence was eroded. In London, for example, right-wing candidates were increasingly successful in elections to decision-making bodies. In 1928 one of the London delegates to the NC[36] sponsored a motion denouncing the CP and NMM and authorising the EC 'to take such steps as may be appropriate' to defeat disruption within the union. This resolution (carried by 41:11)[37] encouraged the Executive for the next decade to a degree of authoritarianism unprecedented in the union's history. Employers' proposals in 1931 for a deterioration in nationally determined conditions were agreed without submitting the question to a ballot. AEU members who wrote a letter of protest to the *Daily Worker*, and Manchester activists who sought to organise local resistance, were temporarily expelled from the union.[38]

A Members' Rights Movement was launched to oppose the expulsions, and produced a paper, the *Monkey Wrench*. There is little evidence that its campaign gained extensive support, though the expelled members did win reinstatement at the 1932 Final Appeal Court (FAC).[39] Renewed CP influence in the AEU only became significant after rearmament brought a recovery in employment and shopfloor organisation; as has been seen, Party activists played an important part in the revival of militancy and in the formation of the ASSNC. In the expanding areas of 'new' engineering production, the CP was increasingly to the fore: a prominence reflected in the growth of Party members elected to official positions during the latter 1930s. Yet those 'new' areas were always a minority within the union as a whole, and the EC remained deeply suspicious of 'unofficial' organising initiatives. The ASSNC itself was regularly denounced in the pages of the AEU *Monthly Journal*.[40]

From 1937, with the national shift in CP policy, engineering militants displayed a consequential change of strategy.[41] The ASSNC dropped its demands for a separate national agreement for aircraft workers. A new, more general paper was launched for engineers; its first issue in January 1937 began with the declaration that 'The *Conveyor* is not an "opposition" paper'. As Croucher has indicated,[42] this was part of a deliberate 'accommodation to the AEU's official apparatus'; 'it became increasingly apparent that left-wing opposition within the AEU was being actively discouraged, in favour of a more conciliatory approach to the Executive which emphasised the wish of the left to respect the union's machinery and not to be seen to be breaking ranks by trying to build a "divisive" rank-and-file movement'.

Experience among railwaymen involved many sharp contrasts with that in engineering. Traditionally the numerous companies sought to maintain a subservient workforce, imposing quasi-military discipline and encouraging divisive loyalties to the various occupational grades. Working hours were exceptionally long, and the rates of pay of many grades distressingly low. Employers' hostility kept unions weak, and fear of victimisation made members dependent on their full-time officials. But the pre-war 'labour unrest' brought unprecedented assertiveness on the railways: syndicalist ideas won significant support, a national strike in 1911 developed from unofficial origins, union membership grew rapidly, and the National Union of Railwaymen (NUR) was formed by amalgamation.

Aspirations for major improvements were cut short by the outbreak of war and the union's agreement to an industrial truce. Real wages fell sharply while the pressure of work increased; a potent recipe for unofficial militancy and challenges to the national leadership—most notably J. H. Thomas, who become General Secretary in 1916 after several years as the power behind his ailing predecessor. Many of the NUR district councils—whose functions under the rulebook did not extend beyond recruitment and propaganda—sought to mobilise membership support for demands for substantial pay increases. Unofficial all-grades vigilance committees became centres of opposition in some areas, notably Liverpool.[43] By 1917 these tendencies were uniting: in March the London District Council convened a 'Rank-and-File Meeting' at the Albert Hall to formulate a wage claim; in August, a National Conference of District Councils and Vigilance Committees was held—the first of a series.

There was however an inherent ambivalence in the rise of wartime opposition in the NUR. While some militants pursued ideas of 'spontaneous' localised struggle, most were committed to the principle of disciplined and coordinated national action, seeing their unofficial bodies as 'ginger groups' maintaining pressure on the union's leadership and complementing their participation in the official decision-making structures. And indeed, such participation yielded considerable results: left-wing activists gained an effective presence in the Annual General Meeting (AGM), pressed through a change of rule giving that body rather than the Executive the power to accept or reject settlements, and in November 1917 achieved a highly ambitious programme of demands to be pressed as soon as the war was over. In addition, militants began to win election to the Executive itself, aided by the rule requiring its members to retire after three years' service.

Yet the wartime initiative demonstrated by grassroots activists was short-lived; soon J. H. Thomas succeeded in establishing a firm personal hegemony. Central to this process was the national strike in the autumn of 1919 over the post-war wages programme. Though Thomas had sought from the outset to prevent a stoppage, and concluded it on terms which brought no significant improvement on the previous offers, he emerged with the reputation of a triumphant victor. Thereafter throughout the 1920s, though General Meetings at times came almost to the brink of strike action over wages issues, he always succeeded in persuading a majority to back down. His role as the most provocative of the labour movement's right-wing leaders won him many enemies outside the NUR but caused no serious challenge inside. Following 'Black Friday' in 1921, the AGM supported the Executive's position by a 3:1 majority and brushed aside a challenge to Thomas himself: 'another outstanding personal triumph'.[44] Five years later a similar explanation of the ending of the General Strike was approved 56:21, while a call for the resignation of the leading officials was rejected overwhelmingly. An energetic cadre of CP activists achieved little headway; indeed, Thomas revelled in their hostility, successfully presenting criticism as evidence of communist conspiracy. A remarkable example of the weakness of internal opposition was the 1928 agreement for a cut in wages which the AGM approved 77:2, despite a strenuous campaign by the Transport Workers' Minority Movement.[45]

In the 1930s the situation was transformed. Thomas, who took leave of office during his membership of the 1929–31 Labour

Cabinet, resigned after joining Macdonald's 'national' government. C. T. Cramp, in effect Thomas's deputy as Industrial General Secretary throughout the 1920s, died in 1933. His successor Marchbank was a weaker figure, often overruled by an Executive which was itself divided and regularly rebuffed by the AGM. From the turn of the decade the CP's strategy of developing organisation and agitation at depot level began to yield results, and a growing number of strikes and go-slows occurred—many, though by no means all, led by Party members. The revival of grassroots opposition culminated in the merging of various local rank-and-file bodies in 1933 to form the Railwaymen's Vigilance Movement—a name consciously based on the traditions of wartime militancy. Left-wingers were again increasingly elected to the AGM, to the Executive[46] and to full-time office; perhaps the most notable success was the election of the relatively inexperienced and little-known J. Potts as President in 1938.

One lesson of the experience of these two unions in 1914–39 is that patterns of leadership and opposition and the relative efficacy of each must be perceived very much in their distinctive contexts. The consolidation of official control in the AEU from the 1920s, and the limited *national* impact of the 1930s shop stewards' movement, reflect what may be regarded as a highly artificial form of internal politics, in which the mechanisms of union democracy were divorced from the rhythms of engineering production. In the collapse of membership (from 460,000 in 1920 to 190,000 in 1933), the worst disorganisation was in the newer sectors of the industry where the union's roots were weakest; workplace organisation and branch participation survived best in the traditional strongholds of craft conservatism. Moreover the *district*, which had been eclipsed as a focus of collective bargaining and job control, remained pivotal within the union's constitution. To the extent that left-wing opposition concentrated on the official mechanisms at branch and district level, it was divorced from the realities of the workplace.

Conversely, the revival of shopfloor struggle in the 1930s could not translate into a coordinated challenge to conservative traditions and conservative leadership. For workplace experience was increasingly *uneven* as new sectors of engineering expanded while others stagnated. 'Rationalisation'—the introduction of new forms of work organisation, speed-up, intensified supervisory control—was an extensive feature which inspired rank-and-file protest; but its impact was far from universal, and assumed varying forms in different companies and areas. There was thus little basis for generalisation of conflicts over immediate work experience; while the potency of wages issues as a unifying force was eroded by the spread of payment by results.

In the NUR, by contrast, internal politics were more closely linked to members' work situation. Leadership ascendancy rested on a number of foundations which were to prove unstable. The personal charisma and political skills of Thomas and Cramp were not matched by their successors. Wage reductions in the 1920s were less severe than in most other industries, but this relatively favourable position was increasingly threatened by a deterioration in the economic position of the railways. Many of the leading wartime militants were absorbed into the union hierarchy or the new machinery of local collective bargaining; but a new generation of activists eventually built up influence.

They were aided in the 1930s by a significant worsening in workers' material conditions. Wage reductions imposed in 1931 (shortly after the termination of the 1928 cuts) were not fully restored until 1937, while workers in other industries fared better. The promotion system, which traditionally acted as a brake on militancy, became blocked as companies enforced redundancies, dashing expectations of career progression. 'Rationalisation' was imposed so extensively that despite its divergent forms in different types of occupation, the resulting grievances could have a unifying effect. And the *national* determination of conditions between the union and the tightly-knit railway companies[47] ensured that discontent would be directed at the NUR decision-making centres. Hence the possibility for oppositional activists to coordinate members' discontents and tap the union's own 'all-grades' tradition in mounting an effective challenge to the national leadership.

Analysis of the successes and failures of rank-and-file movements in other unions would require a similar specificity of focus. Some generalisation is nevertheless possible. During the wartime industrial truce, and between the wars under the dual impact of economic recession and a commitment to conciliatory bargaining institutions, union leaderships deployed their enhanced powers in the direction of conservatism, routinism and the appeasement of employers. The scope for membership perception of a conflict of interests with their leaders was accordingly enhanced.

In this context, the complex processes of mediation between the members and the national leaderships were of crucial importance. In the AEU, the politics and perspectives of the local activists who controlled the district committees and were delegated to the National Committee were of fundamental importance; without their support the writ of the national leadership would have had little force outside their Peckham Road headquarters. Similarly, in the NUR the leadership was secure only so long as it won the backing of Executive members and AGM delegates, who were themselves attuned to the official view through their involvement in branch administration and representation on local departmental committees. What might be termed a 'semi-bureaucracy' of lay activists with quasi-official functions served (and indeed still serves) in many unions as a vital reinforcement of the authority of full-time officialdom.

As has also been suggested, experience in the years 1914–39 demonstrated some of the problems of 'rank-and-filism'. In many contexts there was a clear differentiation between activists and the mass of members; the label 'Rank-and-File' was frequently used tendentiously. This gave union leaders the dual option of appealing to the members over the heads of their representatives (a technique employed with considerable skill by J. H. Thomas) or seeking to incorporate the latter within official structures. Both strategies were facilitated by the fact that lay activists in most unions derived disproportionately from the same minority sections of the work-force as the leaders themselves: male, relatively skilled, higher paid and more secure than the majority of members.[48]

A common obstacle to opposition movements was the strength of ideologies of discipline and loyalty. As was indicated earlier, the cause of centralisation and organisational consolidation was a characteristic of the left in many unions around the turn of the century and even in the period of the present discussion. Fragmented action conflicted with the rhetoric of unity and solidarity, as right-wing leaders found to their advantage. In the NUR, the charge of 'sectionalism' had a special resonance, because of the existence of the separate footplate union ASLEF and the breakaway of signalmen in 1924. Yet members' discontents, rooted in varying local conditions, were inevitably uneven; how could they be generalised without creating a 'union within a union' or else betraying the involvement of 'politically motivated' organisations?

Underlying all these issues was the evolution of bureaucratic practices in the terms identified at the outset of this chapter. Before 1914, British unionism relied substantially on 'do-it-yourself' action at the grassroots: informal job control, local 'trade movements', spontaneous initiative from below. In 1914–20, the traditions of 'primitive democracy' clashed explosively or coexisted uneasily with the newer principles of centralised collective bargaining and collaborative industrial relations. In the 1920s and 1930s, loyalty to this joint determination of conditions by employers and union officialdom became the latter's insistent demand. 'Official trade unionism', as Cole wrote at the end of this period, 'has endeavoured, not to challenge capitalism, but to make terms with it; and it has regarded as its worst enemies, not the employers, but those Trade Unionists who have endeavoured to recall it to a more militant policy.'[49] Necessarily involved in such attempts was the monopolisation of initiative at leadership level and hence the *demobilisation* of the membership as an active collectivity. To the extent that this succeeded, the rank and file became a discrete aggregation of individuals rather than a collective actor on the trade union scene; hence 'rank-and-file movements' increasingly represented artifical constructs.

In his powerful 1917 pamphlet, J. T. Murphy had written that 'it matters little to us whether leaders are official or unofficial, so long as they sway the mass. . . . If one man can sway the crowd in one direction, another man can move them in the opposite direction. We desire the mass of men and women to think for themselves, and until they do this no progress is made, democracy becomes a farce . . .'[50] Bureaucracy—which is best defined in terms of a mode of social relations—is clearly corrosive of such forms of *collective* thought and initiative. This in turn necessitates that any oppositional or 'rank-and-file' movement, to be effective, must transcend spontaneity and must in practice be the product of political direction. Perhaps the most fateful aspect of trade union development during our period was to render Murphy's sentiments utopian.

## Notes

1   See for example the critical comments by Van Gore, 'Rank-and-File Dissent', in C. J. Wrigley, *A History of British Industrial Relations 1875–1914* (1982).

2   See James Hinton, *The First Shop Stewards' Movement* (1973), Ch. 2.

3   See, for example, Richard Price, *Masters Unions and Men* (1980).

4   *Workshop Organisation* (1923), pp. 3–4.

5   December 1917.

6   J. T. Murphy, quoted in Hinton, p. 93.

7   *British Trade Unionism Today* (1939) pp. 169–70.

8   See Carter L. Goodrich, *The Frontier of Control* (1920; reprinted 1975).

9   Quoted in Hinton, p. 119.

10  ASE Annual Report, 1903, quoted in J. B. Jefferys, *The Story of The Engineers* (1945), p. 167.

11  Arthur Gleason, *What the Workers Want* (1920), p. 184.

12  J. B. F. Goodman and T. Whittingham, *Shop Stewards* (1973), p. 39.

13  See Frank Carr, 'Engineering Workers and the Rise of Labour in Coventry, 1914–1939' (Warwick University PhD, 1978), pp. 468–9.

14  George Chester, 'The Boot and Shoe Operatives' in Cole (1938), pp. 422–3. As a branch officer in 1920, Chester had helped persuade the union's conference to establish workplace organisation as a subordinate element in the structure; see Alan Fox, *A History of the National Union of Boot and Shoe Operatives* (1958), pp. 401–2.

15  J. H. Richardson, *Industrial Relations in Great Britain* (1933), p. 140; see also the *Survey of Industrial Relations* published by the Balfour Committee in 1926.

16  Richard Croucher, *Engineers at War* (1982), pp. 25–6.

17  Thus Richard Croucher comments that 'the question of what shop stewards were able to do remains an important, and unanswered one' ('Communist Politics and Shop Stewards in Engineering 1935–46'; Warwick PhD thesis, 1977, p. 40). He suggests from his own local studies that while AEU stewards in the North remained predominantly concerned with traditional 'craft' defence, their Coventry counterparts were preoccupied with piecework. In *Engineers at War* he comments (p. 25) on the situation at Leyland: 'at first sight it is surprising to see the shop stewards' committee there printing a glossy journal in 1927, until we read the introduction, written by the managing director and complimenting the stewards on the fact that no serious matters of contention had been discussed during the previous year.'

18  Even the Minority Movement, soon to proclaim the principle of 'independent leadership', could in 1928 emphasise the need for official union support for stewards; see *The AEU—a Review and a Policy*, pp. 8–9.

19  For a detailed discussion of the relation between pre-war syndicalism

and wartime workers' control, see Branko Pribićević, *The Shop Stewards' Movement and Workers' Control* (1959).

20   Ibid., p. 79. At the time, possibly because it was the first national 'rank-and-filist' body, it appeared more prominent than the workplace-based committees. The first six issues of *Industrial Peace* each contained an article on 'The Rank-and-File Movement', concentrating on the role of W. F. Watson, Tom Mann and other amalgamationists.

21   As one of the leading Clydeside militants later commented, 'one of the biggest weaknesses I found in the National Shop Stewards' Movement . . . was the gap between the committee and the workers. Comrades would solemnly discuss proposals for action, and when it was put to them, "Well, what is your shop, or what are workers in your town, likely to do?" too often the reply was non-committal, because they knew they were not speaking *for* anybody but themselves, or a few militants' (Tom Bell, *Pioneering Days*, 1941, p. 139).

22   Hinton, *op. cit.*, p. 270.

23   Among the varied accounts of this process see ibid.; Walter Kendall, *The Revolutionary Movement in Britain* (1969); L. J. Macfarlane, *The British Communist Party* (1966); Michael Woodhouse and Brian Pearce, *Communism in Britain* (1975); Hugo Dewar, *Communist Politics in Britain* (1976); James Hinton and Richard Hyman, *Trade Unions and Revolution* (1975).

24   Both undated.

25   *Report on Organisation* (1922), p. 36.

26   29 March 1919.

27   12 April 1919.

28   For a detailed account of the history of the NMM, see Roderick Martin, *Communism and the British Trade Unions* (1969). The present writer's detailed assessment of the Movement's record can be found in Hinton and Hyman, *op. cit.*, and is not repeated here.

29   Doctrinaire enthusiasts of the 'new line' bemoaned the lack of commitment of most Party activists to its sectarian implications. Breakaway unions were not seriously encouraged (the two which were formed, the United Clothing Workers and the Scottish Mine Workers, both resulted from exceptional provocation by incumbent right-wing leaders); nor were independent factory committees of non-unionists established. Arthur Horner, the most prominent CP activist among the South Wales miners, was disciplined for his 'trade union legalism' but never expelled from the Party; the position he expressed, more tactlessly than some, was widespread among the CP's industrial militants.

30   An important element in this decline was the decision, after the TUC in 1927 threatened to blacklist trades councils which were affiliated to the NMM, to advise such councils to disaffiliate. Party influence within the trades councils—an important arena of activity during the 1920s—was gravely weakened.

31   NMM, *Points for Members of Industrial Committees*, 4 December 1930.

32 This powerful lay negotiating body—unique to the London busmen—reflected the strong democratic traditions of their formerly separate union which were carried over into the new T&GWU in 1921.

33 'Trade Unions and the Fight', *Labour Monthly*, March 1932.

34 Croucher, *Engineers at War*, p. 40.

35 Leading non-communists in the Movement formed an unsuccessful breakaway union.

36 J. D. Lawrence, a former communist.

37 In the following year is was reaffirmed by a smaller majority.

38 See Edmund and Ruth Frow, *Engineering Struggles* (1982). All but one of those involved refused to make the retraction demanded by the Executive. The exception was Jack Tanner, a pre-war syndicalist and leading figure in the shop stewards' movement who did not join the CP but nevertheless worked closely with it in the 1920s, becoming the most prominent of the leaders of the MWMM. In 1931 he was elected a full-time official in London. For retracting his signature to the *Daily Worker* letter he was denounced by the CP and expelled from the NMM; this did not prevent him winning election to the EC in 1935 and the Presidency in 1939.

39 The Court, an elected lay body, ruled that the penalty of expulsion was too severe for the offence, proposing a fine instead. A curious episode at the same FAC was the appeal of an AEU district against the EC's refusal to discipline the President, W. H. Hutchinson, for alleged drunkenness at a local function; the FAC ruled that he should be removed from office. Both decisions appear to reflect the constitutional legalism traditionally displayed by the FAC, rather than political influence. Indeed Hutchinson was less right-wing than many of his EC colleagues. In the 1920s, as a member of the Labour Party National Executive, he had been one of the strongest supporters of the attempts by the CP to gain affiliation; and he had written for the CP-controlled Labour Research Department.

40 The General Secretary, F. A. Smith, displayed remarkable flights of rhetoric in his report in the *Monthly Journal* of June 1937: 'Shop Stewards holding office in the AEU have been definitely appraised that this body is in no way or in any sense a part of the union's official machinery, and that participation in it is contrary to union rules, and a violation of the principle of loyalty to the union and the individual undertaking given by each applicant for membership. We have publicly disclaimed any responsibility as a union for action emanating from this body, neither do we intend, whatever the consequences, to allow the funds of the organisation to be dissipated at the whim and fancy of a self-appointed caucus. This predatory body possesses a fundamental difference of outlook than that usually associated with democracy, and relies on an emotional spur instead of a conservation of human and financial resources, and is an attempt by shameless advocacy to shorten a straight line to reach its objectives.

Their fierce claims can only terminate in rebellious disillusionment, and enlightened self-interest is ready for their blistering challenge.'

41  An earlier indication of the potency of 'popular front' principles was the inclusion in *Labour Monthly* of June 1936 of an article by J. D. Lawrence, erstwhile hammer of the left in the AEU.

42  *Engineers at War*, p. 64.

43  The secretary of the Liverpool committee, C. J. Edwards, described its role in terms which echoed the declaration of the engineering shop stewards' movement: 'Vigilance Committees are not subservient to the rules and constitution of the union, their hands are free and unfettered. The only people whom they are responsible to are their constituents' (*Railway Review*, 1 March 1918).

44  P. S. Bagwell, *The Railwaymen* (1963), p. 464.

45  The CP Central Committee reported to the 1929 Party Congress that 'it must be recognised as a serious weakness of the Party that it was unable to lead any unofficial action on this issue'.

46  Most notably W. C. Loeber, a leading national member of the CP and the most prominent railwayman in the NMM, in 1937; and J. B. Figgins, the best-known leader of the RVM, in 1930. He became a full-time official in 1938 and General Secretary in 1947.

47  The four companies established in 1923 collaborated closely over operations as well as negotiating in combination.

48  Until rule changes during the 1939–45 war the AEU was exclusively male though in theory multi-occupational; but both leaders and unofficial militants derived from the ranks of skilled men. Women engineers and men classed as lower-skilled were often members of the general unions—and hence not available to boost opposition within the AEU. In the NUR, as with railway employment generally, there were few women; the higher-paid grades of more senior employees dominated official and unofficial activities alike.

49  *British Trade Unionism Today*, p. 77.

50  *The Workers' Committee* (1972 reprint), pp. 14–15.

# 4

# Employers and Managers: Organisation and Strategy 1914–39

*Howard F. Gospel*

On the eve of the First World War the main employers of labour, outside of agriculture and domestic service, were the metal manufacturing, transport, mining, building and textiles industries. Of the ten largest manufacturing employers there were three in metal working and engineering, three were provided by the railway workshops, two were in textiles, and the other two were the Royal Dockyards and Royal Ordnance factories. By 1939 mining and textiles had already declined absolutely and of the ten largest manufacturing firms two each were provided by traditional heavy metal working and by the railway workshops; there was one in textiles; the Naval Dockyards were still included; but now added to the list were Unilever, ICI, Imperial Tobacco and the manufacturing facilities of the Coop.[1] Within the industrial structure there had been a number of important changes in the pattern of employment.

In the late nineteenth and early twentieth centuries Britain had been slow in moving into new industries, but in the interwar years, especially in the 1930s, there was a considerable growth in areas such as electrical engineering, motor vehicles, chemicals and pharmaceuticals. The ground which Britain had earlier lost to Germany and the USA was partly made up in these years. Equally, though internal growth and the merger wave of the 1890s had produced some large-scale enterprises in Britain, in 1914 British industry was still for the most part dominated by medium and small firms, still largely controlled by owning families. The merger wave and growth of the 1920s went a long way to change this. Firms such as ICI and Unilever were a creation of major mergers; other firms such as Courtaulds, Dunlop, Austin and Morris grew internally; the electrical engineering firms, GEC, English Electric, AEI, were a result of both internal growth and merger. The outcome of this was that by the 1930s there were at least ten manufacturing businesses employing 30,000 or more people, the largest of which, Unilever and ICI, employed 50,000 or more.[2] By 1935, of the 5.2 million workers covered by the Census of Production, 28.1 per cent worked in firms employing 1000 or over, and another 12.9 per cent in firms employing 500–999 workers; in other words, nearly half the labour force was to be found in firms employing more than 500 workers.[3]

The economic climate in which firms operated during the quarter-century covered by this volume saw fluctuations of an unprecedented nature. The years 1914–20 were a period of high levels of demand and employment such as had not been seen since the Napoleonic Wars. The next 13 years witnessed two of the deepest depressions in British history, separated by six years in which, though the level of industrial production revived, the unemployment figure remained around 10 per cent. During the 1920s British industrialists tried, with varying degrees of determination and success, to rationalise their industries and to develop new enterprise structures in the face of contracting markets and falling profits. From 1933 onwards the economy slowly revived and, protected also by tariffs, industry found itself in a more favourable market environment.

As other chapters in this volume have pointed out, the period 1910–1920 saw a massive increase in trade union membership. It also witnessed considerable changes in the organisation of British employers for labour purposes. Internal changes in the structure of the firm are dealt with below. At this point emphasis is placed on changes in the organisation of employers at industry and national level. Before 1914 most, though by no means all, British industries had trade associations and employers' organisations for industrial relations purposes. During and immediately after the war there was a period of growth in the number and stability of these organisations. Undoubtedly the rise in union membership and militancy was an important factor. In addition, however, the growth was assisted by the desire of government during the war to improve consultative relations with businessmen and to have representative organisations which could make and administer agreements for the whole of their industries. The latter desire is illustrated by the Whitley Report, one of whose conclusions stated: 'an essential condition of securing a permanent improvement in the relations between employers and employed is that there should be adequate organisation on the part of both employers and workpeople'.[4]

In 1914, there were 1487 employers' organisations. By 1925 this had risen to 2403. Subsequently, during the depression years the number fell to 1550 in 1936.[5] However, this reduction was mainly the result of mergers rather than failures and it was estimated in 1938 that half of all British workers were employed by firms belonging to employers' organisations and in the main manufacturing industries the proportion was much higher.[6]

Before 1914 there had been several attempts to create a central employers' organisation but all these had failed. Wartime conditions proved an effective catalyst. In 1915 a number of protectionist firms, drawn largely from the Midlands, formed the British Manufacturers' Association.[7] This comprised mainly small firms and its main interests were in the commercial field. In the following year the Federation of British Industries (FBI) was founded and proved the most successful employers' body to that date. However, the individual industry employers' organisations were extremely jealous of their independence and were determined not to see what they perceived as their prerogatives undermined by these peak associations. In 1917, led by the Engineering Employers' Federation (EEF), they forced the FBI to withdraw a progressive report it had produced on sickness and unemployment benefit, redundancy payments and the guaranteed week. Moreover they insisted that henceforward the FBI desist from dealing with labour relations.[8]

However, the need for a central organisation to deal with such matters became evident during the National Industrial Conference called by Lloyd George in February 1919 to consider the resurgence of industrial unrest. A new National Confederation of Employers' Organisations (NCEO) was thus formed to coordinate the employers' position and to constitute their side of the permanent National Industrial Council which it was proposed to establish. The NCEO had in membership most of the employers' organisations in Britain and by 1920 claimed to cover over 7 million workers and nearly 90 per cent of the organised employers in the country.[9] From the start it was dominated by the employers' organisations in engineering, coal mining, railways, shipping, and iron and steel. As will be shown later, in large part at their insistence, the Confederation developed only a limited role in procedural and substantive rule-making. Nothing came of the National Industrial Conference nor of a proposal to coordinate action to resist union wage claims in 1919–20.[10]

Thus by 1920 the pattern of employers' organisation external to the firm had been set. This was one where employers, including most of the largest firms, relied on strong employers' organisation at the industry level, but where central inter-industry organisation was weak. This was to bias the British system to industry level dealings between employers and labour.

To appreciate these developments on the employers' side it is necessary to place them in the context of the historical events of the war and immediate post-war years. The decade 1910–1920 had rendered British employers less secure in their position and self-confidence. A number of factors combined to make them fearful for their future. Union membership and militancy of course began to increase before the First World War. During the war, trade unions gained in status and power, not least at shopfloor level where employers constantly found themselves having to seek the consent of labour in order to execute their plans. Shop stewards, though they had existed previously, became more active, especially in the engineering and shipbuilding industries. At national level the revival of the Triple Alliance of miners, railwaymen and dockers intensified employers' fears. Wartime state control of industries such as coal-mining and the railways made some employers concerned for the future of the capitalist enterprise, in particular in a situation where allegations of unequal sacrifice and excessive profits were rife, where the miners were campaigning against decontrol, and where syndicalist ideas seemed to be increasingly popular in the union movement. The events in Russia in 1917 added further substance to the fears of the capitalist élite in Britain. Meanwhile the number of working days lost rose from 5.6 million in 1917, to 5.9 million in 1918, and to 35 million in 1919.[11]

As we have seen, the reaction of British employers was to strengthen their organisation, while also pursuing a largely cooperative policy. Many employers supported the establishment of the Whitley Committee in 1916 and, outside the staple industries, welcomed its recommendations for reconstruction in industrial relations. They felt that Whitley, with its emphasis on constitutions and procedures, accorded well with British traditions. Of course Whitley was based on trade union recognition, but the war had already made this a foregone conclusion in most British industries. Whitley did not, however, seriously invade managerial prerogatives in internal matters within the firm. Though employers in the staple industries could argue that it was not for them, since they had already devised their own machinery, they were not overtly hostile to the creation of Whitley Councils elsewhere. In other industries, it was hoped that Whitley would provide a basis for cooperation rather than class-conflict.[12]

Whitley did not, however, defuse the industrial situation. In 1919–1920 there was a massive outburst of industrial unrest, among engineering and shipbuilding workers, on the railways, and in the mines. In the spring of 1919 Lloyd George called a National Industrial Conference of employers and unions to seek a remedy for the mounting conflict. However, the miners, railwaymen, transport workers and engineers refused to take part. On the employers' side the FBI was supportive, but it was the lack of a coordinated employers' response which led to the establishment of the NCEO. The conference proposed a universal 40-hour week, an extension of the minimum wage system, and the establishment of a permanent joint council of employers and trade unions to advise the government on economic matters. However, both the government and the NCEO soon started to prevaricate as the immediate crisis of spring 1919 passed.

From mid-1920 with the onset of economic depression the cooperative spirit of wartime and Whitleyism within the employers' counsels was displaced by the more belligerent and hard-headed groups within the NCEO who were concerned to win back control on the shopfloor and meet overseas competition as best they thought fit. The depression strengthened the hard-liners among British employers and created the opportunity for a counter-offensive. But the counter-offensive was to be different from that of the 1850s and 1890s in that trade unionism and collective bargaining had since then become more entrenched.

To understand the policies of the employers it is necessary to examine in more detail developments in the collective bargaining system which had occurred up to 1920 and to trace these through the rest of the interwar period.

In the basic industries of Britain employer recognition of trade unions had developed through the late nineteenth and early twentieth centuries. The most important groups of employers who held out against recognition were the shipowners and the railway companies. For the rest, where trade unions had some organisational strength, British employers had increasingly concluded that unions could not be permanently ignored. Moreover to exclude unions was becoming increasingly expensive and a growing number of employers had realised that there might even be advantages in recognising unions and dealing with them, especially if this could be done on a collective basis through their employers' organisations. Indeed in the years before the war this realisation had already affected the shipping and railway companies.[13] But, still, full recognition on a regular basis did not come in these two industries until the war. It is probably true to say, however, that even before the war the days of union exclusion via 'free labour' and union-busting activities, such as had been used in the gas and shipping industries in the late nineteenth century, were over.[14]

Engineering provides an interesting case of the extent and limits of employer recognition. In the case of manual unions, federated employers had since 1898 been obliged to recognise unions covered by the Terms of Settlement of that year. Later the EEF was prepared to recognise other manual unions which could prove membership and which were ready to accept the 1898 Provisions for Avoiding Disputes. In this way, for example, the Workers Union was recognised in 1914. The process of formal recognition at national level was completed during the First World War when in 1917 the EEF signed its first National Wages Agreement with 47 unions.

At local level before the war there had been some informal *de facto* recognition of shop stewards in engineering. Again it was during and immediately after the war that formal recognition was extended to shop stewards. A strike in Coventry in November 1917 first forced the employers to grant a limited amount of recognition. In May 1919 this was widened at the insistence of the Amalgamated Society of Engineers (ASE): workers were to be allowed to elect shop stewards; the names of stewards, their constituencies, and the unions to which they belonged were to be passed on officially by the unions concerned to management; stewards were to be offered facilities 'to deal with questions raised in the shop or portion of a shop in which they were employed'; and stewards on works committees were allowed to visit parts of the plant outside their own constituency.[15] As with recognition of the manual unions, so with recognition of shop stewards, the EEF's aim was to bring them into the Provisions for Avoiding Disputes and to put definite limits to their activities. In this way they hoped to contain stewards by putting them under tighter union control and making them subject to what they termed 'constitutionalism'.[16]

There were a number of further limits which the Engineering Employers placed on recognition. First, they always insisted on what they termed 'freedom of employment' and resisted all attempts to obtain a formal closed shop. The most dramatic opposition to the imposition of a closed shop was in 1920 when the EEF locked out all Electrical Trade Union (ETU) members after electricians at the Penistone works of Cammell Lairds came out on strike in objection to the employment of a non-union foreman.[17] This is not to say that informally closed shops did not exist in some engineering firms, especially among the more skilled craftsmen. The same did, of course, apply to other industries such as printing, iron and steel, shipbuilding, and some workers in cotton textiles. However, with the exception of the ship-owners and National Union of Seamen from 1921 onwards, more formal closed shops were rare and opposed by British employers throughout the interwar years.[18]

The second limit which employers placed on recognition related to white-collar workers. The EEF, for example, grudgingly recognised the National Union of Clerks in 1920 and the Association of Engineering and Shipbuilding Draughtsmen in 1924. This recognition was, however, only for procedural purposes and the two unions had to accept the Provisions for Avoiding Disputes.[19] Other weaker white-collar unions it refused to recognise. More in line with the predominant ethos of British employers, the EEF adamantly refused to recognise unions for foremen and supervisors, holding that the 'foreman is the agent of the employer in the works'.[20] The Federation encouraged the Foreman's Mutural Benefit Society, one of whose membership requirements was that members should not be trade unionists.[21] The only other group of employers who conceded some recognition of white-collar unions in this period were the printing employers. The Newspaper Proprietors Association (NPA) recognised the National Union of Journalists in 1917 and were followed by the Newspaper Society in 1918 and the Scottish Daily Newspaper Society in 1921. The NPA also recognised the National Union of Printing Bookbinding and Paper Workers for circulation representatives in 1919 and the National Society of Operative Printers and Assistants for clerical workers in 1920.[22]

A third limit which employers often still put on recognition was union membership for apprentices, boys and youths. The EEF, for example, refused to recognise unions for these groups. In the eyes of the Amalgamated Engineering Union (AEU), the employers took an 'old-fashioned' view of their prerogatives in this area and chose to see the relationship 'as in the nature of an individual contract between the employer and the parents or guardians, in which an undertaking is given to teach the apprentice his trade, and the apprentice on his side undertakes obligations to his "master"'.[23] Recognition came in the late 1930s only after a series of strikes which led the employers to see recognition as the best means of 'bringing matters under constitutional authority'.[24] Apprentices under written indenture were excluded; a tight disputes procedure was laid down; and no fixed proportion of apprentices and other junior males to journeymen was to be allowed.

Thus, though it is true that the attitude towards union recognition had changed, it must be added that unions had still to fight for recognition and show their strength or disruptive potential before they were recognised. Equally employers could still occasionally try to exclude trade unions once they had been weakened. The classic case of this in the interwar years was the support of many mining companies for the so-called 'non-political' or 'Spencer' unions in the coalfields after 1926.[25] However this kind of abrogation of recognition and such support for company unionism was the exception rather than the rule.

Two further points may be made about employer recognition. In the first place, recognition on a catch-all basis such as occurred in engineering, though at the time it might seem to have merits in terms of 'divide and rule', subsequently had the disadvantage for employers of establishing or consolidating multiunionism, later seen as such a severe problem for British industry. Secondly, formal recognition of shop stewards, white-collar unions, and indeed also manual unions, was vitally important for it constituted a base from which later trade unionism could grow from the late 1930s onwards.

Recognition however, is only the first stage in developing a system of collective relations. Along with it went the establishment of machinery for negotiating and administering agreements and for resolving disputes. On the eve of the First World War the form which such machinery was to take in Britain was by no means certain.

In some firms there were rudimentary factory or site arrangements for negotiations, almost always *ad hoc*. In certain industries such as engineering *ad hoc* machinery existed at district level. In other sectors such as coal-mining the district conciliation boards and minimum wage boards established before the war were rather more formalised. In cotton, engineering, shipbuilding and a number of other industries more formal disputes procedures had been developed, largely at the employers' initiative, and these had industry-wide stages. However, this procedural development received some major setbacks in the period before the First World War. In 1912 the Boilermakers withdrew from their national disputes procedure established in 1909; the system in building came under increasing pressure; in 1913 the cotton spinners withdrew from the Brooklands Agreement and were followed subsequently by the cardroom operatives; and just before the war the ASE withdrew from the national engineering procedure.

The war was to reset the mould and establish in most industries a framework of district and national machinery for negotiations and for handling disputes. This was, of course, formalised in the Whitley industries with their national joint industrial councils, district councils and works committees (though the latter, where they were established, were relatively weak consultative forums). In most other industries similar kinds of machinery and procedures were put into place, on which the employers placed great reliance and for which they were largely responsible.

The elaborate Procedure for Avoiding Disputes in engineering was the most famous. The Engineering Employers were determined to maintain this in the form of the York Memorandum which they persuaded the ASE to accept in 1914; to achieve this they were prepared to make concessions by shortening the stages of the procedure, writing in works conferences, and leaving out the 'current conditions' clause which had stipulated since 1898 that while an issue was in dispute work was to continue on terms imposed by management.[26] Important objectives of the 1922 national engineering lock-out were to reaffirm the procedural framework, to extend it to all the unions in the industry, and to define the conditions under which work was to be carried out more closely in management's favour.

The employers liked to stress the judicial, conciliatory and peace-keeping aspects of their procedural systems.[27] But procedure also performed other functions. In engineering its rationale cannot be separated from the question of managerial prerogatives. It should be remembered that the procedure had its origins in the 1897–98 lock-out and that it was reaffirmed in the 1922 lock-out. The managerial functions clause and the peace clause reinforced management's right to make decisions in their workshops. The system of employer panels safeguarded management's interests and prevented the establishment of embarrassing precedents. Once a question had been considered centrally, the procedure allowed the whole power of the federated employers to be deployed on behalf of a member firm to protect managerial interests in what were seen as matters of principle. The procedure was also used to maintain the national wage system, for in the interwar years procedure was used to choke off district wage movements (such as had existed pre-war) and to prevent claims being submitted by more prosperous sections of the industry (such as aeroplane construction).

The advantages which management obtained should not, however, hide the fact that the union, especially the leadership, got some benefits out of these procedural arrangements. The union, of course, got recognition; the leadership enhanced its own position;[28] and the membership in less well-organised shops got better terms and conditions than they might otherwise have secured. The unions, however, were always restless under the procedure. But after 1922 there was no chance that the Engineering Employers would let them terminate it. Any such stirrings elicited a lock-out threat from the EEF or a threat not to negotiate on wage matters. However, from the mid-1930s onwards, there is evidence that the EEF was prepared to proceed more carefully and to operate the procedure with greater flexibility.[29]

As with the procedural system, so with the substantive systems of wages and conditions, it was unclear in 1914 what kind of wage-bargaining arrangements were to solidify in British industry. Where collective bargaining over wages and conditions existed it was usually on an *ad hoc* informal basis at factory, site, or mill level. In some industries superimposed on top of this were district agreements. Such, for example, was the system in engineering and building. In a few industries such as coal mining and shipbuilding national adjustments to district rates were negotiated, but still a large number of district rates remained in a haphazard fashion. It was really only in some of the textile trades and some small homogeneous industries that national wage systems had been established.

The war was to change this. First, enhanced union strength and pushfulness increased the employers' fear of leapfrogging and created on their part a perceived need for them to coordinate their wage policies on an industry-wide basis. Second, the activities of the government arbitration body, the Committee on Production, and its awards of national wage increases familiarised both employers and unions with the notion of industry-wide settlements. Third, the Whitley Committee gave a considerable impetus to national bargaining in a broad spread of industries.

There was considerable variation in the comprehensiveness and tightness of these agreements. As will be shown in a later chapter,[30] some attempted to set standard rates and conditions. In the majority this was not the case. In engineering, for example, where national wage negotiations had been established in 1917, the national wage system was composed of a series of pre-war district minimum rates for certain classes of labour and a national bonus, to which across-the-board additions and subtractions were made. Within this framework the actual level of earnings was determined at the workplace by a combination of unilateral management regulation, workplace bargaining and informal understandings. During the war and the immediate post-war boom, domestic wage-bargaining attained a new importance because of full employment, wartime changes in production, and the extension of payment by results. There could thus be a considerable gap between, on the one hand, national rates and national regulation and, on the other hand, what actually happened at workplace level. The same drift occurred again from the mid-1930s onwards. In periods of depression, though the national wage system was more likely to regulate actual earnings, there was downward deviation in the form of wage undercutting.

A pattern of national bargaining and a tendency on the part of British employers towards cooperation had thus been established between 1914 and 1920. The onset of depression in 1920 was severely to test this pattern, to shift the balance of power, and to change the employer strategy from one of cooperation to one of confrontation. In the forefront of this attack were the employers in engineering and coalmining.

In engineering the main battle was over managerial prerogatives. The 1898 Terms of Settlement had been a statement of formal rights. In reality in many workshops traditional practices continued and employers did not always get their own way. In the course of time the managerial victory weakened especially during boom periods and when short-term production needs dominated over long-term industrial relations principles. During the war, a combination of labour shortage, the need to meet production targets, the rise in union membership, and the development of shop steward organisation further weakened management's position. Though during the war new work practices contrary to craft traditions were introduced on a large scale, work groups and their representatives were able to claim a greater say in decision-making and impose restrictions on management.

In 1920 when the boom broke and unemployment rose, the engineering unions' policies became more defensive in particular on overtime working, the introduction of payment by results, and machine manning. The Engineering Employers were determined not to see their perogatives further undermined and to re-establish management control in areas invaded by the unions during the war. Moreover, under wartime production they had seen the advantages of mass-production methods and of greater flexibility in work organisation.[31] Thus, from 1920 onwards, as the market situation deteriorated, they felt the need to reduce costs and remove union restrictive practices. In early 1921 the Federation nearly locked out AEU members on three occasions: over a union embargo on overtime; the refusal of the union in one federated firm to allow apprentices to work on payment by results; and union refusal to allow firms to operate certain machines except on conditions laid down by the union.[32] In late 1921 the Federation, now set on a confrontation, forced the AEU Executive, increasingly conscious of its weakness in the face of mass unemployment, to sign a memorandum allowing management to decide when overtime was necessary, abandoning the union position on status quo, and accepting a new managerial functions clause. When the AEU membership rejected this memorandum, in March 1922 the Engineering Employers locked them out. The Federation then served an ultimatum on 50 other unions in the industry demanding that they also accept the memorandum. When they refused they were in turn locked-out.

The lock-out lasted until June and ended with the unions returning to work on the employers' terms. Just as in 1898 the employers had chosen the eight-hour question, so in 1922 they chose overtime working as a particular issue on which to make a stand and had broadened out the ensuing conflict to cover the whole question of managerial prerogatives. The EEF made this clear in a public statement: 'The question at issue is not one of overtime. . . . The issue is a refusal by the trade unions to continue the recognition of the Employers' right to exercise managerial functions unless with the prior consent and approval of the unions.'[33]

The employers were determined, in the light of production and market conditions, to show that there were certain areas where management had discretion and where there could be no 'dual control or veto on management'.[34] The question of status quo had not been particularly clearly decided in 1898 and had been fudged in 1914, but it was an issue which was inevitable given management's claim to be able to introduce changes, the workers right to object, and the delay subsequently involved in the disputes procedure. The employers strongly denied the need to obtain union consent before changing working practices and held that a settlement of this issue on their terms was a necessary requirement for the efficient operation of their businesses.

The agreement which ended the 1922 lock-out stated explicitly that 'the employers have the right to manage their establishments and the trade unions have the right to exercise their functions'. The unions were forced to recognise the employers' right of initiatory discretion and henceforward, while cases were going through procedure, work was to be carried out 'under the conditions following the act of management'.[35] The 1922 victory was substantial and was to undermine the position of the engineering unions, especially at shopfloor level, for over a decade.

In coal mining the employers, faced from the early 1920s onwards with falling prices, low productivity and profitability, and intense competition in foreign markets, concentrated on the wage-bargaining system and on reducing wage costs. Their employers' organisation, the Mining Association, demanded wage-cost adjustments according to the economic capacity of the different colliery districts. After the bitter seven months national lock-out in 1926 and the collapse of sympathetic trade union support for the miners, the coal-owners insisted on the abolition of the national wage bargaining system, the need for district wage reductions, and a longer working day. Supported by other employers' organisations and the NCEO, they resisted government attempts to find a compromise and ultimately drove the union back to district agreements. They followed up their victory with open victimisation, the encouragement of the so-called 'non-political' unions, and a vigorous reassertion of managerial prerogatives, especially in South Wales and the Midlands. The mine-owners' obdurate stance has been described as 'a classic example of employer militancy'. [36] Keynes at the time described their policy as 'half-witted'. [37] Their insistence on lower wages, longer hours and management prerogatives, though not irrational in the circumstances in which they found themselves, was a short-sighted alternative to rationalisation, investment in mechanisation and increased productivity.

In the other staple industry, cotton, the employers' attack developed in the late 1920s and early 1930s as competitive pressures intensified. In the winter of 1930–31 the weaving employers locked out all their workers in order to force them to accept a larger complement of looms per weaver in the interests of cost-reduction. This was not a new idea, but some employers now regarded it as a crucial aspect of managerial prerogatives. 'The question has resolved itself', said one millowner, 'into whether or not an employer should be allowed to use his machinery in the manner in which he thinks best, or whether he must be governed by the operatives' association.' [38] Despite the recession, the employers, however, failed because of strong union opposition and because the weaving employers as a whole were not sufficiently committed to the more-looms strategy. As a result the lock-out was called off unconditionally after seven weeks. Frustration over this failure and union resistance to industry-wide wage cuts and hours increases led both the weaving and spinning employers to suspend all collective agreements in 1932 and leave their members free to wring whatever concessions they could out of their workforces at mill level. After several months the government intervened, collective bargaining was re-established, and abrogated agreements restored. However, a more indirect attack continued in the form of furtive undercutting of collectively agreed rates. This led in 1935 to the agreement of the weaving section of the industry to the imposition of legally enforcable wage lists. As with the mine-owners, so the cotton employers sought wage-cost reductions rather than extensive changes in the structure of their industry or expensive investment in new equipment as the solution to their problems.

In other industries employers also used the economic depressions of the 1920s and 1930s to reassert their control. Equally, in a number of industries national wage bargaining collapsed—road haulage, wool, rubber. Union membership in most industries fell considerably and employers used the opportunity offered to claw back union gains. However, a number of qualifications to this picture must be added. First, in more sheltered and growing industries employers were not forced to adjust to such drastic changes in their market situation and, though they pushed for wage reductions, they avoided the belligerent confrontations of the engineering and coal employers. Second, in a number of industries, relations remained reasonably close and cooperative—iron and steel, footwear, printing, food processing.[39] This included the two sectors of transport—shipping and railways—where before the war employers had been most belligerent. Third, even in coal and engineering, the collective bargaining system, though severely challenged and weakened, did not collapse. As economic conditions improved from the mid-1930s onwards, there were signs of more conciliatory attitudes on the part of the employers.

The episode of the Mond–Turner Talks is well known, but needs to be covered in any assessment of British employers in the interwar years not so much for what it achieved, but for what it signified.

After the General Strike there was a tightening of employers' attitudes towards trade unions and widespread retaliation against activists. The NCEO pressed the Conservative government for a wholesale reform of labour law and the removal of the immunities established under the Trades Disputes Act 1906. In the end they achieved less than they wanted with the passage of the Trades Disputes Act 1927. However, this belligerent stance was not the reaction of all employers. In November 1927 Sir Alfred Mond (chairman of the newly-created ICI) approached the TUC with proposals for talks to discuss compulsory conciliation, security of employment, disclosure of information to trade unions, schemes for worker participation and the rationalisation of industry. He associated with himself some of the leading businessmen from some of Britain's largest companies—GEC, Dunlop, the railway companies, Dorman Long, Courtaulds, John Brown, Bolckow Vaughan, Richard Thomas, Hadfields, Austin Motors, BP, Bowater, Distillers, and the major banks. Thus, though the older industries were represented, among the employers there was a very significant group from the newer and expanding industries and from recently merged large corporations. In the discussions which developed with the TUC no limitations were placed on the topics covered and as a sign of equality it was agreed that the chair should alternate between Mond and Ben Turner (Textile Workers and TUC President)—hence the name of the Talks.

In July 1928 the Talks produced a report which by the standards of the time was remarkably progressive and enlightened. It made recommendations in five areas. First, it recommended trade union recognition. The TUC was acknowledged to be 'the most effective organisation' on the union side and the only body which possessed the authority to 'discuss and negotiate' on all questions relating to industrial matters.[40] In individual industries it recommended that cooperation could best be obtained by 'negotiations with the accredited representatives of affiliated unions or of unions recognised by the General Council of the TUC as *bona fide* trade unions'. Such negotiations should not be confined to wages and conditions, but should go beyond this and cover 'other matters of common interest to the trade and industry concerned'. Secondly, it condemned victimisation of workers for being members of unions or of union representatives for acting in pursuit of 'legitimate trade union activities'. Those dismissed because of their activities in the General Strike were to be reinstated and appeals procedures established to hear complaints of unfair dismissal.

A third recommendation was that a National Industrial Council (NIC) should be established, comprising an equal number of representatives of the TUC on the one side and of the NCEO and FBI on the other. The Council, once established, was to hold regular quarterly meetings to investigate and discuss general industrial relations questions. At the request of either side to a dispute the NIC should appoint a Joint Conciliation Committee to investigate and by persuasion bring about a settlement. Fourthly, the report welcomed the rationalisation of industry, including the relaxation of union restrictive practices. Mergers and reorganisation were to be encouraged where they brought about efficiency and higher real wages. Such rationalisation, it was stated, was best achieved by the cooperation of unions and employers. At the same time the report recognised that the interests of workers displaced by rationalisation would have to be safeguarded. Mond and his fellow employers saw this encouragement of union support for rationalisation as important.

Finally, the report expressed doubts about the Gold Standard to which Britain had returned in 1925. It argued that this restricted the supply of money and credit available to industry, held back economic expansion, and that an overvalued pound handicapped Britain's export trades. The Mond employers persuaded the trade union side of the Talks to join them in addressing a memorandum on this subject to the Chancellor of the Exchequer, Winston Churchill, in April 1928. From the employers' point of view, of course, it was realised that such union support in lobbying government would be even more valuable in the event of a Labour government.

A further report, on unemployment, was adopted by the joint conference in March 1929. Among other things this recommended government financial assistance to promote amalgamations; joint management and union discussions on rationalisations in the coal, iron and steel, and shipbuilding industries and in certain branches of the engineering and textile trades; a state development fund large enough to stimulate the economy during depression; an increase in old age pensions to encourage older workers to retire and to make place for younger unemployed workers; the raising of the school-leaving age from 14 to 15 to withdraw an estimated half million young people from industry; and finally a full enquiry, on which employers and unions would be represented, into how Bank of England and Treasury monetary policy might be adapted to encourage industrial expansion.[41]

The two central employers' organisations, the FBI and the NCEO, especially the latter and its members, rejected the proposed NIC and the conciliation machinery. They feared that the outcome of the proposals would re-establish the power of the unions and constitute an invasion of managerial prerogatives. However, for public relations reasons and anticipating some advantages in discussions in the event of a Labour government, they agreed to enter into talks about talks.

In the early 1930s a series of talks were held in which the TUC and the FBI took the initiative, while the NCEO played a passive and obstructive role. The FBI met with the TUC to discuss monetary policy, interest rates and protection. For its part the NCEO made no proposals for meetings, but it was invited by the TUC to discuss rationalisation and unemployment. Reluctantly it agreed, but, as the depression deepened, it tried to get out of the talks. The Engineering Employers came out in opposition to the meetings and told the Confederation that discussion of rationalisation, new technologies and redundancies constituted an invasion of managerial prerogatives.[42] Engineering Employers could not accept that changes should only occur with union consent: 'in 1897 and again in 1922', said the EEF, 'the Federation was compelled to take action of a very serious nature for the purpose of securing the retention of the employers' freedom in this respect'.[43] It was not going to retreat from this.

A pamphlet issued at this time by the NCEO shows how far apart were the organised employers and unions on economic policy and industrial relations. This pamphlet argued that the solution to the economic crisis was to reduce wages, to let export industries, not sheltered industries, set the wage pattern, to cut unemployment benefit and to reduce government expenditure. The TUC, on the other hand, in part influenced by the Mond–Turner Talks, was at this time developing its own under-consumptionist and Keynsian demand theories. In reply to the NCEO document the TUC stated:

> Reductions in social services, restrictions on wage fixing machinery, the cutting down of unemployment benefit, the reduction of wages in the public services, these are apparently the only remedies this organisation [NCEO] can offer in the present emergency. From beginning to end of their manifesto there appears to be nothing of a constructive character. There is no recognition of the fundamentals of the problem, and indeed nothing to indicate that the writers are living in 1931 and not 1881. Such a policy is merely a confession of intellectual and moral bankruptcy.[44]

In these circumstances the cycle of talks which had begun in 1927 came to an end in the early 1930s.

Whether an opportunity was missed to restructure British industrial relations, to develop national level arrangements and to make British industry more productive, it is difficult to say. It must be remembered that many of the Mond employers could take a broader view but had little first-hand experience of industrial relations matters. For many of them, concessions and grand gestures were easier than for most British employers. Probably on the whole the attitudes and reactions of the NCEO and its members were more representative of British industry, certainly of medium and smaller firms in the older trades. Also their insistence on managerial prerogatives and lower wages as a means of dealing with competitiveness was traditional in many industries. In essence, then, the sequel to the Mond–Turner Talks indicated a reluctance on the part of many employers to take new initiatives and a complacent satisfaction by the early 1930s with the existing industrial relations system and with the equilibrium which had been established in their favour.

This is not to say that there were no further changes or developments at company and plant level. Let us turn therefore to changes in the internal management hierarchy. By the outbreak of the First World War, subcontracting, which had been so widespread in the nineteenth century, had died out in most British industries. It continued to exist, however, in some sectors of more casual industry, such as building and the docks. In other industries something like it in the form of the helper system continued to exist, e.g. spinners and their piecers in cotton and ship's platers and their helpers in shipbuilding. Meanwhile in coal mining the so-called 'little butty' system continued in certain coalfields such as Nottinghamshire and Kent.[45]

As to the foreman, he very often retained considerable power up to the First World War and beyond. As one observer commented in 1917, 'In most works, in the engineering trade at least, the whole industrial life of the workman is in the hands of the foreman.'[46] He went on to describe how the foreman hired and fired, set workers to work, maintained discipline and fixed wages. 'A tyranny could often be established, which the higher management, even if it had the desire, has very little power to soften or control.' Thus the foreman remained a key figure in labour management within the firm. However, a gradual diminution in power and authority, begun before the war, was carried further during the war, with the rise in trade union power, the spread of more sophisticated incentive systems, and the rise of staff specialisms. Thus Sidney Webb could write in 1917 that, following American practice, increasingly appointments, dismissals and other decisions were increasingly being made, not by the foreman, but by more senior managers or by specialist employment departments.[47]

In the interwar years, though the number of foremen increased, they were on the whole less powerful, more dependent on top management for their authority, and had more to enforce company rules rather than their own. Their greater dependence did not mean a closer relationship with top management; rather the contrary, for the rise in the number of foremen, the increasing size of companies and plants, and the growing differentiation in the management hierarchy probably reduced the personal contact with senior managers. As a result, when circumstances were favourable, foremen increasingly started to turn to trade unions, much to the alarm of employers who reacted by providing benefits in terms of wages and conditions, by the encouragement of the Foremen's Mutual Benefit Society, and by providing company training programmes.[48]

From the late nineteenth century onwards some of the larger firms had been employing specialist record-keepers, wages clerks, production engineers and 'feed and speed' men. Before the war, some of the more progressive firms in the lighter industries had appointed full-time internal 'welfare workers' to oversee working conditions and recreational facilities. Some of these had come to deal with recruitment, factory discipline, wages and even trade union negotiations. However, in 1914 these welfare workers, or 'social secretaries' as they were sometimes called, still had limited functions, were employed mainly in female industries, and themselves numbered fewer than 100.[49]

The extension and systematisation of welfare work was taken further during the First World War. The Health of Munitions Workers Committee recommended that welfare workers should be appointed in all factories where women were employed. Subsequently this became compulsory in all government-owned factories. In January 1916 Seebohm Rowntree was appointed head of a newly-formed Welfare Department of the Ministry of Munitions. This Department further encouraged the appointment of welfare workers and established a programme to train them. By 1917 there were 600 welfare workers and by the end of the war 1000. Firms' welfare work was also encouraged and by 1918 there were nearly 300 company officers engaged in this.[50] Some of these welfare officers dealt with aspects of adult male employment.

There was, however, some opposition to the extension of welfare work, some workers and their unions objected seeing it as excessive interference and as a manifestation of American-style scientific management.[51] Foremen were suspicious that welfare workers would undermine their position. Some employers saw welfarism as an unnecessary and costly luxury which might work in prosperous industries and firms where trade unions were weak such as Rowntrees, Cadburys or Lever Bros but which were less appropriate in the harsher climate of the staple industries. Some of those who had welfare workers imposed upon them during the war saw it as an infringement of their managerial prerogatives and dismissed their welfare workers immediately wartime regulations lapsed.

However, after the war, possibly after a temporary decline, there was an increase in the number of firms employing welfare officers. Increasingly they were themselves men and paid more attention to male workers. Slowly welfare work developed by way of what was first called 'employment management' into 'labour management' and then 'personnel management'. Increasingly in employment and personnel departments more emphasis was placed on systematic recruitment. Also, through the interwar years, wage and salary administration became more formalised and technical, as along with new forms of incentive systems, there was the beginnings of job analysis and job grading—the forerunners of modern job evaluation and merit rating. However, the speed of these changes should not be exaggerated. In 1939 there were still only about 1800 welfare workers and labour managers in Britain, and probably still less than 50 per cent of them were men. For the most part it is probably also true to say that there were more 'welfare workers' than 'personnel managers' and many of them were still not involved in those aspects of industrial relations which covered collective bargaining with trade unions.[52]

Employers, often through this new personnel, deployed a range of strategies and techniques of labour management within the firm. In terms of what might be called 'welfarist' measures, there was still some reliance on profit-sharing and co-partnership-type schemes. However, though there were some prominent exponents of this (such as ICI), there were other firms which abandoned their schemes in the interwar years (such as Unilever), while the majority of British employers, though they might talk about the 'human touch',[53] did little to develop new schemes. One significant development, however, was the growth of company-based pension schemes. Though notable examples of such schemes existed from the nineteenth century, such as among the railway and gas companies, there seems to have been an increase in the number of schemes from about 1910 onwards and a more rapid increase in the 1920s. As with other welfare-type measures, though undoubtedly introduced with a degree of benevolence on the part of some employers, they were also aimed at directing workers' loyalty to the firm, containing industrial conflict, and undermining the power and influence of trade unions.[54]

In terms of 'scientific management' British employers had been slow to adopt Taylorist ideas and techniques and this continued throughout the interwar years. However, in the 1930s the consulting firm of Bedaux did have an influence on some firms, especially in the newer and expanding sectors, in particular with its techniques of work measurement and new wage systems.[55] More significant than formal scientific management, British employers were slowly doing what came naturally to them. There was a continued spread of piecework. In engineering, for example, in 1906 24 per cent of fitters and 36 per cent of turners were on piecework; by 1938 this had risen to 62 per cent of fitters and 61 per cent of turners and machinemen.[56] There was also an introduction of new machines and methods of work organisation, especially during the war and in the 1930s. In engineering, for example, with the introduction of automatic machine tools, greater mechanisation, and mass production in certain sectors and firms, the percentage of skilled workers declined. Though the figures must be treated with some caution, the proportion of skilled workers in engineering fell from approximately 60 per cent in 1914 to 32 per cent in 1933. During the same period the proportion of unskilled workers also declined and it was the semi-skilled who grew from about 20 per cent to 57 per cent of the labour force.[57] However, traditional and newer types of technology and work organisation continued to exist side by side in differing proportions within sectors, firms, and even different shops within the same firm. During depression years and in less prosperous sectors, the introduction of new equipment and new methods was slowed down. During years of prosperity workers and their unions were able more successfully to influence management plans. Thus, overall there was no dramatic transformation of work organisation on scientific management lines in British industry during this period.

This essay has shown that British employers were not a monolithic group. There was great variety in their attitudes and policies. It would be too simple to say that there was a basic divide between those who wanted cooperation with their workforces and with the trade unions and those who favoured a more belligerent insistence on managerial prerogatives. Various policies coexisted and certainly as time passed and circumstances changed, employer strategies adapted. The coal-owners and traditional engineering employers might represent a predominant strand, but different traditions existed and new strategies were being tentatively developed. Overall, in the period 1914–39 employers played an important part—perhaps *the* most important part—in creating and maintaining the British system of industrial relations. It was largely at their initiative that a national system of collective bargaining was created; in the depression years, though the employers sought to shift the balance within this system, they maintained the basic arrangements. Over the years covered by this volume there were some significant developments in company and plant level strategy, in particular the slow development of the personnel function and the replacement of *ad hoc* informal methods of labour management with more bureaucratic forms. However, it is probably true to say that there was an over-reliance on the national system at the expense of company and plant level policies. This did not represent an immediate problem for British employers in the interwar years. However, after the Second World War, with a change in the balance of power within industry and an increased competitive challenge in world markets, this was to constitute for British employers a major deficiency in the industrial relations system.

## Notes

1 Department of Employment, *British Labour Statistics Historical Abstract 1886–1968* (1971), pp. 102, 111, 116. For information on enterprise employment, see C. Shaw, 'The Large Manufacturing Employers of 1907', *Business History*, 25 (1983); and for the 1930s unpublished work by the Business History Unit, London School of Economics.

2 See L. Hannah, *The Rise of the Corporate Economy* (1983), Ch. 7.

3 P. Sargant Florence, *The Logic of British and American Industry* (1953), pp. 24, 34.

4 Ministry of Reconstruction, *Interim Report of the Committee on Relations between Employers and Employed*, Cd. 8606 (1917–18), para. 23.

5   PRO/Lab 2/427/259/1918; Ministry of Labour, *Eighteenth Abstract of Labour Statistics*, Cmd. 2740 (1926), p. 191; *Twenty-Second Abstract of Labour Statistics*, Cmd. 5556 (1936–37), p. 136.

6   J. H. Richardson, *Industrial Relations in Great Britain* (1938), p. 83.

7   In 1917 this became the National Union of Manufacturers.

8   For more details see H. F. Gospel, 'Employers' Organisations: Their Growth and Function in the British System of Industrial Relations in the Period 1918–1939'. Unpublished PhD (London, 1974), pp. 304–6.

9   NCEO/C66/VII, Notes 28 February 1929. See also NCEO Annual Report 1924, NC 1215, p. 12.

10  See Gospel, *op. cit.*, pp. 307–8, 352.

11  Department of Employment, *op. cit.*, Table 197.

12  For the fullest account, see R. Charles, *The Development of Industrial Relations in Britain 1911–1939* (1973).

13  B. Mogridge, 'Militancy and Inter-Union, Rivalry in British Shipping, 1911–1929', *International Review of Social History*, 6 (1961); G. Alderman, 'The Railway Companies and the Growth of Trade Unionism in the late Nineteenth and early Twentieth Centuries', *Historical Journal*, 14 (1971).

14  The National Free Labour Association seems to have faded out around this time and, though a body called the United Kingdom Employers' Defence Union was still making belligerent gestures in 1913, it seems to have attracted little or no support. *The Times* 25 and 27 September 1913.

15  G. D. H. Cole, *Workshop Organisation* (1923); G. Pribićević, *The Shop Stewards' Movement and Workers' Control 1910–1922* (1959).

16  EEF/XIV/Memorandum as to the Effect of the Conflict between Industrial Trade Unionism and Craft Trade Unionism (1918), p. 1.

17  For more details see Gospel, *op. cit.*, p. 131.

18  See W. E. J. McCarthy, *The Closed Shops in Britain* (1964), passim.

19  Gospel, *op. cit.*, pp. 138–41.

20  EEF/XXII/Management Committee minutes/26 January 1923; EEF/XVIII/Executive Board/6 July 1920.

21  See J. Melling in this volume, pp. 243–83.

22  G. S. Bain, *The Growth of White Collar Unionism* (1970), pp. 142–75.

23  *AEU Monthly Journal*, June 1937, p. 225.

24  EEF/XXXVI/General Council/20 October 1937.

25  After the General Strike G. A. Spencer established the Nottinghamshire and District Miners' Industrial Union. This spread to other coalfields and was financially assisted by the owners.

26  See EEF, *Decisions of Central Conference 1898–1925*, Case No. 772, 10 November 1898, for a definition of 'current conditions'. See E. Wigham, *The Power to Manage* (1973), pp. 84–5 on the York Memorandum.

27  See, for example, Engineering and Allied Employers National Federation, *Thirty Years of Industrial Conciliation* (1927), passim.

28  R. Hyman, *The Workers Union* (1971) pp. 61, 88–9; B. C. M. Weekes, 'The Amalgamated Society of Engineers 1880–1914', Unpublished PhD (Warwick, 1970), pp. 132–3, 228, 357.
29  Gospel, *op. cit.*, p. 163.
30  See Chapter 8 below.
31  EEF/XIV/*Interim Report on Post-War Industrial Problems*/29 July 1918.
32  See Scrapbook of North-East Coast Engineering Employers' Association, entitled 'Engineers' Lock-out 1922', pp. 1–25; EEF/XX/E.B./ 18 March 1921. The pamphlet, 'Maintenance of Right of Employers to Exercise Managerial Functions', issued by the Federation in March 1922, emphasises the importance of the machine question in the dispute.
33  Scrapbook referred to above, leaflet entitled 'Maintenance of Rights of Employers to Exercise Managerial Functions'.
34  Speech by Sir A. Smith in Commons debate on 1922 dispute, *House of Commons Debates*, Vol. 152, 20 March 1922, col. 122.
35  See Gospel, *op. cit.*, pp. 180–3 for a more detailed analysis.
36  G. W. McDonald, 'The Role of British Industry in 1926', in M. Morris (ed.), *The General Strike*, p. 310.
37  J. M. Keynes, 'The Need of Peace by Negotiation', *New Republic*, 19 May 1926, p. 395, quoted in J. E. Williams, *The Derbyshire Miners* (1962), p. 734.
38  J. H. Grey, President of the Cotton Spinners and Manufacturers' Association, in the Burnley Cotton Spinners and Manufacturers Association, Minutes, 7 January 1931, quoted in A. McIvor, 'Cotton Employers' Organisation and Labour Relations Strategy 1890–1939', Polytechnic of Central London, Working Paper No. 18 (1982), pp. 35–6. I am endebted to A. McIvor for information on the cotton employers.
39  W. R. Garside, 'Management and Men: Aspects of British Industrial Relations in the Inter-war Period', in B. Supple (ed.), *Essays in British Business History* (1977), adds other industries.
40  All the quotations are taken from Conference on Industrial Reorganisation and Industrial Relations, *Interim Joint Report* (1928).
41  Conference on Industrial Reorganisation and Industrial Relations, *Interim Joint Report on Unemployment* (1929).
42  For the full details of these talks, see Gospel, *op. cit.*, pp. 339–50.
43  NCEO/C530/I/Letter, EEF to NCEO/1 September 1930.
44  FBI/330 K2 (A)/IV/TUC General Council Economic Committee, *Short Statement on Economic Policy* (1931).
45  For a good account of one such system of subcontracting during this period, see R. E. Goffee, 'The butty system and the Kent coalfield', *Bulletin of the Society for the Study of Labour History*, 34 (1977).
46  'Industrial Reconstruction: An Employer's View', *The Athenaeum*, March 1917.
47  S. Webb, *The Works Manager Today* (1917), pp. 21, 23.
48  See J. Melling, Ch. 7 below.

49   M. M. Niven, *Personnel Management 1913–1963* (1967), pp. 24–9.
50   Ibid., pp. 40–5; A. Briggs, *Social Thought and Social Action: A Study of the Work of Seebohm Rowntree 1871–1954* (1961), pp. 120, 125; *Official History of the Ministry of Munitions*, vol. V, Part III, pp. 37, 42.
51   Niven, *op. cit.*, p. 74; L. Urwick and E. F. L. Brech, *The Human Factor in Management* (1944), pp. 24–5.
52   Niven, *op. cit.*, pp. 79, 81.
53   W. Lewchuk, 'Fordism and British Motor Car Employers 1896–1932', in H. F. Gospel and C. R. Littler (eds.), *Managerial Strategies and Industrial Relations* (1983), pp. 82–100.
54   I am endebted, for this brief reference to pensions, to conversations with Professor L. Hannah, Business History Unit, London School of Economics.
55   C. R. Littler, *The Development of the Labour Process in Capitalist Societies* (1982), Chapter 8.
56   M. L. Yates, *Wages and Labour Conditions in British Engineering* (1937), p. 97; K. G. J. C. Knowles and D. J. Robertson, 'Earnings in Engineering, 1926–1948', *Bulletin of the Oxford University Institute of Statistics*, 13 (1951).
57   See Gospel, *op. cit.*, pp. 50–1.

# 5

# The Government and Industrial Relations, 1919–39

*Rodney Lowe*

Three problems immediately confront any analysis of government involvement in industrial relations during the interwar period in Britain. First, what is meant by the terms 'government' and 'industrial relations'? Secondly, once defined, what is the nature of the relationship between the two? Thirdly, what peculiar significance—if any—did the interwar period have for this relationship? This chapter, by providing what (for some) will be a rather narrow answer to the first question will inevitably prejudge the answers to the other two; but it is not the intention wholly to emulate an ostrich. Alternative interpretations, based on different ideological assumptions, will be duly—and possibly even fairly—examined.

The focus of this chapter is narrow because 'government' is defined as central government or, more specifically, the Cabinet and the Civil Service. Thus local government is excluded although (owing to the extension of the franchise and their increasing significance as employers) the role of local authorities in industrial relations at this time was becoming increasingly important and controversial.[1] Excluded also are other agencies of the 'state', such as the judiciary, the military and the police.[2] Such omissions might be justified solely by the current inadequacies of historical research, but a more important constraint is lack of space. Then, as now, neither the Cabinet nor the Civil Service were homogeneous bodies and so any serious study must examine in some detail their diverse, and often contradictory, behaviour. Is it realistic, for example, to assume—as have some historians—that Cabinets headed by the interventionist Lloyd George and by those dedicated to eradicating his influence on British government (Baldwin, MacDonald and Chamberlain) had common objectives? Moreover, did the displacement of the Liberal by the Labour Party and the subsequent alternation of government between two Parties, representing the opposing sides of industry, have no impact at all on 'government' policy? As for the Civil Service, the Ministry of Labour was established in 1916 ostensibly to centralise administrative responsibility for industrial relations, but before 1940 its authority was far from complete. Industrial relations in several key industries remained the direct responsibility of other Departments (the coal industry, for example, was the responsibility of the Board of Trade). Working conditions continued to be supervised by the Home Office. The government's role as an employer was also dominated by the Treasury and, in the 1930s, by the Defence Departments. Such diverse political and administrative influences on policy cannot simply be ignored.

'Industrial relations' is another term which is open to a variety of interpretations. Here it is defined as 'industrial disputes' and so the ensuing analysis concentrates on the attempt by central government both to resolve disputes (through its conciliation and arbitration service) and to prevent them (either through its evolving relationship with both sides of industry or through legislative and administrative action designed to improve working conditions and industrial practice).[3] It rejects the Marxist assumption that industrial relations is a 'consecrated euphemism' for the class war and that, consequently, any action—or, indeed, inaction—by government must be interpreted in the wider context of a fundamental clash of interest between the capitalist élite and the oppressed working class.[4] Moreover, it does not specifically analyse the impact which the government's broad economic and social policy had—and was designed to have—on the shopfloor. By helping to determine levels of employment and poverty it clearly had some impact. But what exactly was it? Were trade unions strengthened or weakened, for instance, by the continued extension of unemployment insurance and assistance? Did the loss of their traditional role as friendly societies enable unions to concentrate their attention and funds on strikes; or did the expansion of state social services undermine members' loyalty to their unions? Did the reduction of poverty enable strikes to be sustained over longer periods; or, by decreasing the sense of inequality and injustice, did it sap the will to strike? By providing in effect a floor below which wages could not fall, did unemployment benefit assist trade union negotiators; or, by increasing industrial costs, did it increase unemployment (by discouraging investment and undermining export competitiveness) and thereby erode trade union strength? Such issues are extremely important but they cannot be adequately examined in the space available here.[5]

On the basis of these definitions, it can but be concluded that, contrary to much received opinion, the influence of government on industrial relations during the interwar period was relatively weak and that there occurred no momentous change in government policy. On the one hand, despite such political crises as the 1926 General Strike, the real initiative in industrial relations continued to lie—as indeed the government's voluntarist policy intended it to lie—within industry itself. In the settlement of disputes, for instance, government action was constrained by the realisation that, in the absence of any coercive powers, its influence was dependent upon the goodwill of both sides of industry; and, in the improvement of working conditions and industrial practice, memories of non-compliance during and immediately after the First World War discouraged the active advocacy of reforms that had not the prior consent of industry. On the other hand, despite the ending in 1926 of a 16-year period of 'direct action' which has assumed such significance in labour history, there was no 'revolution' in government policy comparable to that of the 1890s (when government first trespassed into what had been regarded previously as the 'private preserve' of employers), or of the 1950s (when the government's traditional 'neutrality' was compromised by its newly-acquired responsibility for managing the economy). Policy-makers in fact consistently sought continuity. 'The machinery for the settlement of disputes is now fundamentally the same as in pre-war times,' boasted a Ministry of Labour memorandum in 1921, which was to provide the basis for interwar policy;[6] and, in the 1940s, the same Ministry successfully used its new-found authority to resist the attempt by economic ministries, seeking to minimise the risk of wage-inflation, to replace the interwar pattern of free collective bargaining. In industrial relations, as in so many other areas of policy, the interwar period was significant for what did not, rather than for what did, change.

Given these somewhat unheroic assumptions, three important questions can nevertheless be asked. First, given the increased pluralism of politics (following the trebling of the electorate in 1918), the greater industrial and political strength of trade unions (following the First World War) and the actual attainment of power by the Labour Party, were there no political modifications to industrial relations policy? Secondly, what caused the dramatic change in the temper of industrial relations between the First and Second World Wars? During the First World War, an annual average of 4.2 million working days were lost and industrial relations were particularly bitter during the period of reconstruction but, in contrast, during the Second an average of only 2 million days were lost, official strikes were voluntarily suspended until 1951 and an effective prices and incomes policy was achieved. Clearly, this remarkable transformation can be largely explained by non-governmental factors such as (in the 1930s) mass unemployment, changes in the occupational structure of industry and the bureaucratisation of both employers' organisations and trade unions; and (in the 1940s) the wartime alliance with Russia and the election of a majority Labour government committed to implementing a welfare state. But was it in no way the conscious achievement of interwar industrial relations policy? Finally, given the problems that were to beset industrial relations policy after 1944 as a result of the government's acceptance of responsibility for the management of the economy, were not these problems anticipated and was no countervailing action taken in the 1930s as government influence, both in the economy and as an employer, gradually expanded? These questions will dominate the ensuing analysis.

## The Cabinet and industrial relations

The involvement of successive Cabinets in industrial relations, and hence the political modification of policy, is best analysed in three overlapping stages, and will be subject to two further assumptions. The first is that the involvement of politicians in industrial relations was sporadic and occasioned largely by specific crises, whilst the continuity of policy—such as the provision of advice to prevent disputes—was maintained by the Civil Service (whose activities will be discussed in the next section). The second is that, as vigorously argued at the time, 'in the whole field of industrial relations, a lengthy record of positive achievement is more likely to be suspect of failure than of success'.[7] Consequently, although the Cabinet scarcely discussed industrial relations between 1926 and 1939, there is no a priori reason why this period should be portrayed—as so frequently it has been—as a sorry anti-climax to the heroic confrontations of the early 1920s. The three overlapping stages are: the unions' flirtation with 'direct action' between 1919 and 1926, the Labour governments of 1924 and 1929–31, and the consolidation (largely after 1926) of a permanent peacetime working relationship between government, employers and unions.

The years between 1919 and 1926 have been conventionally represented by Marxist historians as a unified period in which government eroded the wartime solidarity of a potentially revolutionary working class and gradually reasserted the legitimacy of capitalism. To its economic weapons of mass unemployment and the return to the Gold Standard, government added a subtle political strategy by which it promised reform (whilst the trade unions were strong), assumed coercive powers (when they weakened) and then abstained from active intervention in industrial disputes (once employers had fully regained their self-confidence). The logical climax to this concerted economic and political campaign was the provocation of the General Strike in 1926 and the passage of the vindictive Trade Disputes and Trade Unions Act in 1927.[8] However, for other historians the period has no such unity and class conflict was not the consistent motivation of successive governments. Rather, post-war adjustment—as will be demonstrated—had four distinct phases and was largely complete by 1922; throughout the unwelcome depression, moreover, the principal objective of successive governments was always to force industry, in the absence of any spontaneous consensus, to confront and then to resolve its own problems.

The first phase of post-war adjustment lasted until September 1919. During these months, the Lloyd George coalition, alarmed not only by union rhetoric but also by strikes in the police force and in government-controlled industries, was genuinely concerned that some unrest was part of a 'deliberate anti-social movement'.[9] In order to contain it, the Cabinet was prepared to make radical concessions—but only on condition that industrial consensus could be attained. Thus, in February 1919, the National Industrial Conference was summoned to encourage industry to devise an agreed programme of reform and the Sankey Commission was appointed to determine the future of the coal industry, then under government control. These initiatives were not, as has been suggested, part of a 'deliberately devious plot of delay and concession' to help dissipate trade union strength but, initially at least, genuine attempts to attain reform.[10]

The attempt failed, not because of government duplicity but because the necessary conditions for industrial consensus did not exist. The trade unions were divided over both tactics and strategy: five of the most powerful unions (the Triple Alliance, the ASE and the Steelworkers) refused, for instance, to attend the NIC and no definition, let alone a blueprint, for nationalisation could be agreed. Moreover, the employers were preoccupied by their own organisational problems and were led by the most subtle of procrastinators, Sir Allan Smith. Hence, the Sankey Commission failed to produce a unanimous report on which the government could act and the supposed agreements that were reached by the NIC contained contradictions and mutual misunderstandings that made their translation into effective legislation impossible. That failure was largely the responsibility of industry not government is confirmed by the concurrent drafting of the Industrial Courts Act. This Act, which was to provide the legislative basis for government intervention throughout the interwar period, was a government initiative and realised two ambitions of pre-war reformers: provision was made for a permanent court of arbitration and for courts of enquiry (which, by openly examining the causes of major disputes, could enable the public as the third party to any dispute to exercise some influence on the combatants). The government's original objectives, however, had been even more ambitious. The Act was to have rationalised wage-bargaining not only by enabling the Industrial Court to develop a consistent set of principles on which all awards might be based, but also by permitting the legal enforcement of the Court's awards both on the actual disputants and throughout the relevant industry. Such ambitions, however, had to be abandoned in the face of TUC opposition.[11] The one thing, indeed, upon which both sides of industry seemed genuinely to agree was that government intervention in industrial relations should be minimised.

The first major break in government policy followed the rail strike of September 1919, during which the NUR won the propaganda battle with the government and few volunteers responded to the call for special constables. Junior Ministers started so seriously to panic that they suffered visions of the Cooperative Society as a nationwide system of communist cells storing up 'reserves of food for their own people for enabling them to fight the community'.[12] Neither Lloyd George nor Bonar Law appeared affected—except, of course, when it was politically convenient—but both grew increasingly exasperated by Labour's inability to respond (as promised) to decreased working hours and continuing state control with increased productivity and industrial peace. Consequently, the Cabinet agreed that although reform should not be shelved, it should be contained within more conventional economic and constitutional limits. As Lloyd George wrote to Bonar Law in September 1920:

> I have become more and more convinced that the time has arrived for coming to grips with the conspiracy which is seeking to utilize labour for the purpose of overthrowing the existing organization of the time ... We must show Labour that the Government mean to be masters – I need hardly say this Government, but the Government of the land; but we must carry with us every phase of rational sane well-ordered opinion. ... There must be no suspicion that we are utilizing conditions in order to carry out a return to a reactionary regime.[13]

Whereas in 1919, therefore, the Gold Standard had been suspended in order to facilitate reform, economic orthodoxy was now restored; and whereas the devolution of political power to an 'industrial parliament' had been seriously considered, the constitution was now stoutly defended. In the first place, this meant the decontrol of those industries still under government control and cuts in public expenditure (and hence in the number of civil servants employed to improve industrial practice through, for example, the establishment of Whitley Councils). Reforms designed to improve pay and working conditions (such as Trade Boards) were also actively discouraged on the grounds that they increased industrial costs and thereby impeded economic recovery. In the second place, a permanent emergency organisation (the Supply and Transport Organisation) was established and the Emergency Powers Act passed in October 1920 to safeguard the supply and distribution of essential goods during a national crisis.[14] These latter measures were largely defensive, their principal object being to prevent the government from appearing impotent during a major industrial strike. The Emergency Powers Act, for instance, potentially gave the government dictatorial powers by enabling it to rule by regulation for a month but, in fact, these powers were subject to strict controls. All regulations had to be approved by Parliament within seven days and their use to impose conscription and to suspend the right to strike or picket was specifically debarred. Inevitably, however, these essentially defensive measures were construed in some quarters as offensive. Given that the purpose of major strikes was to maximise public inconvenience and thereby bring political pressure to bear on employers to settle, any action which strengthened the government's resolve and minimised public inconvenience could always be interpreted as 'strike-breaking'. Indeed this was—and is—a logical inference to be drawn by those who would place a union's right to strike above the public's right to receive essential services.

The third phase of post-war adjustment commenced in the summer of 1921 when, following the defeat of the miners after Black Friday and in the continuing depression, the Cabinet's commitment to reform ended. The experiment of devolving political power to industry was abandoned, with the formal resignation of the NIC and the government's refusal to ratify the first major convention of the International Labour Organisation (a body created in 1919 to improve industrial practice throughout the world, in which both industry and government enjoyed equal voting rights). The commitment to improve working conditions was also abandoned with the abolition of Agricultural Wages Boards, the termination of the Trade Board expansion programme and the Cabinet's unconstitutional veto on the enforcement of minimum wages in the retail distributive trades.[15] Like the emergency precautions, such actions could be, and have been, interpreted as a specific attack on trade unions; but, as the epitome of economy measures at the time (the Geddes Axe) demonstrated, all they really represented was the final dissolution of reconstruction ideals in the face of hard economic and political fact. The Geddes Axe, it should be remembered, fell not only on social and industrial reforms but also its chairman's own offspring, the Supply and Transport Organisation. The reduction of its annual expenditure to under £2000 hardly betokened a major capitalist offensive. Moreover, the justification for the cut was highly significant. As Geddes informed the Cabinet:

The machinery has been in existence for two years and has, I think, served its purpose well. It was essential for the maintenance of order and decent living that Government should take upon itself during the period of unrest which followed the war, the duty of protecting the community from the irresponsible attitude of extremists. The war had created in people a habit of looking to the Government for direction and initiative in almost every department of life. . . . This state of things has now passed. Private initiative has once more reasserted itself.[16]

By 1922 private initiative was deemed to be so resurgent that, after the collapse of the Lloyd George coalition, successive Cabinets sought to withdraw not only from industrial legislation but also industrial negotiations. This marked the start of the fourth and final phase of post-war adjustment, after which the dominant principle in industrial relations was non-intervention. There were three major justifications for this principle, of which the first was tactical: the desire of Ministers to distance themselves from Lloyd George in order both to exorcise his memory and to avoid his mistakes. Lloyd George's ever-willingness to negotiate in industrial disputes may initially have maintained a vital link between government and moderate labour leaders but, eventually, his mercurial tactics—alternating between consensus, coercion and bluff—had confused rather than resolved problems. The other two justifications were strategic: the desire to elevate government above sectional interest and to conform to prevailing cultural values. The first was well summarised in 1922 by the new Minister of Labour, who stated:

In his capacity as conciliator he must in the industrial world hold the balance with severe impartiality between capital and labour. As a member of the Government he had to face representatives of one of those two antagonists—labour—as a political opponent. The sound basis for general policy was that the State would require employers and workers to manage their own affairs.[17]

The second was well expressed by Baldwin, who argued with typical conviction:

What this Government will not do is to attempt to control the industries of the country. . . . The people have repudiated socialism. They have repudiated nationalization. They have repudiated the goal of a Britain controlled whether from London or Moscow. . . . By the natural evolution of our industrial life in England, we are confronted today and shall be more and more with great consolidations of capital, managed by small concentrated groups, and by great organizations of labour led by experienced and responsible leaders. That position must be accepted. ... It is little that the Government can do: these reforms, these revolutions, must come from the people themselves.

Such attitudes have subsequently been attacked as hypocritical with the perceived distinction between political and industrial issues being, in particular, scornfully dismissed as both artificial and partial. These attacks are misguided. However artificial in theory, the distinction between political and industrial issues was understood, and more importantly demanded, by both sides of industry at the time.[18] Moreover, as Baldwin's famous 'peace in our time' speech made explicit, government abstention from intervention required of politicians, however deep their convictions, a commitment not to 'reform' (to their own advantage) industrial relations law.

The continuing unrest in the coal industry, which culminated in the 1926 General Strike, demonstrated that the new non-interventionist policy was not immediately successful. Baldwin initially stretched the policy to its limit in an attempt to avert a crisis: he provided the coal industry with a subsidy for nine months during which he hoped a Royal Commission would find a formula by which the industry could solve its own problems.[19] 'Red Friday' should be seen, therefore, not as the consequence of the union's successful coercion of government or as a tactical delay by the government (so that it might perfect its emergency organisation) but as a genuine attempt to resolve the fundamental industrial problem that was to provoke the General Strike. The attempt, however, failed and then, in May 1926, the Cabinet did precipitate the final crisis, either because Ministers were fully confident in the Supply and Transport Organisation or, more reasonably, because they were collectively irritated by the prevarication of the trade union movement on an issue which could reasonably be construed as a challenge to constitutional government. This last-minute belligerency, however, should not be taken as evidence that the government had long sought confrontation. Undoubtedly there was in the Baldwin Cabinet, as in all Conservative Cabinets, a minority of Ministers who sought confrontation with the unions but in 1926, as throughout the interwar period, this minority was always eventually defeated. Similarly, the government's 'total victory' in the General Strike should not be regarded as indicative of its strength in relation to either side of industry. The reputation of the Supply and Transport Organisation only survived because of the strike's brief duration and the cooperation of the strikers; and the government's 'victory' still left the coal industry (on which the nation largely depended for its energy supplies) unreformed and inefficient.

The final test of any analysis of post-war adjustment is the 1927 Trade Disputes and Trade Unions Act. This Act made illegal general or sympathetic strikes designed to coerce the government; strengthened the law on picketing; substituted contracting in for contracting out of subscriptions to trade unions' political funds; banned civil servants from joining outside unions or from being affiliated to the TUC; and forbade the imposition of a 'closed shop' by local authorities or their contractors. It is scarcely surprising, therefore, that it has been portrayed by partial observers, both at the time and since, as a vindictive act of retribution against the unions. However, as Alan Anderson has convincingly argued, what is most remarkable about the Act is not what it included, but what it excluded.[20] It contained no attack on trade unions' funds, as had been demanded in times of crisis from 1919 to 1926. Criminal law was not substituted for civil law in industrial relations, as demanded by the Lord Chancellor. Neither the Trade Disputes Act 1906 was repealed nor the Conspiracy Act 1875 extended, as requested by employers' organisations. Compulsory strike ballots and compulsory arbitration, as demanded by Neville Chamberlain and Conservative Party Central Office, were also rejected. In short, 'the very minimum' that was acceptable to employers and the Conservative Party was conceded and the main thrust of government policy—the bringing together of the two sides of industry as in the Mond–Turner talks—was only temporarily delayed. Consequently the Act supports, and does not controvert, the interpretation of post-war adjustment that, having failed (in the absence of industrial consensus and economic prosperity) to pioneer reform before 1921, Liberal and Conservative Cabinets then resorted to a 'second-best' solution of non-intervention in order to force industry to face up to and resolve its own problems.

What, however, of the minority Labour government of 1924 and its successor of 1929–31? Did not their election make any significant difference to policy? The simple answer is no, because bound within powerful industrial and cultural conventions the influence of government on industrial relations was relatively weak. In the settlement of disputes, the formal neutrality of the state (as desired by the unions) was maintained. In the pioneering of change, vested interest again triumphed (as in 1924, when the Cooperative Society resisted attempts to revive the Grocery Trade Board and, in 1930, when internecine warfare between the NUR and TGWU obstructed the ratification of the ILO's convention on maximum hours of work).[21] In defence of the community's essential services, the emergency organisation was also kept in readiness (so that, during the transport strike of March 1924, a state of emergency was declared and draft regulations prepared, which included the use of the Navy to maintain the electricity supply). The one exceptional thing which the Labour government did demonstrate was that, within the formal policy of voluntarism, there was considerable scope for flexibility. Thus, in the settlement of disputes, greater pressure was brought to bear on employers to reach a settlement and, in 1924, more courts of enquiry were set up (seven in comparison to only six over the previous four years) in the belief that public opinion could be won over to the trade unions' point of view. Greater political and administrative effort was also made to prepare the ground for the improvement of working conditions; and, in order to demystify the emergency services, the public were taken into the government's confidence to the extent that trade unions were invited to cooperate in the distribution of essential supplies. Most significantly of all, especially for the evolving relationship between government and industry, Labour governments—either because of their lack of viable short-term policies or because of their minority position in Parliament—were ever-willing to involve both employers and trade union leaders in the planning of general government policy.

As central government strove to follow a policy of non-intervention in industrial relations, it was ironic that it should simultaneously start to consult industry more frequently on general industrial matters. However, given the persistence of mass unemployment, and the government's need to be seen by the electorate to be doing something constructive, such consultations were perhaps inevitable. Moreover, they were encouraged by the personal contacts established between businessmen and civil servants during the First World War and the growth of centralised industrial pressure groups with which the government might negotiate: the

TUC (which became increasingly professional under Citrine as General Secretary), the Federation of British Industries and the National Confederation of Employers' Organisations (a body whose creation in 1919 had been actively encouraged by government in order to unify employers' attitudes towards industrial relations and social policy). What, however, was the real significance of these consultations? Were they important or not? For several historians, they are of supreme importance for they are seen as the mechanism by which both industrial unrest was contained after the First World War and Britain's relative social stability thereafter sustained. As Keith Middlemas has argued, for example, it was through these liaisons that government conceded to major industrial pressure groups a certain political power and authority and thereby transformed them into 'governing institutions'. In return, they agreed to control their members and thereby 'marginalised' dissent. The process was secret and depended on informal understandings, and so has been described not as corporatism but as 'corporate bias'.[22]

The concept of 'corporate bias' has a superficial attraction. Employers' organisations and trade unions were certainly able openly to assume the guise of 'governing institutions' on bodies such as the International Labour Organisation and the Economic Advisory Council. They were represented also on innumerable government commissions and committees; and the proceedings of at least one such committee, the Ross Committee on Fair Wages (which was established in 1937 to determine the government's role as a model employer) were suspended so that the NCEO and the TUC could negotiate a private agreement.[23] The TUC, moreover, was useful to the government in 'educating' the trade union movement. Immediately after the General Strike, for instance, Bevin was transported (together with employers' representatives) to the USA so that he—and through him his colleagues—might appreciate that higher productivity, and not lower wages, was the solution to depression; and a remarkable series of secret meetings took place in 1937 between Citrine and Sir Horace Wilson so that, in the interest of expediting rearmament, Chamberlain might know how best to overcome the passive resistance of the craft unions.[24] Finally, the relationship between employers and trade union leaders could, in private, be extremely cordial. This was true of informal, as opposed to formal, meetings at the ILO; and, in 1938, at a meeting of the Amulree Committee on Holidays with Pay, the

NCEO and TUC representatives changed places to argue, with the utmost conviction, their opponents' case.[25]

The concept of 'corporate bias', however, cannot be sustained. Its validity depends on the basic assumption that the government, throughout the interwar period, had continually to suppress incipient unrest and that its containment was the achievement of high politics. Such an assumption cannot be sustained in the light of contrary evidence which suggests that post-war unrest subsided and remained dormant for far more subtle cultural and economic reasons.[26] In any case, the so-called 'governing institutions' patently lacked the authority to control the behaviour of their members. After the Mond–Turner talks, for instance, the Engineering, Shipbuilding and Mining employers threatened to secede from the NCEO if even the bland recommendation of trade union recognition was accepted; and the AEU vigorously rejected the TUC's lead over rearmament in 1938, refusing even to sell the TUC its monthly journal on the grounds that it was 'unavailable to the public'.[27] The 'governing institutions' were in fact inherently weak and, rather than the government needing them, they needed regular contact with government to validate their status and so assert some authority over their membership. To attract more members, their recruiting literature grossly exaggerated the political importance of these contacts and it is these claims that the proponents of 'corporate bias' have mistakenly taken at face value.

Throughout the interwar period, indeed, there is little hard evidence either of any sustained, clandestine relationship between government and industry or of any exceptional influence on government legislation from the alleged 'governing institutions'. Formal attempts at cooperation, such as the National Industrial Conference, the Mond–Turner talks or the Economic Advisory Council, rapidly collapsed because, after the initial identification of mutual problems, employers and trade union leaders were prevented by rival economic philosophies and suspicion from reaching constructive agreements.[28] Successive governments also remained on bad terms with their attendant interest groups. Over social service expenditure, for example, the Baldwin Cabinet countered the NCEO's vilification of socialist intentions with charges of 'obstructive inertia' and the second Labour government was actually brought down by a TUC revolt.[29] As for legislative influence, the real position was well summarised by the Trade

Disputes Act 1927, which the NCEO was able only marginally to affect and which the TUC, between 1929–31, was unable to repeal. Certainly the 'governing institutions' themselves would have been astounded by their retrospective importance. Their own perception was entirely different. During rearmament in the late 1930s, for example, Bevin was furious with the government's attitude towards the TUC, which has correctly been described as one of 'avoidance' not 'cooperation'. The historian of the FBI has concluded:

> The image of the Federation pulling the strings behind the National Government cannot be supported by the facts. The dominant preoccupation of the FBI leadership remained the avoidance of divisions within the organization. Issues likely to cause a split were consistently sidestepped and thus the Federation failed to take significant roles in the most important questions of the period.

The NCEO, during its planning for reconstruction during the Second World War, accepted a similar verdict on its own influence.[30]

'Corporate bias' therefore is an inadequate description of government's evolving relationship with industry between the wars. Unquestionably, during the interwar period, government did regularly consult both sides of industry; but this was only natural, given the increased pluralism of politics after the extension of the franchise in 1918. Employers and trade unionists were also regularly invited to sit on government committees; but this again was only natural, since they alone had the technical knowledge which government required as it was reluctantly drawn back into industrial problems. Government policy in fact remained resolutely the decentralisation, not the centralisation, of responsibility. Each industry was to be responsible for its own affairs whilst government itself stood above the fray, free to defend its perception of the 'national' interest. Corporatism or 'corporate bias' had to await the Second World War when economically the two sides of industry were more equally matched and, politically, the purpose of such a deal was uncontentious.

### The Civil Service and industrial relations

The assertions of the previous sections can be better defended when the sporadic intervention of transient Ministers is correlated with the continuous activities of permanent civil servants. Throughout the interwar period, the Civil Service—like successive Cabinets—was largely committed to a policy of 'home rule for industry' and thus to the minimising of the role of central government in industrial relations. There were, however, two exceptions. First, some degree of intervention was accepted as inevitable in order to defend the 'national' interest, to maintain minimum standards of industrial practice and to encourage collective bargaining (through the free and voluntary conciliation and arbitration service); and this concession, as the Labour governments showed, permitted a considerable degree of flexibility. What, after all, was the 'national interest'? What were 'minimum standards'? How much covert persuasion might be exercised to secure industrial peace? The second exception arose from the different departmental responses to these questions. On the one hand, the Home Office was always prepared to use the threat of a new Factory Act to encourage improvements in industrial practice whilst, on the other, the Board of Trade and the Defence Departments (especially in the 1930s when they were seeking, respectively, to revive the market economy and to rearm) appeared incapable of appreciating anything but strict commercial criteria.[31] The policy of the Treasury was rather more complex. As the controller of both public finance and the conditions of public employment, it opposed any expenditure that might unbalance the budget or impede the free market whilst, as the upholder of the concept of 'public service', it opposed secret corporate deals with industrial—if perhaps not financial—interests. The main focus of this section, however, will be the department officially responsible for industrial relations policy, the Ministry of Labour. In harmony with the political commitment to reform, its officials actively promoted industrial change before 1921, but thereafter (as will be seen) they were more restrained.

Between 1919 and 1921, official involvement in industrial negotiations largely concerned the coal industry and the railways and thus the Board of Trade and the Ministry of Transport. This helps to explain the exceptional degree of 'mutual incomprehension' that existed between the government and unions at the time.[32] However, behind the scenes Ministry of Labour officials, under the exceptional leadership of Harold Butler, did actively strive (within a voluntarist policy) to realise the new ideals of pre-war liberalism and wartime conservatism: the expansion of social expenditure, as productive expenditure, and the stimulation of industrial productivity. Hence, at an international and national level, the ILO and NIC were established as authoritative industrial fora to which real legislative power might be devolved. At an industrial level, Whitleyism was promoted to minimise the chances of friction and to maximise the opportunity for cooperation at all levels within the firm. Finally, the number of Trade Boards was trebled and an attempt made to coordinate wage awards through the Industrial Court, in order to improve minimum conditions of work and to rationalise industrial negotiations. The consistent objective of such a policy was the achievement of an 'ordered freedom' in which economic growth might be sustained and some redistribution of responsibility and wealth attained.[33]

The policy failed. Neither the industrial consensus nor the political will existed to permit such a devolution of power: democracy could not be so easily correlated with industrial efficiency. Moreover, with the deterioration of the economy, the Treasury grew concerned about not only the cost of such reforms but also the very principle of state intervention. During 1919, with the inauguration of Whitleyism and an arbitration board for civil servants, its own managerial power within the Civil Service had been challenged.[34] It reacted vigorously by attacking the very existence of a permanent conciliation staff. The justification for its attack, which was to be well aired before the Geddes Committee, was that in two ways such a staff impeded economic recovery. First, it increased public expenditure and secondly, by increasing working-class expectations and weakening industrial self-discipline, it strengthened trade unionism, discouraged the downward flexibility of wages and consequently caused strikes. The obvious analogy, as one Ministry of Labour official remarked, was that the existence of the fire brigade caused fires.

The Ministry successfully defended the existence of its conciliation staff. It argued that the costs incurred were 'productive expenditure', since the 'greatest economy to the nation' was 'the avoidance of industrial disputes and the consequent loss of production and efficiency'. Moreover (in a clear reference to Lloyd George's antics) it maintained that all modern governments, as trustees for the community, had to intervene in major disputes and that 'the most wasteful and mischievous form of intervention was intervention decided upon ... hurriedly in response to public clamour with no expert advice'.[35] Its victory, however, was Pyrrhic for the number of conciliation staff was permanently reduced from its post-war peak of 229 to under 30, and the positive idealism of Butler was lost. Coinciding with the change in political climate, official policy after 1921 came firmly to be based on the premise that 'the efficacy of State action depends very largely upon the care with which the responsible Department ordinarily refrains from active intervention'; and local officials were duly advised to

> strive to the utmost to avoid active intervention while at the same time maintaining just sufficient contact with the progress of affairs to let those in authority know, as and when necessary, what is happening or is likely to happen by way of industrial conflict ... to be acquainted with matters of importance without anyone concerned knowing that they are acquainted.[36]

The consequent decline in the formal influence of the Ministry, and hence of central government, in industrial negotiations is demonstrated by table 5.1.[37]

Under the dominant personalities of first Sir Horace Wilson in the 1920s, and Sir Frederick Leggett in the 1930s, however, ministerial policy was not without its positive, informal influence. Conciliators respected the traditions and autonomy of each industry but, as before the war (when Sir George Askwith had been chief industrial commissioner), they constantly strove to encourage both sides of industry to accept practices which would foster self-restraint and responsibility. 'The preservation of order in a democracy', remarked Leggett, 'depends on a personal sense of responsibility' and this could only be achieved from below by slowly building up 'organisation and knowledge and goodwill'.[38] Strikes and lock-outs were thus, in the last resort, to be welcomed if they forced both sides of industry to face hard economic 'facts'; and by these criteria the General Strike was, in the end, welcomed and later 'justified' by the readiness of employers and the TUC to meet at the Mond–Turner talks. The more common objective of policy, however, was (as in the road haulage industry in the 1930s) the peaceful development of conciliation machinery.

By definition, the 'success' of such a policy is hard to establish. Written records inadequately chronicle the continuous effort at

Table 5.1: The Ministry of Labour and Industrial Settlements 1920–38

|      | Arbitration settlements | | | Conciliation settlements | Courts of Enquiry |
|      | Industrial Court | Single arbitration | Ad hoc board | | |
|------|------|------|------|------|------|
| 1920 | 540 | 73 | 15 | 286 | 3 |
| 1921 | 122 | 19 | 7 | 123 | 1 |
| 1922 | 37 | 9 | 8 | 48 | 1 |
| 1923 | 113 | 14 | 6 | 33 | 1 |
| 1924 | 143 | 7 | 12 | 83 | 7 |
| 1925 | 165 | 8 | 8 | 73 | 3 |
| 1926 | 104 | 5 | 4 | 24 | — |
| 1927 | 82 | 6 | 1 | 14 | — |
| 1928 | 52 | 10 | 5 | 42 | — |
| 1929 | 39 | 14 | 3 | 38 | — |
| 1930 | 43 | 6 | 3 | 31 | 1 |
| 1931 | 35 | 7 | 6 | 48 | — |
| 1932 | 28 | 3 | 1 | 45 | — |
| 1933 | 26 | 3 | 1 | 22 | — |
| 1934 | 30 | 6 | 4 | 29 | — |
| 1935 | 29 | 10 | — | 41 | 1 |
| 1936 | 35 | 9 | 1 | 45 | — |
| 1937 | 20 | 6 | 2 | 66 | 2 |
| 1938 | 26 | 6 | 2 | 83 | — |

informal persuasion, the more so since Leggett (like Askwith) liked to shroud conciliation in mystery. Moreover 'success' can only be fairly judged against the particular economic and social circumstances of each industry and this has yet to be seriously attempted by business historians. However, the most authoritative account of interwar industrial relations has concluded that 'the practice of conciliation and arbitration, and the setting-up of standing joint bodies for negotiations, have contributed to a real change of attitude between employers and unions and have much reduced the severity of strikes'.[39] On such an interim judgement, it may be concluded that policy was reasonably successful and that the constructive consensus of the 1940s was, in no small way, the direct consequence of official interwar policy.

Ministry of Labour officials also strenuously opposed the amendment of industrial relations law and corporatist experiment. As in the drafting of the Trade Disputes Act 1927, they opposed legislative change because it was impractical, irrelevant and potentially self-defeating.[40] In relation to secret ballots, for instance, they questioned how large a vote would have to be to become representative and how the legislation could be enforced; they also warned that ballots might exaggerate industrial friction because, by providing 'a new line of least resistance', they would discourage moderate leaders from standing up to their extremists and then bind them to the 'embarrassment of a written vote ... cast without full appreciation of the facts'. In relation to cooling-off periods and compulsory arbitration, they noted the failure in practice of governments to invoke such laws when they were on the statute book, the danger of non-compliance and the undermining of free collective bargaining (as negotiators jockeyed for position, rather than seeking genuinely independent settlements). Any change to the political levy, it was correctly predicted, would be 'a boomerang which will inflict more hurt on the attackers than the object of the attack'. In short, easy political panaceas (which have a distinctly modern ring) were rejected and the conviction maintained that a new will and genuine cooperation could only be achieved in industrial relations by the patient encouragement of moderate industrial leaders. Especially in relation to trade unions, legislation was positively dangerous because, by causing union officials to relax, it could open a gap between the national leaders and their rank and file—a gap which, as in the First World War, might be exploited by militants.

Memories of the war and its immediate aftermath also caused officials to reject corporatist experiment. After the experience of 1919, for instance, officials opposed sporadic proposals to resurrect the NIC, on the grounds that such a body could but exaggerate national political rivalries at the expense of mutual sectional interests and would, therefore, be an 'obstacle to reasoned consideration'.[41] The submission of draft legislation to outside pressure groups before the House of Commons were also banned, for fear of jeopardising Parliament's authority. Most importantly of all, during rearmament in the 1930s, memories of the exploitation of government by vested interest in the First World War deterred officials from entering tripartite deals. Even in 1938, when the TUC legitimately complained about the lack of information it was receiving in relation to employers, the establishment of a formal trade union consultative committee was vigorously opposed. Owing to the problem of confidentiality, it was argued, the general effect would be that while the Committee themselves might feel they were not being told very much, and would be correspondingly dissatisfied, the trade unions in general would regard them as being 'in the pocket of government' and the object of cooperation would not be advanced.[42]

There is little evidence here of 'corporate bias'. Ministry policy was indeed identical to that of the Cabinet (which of course not only controlled, but was also itself heavily influenced by, the Ministry): the transformation was sought not of national pressure groups into 'governing institutions', but of individual industries into self-governing and efficient entities.

### Anticipating the Future

As government's responsibilities as an employer, contractor and manager of the economy gradually expanded in the interwar period, its influence on industrial relations was not just as a legislator and a conciliator but also as an independent economic power. This power it used with extreme caution. Hence, when the TUC requested that—as in the 1890s—government should act as a 'model employer', it was firmly rebuffed. In the mid-1930s, for instance, a reduction in civil servants' hours of work was refused on the grounds that, by increasing taxation and implying approval of a new 'norm', it would add directly and indirectly to industry's costs and thereby increase, not decrease, unemployment as the TUC had assumed. As a contractor, the government also allowed the Fair Wages Resolution—another symbol of the good intentions of the 1890s—to fall into disuse and abuse. Its complete agnosticism was, indeed, well reflected by its attitude to wages, which the Ministry of Labour summarised thus:

> Government wages policy is a 'fair wages' policy', i.e. to take wages as they are in outside industry, to take no responsibility for fixing wages and, in the expenditure of public money, to do nothing calculated to disturb the level or influence the course of wages in outside industry.[43]

Such conservatism may be justified on two counts. First, whenever (as a legislator) government attempted to pioneer change, it was defeated by industry's non-compliance. Neither the Labour government, for instance, could persuade mine-owners to accept national wage negotiations as specified in the Coal Mines Act

1930, nor could the National government force employers to rationalise their industries once protection had been granted. Secondly (as a contractor), not only did government share the basic economic and industrial assumptions of employers—as demonstrated by the establishment of departmental advisory panels of industrialists, not trade unionists—but it was also fully aware that, in the absence of a bureaucracy well-qualified in managerial and technical skills, it was dependent on their goodwill. However, government's increasing unwillingness to take calculated risks in the public interest did bode ill for the future. Immediately after the First World War, for instance, all plans for nationalisation had included special provisions to defend the consumers' interest; but by the 1930s, as was demonstrated by the drafting of the 1937 British Overseas Airways Bill (which set a precedent for post-war nationalisation), this consideration had been shelved. In 1937, Leggett successfully argued against any new elaborate conciliation machinery on the grounds that it was

> desirable in the case of Imperial Airways, as of all other employers in the country, to leave the existence of collective arrangements to be determined by the facts. President Roosevelt has had some unfortunate experience in regard to his legislation for imposing collective agreements . . . and that experience is not encouraging for similar action in this country. I see no reason for distinguishing between a company, upon which in any case the Government would be able to exercise considerable moral influence, and other employers.[44]

Rather spuriously, therefore, industrial goodwill and moral suasion were deemed sufficient safeguards for both public money and the public interest.

### Conclusion

The actions of both politicians and civil servants in the interwar period, as can be seen, readily lend themselves to a Marxist interpretation of industrial relations. The commitment to reform before 1921 might be taken as an attempt to 'humanise' or 'moralise' capitalism at a time when it was under pressure. Thereafter the resort to voluntarism might be interpreted as an abstention by the state in favour of employers once their fortunes had revived; and the insistence on sectional negotiations rather than the renewal of the *National* Industrial Conference might be taken as an attempt to 'depoliticise' industrial relations. The purpose of the Ministry of Labour, moreover, was implicitly to use trade union leaders as a means of 'social control'; and the departmental views of the Treasury, the Defence Departments and the Board of Trade shared the basic economic and industrial assumptions of employers.

Such an interpretation, however, is hard to sustain. Its first weakness is that it overestimates the influence of government: between 1919 and 1921, for example, it was not any political or bureaucratic conspiracy which stifled radical reform but a lack of industrial and social consensus. Secondly, it denies the fact that the reversion to voluntarism was at the request of both sides of industry and that the continuing success of that policy was dependent on the willingness of both trade union leaders and the rank and file to accept sectional agreements. Thirdly, it overlooks the further fact that for every trade union complaint about government intervention there was at least one from the employers. Trade union complacency might, admittedly, be explained by 'false consciousness' and employer belligerency by disagreement over the government's choice of tactics in the class war; but there is little evidence that can support such contentions. Rather, what there is evidence for is the charge that government policy, for all its apparent short-term success, betrayed the long-term interests not just of the working class but of all consumers. In 1919 there had been a genuine attempt to realise the pre-war hope that the 'public' interest could be openly defined and resolutely defended. Except for the extreme measure of the Emergency Powers Act and the under-used provision for courts of enquiry, this attempt, with its ominous consequences for the future, had largely been abandoned by 1939.

There is, however, one major qualification to so definite a conclusion. Historians—like the post-1945 Treasury, when dealing with prices and incomes policy—can perhaps be too easily misled by an implicit belief that rational solutions can be achieved in industrial relations. No such belief was held by interwar conciliators, whose practical experience convinced them that permanent industrial settlements could be achieved only by the balancing of opposing forces, not by reason. If this instinct was correct, then perhaps interwar government through its unobtrusive policy of 'home rule for industry' achieved all that, in the given circumstances, it could reasonably have hoped to achieve.

## Notes

1   The increasing number of Labour-controlled councils, as was recognised by the Trade Disputes and Trade Unions Act 1927, resulted in local government and their contractors acting as a 'model employer' on issues such as union recognition and the closed shop.
2   For the restrained role of the military, see K. Jeffery and P. Hennessy, *States of Emergency* (1983), passim.
3   Ernest Bevin, for instance, on his translation from trade union leader to Cabinet Minister in 1940, defined government responsibility as not only the settlement of disputes but also the provision of a comprehensive code of 'conduct, inspection, enforcement and welfare'. See PRO, Lab 10/248, 19 October 1942.
4   R. Miliband, *The State in Capitalist Society* (1973 edn), p. 73.
5   Chapter 6 of this book is a pioneering attempt to analyse the impact of state welfare on industrial relations.
6   PRO, Lab 2/921/IR 190/1922, Part 2.
7   PRO, Lab 2/1804/CEB (G) 111/1928, Chapter 3.
8   For variations on this theme see, in particular, J. E. Cronin and J. Schneer, *Social Conflict and the Political Order in Modern Britain* (1982), Chapter 6; K. Burgess, *The Challenge of Labour* (1980); and J. Skelley (ed.), *The General Strike, 1926* (1976).
9   PRO, Cab 23/9, WC 526, 4 February 1919. The phrase is Bonar Law's.
10  S. Armitage, *The Politics of Decontrol of Industry* (1969), p. 160. For a fuller justification of the argument in the succeeding paragraph, see R. Lowe, 'The failure of consensus in Britain: the National Industrial Conference, 1919–21', *The Historical Journal*, 21 (1978), pp. 649–75.
11  PRO Lab 10/66. TUC opposition was aroused despite the fact that the initial resort to arbitration was the voluntary decision of both parties and (inevitably) that the trade union side at the NIC had demanded such a reform.
12  Sir R. Horne to Lloyd George, 14 December 1919; Lloyd George Papers, House of Lords Record Office, F27/6/27.
13  PRO Cab 63/29. For the best analysis of Lloyd George's contribution to industrial relations after 1918, see P. Rowland, *Lloyd George* (1975); and K. O. Morgan, *Consensus and Disunity* (1979). See also W. S. Adams, 'Lloyd George and the Labour Movement', *Past and Present*, 3 (1953), pp. 55–64.
14  The definitive account of Britain's emergency services is K. Jeffery and P. Hennessy, *States of Emergency* (1983).
15  R. Lowe, 'The erosion of state intervention in Britain, 1917–24', *Economic History Review*, 31 (1978), pp. 270–86.

16   Cab 24/128, CP 3308, 15 September 1921.

17   *The Times*, 7 November 1923. The succeeding remarks by Baldwin are quoted in K. Middlemas and J. Barnes, *Baldwin* (1969), pp. 297, 380–1.

18   Hence Bevin's statement to the TUC Conference in 1928 that 'the difference between a politician and an industrial leader is this: that our party is working for change, but the industrial leader has every day of his life to deal with facts as they are'. TUC, *Annual Report* (1928), p. 448.

19   Hence Baldwin's observation that 'what is called political interference in the mining industry has been entirely due to the incapacity of that industry unlike other industries . . . to settle its disputes for itself'. Quoted in E. Wigham, *Strikes and the Government, 1893–1974* (1976), p. 65. The best accounts of the General Strike are G. Phillips, *The General Strike* (1976); and M. Morris, *The General Strike* (1976). See also A. Mason, 'The Government and the General Strike', *International Review of Social History*, 14 (1968), pp. 1–21.

20   The definitive analysis of the Act is A. Anderson, 'The Labour Laws and the Cabinet Legislative Committee of 1926–7', *Bulletin of the Society for the Study of Labour History*, 23 (1971), pp. 39–52. Significantly, at a time when the Labour Party controlled a minority of authorities, the victimisation of trade unionists was also banned by the Act; but, as with the Emergency Powers Act, the vagueness of the Act's wording makes its interpretation a matter not just of the empirical observation of ministers' recorded intentions but also of faith.

21   PRO, Lab 2/1029/TB 357/1924; R. Lowe, 'Hours of Labour', *Economic History Review*, 35 (1982), pp. 258–9. See also, Jeffery and Hennessy, *op. cit.*, Chapter 4, which conclusively refutes J. C. C. Davidson's gossip about the Labour Cabinet's ignorance of the STO.

22   K. Middlemas, *Politics in Industrial Society* (1979), passim.

23   B. Bercusson, *Fair Wages Resolutions* (1978), p. 219.

24   Thus Wilson reported in May 1938: 'Sir Walter Citrine reminds me that if it were suggested by any of his colleagues that the armaments industry should be nationalized so as to avoid profiteering, it would be well to point out that the experience of France shows the difficulty of getting adequate production when armament firms are nationalized.' PRO Prem 1/251.

25   R. V. Vernon and N. Mansergh, *Advisory Bodies* (1940), p. 296.

26   See above, p. 188. See also K. G. J. C. Knowles, *Strikes* (1954), Ch. 2; and the review of *Politics in Industrial Society* by B. Supple in *Economic History Review*, 33 (1980), pp. 432–7.

27   R. A. C. Parker, 'British Rearmament 1936–9', *English Historical Review*, 96 (1981), p. 339.

28   Whereas the EAC collapsed, its sub-committees survived as a vital point of contact for civil servants and economists.

29   Lowe, 'Hours of Labour', *op. cit.*, pp. 268–71.

30   R. P. Shay, *British Rearmament in the Thirties* (1977), p. 125; S.

Blank, *Industry and Government in Britain* (1973), p. 30; 'Reconstruction Policy', October 1942, in Lithgow Papers, 34; Glasgow University.

31  H. Jones, 'Employers' welfare schemes and industrial relations in inter-war Britain', *Business History*, 25 (1983), p. 72. R. Roberts 'The Board of Trade, 1925–39' (unpublished D. Phil, Oxford University, 1986). I am indebted to Dr Roberts for exhaustive discussions on the interwar Board of Trade.

32  Morgan, *op. cit.*, p. 51.

33  The phrase is that of A. E. Zimmern in Tom Jones Papers, C19; National Library of Wales. Zimmern was a mentor of Butler who left the Ministry in 1919 to become deputy director of the ILO.

34  Thus the head of the Treasury's Establishment Division protested: 'The Government is trying to set up a new state of things and the Treasury veto cannot be left in the state it has been.' PRO Lab 10/67. The Treasury soon gained its revenge, with the temporary suspension of arbitration (1922–25) and the permanent translation of Whitley councils, in Citrine's phrase, into circumlocution offices.

35  For the Ministry's full case, see PRO Lab 2/1822/CEB 451/2/1922 and Cab 27/167/E (Labour). In 1935, for instance, the Ministry had only 13 conciliation offices at headquarters and 10 in the provinces.

36  PRO Lab 2/921/IR 921/1922 and 933/IR 549/1922.

37  Vernon and Mansergh, *op. cit.*, p. 305, supplemented by *Annual Reports* of the Ministry of Labour. The formal decline in government influence between 1920 and 1939 is also reflected by the reduction of Whitley Councils, from 106 to 87, and of workers covered by trade boards from 3 to 1¼ million.

38  F. W. Leggett, 'The settlement of labour disputes in Great Britain', in E. Jackson, *Meeting of Minds* (1952), p. 674. Steel–Maitland Papers, GD 193/319; National Library of Scotland.

39  K. G. J. C. Knowles, *Strikes*, p. 65.

40  PRO Lab 2/880/IR 688 and 921/IR 190; Cab 27/327; Cab 24/182/CP 344 (26).

41  PRO 30/69/1/359 (12), Appendix 3, 1934. On the refusal, even by Labour governments, to submit draft legislation to the TUC before Parliament following the Hours Bill (which was an NIC Bill) and the Industrial Courts Act (deemed to be of special importance) in 1919, see PRO Lab 10/1 and 525.

42  Prem 1/251. T. W. Phillips (Permanent Secretary, Ministry of Labour), June 1938. His Ministry's considered opinion was that 'the boilermakers' district delegates in Barrow and Glasgow are of greater importance in regard to shipbuilding than all the members of the General Council'. PRO Cab 21/702.

43  PRO Lab 10/276 and 73. See also Bercusson, *op. cit.*, p. xix, 179.

44  PRO Lab 10/100. For the virtues of the earlier period see, for instance, PRO Lab 2/767/HQ 12018/7 and 433/WA 2419/1919.

# 6
# Social Welfare and Industrial Relations 1914–1939

*Noel Whiteside*

Throughout the twentieth century—and arguably well before that—central government has influenced both levels of wages and workers' access to the basics necessary for social support. This interference has included policies designed to encourage lower prices, the levying of indirect taxes, state subsidies to industry and the public funding of essential social services. Even complete non-intervention actually follows the same pattern; implicitly, such a policy assumes that market forces are the sole agencies capable of achieving the desired balance. Hence government policy has helped determine the cost of living and the spending power of the working population in a variety of ways, which are well removed from its activities in the field of industrial arbitration. Changes in policy have influenced—and have been influenced by—patterns of wage-bargaining and the nature of working-class organisation and politics.

From the late nineteenth century, arguments developed both within official and industrial circles over whether a minimum acceptable level of subsistence was to be obtained from industrial bargaining in a free market, or from state-provided welfare services. Such debates continued throughout the interwar period, reflecting changing assumptions about the demarcation between public and private responsibility in the provision of social support. Until the eve of the First World War itself, wages were assumed to be the mainstay of the worker and his dependants. Public expenditure on welfare was overwhelmingly directed to the very young, through elementary education, and latterly to the very old, through non-contributory pensions. While, arguably, pensions did provide a small means-tested supplement for the wage-earner, compulsory education positively added to working-class burdens because it removed the possibility of children contributing to the collective family income. By the outbreak of the Second World War, this pattern had been broken. The Exchequer was providing direct subsidies to wage-earners, principally through housing and financial help for the unemployed.

Of course, welfare issues had long exerted an influence on industrial relations. Organised labour had traditionally viewed with some suspicion those private systems, sponsored by some employers, which aimed to increase workers' loyalty to the firm, to contain—even pre-empt—the development of union organisation, and thus to prevent pressure on wages. Such industrial welfare schemes had sometimes developed in direct response to union-run benefit systems which were found among skilled workers' organisations in the late nineteenth century.[1] The growing intervention of the state had important new implications for industrial relations in the early twentieth century. First, the nature and purpose of the industrial wage changed and this required a re-evaluation of the scope of collective bargaining. Second, as a result of the rising importance of the 'social wage', trade union activities became directed not just to industry but, increasingly, to Whitehall and Parliament. This provoked a shift in the balance between the industrial and political wings of the labour movement. Finally, partly as a result of these developments, the ideological assumptions on which union organisation was based underwent a subtle change. By the outbreak of the Second World War, a much weaker movement was generally placing far less emphasis on the extension of union autonomy and control through the bargaining process and far more on the benefits to be gained from cooperation with central government. This was chiefly evident in labour policies promoting a centrally planned economy and state services.

This transformation of the nature of union politics and the purpose of collective bargaining is important. It is too often assumed that the extension of state welfare was simply the consequence of political pressure from organised labour and that official national insurance schemes were an extension of earlier trade union practices. Closer examination shows this analysis is partial. Collective solutions to social problems did not command the universal support of the industrial labour movement in the early twentieth century. While consensus existed among trade unionists about the desirability of publicly-funded schemes for education and housing, it collapsed abruptly in areas where industrial bargaining and potential state welfare overlapped—for example, in debates over the maintenance of schoolchildren and the introduction of national social insurance. Established skilled unions suspected that extensive systems of state support might limit the scope for industrial bargaining and provide employers with a ready excuse for reducing wages. Moreover, a public alternative to the benefits such unions provided might corrode membership loyalty and weaken organisation. It is only among general labour leaders, whose bargaining powers were weak and organisation unstable, that support for extensive state intervention was found. Aside from these conflicts over the demarcation between industrial and political spheres, further disagreements existed over the degree of central control necessary or desirable for the promotion of working class interests. In the immediate post-war years at least, the labour movement wanted central regulations to be disbanded and, in keeping with its democratic tradition, greater autonomy to be restored to the local authority and to shopfloor bargaining. Universality and uniformity were less important aims than the desire to extend rank-and-file influence over local political and industrial conditions.

The following analysis of the changing relationship between the 'social' and 'industrial' wage, and its importance for our understanding of the interwar period, draws on two areas of historical study which are commonly discussed separately. Recent research in the field of industrial relations has been largely preoccupied with analysing the struggle for control over the production process, while social policy history has tended to concentrate on tracing the antecedents of the 'welfare state'. By looking at both these fields, this chapter will focus on the general political debate linking these issues. It will look specifically at state social insurance; the opposition, found among certain unions, to the extension of official unemployment insurance during and after the First World War contrasts strongly with the general acclaim greeting Beveridge's plan for a comprehensive scheme in 1942. The first section will show why union-based benefits lost their viability as an alternative to state welfare in the interwar period; the second demonstrates how the impact of mass unemployment changed the attitudes of both sides of industry towards state social insurance. This is followed by an assessment of how the provision of state benefits influenced industrial bargaining and wages and a short concluding section on the changes found in the scope of industrial relations and the nature of trade unionism which occurred in the interwar period.

## II

Many major trade unions gave their members some form of protection against the threat of destitution before the First World War. This provision of 'friendly' and 'trade' benefits offered advantages to both members and organisation: it helped the trade unionist in his search for work while offering some income when sickness, accident, redundancy or trade dispute removed his chance of employment. It also reinforced loyalty to the trade (as lapsed contributions meant forfeiting the right to benefit). It thus allowed the union branch the means to police working agreements and trade practices and to discipline members who transgressed them. In certain trades, the union branch would expect members to come automatically on to dispute or unemployment pay should their employer break an established industrial agreement. Hence the process of industrial bargaining, in a number of unions, was reinforced by the provision of benefits which served to enforce the rulebook. These practices were most successful in older craft or skilled unions, where bargaining procedures were recognised and wages could be maintained at the high level necessary to maintain heavy union dues, which were required to fund such schemes. Union benefits were less important for the numbers they covered (which were small) than for the tradition they embodied and the example they set. They were even imitated by general labour organisations, notably the Workers' Union, whose remarkable expansion in the early decades of the twentieth century probably owed much to its provision of cash benefits to unemployed members.[2]

Hence industrial labour regarded the expansion of state social welfare with some ambivalence. While arguing strongly in favour of greater public expenditure on housing and education, the TUC looked to the government to guarantee full employment and to enforce fair wages, not to sponsor state social insurance. In the event, the National Insurance Act 1911, which provided universal health benefits and protection against unemployment in a limited number of trades, was accepted (if not universally welcomed) because it allowed unions to register as official agencies for the provision of benefits under both insurance schemes. These apparent advantages, however, could not compensate for the schemes' drawbacks, which, basically, stemmed from the introduction of uniform regulations and central supervision over a wide variety of trade practices. This was particularly true in the area of unemployment. First, benefit was refused to all losing work due to an industrial dispute (whether or not they were directly involved) and to any workers who left work voluntarily or were dismissed by their employer for whatever reason. Hence the preoccupation of official regulations—namely, to safeguard the taxpayer's contribution from 'abuse'—came into direct conflict with the purpose of trade union schemes, which aimed to use benefits to enforce trade agreements. Moreover, the state scheme assumed that the common response to industrial recession was redundancy; in some sectors—notably coal mining and textiles (as well as other quasi-casual trades)—falling production was traditionally met by systems of work-sharing and short-time employment. These workers would gain nothing from the official scheme; they would be required to pay contributions while working arrangements would disqualify them from receipt of benefit.

Hence the opposition within the TUC to the state unemployment scheme revived when its official extension was before Parliament both in 1916 and in 1919–20.[3] General labour leaders had always objected to an official contributory system as being an unfair tax on the low paid; it was this group who gave the most vociferous support to the slogan 'work or maintenance' and demanded that the taxpayer bear the cost of supporting the unemployed. At the other end of the spectrum, a number of labour leaders could boast—in the context of full employment—that their unions could offer better benefits for lower contributions than could the official alternative. There was no reason why other members of the working class should subsidise the cost of unemployment in less stable sectors of the community. Again, an appeal was made for the Exchequer to make up the difference. In general, unions agreed that membership of the official unemployment scheme should be voluntary and that specific industries or trades be allowed to 'contract out' of its provisions. In 1920, woollen textiles, printing, boots and shoes, wire-making, and insurance and banking all tried to negotiate their way out of national unemployment insurance. Similarly, the cotton unions tried to perpetuate the system, established by the Cotton Control Board during the war, of a 'make-up' wage to subsidise short-time workers. This had been funded not by contributions but by a levy on the trade and administered through union branches. Likewise Ernest Bevin, seeking to remedy the under-employment experienced by casual dock workers, argued before a public enquiry that a levy on goods going through the ports should be introduced to finance a minimum maintenance wage for port workers.[4]

Increased union organisation and the rising power of labour at the workplace, both the consequence of the war, help explain the evident shift of opinion away from state regulation and towards 'home rule for industry' after the Armistice. Hence central control of the unemployed was, in a number of sectors, rejected in favour of restoring powers over the allocation of work to the union branch. This not only reinforced organisation, but allowed both access to the job market and the provision of relief to be negotiated according to prevailing industrial conditions and agreements, rather than be subject to uniform—sometimes alien—regulations. Disenchantment with collectivist solutions to labour market problems was not confined to the unions alone. Evidence presented to official enquiries in 1919 and 1920 demonstrated repeatedly that many employers still preferred to use the union branch when recruiting extra hands; local union officers knew their members and the nature of the work in a way the employment exchange officials never could.[5] The prevailing trend towards this extension of the sphere of industrial bargaining is reflected in the membership figures for unions providing benefit; in 1916, these had stood at 1,016,500 and rose to 4,108,000 by 1921, or around half the membership of the TUC.[6] Even the London Dockers' Union managed to initiate its own, rather short-lived, unemployment benefit scheme in the summer of 1920.

Yet the years immediately after the Armistice proved to be the high point not only of union organisation, but also of this drive to broaden the sphere of collective bargaining, thereby reinforcing union autonomy. From 1922, TUC policy became more coherent; interest in 'insurance by industry' or 'contracting out' of the state scheme waned dramatically. A ballot of trade unions conducted by the TUC in 1923 revealed that, although a number of small organisations—chiefly in textiles, printing, iron and steel and the distributive trades—still supported the principle, twice as many trade unionists (led by the Triple Alliance) opposed it.[7] Sectional special pleading was rejected in favour of working-class unity; the problem of unemployment was a national one and its solution demanded legislative action. Hence the TUC started promoting policies designed to secure industrial recovery, to vest government with the responsibility of providing work and, by the late 1920s, to restrict the numbers competing on the labour market.[8] As always, the provision of work took precedence over questions of maintenance; however, in this sector, industrial solutions were rejected in favour of non-contributory Exchequer-funded benefits, at subsistence levels, which were to be administered through the trade unions themselves.[9]

This conversion from industry-based to government-based solutions to the problems of the labour market is chiefly explained by developments in industrial relations in the early 1920s and by the corrosion of union bargaining power. Three aspects merit particular attention: first the impact of the war generally on industrial wage structures; second, the collapse of the staple export trades where the tradition of union benefits was particularly strong; and finally, the concessions won by the labour movement from central government on behalf of the unemployed. By the mid-1920s, official insurance schemes were operating on the principle of 'work or maintenance' in all but name.

The first of these developments sprang from broad, structural changes in the nature of industrial production during the war and the strategies developed by skilled unions to contain the impact of technological advance on their bargaining position. Union benefits reflected and reinforced craft autonomy and craft control; these had been under attack in specific sectors for some time and were further undermined by the impact of the war emergency.[10] Compulsory official arbitration in industrial disputes also changed the basis for assessing wage claims. In the absence (in many industrial sectors) of a 'free market' within which the value of the product could be determined and thus the value of labour ascertained, the Committee on Production pioneered the use of the cost of living index for the purposes of fixing wages and war bonuses. Rising prices hit the skilled and the unskilled alike; the result was a narrowing of differentials.[11] Although the 'state of trade' was made an additional criterion by the Industrial Court in 1919, the wages of a large number of workers—about 2.75 million by 1921—remained pegged to sliding-scale agreements. As a result, falling prices introduced about half the wage cuts imposed in 1921 and 40 per cent of the reductions imposed the following year.[12] Although the official cost of living index was subject to fierce criticism by the union movement—and not without justification—industrial labour was not able to withstand this onslaught on wages, especially in the traditional export trades.

An official survey carried out in the mid-1920s revealed the impact of these developments on the structure of wages.[13] Although, overall, wages had stayed marginally ahead of the cost of living, this average concealed very wide variations in experience. Builders' labourers, electricity and gas workers, railway workers and those in the printing trades had doubled their wage rates since the pre-war period. By contrast, skilled men in engineering, ship-building and iron and steel had failed to keep up with the cost of living. Hence considerable overlap existed in the wage rates for skilled and unskilled; in London, bus drivers and dustmen could get paid more than engineers. Higher unemployment and proportionately lower wages among skilled workers in the old staple export trades made it increasingly difficult for their unions to raise the high contributions necessary to fund comprehensive systems of support.

The effects of general structural factors were, of course, exacerbated by the extension of membership by the Engineers, the Iron-founders and other skilled unions in metals and ship-building to semi-skilled men.[14] This strategy was designed to contain the impact of machine tools and mechanised production processes on union control over the nature and distribution of work. New recruits were attracted by the benefits these unions offered; they were, however, less capable of paying heavy dues, more liable to unemployment and therefore most likely to claim on union funds. Engineering, ship-building and metals had all expanded their capacity during the war; the collapse of these industries in the 1920s therefore placed enormous strains on union finances.

The experience of the ironfounders in the early 1920s proved fairly typical. The option of raising contributions or imposing regular levies risked alienating those members in work, especially as wages here were lower, in real terms, than they had been before the war. With the bank balance badly depleted by a lengthy strike in 1919 and the gap between income and liabilities showing no signs of diminishing, the Foundry Workers' Union drifted through the 1920s, keeping the ship afloat by cutting benefit rates, restricting periods of access and raising loans from a variety of sources.[15] The engineers were less fortunate; during 1921, the AEU paid out £2 million in unemployment pay alone. Between March and June the following year, the Engineering Employers' Federation locked out union members. Between 1920 and 1922 financial reserves fell from £3.25 million to £32,572; all benefits (except superannuation) were suspended and, by January 1923, 25 per cent of the AEU's members were lost.[16] Of course, the few unions recruiting unskilled workers and paying friendly benefits proved the most vulnerable of all. The largest general union in 1920, the Workers' Union, maintained its commitment to support its unemployed. In 1928, its finances exhausted and membership gone, the sad remnant merged with the Transport and General Workers' Union.[17] During 1921 alone, the union movement paid out £15.5 million in unemployment pay. The ability to maintain this commitment was limited; by 1925, the numbers able to claim unemployment benefit from their union had fallen from over 4 million to under 1 million.[18] Numbers registered with trade union 'approved societies' under the state health insurance scheme were little higher.[19] Although these included members of small, relatively well-funded craft societies, a substantial proportion covered workers no commercial society would recruit, like the miners. The old association between industrial organisation and welfare protection had apparently been broken.

This is not to argue that industrial labour was unsuccessful in winning protection for its members in this period; if anything, the opposite was the case. The extension of the franchise in 1918, coupled with pressure by the TUC and the National Unemployed Workers' Movement on central and local government, paid off very well. In a variety of Labour-dominated Poor Law Unions—notably in South Wales, East London and the North-East—outdoor relief for the unemployed became increasingly generous; between 1921 and 1922 expenditure in this sector rose by £10 million.[20] Concessions from the coalition government (1918–22) were even more impressive. Out-of-Work Donation, introduced to civilian and military unemployed after the Armistice and extended in 1919, offered rates of pay on a non-contributory basis to the unemployed and their families, which put the 7 shillings available under the National Insurance Act 1911 in the shade.[21] Before the Unemployment Insurance Act 1920 was barely operative, amending legislation raised the basic rates of benefit from 15 shillings to 20 shillings a week, extended periods of access and, later, introduced allowances for dependants. Public expenditure in support of the unemployed nearly doubled between 1921 and 1922; the Unemployment Fund lost its actuarial viability as benefits available under the state insurance scheme alone rose from £9.7 million to £62.17 million in this period.[22] As a result, the relationship between union and state benefits changed. In 1911, the state benefit of 7 shillings had supplemented the 10 shillings, 12 shillings or even 14 shillings which some unions could offer as unemployment pay.[23] After the war, the position was reversed; many societies experienced serious difficulties in providing benefit at one third the national rate. Indeed, between 1921 and 1925, 75 per cent actually failed to do so.[24] As prices fell, especially during the slump, the real value of state benefits rose; revisions in basic rates introduced between 1920 and 1932 never reversed this general trend. Although access to 'extended benefit' (claimed without adequate contributions) was discretionary, all successful claims were paid at the full rate. Hence the advent of the means test in the 1930s, with its concomitant reductions and disallowances, was so unpopular because it not only contravened the principle of benefit as of right but also reduced, in some cases substantially, the rate of relief available to claimants.

In the interim, however, the greater part of the union movement became convinced of the advantages to be gained by bargaining with the state, especially as the uneven impact of the recession made trade-based benefits less feasible in many sectors. However, this conversion was neither universal nor uniform. In sheltered sectors of employment—notably in printing, among skilled workers in specialist sectors such as book-binding, lace-making, furniture-making and among the distributive trades—the tradition of union-funded benefits survived the interwar period.[25] Moreover, state-based welfare was welcome as long as it supported wage rates and reinforced collective bargaining, which unemployment insurance arguably did. Other measures which might be used to reduce wages, notably the introduction of family allowances, met with a much more equivocal response.[26] For similar reasons, the industrial labour movement came to support the idea of contributory welfare, or a 'levy on incomes' as the TUC phrased it in the early 1930s, because such a system associated welfare rights with the earning of wages and thus helped the trade union member.[27] In the 1930s the Association of Trade Union Approved Societies continued to maintain that access to the Labour Party's proposed free national system of health care ought to be based on contributions.[28] This was not to argue that deductions from the wage packet should be the sole source of welfare funding; in order to gain greater financial support from the national Exchequer, the TUC became more involved in broader political debates surrounding social insurance issues.

### III

It was the measures passed by the Lloyd George government in the years following the Armistice—both in extending the unemployment insurance scheme and in granting 'temporary' extended access to all forms of state benefits for the unemployed—which transformed the assumptions on which national insurance had been founded. Both parts of the 1911 Act had included various financial incentives to encourage employers to regularise employment; under unemployment insurance, reimbursement was available to both contributors if claims were low.[29] Beveridge himself, as one of the principal architects of the original unemployment scheme, subsequently claimed that the system aimed to be flexible. It was designed to foster the growth of insurance by individual industries, to allow a little variance in contributory rates between trades, to make the state contribution compensate for the higher unemployment experienced in some sectors and to allow payment of the premium generally to come more in line with the level of risk, as was (and is) the practice under commercial insurance systems.[30] Such considerations largely went by the board in 1920, thanks to the preoccupation inside Whitehall in general and the Treasury in particular with the need to contain public expenditure and to limit future official liability. Hence the 1920 Act extended the unemployment scheme designed for engineering, construction and ship-building to virtually all manual trades. Provision to allow whole industries (not trades) to contract out of the state scheme, thus allowing unemployment pay to correspond with work patterns in particular sectors, was included—but only on the most disadvantageous terms. The Treasury made no secret of the reasons behind this policy of universal uniformity; under the extended system, 'good' trades would indirectly compensate for the bad.[31] In the event, this meant not that skilled workers' contributions paid for unskilled benefits (as many in the TUC had argued they would) but that the scheme allowed sheltered trades, where wages tended to be higher, to provide a subsidy to the staple export sector, where unemployment proved most long-lived.

Pre-war legislation had been based on the assumption that social insurance was essentially a system of wage spreading; as Beveridge put it to the Royal Commission on Unemployment Insurance:

> we want to insist that everybody keeps something in hand for a rainy day—not all that is wanted, and that is all that insurance was—a compulsory spreading of the remuneration of labour from good times into bad times so that there might be something for the rainy day and we hoped that each individual would have other resources as well.[32]

Although the 1920 Act went some way towards modifying this individualistic approach, the most fundamental breach in the principle developed from the introduction in 1921 of 'uncovenanted' benefits, later termed 'extended' benefits and (after 1928) 'transitional' benefits, all of which allowed claims to be lodged in advance of contributions. The burden imposed on the Unemployment Fund was exacerbated by the introduction of dependants' allowances the same year. Between November 1920 and July 1923, the unemployment scheme collected £73.5 million in contributions and paid out £128 million in benefits.[33] The surplus accumulated in the period 1911–20 vanished abruptly and the first in a long series of Exchequer loans, designed to meet a temporary emergency, was introduced to bridge the gap between contributions and claims. All clauses allowing 'contracting out' or refunds to industry were suspended (later abolished) in the early 1920s. Mass unemployment undermined the actuarial viability of unemployment insurance; the Fund's debts seemed irredeemable. By the early 1930s, these developments, coupled with the falling importance of union benefits, had changed the national unemployment scheme from an officially sponsored system designed to foster voluntary insurance to a publicly-funded state service.[34]

Unemployment insurance was not the only scheme so trans-formed. Contributory social insurance enjoyed a period of considerable popularity in ruling circles during the years following the First World War; it appeared to offer the extension of social protection in the immediate term while limiting, even perhaps reducing, public expenditure in the long run. Extensive investigations took place in the early 1920s with the aim of rationalising existing national schemes and extending the scope of state insurance. This type of solution also promised to solve the vexed problem of the Poor Law. Such a programme won the support of all three political parties during the general election in 1923.[35] Contributory pensions for the 65–70 age group, with coverage for widows and orphans, were introduced in 1925, on the assumption that the joint contributions to the fund set up to provide these benefits would eventually finance all old age pensions. Thus industry would relieve the Exchequer of the burden imposed by the non-contributory pension scheme for those over 70 years. The impact of the recession made this objective unfeasible during the interwar period.[36] In an era of mass unemployment, it proved impossible for any contributory insurance scheme to remain both universal in coverage and financially sound; contributions fell while claims rose. In practice, furthermore, it was politically suicidal to resist the claims of those whose contributory record had lapsed. Rights to health benefits and pensions were periodically redefined and extended, in much the same fashion as occurred with the unemployment scheme, and this prevented any reduction in public liability. In an effort to contain benefit expenditure, officials in the Ministries of Health and Labour encouraged the stricter surveillance of claimants by approved societies, labour exchanges and relieving officers during the 1920s.[37] The following decade, similar motives lay behind the introduction of comprehensive means testing.

The question of who was to pay for these extensions and concessions dominated social policy debates until the mid 1930s. State insurance assumed tripartite funding; as unemployment rose and resources dwindled, governments raised the joint industrial contribution in order to rescue the Unemployment Fund from debt. Between 1920 and 1922, the industrial contribution under the unemployment scheme alone rose from 8d to 1s 7d.[38] With the Widows, Orphans and Old Age Pensions Bill pending in 1924–25, this looked set for further expansion—a development welcomed by neither side of industry. Naturally the TUC welcomed the introduction of extended benefits under both health and unemployment schemes, together with Lloyd George's expanded programme of public works, as an initial step towards state provision of 'work or maintenance'. On the other hand, unions remained in constant opposition to official restrictions on rates of benefit and terms of access and opposed the retention of a contributory principle. Using assumptions based loosely on Hobson's theories of economic growth, union spokesmen at a variety of public enquiries denied the validity of wage cuts as a stimulus to industrial expansion and continued to demand that the 'insurance principle' be formally abandoned, that the financial basis of state-sponsored benefits be broadened, that rates be equivalent to 'full maintenance', and that distinctions between different 'classes' of unemployed (granting of extended benefits was subject to official discretion) be abolished.[39] At grassroots level, labour activists sought to achieve their aims through other means, notably the more generous provision of outdoor relief to the unemployed. In the winter of 1921–22, about 200 industrial Poor Law Unions stood officially accused of 'lax' administration. Under pressure from the National Confederation of Employers' Organisations (NCEO), the National Union of Manufacturers (NUM) and the Conservative Party, the coalition government took steps to contain the incidence of 'topping up' unemployment benefit under the Poor Law.[40] Between 1923 and 1927, this officially fell from 10 to 2.4 per cent of the unemployed. As sickness and disablement benefits were at a substantially lower rate, containing claims for outdoor relief in this sector proved less easy.

The NCEO, like the TUC, also resented the rising burden on industry imposed by social insurance systems, but there agreement ended. Far from demanding more liberal access and more generous benefits, organised employers from the early 1920s tended to argue that social welfare expenditure was a barrier to industrial recovery. They therefore supported a return to the principles of 1911—namely, a limited system of state social insurance coupled with a deterrent Poor Law. Indeed, it was the NCEO which first established an explicit link between the 'social' and the 'industrial' wage, for, under the systems operating in the early 1920s, both impinged on the question of overseas competitiveness through their impact on overall industrial costs. Not surprisingly, employers' views on the desirability of national schemes of social insurance were not uniform; their perception varied according to their market position in much the same fashion as the trade unions. The NUM, recruiting largely in new industries and sheltered trades, proved more in favour of promoting insurance by industry than did the NCEO. Confederation members, which included many firms in engineering, ship-building, metals and old staple export trades, feared the financial consequences for themselves if profitable sectors were allowed to waive their obligations under a national scheme. At the same time, there was no inherent reason why those without work should be an industrial charge. Hence the NCEO demanded repeatedly that extended benefits be abolished, that administration be tightened (thereby excluding union adminis- tration of benefits to members), that Exchequer contributions be raised, and that claimants who had exhausted their rights under the scheme be thrown back on the Poor Law.[41]

The formal submission of these demands in the spring of 1925[42], stimulated by the impending extension of social insurance under the Widows, Orphans and Old Age Pensions Bill, made little immediate impact on the Baldwin government's policies. A campaign to tighten up administration of benefits and relief was initiated, but verbal concessions made to the NCEO were subsequently rescinded; the Economy Act of 1925 showed that the Cabinet preferred to save on public expenditure at the expense of industrial costs. Throughout the 1920s, governments continued to transfer the cost of unemployment on to industry and local government. During the late 1920s, overt conflict existed between government and the industrial export sector over financial priorities in this area.[43]

It was only after the fall of the second Labour government in 1931 that the NCEO view fell more in line with Conservative Party policy. At the request of both sides of industry, transitional benefits had been transferred to the Exchequer in 1930. In the same year, Labour backbench pressure reduced restrictions on unemployment benefits; as the slump hit, so public expenditure soared. Following the report of the May Committee, the Labour Cabinet split over its recommendations to cut benefits (which had been vociferously opposed by the TUC) and the government fell. The political settle- ment reached under the 1934 Act was evidently more in line with

NCEO thinking on unemployment relief.[44] Although industrial contributions were not cut, unemployment insurance was restored to an actuarily-sound basis. Means-tested relief, funded by the Exchequer and administered by the Unemployment Assistance Board, was made available to those who had exhausted their rights under the insurance scheme and the provision of cash benefits was thus isolated from political influences. Other claimants for relief came under the aegis of the local rate-funded Public Assistance Committees which had taken over most of the responsibilities of the Poor Law Guardians under the Local Government Act 1929. Albeit that the new national scales of relief were not as stringent as the NCEO would have liked, the whole system was far more in line with the Confederation's philosophy than it was with the policies of the TUC.[45] The assumptions underlying the practice of the Unemployment Assistance Board totally contradicted union arguments that subsistence benefits should be universally provided. As claims could be partially, or even completely, disallowed, the new scheme arguably offered less protection to wages than the system that had prevailed in the 1920s.

However, these changes did not visibly lighten the burden imposed by social welfare on the Exchequer. The most cursory scrutiny of public expenditure in this area shows that the historical reputation of the interwar period, as being one of stagnation in social policy development, is hardly well merited. Repeated official efforts to contain, or even reduce, expenditure on the social services met with little success. Overall costs in the field rose from £62.807 million in 1910 to £306.634 million a decade later. Over the next fifteen years, these expanded further, to reach £503.783 million in 1935, even though prices fell overall during this period.[46] Part of this expansion can be explained by the introduction of new programmes, notably contributory pensions and the extension of public subsidies for housing and slum clearance schemes; these, however, account for less than £82 million of the escalating costs between 1920 and 1935. In any case, expenditure on war pensions fell by £54.53 million in the same period.[47] To explain the balance, we must conclude that rising public liability reflected the consequences of mass unemployment and general increasing reliance on state schemes.

An examination of how state welfare was funded further substantiates this conclusion. As indicated above, mass unemployment played havoc with the actuarial bases of the various state social insurance schemes; the consequences of this are broadly reflected in the following table.

Table 6.1: *Great Britain: Public social services: Analysis of receipts from which annual expenditure was met (local and central government)*[48]

(£ millions)

|  | 1922 | 1932 | 1935 |
|---|---|---|---|
| Receipts from contributions, fees, interest and rents | 182.297 | 131.439 | 147.928 |
| Parliamentary votes (general) | 190.950 | 233.295 | 234.815 |
| Local rates and Parliamentary block grants | 86.901 | 107.645 | 119.584 |

Recipients of welfare were unable to meet their statutory obligations under social welfare schemes; this was particularly evident in the areas of housing and social insurance. In spite of repeated efforts, especially by Conservative governments, to make state welfare financially self-sufficient, even commercially viable, subventions by the taxpayer and the ratepayer proved essential in order to keep the show on the road. Although subject to indirect taxation, only a tiny minority of the industrial workforce earned wages above the income tax threshold. In simple material terms, public funds played an increasingly significant part in supplementing the living standards of the working class.

## IV

It remains to assess how these developments in social insurance and the general expansion of state welfare influenced industrial bargaining in the interwar period. The rising significance of the social wage certainly helps explain why levels of poverty experienced in Edwardian Britain did not reappear in the interwar years. However, it seems that the poorest in the community were not necessarily the main recipients of public largesse. The main beneficiaries of official social benefits were the unionised sectors of the labour force. Those groups who were marginal to industrial production, notably the unorganised, the unskilled and women workers, were the chief victims of official parsimony.

Contemporary and subsequent investigations into unemployment in this period revealed time and again that its incidence was highest among the unorganised and unskilled in the depressed areas, who thereby failed to maintain their contributions, were more likely to be subject to the exercise of official discretion in the 1920s and were subject to means testing in the 1930s.[49] In the drive to eliminate 'scroungers' and 'malingerers' from dependence on public funds, women workers in general and married women workers in particular, received more than their fair share of official attention. Under the employment scheme, they were the principal target for the 'not genuinely seeking work' regulation introduced in 1922, because their family commitments tended to limit their mobility. Under official encouragement, employment exchanges offered many women claimants domestic service. If they refused, benefit could be disallowed under statutory regulations; if they accepted, they left the unemployment scheme altogether as domestic service was not an 'insured trade'.[50] Only in the North-West and parts of the Midlands, where housemaids and cleaners were not in high demand and where married women's industrial employment was commonplace, did women workers retain their right to unemployment benefit in substantial numbers.[51]

Disqualification in one sector was subsequently reflected in another; married women's claims to sickness benefit—already unexpectedly high before the war—grew disproportionately during the 1920s. Again, the official response was directed at the stricter policing of claims from this group, with a view to their disallowance. The impact of the slump further exacerbated the problem. In the new drive for public economy in the early 1930s, married women's benefit rates under both schemes were cut and, under the Anomalies Act 1931, their rights to means-tested transitional payments (later unemployment assistance) virtually disappeared.[52]

Economic historians have concluded, not surprisingly, that state social insurance was generally advantageous to the industrial workforce. During the 1920s, the cost of living fell by 43 per cent, wages by 33 per cent, while unemployment benefit for a family of four doubled from 15 shillings to 30 shillings a week: it was also available for longer periods.[53] By the 1930s, the possibility that state benefits might be higher than wages, especially for large families, excited public controversy; the effects of 'the dole' on wage levels and work incentives has long been a contentious subject. Two American historians have recently sought to demonstrate that levels of unemployment in interwar Britain were raised by the availability of benefits. The unemployed, thanks to state help, were able to prolong their search for work and could thereby avoid low-paid jobs and bad conditions. By contrasting the unemployment experience of women, juveniles and adult males at this time, Benjamin and Kochin have shown that the higher rates of registered unemployment among the latter group were the direct consequence of the comparative ease with which they could get access to the Unemployment Fund.

This argument has provoked a storm of criticism.[54] It is important here because it infers that the existence of state benefits allowed the unemployed to evade low-waged work and therefore helped prevent wages falling in line with prices. If it is true that statutory benefits actually protected wage rates, they also indirectly strengthened the bargaining position of industrial labour. However, the idea that unemployment would have been lower had social insurance benefits not been available is somewhat contentious. For a start, Benjamin and Kochin's analysis assumes that registered unemployment rates and actual unemployment rates were one and the same. This is a mistake. We know that, deprived of the right to benefit, certain groups would cease to sign on but we cannot infer from this that they have either left the labour market or found work. In short, the interwar unemployment statistics are quite inappropriate for the type of analysis Benjamin and Kochin wish to make. They essentially record claims to benefit; there are many unemployed excluded from claiming and discouraged from signing on who never enter the equation at all.

Moreover, to argue that the unemployed preferred the dole to waged work—even for a short space of time—flies in the face of much contemporary evidence which points to quite different conclusions. There is little to suggest that those out of work were deliberately evading it. Although the Unemployment Assistance Board noted that numbers 'retiring' early from the labour market rose in the course of the 1930s, the majority of these were older men in depressed areas—notably miners—who were victims of the structural imbalances in the British economy and unlikely ever to find another job.[55] Numbers of vagrants and tramps rose dramatically in the early 1930s, much as they had done during recessions before the war. This was the result of a growing number of workers searching for work beyond their home district, and being unable to find it. Further, an official, but unpublished, review of attitudes of the unemployed in 1936 reinforced the conclusions already reached in the 1920s. Even the Ministry of Labour—a department with no sympathy for scroungers—could muster little evidence to support the conclusion that the unemployed were malingering at public expense.[56] The attitudes of the unemployed towards work and welfare were also subjected to more detailed scrutiny by a number of contemporary investigations undertaken by philanthropists and social psychologists. These found that the impact of unemployment produced a common set of reactions: initial optimism was swiftly replaced by desperation followed by a growing loss of self-esteem, apathy and depression: a picture fitting ill with the notion of unemployed workers carefully manipulating the system to their best pecuniary advantage.

Of course, the lynchpin of the argument, for present purposes, is less whether the existence of benefit affected the behaviour of the unemployed than whether state help actually reinforced wage rates. On first impression, there appears good reason to conclude that it did. According to the official statistics, the real value of wages certainly rose during the interwar period. Moreover, employment exchanges were required to publicise the trade union rate for the job and were prevented from disallowing benefit to those who refused to work for less than customary wages. Taken from this perspective, state social insurance appears to have helped union organisers by reinforcing industrial agreements.

On closer examination, however, the issue does not appear so clear-cut. Official wage statistics were compiled from collective agreements and these are far from a foolproof guide to changing levels of take-home pay in this period. First, the number of trade union members fell from over 8 million in 1920 to about 4.5 million in the early 1930s. Collective agreements thus covered a little over a quarter of the industrial labour force. It seems, moreover, arguable that those so covered represented the better-paid workers in their particular trades. It is also important to avoid equating wage rates with earnings. Official statistics and other compilations derived from them can take no account of earnings reduced by more intermittent employment experienced in casual trades during recession, by individual sickness or accident or by short-time working. The 'temporarily stopped' category (those who expected to return to their former employer within six weeks) hovered between a quarter and a third of the total number of unemployed throughout the interwar period. Naturally, as the 'count' was based on registrations for a particular day, we must roughly double this to arrive at the total number of the insured workforce subjected to a reduction in working hours or intermittent employment.

Hence the administration of state benefits did not automatically protect the union rate of pay, simply because 'customary wages' were not necessarily those arrived at by industrial bargaining. Furthermore, official benefit regulations were specifically designed to prevent unemployment insurance being used to safeguard wages. The operation of the 'trade dispute disqualification' clause, union spokesmen claimed, positively worked against the protection of negotiated rates of pay. This was particularly the case in the mining industry. The umpire deemed that any quittal of work, stoppage or works closure due to a disagreement over wages and conditions was an industrial dispute and therefore disallowed benefit to those thrown out of work as a result. This ruling covered any refusal by the workforce to accept a wage cut; in the coalfields, therefore, any coal-owner who claimed that he had closed his pit because the miners refused to work for lower wages could prevent them claiming unemployment benefit. This, for example, was happening just before the General Strike in 1926.[57] During the 1930s, benefit was similarly denied those refusing to work for an employer who unilaterally decided to breach a negotiated agreement on wages or hours. Hence the victims were thrown back on means-tested relief.[58] Thus we have no way of knowing how far negotiated wage rates, as reflected in official statistics, were ever observed. Unlike union-based benefits, the national insurance scheme did not provide the means to guarantee their enforcement.

In sectors where industrial relations were sour, welfare benefits did not necessarily help strengthen the position of organised labour and protect wages. Where they were good and employers cooperative, however, the state scheme could be adapted to mutual advantage. In the interwar period, this is chiefly illustrated by the use made by particular industries of state benefits to supplement incomes reduced by short-time working. Following the demise of union schemes and the abolition of 'contracting out', unions and management in particular sectors developed agreements designed to wring maximum possible benefit from the Unemployment Fund.

This response was officially disowned by both the Labour Party and TUC in 1921 because it allowed employers to reduce earnings while enlarging their workforce. The Cabinet saw, however, that subsidising of short-time working was a temporary solution to escalating unemployment and officially condoned the use of unemployment benefits for this purpose.[59] Of 3 million claims lodged at the Exchanges in June that year, one-third came from short-time workers.[60] The arrangement of working practices to comply with the scheme's continuity regulations were negotiated within industries where short-time had been the traditional response to industrial recession—notably in cotton textiles, in some Midlands collieries, in foundries, small metal manufacture, leather, clothing and some sectors of ship-building.[61] Similarly, on the docks, the T& GWU negotiated an agreement which allowed registered casuals to work the system to their advantage; the port transport industry alone contributed £6 million to the Unemployment Fund and drew out £22 million in benefit between 1921 and 1929. By the mid-1920s the Dyers Bleachers and Finishers Union were boasting that, through carefully negotiated working practices, they were 'carrying' a 60 per cent labour surplus in their trade.[62] In some depressed industries, such solutions proved popular by the late 1920s. Unlike the less well-organised unemployed, short-time claimants maintained their contributions and their claims were less liable to be subject to official discretion; similarly, in the 1930s, fewer fell prey to the means test. Official economy drives, notably in 1921 and 1931, attempted to contain the claims of seasonal and short-time workers. However, government policy could not eliminate such practices; it proved impossible to prevent working agreements being negotiated which allowed state benefits to supplement income in a fashion which must have made Edwin Chadwick turn in his grave.

However, the rising value of the social wage and its increasing importance in improving the lot of the industrial worker was not lost on industrial employers. The NCEO, fulfilling the prophecies made by skilled union leaders before the war, argued that the extension of state social services was a justification for lower wages. Hence the growth of state welfare infiltrated discussions at the bargaining table and in public debate; the relationship between the cost of living index and the industrial wage alone was no longer seen as a viable way of determining current trends in the workers' standard of living. Such arguments could also be used within Whitehall to justify the increasingly non-interventionist stance in industrial disputes which developed during the 1930s: 'for a generation past successive Parliaments have been building up a vast structure of social services by which the means of the wage earners are supplemented', a senior Treasury official wrote in a draft speech for the Chancellor. He continued:

> They are assisted in regard to education, health, housing and in the provision to be made against old age and unemployment and through our system of direct taxation a large part of the cost is met from the resources of the well-to-do, including the profits of industrialists and traders. In this way it is possible to improve the position of wage earners without causing the unemployment that would inevitably supervene if profits were encroached upon by a direct increase in wages.[63]

The scope of the argument about the nature and purpose of state welfare had undergone a transformation. Instead of simply giving an alternative means of support for those who were incapable of working, it now provided an essential component in the remuneration of labour. Although the above extract hardly reflects an established 'Treasury view', it does demonstrate the link between state welfare and the propagation of a low-wage economy. While trade unionism was industrially weak, such an equation was viable. The following decade was to demonstrate, however, that state welfare—however welcome—was not universally acceptable as a replacement for higher wages. During the post-war period, in the context of full employment, widespread shortages and the overriding need to increase exports, government came to face this fact and were thus forced to consider how wages also might be subject to greater central control.

## V

The nature and strength of collective bargaining in particular industries and trades provided the foundations for varying union attitudes towards the extension of public welfare. The association between wages and welfare also influenced the development of state social policies—notably during the First World War and in its immediate aftermath—thereby throwing into question traditional assumptions about the proper demarcation between 'political' and 'industrial' spheres of activity. In other words, the division between public provision and wage-bargaining became less distinct. In the post-Armistice period, both sides of industry were generally seeking to broaden the sphere of industrial bargaining and to dismantle central controls, while the Coalition government, disturbed by continuing evidence of extensive social and industrial unrest, sought to appease labour through the introduction of legislative solutions to their social discontents. Industrial recession and rising unemployment reversed this trend. As bargaining power diminished, so labour leaders turned increasingly to the state in order to safeguard their members' interests. Social security became established as an issue of public policy rather than one of individual private responsibility. Within the labour movement itself, this development was reflected in increasing acceptance of central regulation at the expense of local autonomy and in rising support for political—rather than industrial—measures to protect workers' living standards. This trend therefore implied a redefinition—indeed a diminution—in the scope of industrial bargaining and a much greater desire by both sides of industry to influence the development of policies inside Whitehall.

Rising unemployment and the general political commitment to public expenditure constraints transformed the nature of state social insurance and its relationship with the industrial sector. Whereas earlier initiatives were evidently designed to accommodate organised labour, by the late 1920s the emphasis became placed increasingly on the stricter policing of claimants and the exercise of greater central control. By the early 1930s, union involvement in the administration of unemployment benefits was regarded as positively counterproductive by the Ministry of Labour.[64] The chief safeguard against destitution for working people was provided by the state social insurance schemes, not by union benefits. Union branch administration made access to government benefits too easy as local branch secretaries could only place men in their trade with recognised employers; such privileges could not be justified on any grounds. By the 1930s, therefore, arguments supporting official parsimony and administrative uniformity both pointed to the exclusion of the union movement from questions of social security, which had become—for nearly all working people—the provenance of the public sector alone.

To assume that government policy in this area simply reflected the political requirements of industrial capital is both crude and misguided. In general, industrial employers did not support continuing state intervention in the provision of welfare. Such initiatives, the NCEO argued, raised industrial costs, protected wages, exacerbated unemployment by diverting potential funds for investment and by making British goods less competitive on over-seas markets. Social welfare, in short, was a major burden on industry. Little has been said about individual employers' attitudes in this chapter because comparatively little is known; however, it is clear that official unemployment and welfare policies in the interwar period did not reflect industrial employers' views. Although the two did coincide to a greater degree by the mid-1930s, employers appear to have been deeply critical of state initiatives during the 1920s. More advanced groups even sought a collaborative pact with the union movement in order to remove—or at least redirect—some of the more objectionable aspects of state intervention in industrial affairs. The Mond-Turner talks (1927–29) ultimately failed, but none the less showed that advanced employers thought that the recession could only be tackled by a radical change in fiscal policy and that the maintenance of the unemployed was a national problem and should not be viewed as a perpetual industrial liability.[65] Certainly many more conservative employers resented what they saw as lax and over-generous administration of state benefits and proposed that levels of state support should be made more responsive to market forces. Once managerial authority over the unions had been reasserted, the NCEO and its allies argued that high levels of social expenditure—just as much as high wages—were furthering indus-trial decline and undermining the work ethic.[66] How far such attitudes permeated collective bargaining, or were used unilaterally by employers to impose wage reductions or the removal of private welfare benefits, remains an open question.

The effect of interwar recession on union organisation and poli-tics was very marked. The period saw a decline in union autonomy and the scope for collective action and support, alongside a growing recognition that state provision was essential to protect workers' material needs. This change in policy, noted by a number of historians, coincided with a drop in political mobilisation and rank-and-file militancy and the emergence of central union leader-ship dedicated less to the politics of industrial conflict than to cooperation between organised labour, employers and the state.[67] This shift from the industrial to the public sphere was, however, born of union weakness not strength and, in the longer term, industrial impotence became reflected in political ineffectiveness. Although concessions made during the 1920s conferred substantial material benefits on working people, the hallmark of the politics of Citrine and Bevin during the 1930s was its spectacular lack of success. The TUC failed to break the hold of economic orthodoxy over the second Labour government, failed to secure the introduction of retirement pensions or the raising of the school-leaving age, failed to protect benefit rates or to promote any union policies designed to alleviate unemployment and promote industrial recovery. Even so, the importance of the 'social wage' in safeguarding working-class welfare was, by the 1930s, paramount. The TUC, following the tradition established by general labour and industrial unions, was drawn into closer cooperation with the Labour Party; this alliance provided the political foundations for the programme of social reforms in the late 1940s. Union support for Beveridge's social insurance proposals must therefore be understood in terms of the changing sphere of industrial relations and the general decline in union bargaining power.

These changes signified a fundamental alteration in the ideological foundations of British trade unionism. Official perceptions of working-class self-help had, since the late nineteenth century, distinguished the provision of 'friendly' benefits (which should be encouraged) from participation in trade activities (which should be contained). As already demonstrated, many older craft and skilled unions made no such distinction, but valued systems of union benefits because they reinforced industrial autonomy, helped control recruitment to the trade and—within limits—promoted workers' control of the production process at the workplace. Although such systems were more ideal than real, they did provide some kind of blueprint for union organisation and authority and were widely imitated in the early twentieth century. The interwar period witnessed a general change of strategy and the final divorce between 'friendly' and 'trade' activities. Greater material benefits were, however, bought at a price. State welfare was not strictly compatible with earlier union schemes. The latter had always given greatest protection to those losing work in defence of established trade agreements and practices. The official system, by contrast, penalised those whose unemployment was due—however indirectly—to an industrial dispute and gave greatest help to those willing to undertake any work at any price. The purpose and philosophy behind the two systems was very different.

The decline of old methods of craft regulation thus changed the basic nature of trade unionism. The demise of union benefits reflected the gradual disappearance of branch autonomy; organisational structures became increasingly bureaucratic and centralised. At the same time, the general effect of state benefits was to weaken the bonds that tied member to union. As a General Federation of Trades Unions' officer noted sadly in the mid-1930s, men who once had turned to their union in times of trouble now turned to the state. Certainly, in the early 1930s, membership of those organisations still offering union benefits proved more stable than those that did not; the generally helpful treatment of claimants to health or unemployment benefits by union officials contrasted with the more cursory reception found in official employment exchanges or among commercial insurance agencies.[68]

All these developments point to a redefinition in the scope and purpose of industrial bargaining which occurred in the interwar period. In the early twentieth century, established payment systems and working practices had clearly developed with a view to protecting those union members liable to suffer during periods of recession. Union benefits, in many ways, were but the final recourse of the elderly or surplus workers, whose access to work was also frequently protected by negotiated agreements designed to spread work, safeguard jobs and to prevent the ruthless employer from throwing older men on the scrap heap. In this way, the union branch attempted to define and protect the labour force working in the trade. The growth of state support made such safeguards less defensible. It certainly reduced the capacity for both sides of local industry to arrive at negotiated solutions to the problem of recession; state definitions of 'unemployment' and 'incapacity', together with general regulations concerning access to benefits, evidently helped shape industrial working agreements in the interwar period. How far such arrangements were conducive to the interests of industry or workers is hard to say; we might guess that the superimposition of uniform definitions on a wide variety of working practices provoked considerable disruption. Certainly central regulation in this area of social welfare did impinge on the autonomy of both sides of industry and, indirectly, introduced new factors into the field of collective bargaining. The expansion of state provision for working people drew both sides of industry towards Whitehall in order to protect their interests in the policy making process. Thus the sphere of collective bargaining was redefined and the nature of industrial politics was transformed.

## Acknowledgement

The author wishes to thank the Leverhulme Trust for its financial support for her research and Dr R. Lowe and Dr J. Melling for their helpful comments on earlier drafts of this chapter.

## Notes

1   J. Melling, 'Industrial Strife and Business Welfare Philosophy', *Business History*, XXI (1979); idem, 'Non-commissioned Officers: British Employers and their Supervisory Workers', *Social History* V (1980). See also Melling's contribution to H. Gospel and C. Littler (eds), *Management Strategies and Industrial Relations* (1983).
2   R. Hyman, *The Workers' Union* (1971), pp. 6 and 14.
3   N. Whiteside, 'Welfare Legislation and the Unions during the First World War', *Historical Journal*, 23 (1980). Further debate on the issue can be found in contributions by R. Lowe and N. Whiteside in *Historical Journal*, 25 (1982).
4   This debate over dockers' maintenance is fully discussed in G. Phillips and N. Whiteside, *Casual Labour: the Unemployment Question and the Port Transport Industry, (1985)*, Ch. V.
5   See, for example, *Evidence to the Committee of Enquiry into the Work of Employment Exchanges*, PP XI (1921), Cmd. 1140; and *Evidence to the Committee on Procedure and Evidence for the Determination of Claims for Unemployment Insurance Benefit*, PP XVI (1929–30), Cmd. 3415.
6   *Committee on the Audit of Unemployment Benefit: Report*, PP XIV (1916), Cd. 8412, p. 4; and Evidence of the National Joint Standing Advisory Committee: 13 April 1926 to Blanesburgh Committee. Ministry of Labour, *Committee on Unemployment Insurance*, vol. III, *Minutes of Evidence* (1927), p. 149.
7   Ministry of Labour, *Unemployment Insurance by Industries: Report on the Administration of s.18 of the Unemployment Insurance Act 1920*, Sess. II, PP II (1922), Cmd. 1613.
8   See, for example, *Westminster Special Conference: Trade Unions on Unemployment* 24 April 1925 (report in TUC library), TUC *Annual Report* (1925). Also Blanesburgh, *Minutes of Evidence*, vol. III, *op. cit.*, p. 182.

9 By 1932, the system was to be funded by a 'levy on incomes'; union support for an universal contributory system was taking shape. E. Bevin, *My Plan for Two Million Workless* (1933).

10 J. Hinton, *The First Shop Stewards' Movement* (1973), Ch. II.

11 'Notes on general principles of wages adopted by the Industrial Court', May 1920; on file LAB 2/758/WA 5820: Public Record Office (PRO). This includes an account of arbitration 1916–20.

12 *Ministry of Labour Gazette* (August 1921), pp. 390–2. Also G. Routh, *Occupation and Pay in Great Britain* (1980) pp. 201–2.

13 'Present disparities in wages', March 1927; Statistics Division of the Ministry of Labour; on file LAB 2/1436/IR325/1932: PRO.

14 This development started well before the war. K. Burgess, *The Challenge of Labour* (1980), pp. 82–4. Also J. Zeitlin, 'Craft Regulation and the Division of Labour: Engineers and Compositors in Britain 1890–1914', (University of Warwick PhD, 1981), pp. 475–84.

15 National Union of Foundry Workers: discussions of the National Joint Council, January 1922 – MSS 41/NUFW/3/4/30. Also *Annual Reports* of the union. Modern Records Centre (MRC) University of Warwick.

16 J. B. Jeffreys, *The Story of the Engineers* (1959), pp. 197–9, 218–19.

17 Hyman, *op. cit.*, pp. 128–32.

18 See note 6 above.

19 F. Honigsbaum, *The Division in British Medicine* (1979), pp. 220–1.

20 *Annual Returns for Expenditure of the Public Social Services*, PP XIII (1924), p. 397.

21 Out of work donation gave 29 shillings to men and 25 shillings to women, with dependants' allowances. Unemployment benefit was brought in line with the cost of living in 1920 and offered 15 shillings to male and 12 shillings to female claimants.

22 See note 20 above. The figures do not include OWD expenditure, which continued for ex-servicemen in 1921. Even including this, the cost to the Exchequer grew from £34 million in 1921 to nearly £53 million in 1922. See E. M. Burns, *British Unemployment Programmes* (1938), p. 56.

23 Board of Trade Labour Department, *Analysis of the Rules of Trade Unions relating to Unemployed, Sick and Accident Benefits in 1908* (confidential print). Beveridge Papers: Coll. B, vol. XVII. British Library of Political and Economic Science.

24 Unions were empowered under s.17 of the Unemployment Insurance Act 1920 to administer state benefit to their members, as long as they also provided union benefit at one-third of the national rate.

25 Many of the smaller craft unions sheltered under the umbrella provided by the General Federation of Trades Unions, which acted as a mutual insurance agency for member societies. See A. Prochaska, *The General Federation of Trades Unions* (1983).

26 See J. Macnicol, *The Movement for Family Allowance* (1980), Ch. V.

27 See, for example, E. Bevin, *My Plan for Two Million Workless* (1933).

28  R. Earwicker, 'The Labour Movement and the Creation of the National Health Service 1906–48', PhD thesis (University of Birmingham, 1982).

29  Details on pre-war decasualisation policy are described in N. Whiteside, 'Welfare Insurance and Casual Labour', *Economic History Review*, 2nd series, XXXII (1978).

30  *Report on Social Insurance and Allied Services*, PP VI (1942–43), Cmd. 6404, p. 13.

31  Treasury memorandum, 12 March 1917; on file T1/12093/38192/1917, PRO.

32  Beveridge to the Royal Commission on Unemployment Insurance; 31 March 1931, *Minutes of Evidence*, vol. I, p. 728.

33  National Confederation of Employers' Organisations, *Report on Unemployment Insurance* (1924), pp. 14–16. Dependants' allowances were initially based on a separate social insurance scheme; this fund was amalgamated with the main Unemployment Fund in 1922.

34  Evidence: JFG Price to Royal Commission on Unemployment Insurance, 12 February 1932: *Minutes of Evidence*, vol. II, p. 1391.

35  Whitehall had had these issues under serious scrutiny since 1921. See papers of the Watson Committee and the Anderson Committee on files P1N1/1 and P1N 1/2 respectively: PRO.

36  Correspondence and papers on the effects of unemployment on health insurance and pensions in the early 1930s are in PIN 3/41, PRO.

37  Accounts of 'tightening up' can be found in A. Deacon, *In Search of the Scrounger* (1974); and N. Whiteside, 'Private Agencies for Public Purposes', *Journal of Social Policy*, XII (1982), pp. 177–9.

38  This was largely due to the introduction of the new insurance scheme for dependants' allowances in 1921.

39  S. Shaw, 'The Attitude of the TUC towards Unemployment in the Interwar Period', PhD thesis (University of Kent, 1980), esp. Chs. VIII and X. Also evidence of TUC to Royal Commission on Unemployment Insurance, 4 May 1931, *Minutes of Evidence*, vol. I, p. 976.

40  T. Rodgers, 'Work and Welfare: the National Confederation of Employers' Organisations and the Unemployment Problem 1917–1939', PhD thesis (University of Edinburgh, 1982), Ch. V, s.II. I am grateful to Dr Rodgers for letting me read his thesis, from which most of the information about the NCEO has been taken.

41  NCEO, *Report on Unemployment Insurance* (1924) and papers submitted in deputation to the Cabinet, May 1925; on file PIN 7/73, PRO. The NCEO also adopted a similar line in their evidence to the Royal Commission on National Health Insurance and to the Blanesburgh Committee.

42  Papers on files PIN 7/73 and PIN 7/75, PRO.

43  Rodgers, Ch. III, s.IV.

44  Ibid., Ch. IV, s.III.

45  Ibid., Ch. VI, s.IV.

46  *Annual Returns for Expenditure on the Public Social Services*, PP XVI (1937–38), Cmd. 5609, pp. 6–7.

47   Ibid.
48   Figures from published official *Annual Returns for Expenditure on the Public Social Services*, PP XIII (1924), pp. 397–8; PP XII (1934–35) Cmd. 4749, pp. 6–7; PP XVI (1937–38), Cmd. 5609, pp. 6–7. The term 'public social services' covers all local and national expenditure on social insurance and poor relief, as well as costs incurred under housing, public health, old age pensions, education and mental deficiency legislation.
49   All forms of uncovenanted, extended or transitional benefits were granted on a discretionary basis. In the 1930s, recipients of Exchequer funded Transitional Payments (administered through local Public Assistance Committees) or Unemployment Assistance, were required to submit to a household means test.
50   The issue of offering unemployed women war workers domestic service had first been discussed under the OWD scheme in 1918. See LAB2/1463/ED 18453. The decision to take stronger steps towards encouraging unemployed women to take domestic service was ratified by the Cabinet early in 1922. See CAB 23/29 CC9 (22) 15 February 1922, conclusion 1, PRO.
51   Price to Royal Commission on Unemployment Insurance, 31 December 1930, *Minutes of Evidence*, vol. I, p. 80.
52   Burns, p. 115; N. Whiteside, 'Private Agencies for Public Purposes', *JSP*, p. 183.
53   Burns, p. 67.
54   Arguments in favour of widespread 'voluntary' unemployment in the interwar period are to be found in a controversial article by D. K. Benjamin and L. A. Kochin, 'Searching for an Explanation of Unemployment in Interwar Britain', *Journal of Political Economy*, 87 (1979). Issues raised are further discussed in *Jnl. Pol. Econ.* 90 (1982). See also Howson in R. Floud and D. McCloskey (eds), *The Economic History of Britain since 1700*, vol. II (CUP, 1983), pp. 270–1.
55   Numbers on disablement benefit, who 'topped up' on public assistance, rose during the 1930s. These claims appear to have originated principally among elderly workers in depressed industries.
56   M. Krafchik, 'Unemployment and Vagrancy in the 1930s', *Journal of Social Policy*, XII (1983). Also reports from Divisional Controllers on experience of difficulties in persuading claimants to accept low-waged work (October 1936): on file PIN7/167: PRO.
57   T. Jones, *Whitehall Diary* (ed. K. Middlemas), vol. II, p. 82.
58   TUC deputation, January 1939: papers on file PIN 7/309: PRO.
59   Shaw, Ch. III, s.IV. Also Whiteside 'Welfare Insurance and Casual Labour', *op. cit.* The effects of using benefit to supplement short-time earnings were discussed by Price in his evidence to the Royal Commission on Unemployment Insurance, 31 December 1931. *Minutes of Evidence*, vol. I, pp. 107–11.
60   Price to Royal Commission on Unemployment Insurance, 19 December 1930, *Minutes of Evidence*, vol. I, p. 4.

61  Ibid., pp. 107–11. See also memo from Mines Department to MFGB on the Midlands colliery scheme, 9 November 1929: PIN 7/96, PRO.

62  For dockers, see Whiteside, 'Welfare Insurance and Casual Labour', *Ec. Hist. Rev.*, XXXII, pp. 520–1. For Bradford Dyers and Finishers, see correspondence between the union and Citrine on file, 'Unemployed Associations (TC): Unions opinions 1928–1929': 135.61: TUC Filing Department.

63  Hawtrey to Phillips and the Chancellor of the Exchequer, 11 January 1936: on file T 172/1846, PRO.

64  Royal Commission on Unemployment Insurance, *Minutes of Evidence*, vol. II: ML Paper 110, pp. 1388–9.

65  G. W. McDonald and H. F. Gospel, 'The Mond–Turner Talks 1927–1933: a study in industrial cooperation', *Historical Journal*, XVI (1973). Also Shaw, Ch. IV.

66  T. Rodgers, 'Work and Welfare; British Employers and Social Policy between the Wars' (unpublished paper).

67  See, for instance, M. Jacques, 'The Consequences of the General Strike', in J. Skelley (ed.), *The General Strike 1926* (1976).

68  J. Harris, 'Did British workers want the welfare state? G. D. H. Cole's Survey of 1942', in J. Winter (ed.), *The Working Class in Modern British History* (1983), p. 205.

# 7

# Employers and the Rise of Supervisory Unionism, 1914–39

*Joseph Melling*

Industrial supervisors have rarely figured in general accounts of trade union growth and shopfloor organisation. Recent research on the distribution of workplace skills and the growth of machine technology in nineteenth-century industry has emphasised the role of strategic groups and contractual arrangements in the control of production, though the overlooker usually remains an obscure figure in such detailed studies.[1] The role of labour relations and institutions in shaping employers' policies is evident in a variety of industries, though the precise boundaries of management and the arrangements between shop management and capitalist owner are assumed rather than documented. This neglect is in sharp contrast to a sociological literature which has been saturated by interpretations of these 'middlemen' in industry, often presenting the problems of the modern supervisor as symptoms of a deeper dilemma facing the white-collared middle class in post-war society.[2] The most influential account of supervisory unionism was developed by Bain in direct response to the agenda set by the Donovan Commission of the 1960s. Deeply critical of the sociological enterprise and its effort to explain union membership in terms of changing social and class attitudes, Bain continued to place the experience of supervisory organisation within the broad trajectory of 'white-collar' unionism during the twentieth century.[3] In his view, such unions share the common experience of evolving in more specific conditions than the manual unions and depended to a large extent on the favourable circumstances of concentrated employment, employers' recognition of negotiating rights, and the benevolent consequences of state intervention during key periods of growth.[4] Bain largely dismisses the case for unionisation seen as a reaction to changes in the division of work and methods of production, though there remains a recognition of specific market and manufacturing conditions in his analysis.[5]

These arguments were clearly directed against radical interpretations of union growth, as well as current sociological explanations
of white-collar bargaining. Some of Bain's conclusions have been
complemented by a strand of research in social history, providing
strong evidence for the resilience and diffusion of those craft institutions built by key groups of skilled workers in the nineteenth
century.[6] The preservation of hand-based, skilled techniques in the
peculiar environment of the late Victorian economy allowed a wide
variety of trades actively to regulate methods of production and to
circumscribe the attempts of manufacturers to transform the
division of labour.[7] In this view, craft restrictions expressed the
sectional (usually conservative) attitudes of the skilled workers on
the shopfloor, dividing trades as much as journeymen and labourers
from each other. Union policy-making takes on the complexity
of institutions in a pluralistic society rather than reflecting any
fundamental antagonism between classes, or between militant
membership and moderate officials.[8] The survival of craft institutions helped to foreclose certain business strategies and inhibited
employers in their attempts to rationalise production as competition increased during the late nineteenth and early twentieth
centuries. Even the new sectors of industry were overshadowed by
restrictive practices as the techniques of craft regulation survived in
the heavy industries and were transferred to some mass production
sectors.[9] The limited inroads made by British management in the
customs and practices of numerous trades and the problems
subsequently experienced in supervising the shopfloor, when their
own foremen seemed fatally weakened by neglect or their
dangerous proximity to the manual unions, appears to underline
many of these criticisms. Concessions made by employers in the
metal industries—particularly at periods of national crisis and
government control—seemed to provide the foundations for union
growth without delivering efficiency in production.

These arguments have considerable force when applied to the
staple industries during the decades before 1939, exposing deficiencies which arose from the organisation of production as well as
the diverse and uncertain pattern of demand. The changes in tempo
between craft conservatism and political radicalism had been
accompanied by state intervention at critical periods in support of
union recognition. There also remain a number of questions about
the assumptions and the methods of such studies. Research into

the supervision of British industry before 1914 suggests that craft institutions remained of real benefit to the employers and could be manipulated by them to dilute and cheapen labour rather than presenting barriers of regulation.[10] The ambiguities and contradictions of craft work could also be seen in the toleration of brutal foremanship in the most heavily unionised trades. There is also a danger of reducing the distribution of power and authority at work to a pervasive conflict between craft regulation and aggressive management, offset by sectional disputes on the shop floor, rather than assessing craft practices within the context of different struggles. From the late nineteenth century the advance of collective bargaining was largely influenced by the appearance of central employers' organisations and the introduction of national negotiating procedures in many sectors. Business strategies for the use of industrial manpower were developed by these bodies outside the enterprise, as well as by individual firms, though the responsibility for specific decisions remained in the hands of the employer. It is essential to distinguish between the collective endorsement of 'management prerogatives' and the entrepreneurial practices of the industrial firm in explaining the progress of industrial relations.

In defending their right to manage production, employers were responding not only to market opportunities and technical constraints, but to a deeply-held principle of authority in industry. Their understanding of efficiency was necessarily informed by the belief in a particular hierarchy of command and the leadership of the owner at the head of the firm. It was the articulation of 'managerial prerogatives' which provided the cement for associations of individual firms and federations of regional employers during the 1890s, a broad philosophy of authority offering a common platform for disparate interests. The fear of socialist politics amongst the skilled and non-craft unions also sharpened the masters' concern to define their absolute rights over production. Questions of workplace control were accentuated by increased shopfloor activity and a fresh discourse of organised struggle. An emphasis on craft continuities and sectionalism can obscure the significance of such conflicts by divorcing the internal politics of the union from the everyday life of the shopfloor. To pose these politics mainly in terms of an insurgent rank and file versus a moderate union bureaucracy is untenable, but to replace them with craft conservatism and pluralistic unions as the basis of analysis is questionable. Such an approach restricts the focus of industrial relations to the better organised manual workers rather than considering the contribution of lesser skills and the role of non-manual groups in workplace change. In a rather different way, our existing accounts of supervisory unionism is limited by the concern of Bain and others to trace the institutional origins of white-collar bargaining, rather than the supervisors' response to workplace change or their relations with other workers. The deficiencies of these interpretations become evident when we consider the complex origins of supervisory unionism.

### Employers' policies and the origins of supervisory unionism, 1900–18

It is tempting to portray the Victorian industrial supervisor as an isolated and solitary figure, enjoying wide-ranging powers in the workshop and at the factory gates where he hired and fired workmen. In some respects the engineering and shipbuilding industries provided the environment for the rise of the classical foreman, responsible for organising the work and inspecting the finished product as well as leading the hands who served under him.[11] The decades between 1880 and 1914 saw an impressive expansion of heavy engineering and shipyard output as well as the emergence of lighter trades, with employment in the metal industries rising from 927,000 to over 1,800,000.[12] There had been a variety of subcontractors and piecemasters engaged in supervision of engineers during the mid-nineteenth century but piecework was restricted by the 1870s and its subsequent increase from the mid-1880s did not directly threaten the authority of the shop or shipyard foreman.[13] Methods of production were dictated by the diversified market conditions as well as the horizons of technical change, as employers sought to meet the specialist requirements of individual customers rather than imposing standardised production on varied markets.[14] The structure of many industrial firms only encouraged this preference for existing management practices and continued relations with particular customers. On the shipbuilding rivers the scope for specialist supply and the reliance upon established techniques (and methods of payment) during the pre-1914 expansion, appeared to confirm the existing division of labour and the pattern of industrial relations.[15]

Closer examination reveals more substantial progress being made by innovative employers after the 1880s, more especially in the engineering industry. Machine tools were improved, adopted and imported in growing numbers with a sharp rise during the 1890s as the lighter trades exploited the potential of the simpler and faster American lathes.[16] The established 'machine men' on the planing, boring, slotting and drilling operations were joined by less accomplished hands on the new lathes and semi-automatics, particularly in the larger, progressive armaments and sewing machine firms.[17] Experienced craftsmen were generally upgraded to setting these machines and completing more complex jobs or maintenance work, essential in the general engineering works as well as the small jobbing and repair shops. The time-served turner might find that his grinding tasks were removed with the arrival of high-speed tool steel and the specialist grinder, but the new machines actually allowed—and demanded—greater standards of precision and job control which secured the place of the skilled worker amidst the increasing ranks of machinists.[18] Even the exclusive world of the engineering patternmaker was invaded by a series of machine tools in the late nineteenth century, though these remained, along with the art of making intricate moulds, in the hands of the craftsmen.[19]

The introduction of various methods of pieceworking and the periodic attempts to substitute apprentices and boy labourers for the adult workers in the industry, also contributed to a deterioration of shopfloor relations during the 1890s as struggles for control over a wide range of issues set the scene for a major confrontation in 1897–98.[20] The terms of settlement arranged to end the engineering lock-out were drafted to consolidate the employers' victory and establish a clear basis for the exercise of management prerogatives. It quickly became apparent that the leading craft unions retained their power of resistance, engaging in successful campaigns against such policies as the introduction of discharge notes for engineering and shipbuilding tradesmen before 1914.[21] More importantly, the employers built their federations not to break but to contain and regulate the craft societies, relying upon the procedures for avoiding disputes to avert major conflicts in the future. These federations were unable to override the powerful regional interests of the industry and were necessarily confined to the resolution of labour disputes rather than the preparation of any strategy on production. Faced with a series of challenges from organised workers, federation leaders spent the pre-war years striving to bridge the absolute prerogatives asserted in 1898 and the practical problems of constitutional procedures which had been introduced to avert national stoppages. There remained problems not only in securing a united front on any particular issue, but in administering a set of procedures which granted the unions a forum for the discussion of management policies. The aggressive actions of individual firms could carry the whole Federation into battle formation on specific issues, even though national officials on both sides would have preferred some local settlement.[22]

The tensions inherent in the Settlement of 1898 were exposed most visibly in the case of two key groups: apprentices and supervisors. For in the treatment of both grades of worker the engineering and shipbuilding firms expressed the view that their prerogatives gave them a special, intimate relationship with the employees and there could be no interference from the trade unions. In the case of the apprentices the employers held on to the convenient historical fiction that indentures made an apprentice the personal ward of his master, to whom he was bound in low-waged service. The increase of such trainee workers and their widespread use as cheap machine labour was acknowledged by some employers before 1914, though they stubbornly resisted any effort to introduce collective bargaining for the apprentices before the war.[23] Foremen were generally responsible for their adolescent hands at this period, along with most other matters of shop management, though the practical training was left to the tradesmen who demonstrated tasks to his apprentice helper.

Supervisors themselves became the subject of intense scrutiny and debate during the conflicts of the 1890s, as the actual experience of full scale campaigning showed that firms could not rely upon the unqualified obedience of their foremen. The question came on to the Federation agenda after the lock-out, as the leadership under Colonel Dyer introduced a comprehensive benefit scheme designed to detach the supervisors from their craft society membership. Despite the attractive benefits offered by the Foremen's Mutual Benefit Society it enrolled only a few thousand members amongst the tens of thousands of supervisors in the pre-war metal trades, with some recruits apparently maintaining their contacts with the unions against the strict rules of the Mutual.[24] Business organisations in the metalworking industries publicised the advantages of these client societies in their campaigns to counter the influence of wealthy unions offering substantial benefits to the long-serving members promoted to the post of foreman, but they could do little to integrate this specific policy in a wider framework of discussion on the use of industrial manpower. Individual firms continued to rely upon the foreman as the anchor of shopfloor management and believed that the thin line of command could be filled by men of individual ability and masculine leadership who emerged by a process of natural selection from the ranks of the industrial workers. There was little serious discussion of training for this key grade of employee, nor did the question of relations between a new generation of rate-fixers or output inspector and the foreman merit attention in Federation meetings.[25] As with the apprentices, federated firms continued to pursue their own policies whilst depending on their organisations to resist any attempt by the unions to bargain on behalf of their foremen before 1914.

This fulfilment of management prerogatives helped to insulate the supervisors against union pressures after 1898, as the craft societies acknowledged their failure to represent foremen. At the same time, continued shopfloor conflict and the operation of disputes procedures required some participation of foremen in the settlement of disputes. Immediate grievances were carried to the supervisor by individuals or the shop steward, who became increasingly evident as workplace change and local conferences required a line of communication between workers and district officials. In periods of union resurgence, such as that between 1907 and 1914, the wide-ranging struggles over different issues of workplace control could place enormous pressures on individual foremen in the metal industries. Yet the supervisor was accorded no right of representation in the works or district conferences and might be the subject of joint discussions between employers and unions at local or national level. The procedures introduced in 1898 (and confirmed in 1907) suggested a particular logic of constitutional discussion which recognised the rights of employees to representation. Industrial supervisors were inserted as the first line of management authority but were also held to be the personal embodiment of absolute prerogatives as agents of the employer.

They could be conceded no place in bargaining nor any collective interest separate from that of their masters. Trade unions generally avoided the issue and raised particular questions with their foremen members in the privacy of the local branch or district meeting, but the pivotal position of the supervisor in relation to almost every aspect of workplace control meant that the foreman was increasingly seen as a terrain to be captured by the unions engaged in a defence of their customary rights.[26]

The outbreak of war served to intensify the pressures upon industrial foremen and involved them in conflicts which challenged the authority of the state as much as that of munitions manufacturers. Struggles over the introduction of dilution, as the wartime governments moved to engineer the introduction of thousands of untrained workers to the strategic supply industries, have been the subject of considerable debate among historians.[27] It is now clear that few tradesmen were threatened with the prospect of deskilling or immediate unemployment as a result of dilution, the majority being upgraded to setting, preparing or inspecting the work of machinists. There were also significant guarantees to safeguard the sectional interests of craft grades, though employers often circumvented the official provisions on job rates by classing female tasks as 'apprentice' work and moving the trainee craftsmen to skilled output.[28] Organised employers remained deeply critical of many government policies throughout the war and consistently pressed for harsher enforcement of statutory penalties against undisciplined workers.[29] Dissatisfaction also remained within the ranks of the tradesmen, as the bonus earnings and overtime available for repetition work substantially increased the earnings of the semi-skilled after 1915. These piece-rates were also cut by firms pressing for higher productivity and the journeymen campaigned for standard rate rises during 1916–17, as well as resisting efforts to remove the trade card exemptions from conscription in 1917.[30] Resentment at government legislation and administration continued well beyond the Munitions Acts of 1915–16, expressed in renewed shopfloor activity and demands for commitments on post-war reconstruction.[31]

Foremen were particularly vulnerable at this time of rising prices and diminishing trade differentials since their fixed wages were rarely adjusted to take account of the increased earnings enjoyed by the tradesmen and machinists. War bonuses were awarded by individual firms which needed to retain the services of experienced supervisors and to attract new foremen from the ranks, but there was no general practice on the payment for overtime hours worked by staff and real income declined. By 1917 there is evidence of a general deterioration in woodworking as well as metalworking trades, across the shipyards and engineering districts of the munitions centres.[32] Bitter complaints about the neglect of irresponsible employers and the lethargy of government departments which permitted the rising prices and profiteering began to arise in state establishments without any history of strong unionisation, such as the RAF workshops at Farnborough, as well as the large ordnance factories.[33] Disenchanted supervisors reserved their most stringent criticisms for the 'Prussian methods of the government', which had enabled unfair practices as employers used the leaving certificates against their own foremen who sought better-paid positions elsewhere. Whereas most accounts stress the use of the certificates to imprison workers within an enterprise under the control of the foreman, these letters include protests that the recruiting authorities dealt harshly with promoted men who did not enjoy the exemption status of those holding trade cards.[34] Many supervisors concluded that it was their inability to disrupt production on the scale of earlier unrest amongst tradesmen which told against them, since foremen suffered from war increases and were also compelled to operate such 'unsound' legislation as the 1916 Munitions Act without any recourse to the government departments.[35]

These three issues of declining differentials, wartime pressures of production and overtime, and the resentment over government policies (including conscription), persuaded isolated groups of foremen of the need for independent organisation towards the end of 1917. The bulk of the early membership was recruited in the locomotive engineering shops of the great railway companies at Crewe, Swindon and elsewhere, though the shipbuilding rivers of north-east England and west Scotland provided their own limited initiatives in union activity. In early 1918 a National Foremen's Association enrolled hundreds of aggrieved shop foremen, claiming over 2000 members within a year and easily overshadowing the efforts of Amalgamated Societies in Northumberland, Cheshire, Scotland and other districts.[36] Their combined membership represented only a small percentage of the tens of thousands of potential applicants, though the existence of state conciliation machinery meant (as one perceptive contemporary noted) that the new unions could appeal for official arbitration without having to attempt any form of industrial action to sustain their case.[37] The noticeable reluctance of government officials to enter this unfamiliar terrain of internal management relations and the incapacity of the Committee on Production to deal with the supervisors' grievances quickly, helped new unionists to consolidate their position and articulate their claim for separate treatment.[38]

The early direction of the supervisory unions was not apparent from the circumstances of their birth. Many of the first organisers favoured an association closer to the technical fraternities or the friendly societies of the later nineteenth century than a trade union strategy. The National Foremen's Association (NFA) was divided between a strong commitment to the principles of Whitleyism and industrial cooperation in industry, and the clear support for trade union principles amongst a majority of activists in railway and engineering areas.[39] Their leaders preferred to emphasise the difference in titles and perspective between manual unionists and 'association' colleagues, supporting the principle of copartnership rather than conflict in the organisation of industry. In 1921 a federation of supervisory associations was established under the aegis of the Industrial League, with the inauguration conference representing fourteen bodies and over 20,000 supervisors in different industries addressed by Whitley on the benefits of industrial councils and consultation in the post-war world.[40] By the time the conference was convened, however, the industrial climate had changed decisively against co-partnership at the workplace and government sponsorship of conciliation reforms. The formative period for the fresh organisations was to be the years 1918–22, in which struggles over profound issues of workplace control swept through different sectors of the metal trades and which touched directly the status of supervision in the defence of management prerogatives. Foremen were inevitably caught up in shopfloor contests for control over different aspects of production as well as the politicised debates on the future of works committees in collective bargaining. The confrontation of organised employers and the manual unions dictated the circumstances in which foremen struggled to gain an independent voice in industrial relations.

*Supervisors and the limits of workplace control, 1918–22*

The continued expansion of the metal industries after the First World War offset the demobilisation of industrial workers from the munitions plants, as almost 2.5 million people found employment in these industries by 1921. Increased unionisation allowed the most powerful groups of workers to extend wartime bargaining practices and to secure the return of pre-war trade standards. The spread of bonus systems and union surveillance of industrial practices during the dilution process had assisted the rise of the shop steward, especially in districts such as Sheffield and Coventry. District autonomy had been reinforced by the growth of local shop stewards' committees distinct from the official agencies of the craft societies, in areas which possessed a different political complexion from that of Clydeside or Coventry.[41] National executives had allowed the assertion of local precedents against firms unwilling to risk a major stoppage of work on government contracts, thereby underwriting the guarantees given for a restoration of trade practices. The munitions crises of 1915–16 were crucial in the progress of wartime relations, not because of the presence of highly politicised shop stewards at Clydeside but for the attempts of the ASE and other unions to achieve the principle of joint participation in the design and administration of dilution. Faced with the difficulties of holding the craft line amidst the chaos of military emergencies, union leaders and some perceptive stewards recognised the urgent need to move from trade practices to a negotiated settlement policed by both sides in the munitions districts. The resistance of the employers and the limited progress in central discussions forced the official leaders to rely on trade defences in the workshops whilst denying local struggles open support.

The organisation of the semi-skilled and machine grades into separate unions also contributed to a changing scene on the shopfloor, compelling the ASE to reconsider its recruitment policies and improving the position of the non-craft workers in the engineering trades. Some craft societies were able to exploit the pressures of war to extend their hold over charge hands responsible for the most direct form of supervision in the shops or shipyards, consolidating their campaigns in the immediate post-war months.[42] It was generally acknowledged by 1918 that charge hands using the tools of the trade should normally be considered as eligible for membership of the manual unions, participating in them on equal terms with the men they directed. There was no such understanding in the case of full foremen, who had been recognised as the instruments of management authority by the most innovative and aggressive firms in the industry since 1898. Large armaments employers such as Vickers of Barrow had used the opportunities of wartime expansion to promote large numbers of younger, more ambitious, charge hands to supervisory posts and had encouraged the surrender of trade membership amongst these groups.[43] During 1919–20 these men faced demotion as munitions departments contracted or closed, though they could count on a cold welcome from the tradesmen they had abandoned and then driven in the boom years. The Vickers management dealt with the problem by dismissing men in the shop to make room for the disrated supervisors returning to the benches, though they provoked union opposition on this and the related question of union membership for the renegades. To the argument that any dismissals should be made on the grounds of seniority and recent trade experience rather than preference for foremen, local employers insisted that supervisors could not be turned on the open labour market and needed special consideration. The whole discussion was phrased in the vocabulary of workshop control, as the union officials demanded that complete organisation of the shopfloor was required for harmony and efficient production. This had been acknowledged in practice by the widespread recognition of wartime shop stewards 'under pressure from the rank and file', so there could be (argued the union) little force in the claim that all changes in procedure must follow central negotiation.[44] In these circumstances, employers conceded that workers would have some say in 'the conditions of the shop', though the presence of works committees or joint councils could not challenge management's right to sole determination on production and employment questions.[45] Vickers and other firms saw the issue of supervision as part of the wider concern for management prerogatives and the respect for constitutional agreements against the threat of local autonomy or direct action.[46]

A more fundamental challenge came from the Electricians' Trade Union, which had recruited foremen during its early days in the 1890s and had used the First World War to expand its supervisory membership on Merseyside and other areas.[47] The ETU sought to use its success in Liverpool—where a majority of trade supervisors enrolled—as the basis for a campaign in Sheffield and thereby establish a national policy by a series of rolling precedents in the provinces. This strategy would provide the electricians with the means to enforce trade standards in the rapidly growing sectors of electrical engineering, as well as in the essential maintenance work they completed throughout the metal trades. The refusal of an ex-unionist to recognise such customs in the Penistone plant of Cammell Lairds at Sheffield during 1920, provoked one of the most important disputes of the post-war years. Prompted by the foreman's employment of an unqualified improver on craft work, the local district committee of the union supported the strike action of the Lairds electricians. The Engineering Employers' Federation under Allan Smith quickly saw the opportunity to mobilise its membership around the question of selecting supervisors and compulsory unionisation of their foremen. Penistone also offered Allan Smith the chance to force the unions to define their objectives on shopfloor control, as well as the responsibility of national officers for the actions of individual districts. Sheffield members had insisted that the foremen remained a contested terrain until such time as 'the Employers establish their claim' to their exclusion from the unions, justifying their actions in the light of wartime experience and the language of workers' control rather than national agreements.[48] The EEF noted that such phrases as the claim to complete organisation of 'the workers' represented a major advance beyond that of representing the manual workforce and implicitly sanctioned all methods to achieve such control.[49] There was no doubt amongst the employers' leaders of the importance of this case, for as they warned their member firms:[50]

> The right which has been claimed and for which the Federation are at present contending is a right which is of cardinal importance to the industry, and upon which no compromise is possible. The modification of the right or the abandonment of the right would be the first step towards the selection by the workpeople of their superintendence and the control of those superintendents after they were appointed.

Throughout the dispute the Federation emphasised that the employers must establish the principle of absolute and exclusive control over supervision, whatever the particular conditions or prevailing practice within any district, thereby refuting the union's case that existing precedents should form the basis of discussions.[51]

The determined manoeuvring of Smith and his associates exposed the rifts between the ETU and the other unions in the industry, who resented the aggressive drive for a closed shop and hesitated to engage the employers in a general lock-out of the trades. Fending off the efforts of the Ministry of Labour to intervene with a Court of Inquiry into the dispute, the EEF was able to coerce the ETU executive into a voluntary agreement which renounced any pretensions to enforced membership of supervisors and to an effective withdrawal of their campaign at Cammell Lairds.[52] The immediate outcome of the Penistone settlement did not have any dramatic affect on the practices of individual firms towards their supervisors. A large majority of the Federation membership had reported that the individual ability and character of their promoted men remained the criteria for selection, irrespective of union background and most districts opposed the forcible resignation of unwilling foremen from their trade societies.[53] Some large firms had signed agreements actually recognising the right of the ETU to represent their staff foremen, on the strict understanding that the union should not attempt to interfere with the 'internal management and discipline of the works'.[54] Penistone was a landmark in post-war relations because it shifted the focus of debate from general claims for workshop control to the argument that the foreman should not work with the tools, though he should be qualified in the trade he supervised.[55] The terms of the debate were also altered—from the assertion that rights should be decided through direct struggle to the acceptance of official responsibility for local initiatives and their interpretation within the confines of existing procedures.

Management policies did not change suddenly but the more aggressive enterprises used Penistone to step up the Federation's promotion of the Foremen's Mutual Benefit Society (FMBS). Both Vickers and Cammell Lairds had been prominent advocates of the Mutual Society during the war and had attempted to retain their support after the demotion of substantial numbers of foremen, succeeding with important minorities of the ex-supervisors.[56] Society membership reached 7000 in 1919 and despite the contraction of industry, the figures had doubled by 1922 as the north-east coast, west Scotland, Manchester, London and Birkenhead (as well as Barrow and Sheffield) reported heavy clusters of members.[57] Supervisory unionism found it difficult to make headway against this concentrated effort in the marine engineering, shipbuilding and textiles machinery districts, where thousands of foremen accepted the improved benefits of the Society in return for the surrender of their union loyalties.[58] The employers held some of the fallen supervisors by the promise of a future elevation to the staff, though the worsening economic conditions after 1920 made the security of employment at the bench a more realistic proposition than a return to supervision, since the employers frankly confessed that some men were obviously unsuitable in any case.[59] For those seasoned foremen who lost work through no failing of their own, the FMBS functioned as a confidential labour exchange, placing loyal servants in secure posts elsewhere. During the early 1920s the craft societies renewed their campaigns against non-unionism on the shopfloor and many employers were faced with the choice of allowing their former sergeants to drift into unions or of promoting the man once again.[60] For if the supervisor should become unemployed, he could be made to feel the full effects of his isolation from the tradesmen when standing alongside them in the dole queue or labour exchange.[61]

There were also changes in the outlook of FMBS members which gave engineering and shipbuilding firms cause for concern at this period. Previous criticisms of the Society's centralised control in the powerful hands of Thomas Biggart at Glasgow, gave way to disquiet over the efforts of foremen in the north east and elsewhere to transform the Mutual into a consultative body with some negotiating or bargaining functions. Recent concessions by employers in formally recognising shop stewards as part of established procedures, without any consultation with foremen or even permitting the supervisors any right of access to the heads of the firm, troubled those Mutual members who sent deputations to the management at Armstrong Whitworth and Hawthorn Leslie.[62] After initial hostility from the Society and Federation officials to any proposal that the Mutual should assume union functions, the organised employers soon agreed to regular consultation on conditions and appointed a joint committee to settle outstanding grievances.[63] The emergence of a distinct Foremen's Mutual Welfare Association in the Midlands as a formal ancillary of the FMBS to channel these collective views did not meet with approval from the employers, though there was no attempt to crush the

Welfare Association as it moved to more moderate positions after
1922.

The engineering lock-out of 1922 marked the end of the unions'
challenge to management authority and the Federation's victory
sealed employer–supervisory relations within the mentality of
'managerial prerogatives'. One context for the dispute was the
drastic wage reductions imposed on the engineering and shipbuilding trades in 1921–22, as rates fell from over 88 to 56 shillings
in some districts, together with cuts in the piece-rates which large
numbers of workers now performed under.[64] The unions' accession
to these measures had provoked vigorous criticisms in many
districts, where struggles continued over the rating of machine tools
and protection of employment for the thousands of AEU (formerly
ASE) members on the streets in 1921–22.[65] The enforcement of an
overtime ban gave the federated firms a fresh opening for a general
campaign of management prerogatives, as apprentices remained at
their benches under the direction of trade foremen during the
struggle.[66] Charge hands and supervisors working with the tools
were called out, along with the apprentices completing valuable
work for the employers, though the unions only demanded foreman
support in the last desperate stages of the conflict, placing enormous pressure on the card-carrying supervisors.[67] Many firms used
the opportunity to introduce a more disciplined regime in their
works, without the help of foremen who had followed the union
in the crisis.

It was in these unpromising circumstances that the early supervisory unions attempted to establish good relations with the
employers without antagonising the organised workforce on the
shop floor. The National Foremen's Association expanded to 2900
members with 56 branches by the end of 1920 and attempted to
continue its momentum in the early 1920s.[68] There was an initial
and sustained preference amongst the membership for an organisation resembling that of the manual unions, though some officers
pursued a close, cooperative relationship with the federated
employers from 1918. The Association secured a strong following
in large, dynamic firms such as Avery's and the General Electric
Company, as well as the engineering works of the giant railway
companies, though there was little sign of any official or informal
recognition of the supervisors' unions by 1920. Two principles
expressed the strategies of the new presence in the tripartite

relations of industry: that of permitting, or encouraging, membership of both craft and supervisory organisations, and the strict rule
of neutrality during industrial disputes. The new unionists
remained attached to the programme of industrial councils as the
most civilised method of resolving conflicts and of giving the staff
grades a definite, recognised place in the industrial order. In practice, the supervisors were carried along by the struggles around
them and found they could not stand to one side in questions of
workshop control. An important dispute at Avery's in 1920 saw
the NFA membership join with the manual unions in a successful
campaign against a new ratefixing and management regime, as the
employers discovered that even those in the Foremen's Mutual had
taken up NFA cards at Avery's and Thorneycroft's.[69]

These expressions of solidarity did not dispel the hostility of
many craft groups, even though the NFA had adopted a 'skilled'
conception of foremanship from the outset. During the Penistone
dispute the EEF was able to exploit the evident tensions between
the electricians' union and the supervisory and management associations in the industry, although the Federation itself firmly ignored
all correspondence from these bodies when demanding participation in the conference.[70] To overcome these difficulties, the
supervisory unions sought reciprocal agreements with the various
craft societies, binding each not to cooperate with anyone brought
in to replace union members and to observe strict neutrality in
disputes with the employers.[71] During the 1922 lock-out, the NFA
circularised its members against accepting the responsibility for
managing blackleg labour, partly to reassure the AEU of its good
intentions.[72] The members following such policies found that they
left them vulnerable to widespread victimisation on the defeat of
the manual workers, which the supervisory unions were almost
powerless to prevent.[73] They did make some gains in the easing of
manual union opinion, particularly after 1922 when a TUC survey
revealed that bodies representing 1.9 million workers favoured
recognition of special unions for managers and supervisors, as
against 0.98 million failing to endorse such a policy (including the
AEU).[74] Supervisory organisations could now affiliate to the TUC
itself, which the NFA did after various attempts in 1921, though
access was granted at a time of bitter demoralisation in the unions
as unemployment and isolation took their toll, with the three principal bodies struggling to hold a combined membership of 3000

as the employers' Mutual grew to five times that number during the following years.[75]

The hazards posed for independent unionism from the benefit and pensions schemes of the employers had provided the initial impetus for TUC investigation of the supervisory predicament in 1922, though the remarkable burst of interest in 'enlightened' management which accompanied Reconstruction had largely passed by that time. Projects of human factor management and industrial copartnership belonged to the era of Whitley Councils, though the example of the FMBS indicates how reluctantly employers accepted some degree of real consultation in their welfare provisions. More importantly, industrial federations had resolved upon a reassertion of classical prerogatives, with the accommodation of shop stewards within the established structure of negotiating procedures. The dissatisfaction expressed by Mutual members at the recognition of shop stewards gives some measure of the continued neglect of foremen's views within the collective strategy. Federation leaders like Allan Smith did not pretend to legislate for individual managements but only to maintain the principles of capitalist control, leaving firms to pursue their separate interests and peculiar practices without interference. Dealing with the more serious challenge from organised labour and the shop stewards, federations left the firms to deal with foremen. This approach ensured that the subsequent growth of supervisory unions would be largely determined by their relations with individual employers and the wider union movement.

### Industrial supervisors and unionism, 1922–39: the force of craftism?

The progress of supervisory unionism to 1922 suggests that the general explanation offered by Bain and others for the growth of white-collar organisation (concentrated employment, employers' recognition and the benevolent effects of government policies), does not accurately reflect the origins of unionisation amongst foremen and ignores the crucial role of manual trades in the early history of the new unions. Federation policies were shaped by the concern to maintain workshop control in the face of powerful challenges from the shopfloor of industry and the prospect of staff unionism was resisted as a breach of hierarchical discipline. Faced with the continued hostility of their employers, supervisory leaders moved closer to the wider union movement during the early 1920s, whilst attempting to maintain the principle of neutrality in disputes and insisting that independence of foremen was of real value to both masters and men.[76] Federated firms learned from their unhappy experiences of the previous decade and maintained a clear, if rough, differential between the fixed wages of their staff foremen and the earnings of the tradesmen in the 1920s. This may have assisted the spread of some collective identity as supervisors were subjected to standard reductions in line with the rates of manual workers, though there is little sign that the individualistic mentality of the shipyard or engine shop foreman was badly eroded in this period. The conditions of employment and the enormous pressures on the oldest sections of the metal industries allowed the management to resort to some methods of supervision in the years after 1922 which can only be described as primitive.

Unemployment became a serious problem for the engineering and shipbuilding trades during the 1920s, reaching crisis proportions for many firms in the years 1929–35. The impact was most obvious in the heavier sectors of shipbuilding, marine and mechanical engineering, locomotive building and textile machinery, though the manufacture of machine tools and agricultural implements were also badly affected. The contrast with the newer trades of electrical engineering, motor cars, aircraft assembling and assorted lighter occupations could be seen in their increased numbers (including non-craft women) and the comparative rates of unemployment after 1929.[77] Against a background of falling world prices for staple goods and the erratic demand from primary producers, British manufacturers could not rely on a strong and sustained market demand as a basis for reorganising production.[78] There was an understandable reluctance amongst firms in trades such as mechanical engineering to scrap and retool their shops at a period when specialist, jobbing and repair work required the retention of all-round skills or techniques.[79] The Balfour Committee noted the persistence of a diverse range of handicraft skills in response to specialised demand and the slow progress towards standardisation—a criticism which has been underlined in recent research.[80] The severe contraction in trades such as shipbuilding and repairing in the whole period 1921–35 made any consideration of major economies through innovation and redivision of work difficult to conceive.[81]

The obstacles which lay across the road to mass production should not obscure the real advances made in areas of the metal industries during these years.[82] Many firms moved towards batch production as standardisation increased, whilst semi-skilled machine work expanded rapidly and the specialist function of toolmaking was increasingly divorced from the main work of the engineering shop.[83] Trades such as motor cycle manufacture were able to establish world supremacy using handicraft techniques and offering a great range of individual features on their models, whilst car-makers were able to draw on the European markets to secure themselves against North American competition.[84] Even in the sectors which approached most quickly to mass production, such as the six major firms of the car industry, there was a notable emphasis on piecework payments rather than intensive supervision of a Fordist assembly-line to secure productivity.[85] The craft societies pressed for the adoption of simple piecework rates in preference to premium bonus systems, with more than two-thirds of the engineering workforce receiving some form of payment by results in the 1930s.[86] Such schemes did not deliver control over work effort to either management or labour but recast the conditions under which a balance of power could be decided. With an unregulated labour market and weak unionism (as in some car plants), foremen frequently took the opportunity to encourage individual rivalries and manipulate piece rates according to circumstances.[87]

Much more formidable barriers existed in the well-organised heavy trades, such as shipbuilding, where the arrangement of pieceworking and price lists had become a fixed feature in the organisation of production from the late nineteenth century. Unlike the ASE, the ironworking 'black squads' under the Boilermakers' Society leadership had succeeded in avoiding any damaging confrontation with their employers before 1914 and were able to lay strong claim to machine tools introduced in the shipyards rather than permitting a serious disruption of the division of labour.[88] The unions were also able to exploit the deep divisions which existed between the regional organisations of shipbuilding districts that made up the Shipbuilding Employers' Federation (SEF) and the jealousies that undermined projects for unified action by Clydeside and Tyneside firms.[89] Boilermakers' officials encouraged the

Admiralty's aversion to industrial stoppages during the war and pressed forward their case for negotiating on behalf of charge hands in local districts.[90] The Society established a strong hold over the shiprepairing and building yards of the Bristol Channel and Merseyside, as well as forcing Vickers to conclude a closed shop agreement which would not have been possible in the engineering shops at Barrow.[91] In defending their campaign for enforced union membership amongst Mersey foremen after the war, the local officials noted that employers accepted the prevailing situation where the bulk of supervisors were card-holders and the Society's claim for 'freedom from interference [of employers]' in the matter, particularly as they had members 'practically in the position of Managers'.[92] Cammell Lairds of Birkenhead led the resistance, countering the principle that trade apprenticeship provided the essential foundations of any rise to foremanship with the argument that skilled men were not invariably craft unionists and denying the right of the societies 'to control a man as if he were a slave'.[93] Behind this encounter lay a fundamental conflict between the union's attempt to equate full craft credentials with Society recognition and the determination of the employers to distinguish between their approval of skilled supervision (and the tacit concession of complete union organisation) and acceptance of the Society as the embodiment of the craft fraternity. This distinction between the collective recognition of the supervisor's authority over the craft and their participation in the craft society did not deny the union's role in the quality control of journeymen working in the industry but it did dismiss their bid for open acknowledgement of union credentials for promoted men.

Many of the societies found their bargaining position seriously weakened by the catastrophic decline of building orders after 1921, and also by violent wage reductions and the same ultimatum on management functions as the engineering workers in 1922. Activists among the manual and staff grades were victimised amidst the avalanche of unemployment and non-unionists were advanced to promoted posts.[94] This was the experience of woodworking as well as metalworking craftsmen in the yards, as the Joiners' Society retreated from the defence of foremen's wage demands immediately after the War to the shallow support given to Belfast chargehands fighting wage cuts in 1923 and giving the clear impression that such unions were less concerned to improve supervisory conditions than enforce their membership of the society.[95] More vigorous employers canvassed the Foremen's Mutual amongst their staff in the depressed conditions of the early 1920s and union executives avoided raising the issue of management prerogatives, preferring to summons to local branch or district gatherings on sensitive questions.

The situation became more desperate in the crisis years 1929–34, as builders and repair yards reduced their manning standards and the Boilermakers' Society struggled to enforce a work rota and resist the increase of workloads. The limits of craft regulation were graphically outlined when the Society imposed fines on foremen members in breach of customary practices on the Bristol Channel. On appeal from their supervisors, the SEF declared the issue one over which 'the employers should retain complete control', encouraging the foremen to ignore the fines and restricting the access given to union officials seeking to interview employees at their works.[96] Although strike action was called against the foremen's indiscipline under union rules, a district conference of the supervisors at Barry endorsed their stand and insisted on the obligations of foremen in carrying out the policies of management, whilst advocating neutrality during disputes and the recognition of union rights in organising the workforce.[97] Faced with the slack labour market and the determination of the organised shipbuilders to assert their control over terms and conditions of employment, the Boilermakers' officials were unable to compel supervisors to serve as the strict guardians of trade customs. The decline in employment prospects also allowed some SEF leaders to press home their advantage on the subject of supervision.[98] The fundamental distinction between tradesmen and foremen was the restricted access to the tools which any staff supervisor could claim. Lithgows at Greenock undermined this time-honoured principle by offering working charge hands staff status and membership of the Foremen's Mutual, replacing unemployed tradesmen with the demoted foremen of other stricken yards as the firm moved slowly from the bare repair contracts to a limited output in 1932.[99] Whilst the recruitment of apprentices to the metal industries fell sharply after 1929, they represented a large proportion of those at work in the depression under driving charge hands. Demoralisation was so deep that the Boilermakers' officials were reluctant to confront aggressive firms on such questions.[100]

The ironworking trades later regained some of this ground as demand for armaments gave them the confidence to assert that there existed an 'unwritten law' ordering union membership amongst foremen.[101] Individual crafts enforced their demand that their trade should enjoy skilled supervision—against the attempts of shipbuilders to introduce interchangeability of work via the foremen—but they could not guarantee sympathetic treatment nor avoid victimisation by their own trade foremen.[102] Woodworking craftsmen encountered similar setbacks in the interwar years, retreating from the policy of the post-war period when strong efforts were made to compel union membership amongst supervisors and use them as enforcers of trade strategies during disputes.[103] The caution of joiners' officials increased after defeat in a major stoppage of 1924, with Society leaders accepting that general foremen in the building trades were beyond the reach of the union and ordinary supervisors should be left at work during strikes on the understanding that they must not use the tools.[104] This trend continued during the dark days which followed the General Strike of 1926, as major firms sponsored their own client societies for supervisors and woodworkers had to wait until the offending foremen returned to the ranks before exacting their discipline.[105] The employers did not engage in any comprehensive programme of innovation and deskilling in these years but their ability to breach established practices and substitute trade labour was clearly enhanced by their isolation of foremen from the societies. On their part, the unions remained ambiguous about supervisor members, usually excluding them from holding any senior office beyond the branch and excluding the foremen from ordinary business meetings.[106]

The healthy expansion of the lighter sectors of the metal industries appeared to hold out more hope for union initiatives. Organisers faced the problem that the heavy trades which provided the backbone of shopfloor organisation in the early twentieth century had been broken by mass unemployment and the production methods of car manufacturing or aircraft assembling did not possess a comparable network of activists. The assemblers at plants such as Blackburn's Dumbarton works pressed for skilled status and qualified supervision in the 1930s, excluding planning staff from handling mobile tools and gauges and compelling ratefixers to recognise the limits of effort they chose to make.[107] These shops provided the space for renewed shop steward organisation after 1935 and a series of strikes on recognition, pay and bonus systems reported by the *New Propellor*.[108] Lacking the clear structure of trade work and shop organisation found in the older centres, car manufacturing also produced its own variations in methods and supervision between the wars. Firms such as Pressed Steel and Briggs Motor Bodies concentrated on Fordist techniques of metal pressing, accepting a high weekly turnover of labour and the ability to sack (or lay off) men at short notice.[109] Other manufacturers relied upon an adjustable piecework system to secure high output in conditions of changing seasonal employment and more limited shop surveillance, though the bargaining circumstances could vary from the harsh realism of Morris Motors to the recognised shop steward organisation at Leyland.[110] The attempt of Leyland management to crack down on the autonomy achieved by work gangs under a leading hand on piecework, introducing younger supervisors to monitor individual piecework earnings, provoked strenuous opposition from the non-skilled.[111] The role of the foreman remained a critical concern for the workers, though their background and experiences were quite different from those of the craft trades and the relationship of supervisors to unionism varied enormously.

During the early 1930s employers often faced enormous problems in marketing their wares but appeared to have met and rebuffed the challenge from the shopfloor of industry. The declaration of the main federations that employers would exercise their absolute prerogatives in regard to production and control of employment did not give individual firms the practical guidance on organising work that they often needed, but they marked out the broad lines of management ideology. In the highly skilled sectors, employers could tolerate the continued presence of strong craft institutions because of the economies which trade training and organisation of work gave to the firm. Central to the ideology of prerogatives was the understanding that apprentices and supervisors should remain the personal dependants of the employer and could not be introduced to collective bargaining by the unions. Such policies would enable the enterprise to command its own labour market and place the apprentices in a position of the employer's ward. Campaigns before and during the First World War to unionise the apprentices had failed to establish bargaining rights for the craft societies, though the ratio of trainees to journeymen was a vital issue for the unions.[112]

After 1935 the resurgence of activity on the shopfloor in both the old and newer sectors of industry brought these questions into clear focus. Shipyards and marine engine works were using boys on profitable repair work as well as basic machining, sacrificing the training of the workers to the needs of the moment. Wage increases for engineering tradesmen set off the apprentices strikes of spring and autumn 1937, as the unrest spread from west Scotland to aircraft, motor and machine tool plants in Manchester and the Midlands before culminating in a major stoppage at Siemens' electrical engineering works in London.[113] The attempts of the owners' federations to dismiss the movement by references to the indenture contracts failed to stem the tide, as bargaining rights were granted to the young workers and more progressive companies introduced labour superintendants to cater for their trainees. Siemens discovered that their enlightened approach to shop stewards and training only exposed the gulf between the authoritarian style of older supervision and the rights won by the toolroom. A strike by apprentices and tradesmen against the treatment of young employees and a foreman's attitude to shop stewards led to the forced retirement of the supervisor and virtual concession of the AEU argument that civilised collective bargaining had made such brutal individualism amongst foremen unacceptable.[114] Siemens also yielded the point that shop stewards could appeal against a foreman's decision to exclude them from any particular workroom, which pointed to future troubles for supervisors circumvented by able stewards.

These struggles revealed a series of contradictions when the employers' policies are considered as a whole. The absolutist precepts of their federations had remained intact, whilst the arrival of the shop steward and other agents had led to an elaboration of constitutional procedures in which production as well as employment issues were discussed. It was accepted that collective action was necessary for the defence of basic prerogatives in times of union mobilisation, though individual concerns and districts jealously guarded the practical details of work organisation and enterprise strategies against their fellow employers. Apprentices were widely exploited in the difficult conditions of the interwar years whilst owners repeated the convenient fiction that they were the individual responsibility of the employer who provided an all-round training. Foremen were encouraged to drive the workforce and weaken organised resistance, whilst at the same time dealing with the return of the shop steward from the obscurity of the early 1930s. After years when supervisors were widely encouraged to adopt the primitive, commonsense methods of securing adequate output, they were discovered (in the aftermath of rearmament unrest) to be industrial dinosaurs incapable of responding to a changed industrial environment. Labour management experts were invited to diagnose the foreman's problems as workers gained strength and demanded that management behaviour should be regulated by industrial agreements.

Supervisors were subjected to a bewildering array of pressures in these years, as their unions struggled to maintain independence in the face of organised employers and workers. The foremen's organisations drew their members neither from such strongholds of craftism as the shipyards, nor predominantly from the mass-production industries, but mainly from such centres of heavy engineering as the locomotive workshops. The National Foremen's Association was guided by a definition of foremanship which owed more to the skilled conception of work prevalent in the Victorian engineering industry than the principles of functional supervision taught by management theorists. This image of trade supervision was encouraged by the spread of dual unionism as well as the insistence of manual workers that their superiors should have a proper background in the techniques of the workplace. The NFA directed its energies almost exclusively to the engineering industry and its members remained fairly conservative in their attitudes to management, criticising the growing practice of some firms in importing supervisors from outside the immediate shop in which they were to serve. Only men who were clearly 'supervising mechanical details' could apply for union membership and such recruits carried their scepticism of theoretical or academic training into the ranks of the Association.[115] The context for the celebrated disputes between shop foremen and planning or rate-fixing staff at firms such as Avery's can be understood in these terms. Only in the mid-1930s did such unions consider admitting rate-fixers to their ranks and then on an uneven basis.[116] Similarly, the National denied itself the opportunity of recruiting works management to its branches between the wars, refusing entry to interested candidates despite the success of a similar union in enlisting managers and foremen in the North-East.[117]

This failure to develop a rigorous definition of foremanship functions did not commit the supervisory unions to a traditionalist policy on industrial change. After 1922 there were few challenges to the authority of management, with the staff unions endorsing the settlement on managerial functions during the lockout and again in the midst of depression and widespread demotions a decade later.[118] Regardless of their members convictions, supervisory leaders refused to engage in open resistance to the Bedaux schemes of scientific management from 1929, though their experience of rationalisation may have persuaded the unions of the case for organising planning and technical staff in later years.[119] This move helped to carry the NFA beyond the horizons of the railway workshops and towards a more ambitious definition of their role in the evolution of modern management. Over the interwar decades the supervisory unions struggled with 2000–3000 members, scattered in clusters around particular engineering centres and hardly penetrating the new areas of car production and electrical engineering until the rearmament years. Along with shopfloor unionism, supervisory recruitment increased strongly during the pre-war recovery, though the unions depended on their working relations with the railway and omnibus companies and the Air Ministry to sustain them against the continued hostility of manufacturing industry.

The attitude of the majority of employers can only be described as unimaginative when their policies towards supervision are considered. Most firms phrased the problem of labour in terms of cost and control, anxious to avoid the burdens of oncost or ancillary staff who could increase the resources available to the foreman. The collapse of hopes with the Industrial Conference did not prevent the supervisory unions from vigorously advocating the cause of industrial cooperation before and after the General Strike.[120] Railway companies were more familiar with negotiating settlements with a complicated hierarchy of employees, though it was actually their exclusion of foremen from staff superannuation benefits at a time of enforced retirements which sustained the supervisors' unions in the contracting industry.[121] It was a characteristic failing that whilst federated employers promoted the benefits of the Foremen's Mutual and extended its provision to other non-manual grades, many refused to grant supervisors staff status or award a fixed salary and holidays before the war.[122] From 1922 there was no significant change in strategies for supervision and the upsurge of unionism during the Second World War was again to take the industrialists by surprise.

The reasons for this myopia amongst employers cannot be found solely, or even mainly, in the success of craft resistance in these years. To the extent the ideas of craft skill and the value of institutions such as apprenticeship survived into the 1930s, they expressed an industrial culture in which employers participated. Discussions on workshop organisation show a deep belief in the possibilities of ascent through natural selection, as entrepreneurs responded most positively to proposals which emphasised the importance of practical experience and individual character rather than the abstract advantages of improved administration or planning. Such ideas were probably encouraged by market and enterprise structures but had their origins in a shared mythology and experience of personal ability which seemed to be embodied in the personality of the foreman. These men held the line against the forces of disorder and were identified by business federations as the guardians of prerogatives. The unprecedented unemployment of the heavy industries appeared to confirm the 'classical' authority of the foreman, though in fact his powers had always been defined in relation to management needs and prevailing standards in the industry. Changing relations in industry and the evidence of deep discontent amongst the foremen persuaded some employers of the need for a rational bargaining policy to balance the mythology of heroic supervision. Bitter struggles for control of supervision had uncovered the limits of an ideology which merely asserted the obligations of foremen to implement prerogatives and the need to include them in formal procedures. As one employer argued in 1922:[123]

> The advantage of collective bargaining is so great that I should think that it would be an advantage to every foreman to become a Union man. From our point of view of bargaining with him it would simplify the question brought up between the Unions and the Federations . . . as well as the only possible course for him to take.

There were a number of individual firms willing to adopt a flexible or pragmatic attitude towards the unionisation of their foremen but the federation leaders and the bulk of active members were stubbornly opposed to any change of line. The conflicts of the post-war years fortified their belief that supervisors were vital to the maintenance of authority and control in the workplace. Denying the right of manual unions to represent foremen, organised firms stifled the growth of independent unions by their determined support of client societies such as the Foremen's Mutual.

This stand also deprived the employers of any collective strategy on workplace supervision and left the initiative to individual enterprises after 1922. It meant that large sections of British industry lacked any coherent manpower policy which could sustain management rationale and stable bargaining. Manufacturers relied upon the apprenticeship system to provide their best skills without the cost of a serious training programme, as well as providing management with cheap labour over which they could claim absolute control. The supervisors who continued to lead industrial production with their bare hands were taken from a shopfloor rife with customs and practices which they were expected to counter once in office—again without any serious training. Difficulties with supervisors had been symptomatic of a wide range of other problems in the post-war years, which employers allowed unemployment temporarily to resolve. Federation policies allowed firms to shelve the predicament of supervision until labour market conditions changed in the rearmament years and swept away some of the fixed ideas regarding apprenticeship and discipline.

## Conclusions

Supervisory unionism in the metal industries was obviously inhibited by the varied and isolated conditions in which most foremen worked. Organisation was sustained in the large railway shops where groups of engineering supervisors could stand together in defence of their right to separate (and collective) treatment. Yet the growth of unionism cannot be explained by the fact of common employment, any more than by reference to employers' recognition and state intervention. The existence of large firms with a corps of industrial supervisors provided the means, in the shipbuilding and marine engineering districts, for concentrated efforts by the organised firms against staff unionism in favour of sponsored benefit societies. Very few enterprises were willing to give the NFA or other unions any kind of recognition before 1939, though the associations survived in the face of hostility and reached an understanding with the manual unions. Independent unionism had been provoked by unpopular government policies, along with the erosion of differentials and the intense pressures of munitions production during the war, and if the new unions sought to use wartime conciliation procedures they failed to secure official support and weathered the depression of the interwar years with no legislative support. It was the form rather than the fact of state intervention which mattered to the unions.

The question of recognition has also to be placed in a broader, more intricate, context than the decisions of the individual enterprise or the bargaining position of the staff grades. The structure and strategies of employers' organisations proved crucial in shaping the responses to non-manual unionism. Their role was an ideological as well as a strategic one, guardians of absolute prerogatives as well as administrators of the procedural agreements with labour. During the critical years 1914–22 these federations played a key role in the defence of capitalist authority against challenges from the shopfloor, though they remained tenuous coalitions of different firms and regions rather than a force for progressive strategies on production and rationalisation. Their concern was with the problem of labour, defined in terms of cost and control rather than production and participation. Supervisory leaders who appealed to the spirit of Whitleyism and the Industrial Conference found that they were cast as part of a wider confrontation for the control of the shopfloor and were unable to assert themselves as autonomous, equal agents in this dramatic struggle.

Victory for the employers in the pitched battles of 1920–22 allowed the federations to claim success for management prerogatives and stable bargaining arrangements. The settlements really confirmed the preferences of individual firms for pragmatic, diversified, policies in the subsequent years. Older sectors such as shipbuilding were able to cut wages, drive workers and contain craft practices within the boundaries of limited production and repairs. Arguably it was their success with these basic policies which discouraged a more radical reappraisal of the division of labour and the possibilities of innovation, though the collapse of markets obscured the potential of fresh techniques. In the expanding areas of engineering there were important continuities with earlier systems of pieceworking, requiring more varied and flexible kinds of supervision than that associated with the rapid pace of a Fordist assembly-line. This does not prove the backwardness or inefficiency of British management, though it does suggest that firms made few efforts to structure the labour market more rigorously by a coherent training and manpower strategy and this left them open to challenges on a range of issues during the rearmament years.

The reasons for this poverty of imaginative planning can be found in the arena of collective bargaining as well as the strength of enterprise and markets at this period. Business organisations did little to disturb an industrial culture of management which prized the achievements of the able individual in winning a promoted place within a classical hierarchy of command. Formal training was recognised—and frequently dismissed—as belonging to the distinct world of the draughtsmen, rate-fixer and planning engineer rather than austerely masculine surroundings of the shipyard or engine shop. Collective bargaining derived some of its guiding principles from Victorian fictions of apprenticeship and service which were in contrast to the advance of a complex shopfloor bargaining between stewards, foremen and rate-fixers. Progressive firms such as Siemens and Leyland took their own initiatives in regard to these changes, finding their federations unable to prevent or resolve questions of trade training and representation.

Supervisory unionism suffered not only from the determination of industrialists to preserve a hierarchy of clear command. The whole history of their organisation has to be phrased in terms of the changing relationship between employers and different sections of the industrial workforce. It would be misleading to portray these relations as primarily involving a contest between traditional craft defences and an industrial management striving to breach these demarcations. The case of the workplace supervisor shows that craft institutions, such as apprenticeship, delivered major benefits to the employers and did not prevent the drastic deterioration in wages and conditions after 1920. Ambiguities were also apparent in those trades which successfully retained foremen in their ranks, even though unions and employers agreed that skilled work required qualified supervision. When the Boilermakers' Society attempted to call their foremen into line over management policies, they found that the supervisors could take an independent stand without deserting to the camp of the shipyard firms. If shipbuilding foremen carried trade cards longer than some engineering supervisors, they also retained the power of individual brutality and rough discipline in the harsh conditions of Clydeside or the North-East. Supervision could keep within the customary notions of fairness and rights which craft culture endowed on the shipyards, but this might actually prevent the better treatment of workers and provision of decent facilities.

The structure of the older skilled societies gave the districts the autonomy to deal with local conditions but actually inhibited the leaders from moving towards a more coherent strategy for the industries. There are signs from the pre-1914 period, confirmed in the dilution controversy, that officials were ready to translate the customary, direct restrictions of the nineteenth century into a fixed procedure of consultation on innovation. The resistance of the employers to any participation of unions in the decisions of production management (during and after the war), forced the unions into a strategy of campaigns in the workshops and the different districts to defend trade interests. Here lay the significance of post-war debates on the role of shop stewards and works committees, which were never fully resolved in the settlements of 1922. The rise of the shop steward gave the foremen and their unions serious problems, as the account of the NFA and the Foremen's Mutual suggest, opening up the possibility of an employers' alliance with the supervisors.[124] In practice, business attitudes drove the unions into closer alliance with the wider union movement and a closer attachment to the principle of 'skilled' supervision. Mass unemployment broke the back of shop organisation in the heavier trades which figured in wartime struggles, but the resurgence of activity in the lighter trades during the 1930s gave the foremen predictable problems and led their employers to seriously discuss a 'new foremanship'.[125]

The changing tempo of business interest in schemes of enlightened management and human relations in the workplace strongly suggests that industrial conflict rather than management theories guided their attitudes to supervision. Faced with the recovery of manual unionism in the 1930s, foremen found that they had to rely on their skills and personal judgement to secure production rather than clear directives from their employers. The relative weakness of shop floor unionism in the mass production sectors helps to explain the absence of supervisory organisation in car firms, where it was most evident in 1940s America, and its continued strength in the skilled engineering trades.[126] In common with the manual workers, supervisors found that British industry offered only the virtues of voluntaryism as they struggled to define their separate interests.

## Acknowledgements

This essay is based upon research completed with assistance from the Economic and Social Research Council and King's College, Cambridge. Thanks are due to my colleagues Richard Barker and Keith Burgess. Versions of this paper were presented at seminars in Cambridge, Gothenburg, Liverpool and Uppsala, at which participants made many valuable suggestions.

## Notes

1   W. H. Lazonick, 'Production Relations, Labour Productivity, and the Choice of Technique: British and US Cotton Spinning', *Journal of Economic History* XLI (1981), pp. 491–9, 510–13; C. R. Littler, *The Development of the Labour Process in Capitalist Societies* (Heinemann, 1982); S. Wood (ed.), *The Degradation of Work? Skill, deskilling and the labour process* (Hutchinson, 1982); cf. R. Price, *Masters, Unions and Men* (CUP, 1980), for a stimulating discussion of foremanship in the building industry.

2   S. and B. Webb, *The History of Trade Unionism, 1666–1920,* p. 506; G. D. H. Cole, *Workshop Organisation* (OUP, 1923); C. Wright Mills, *White Collar* (OUP, 1956), pp. 87–8, 90–1; A. M. Bowey, 'The changing status of the supervisor', *BJIR* XI (1973), pp. 393–4 and passim for a restatement.

3   G. S. Bain, *The Growth of White-Collar Unionism* (OUP, 1970); cf. R. Crompton, 'Approaches to the study of white-collar unionism', *Sociology* X (1976), pp. 410–12, 416–17 for criticisms; R. Hyman and R. Price, *The New Working Class? White-collar Workers and their Organisations* (Macmillan, 1982), pp. 5–7, 14–15 for a radical appraisal of Bain.

4   Bain, *op. cit.*, pp. 100, 177–8; cf. J. Heritage, 'Class situation, white-collar unionisation and the "Double Proletarianisation" thesis: a comment', *Sociology* XIV (1980), pp. 283–5, 288–9, including suggestion that the business-cycle is a key factor in Bain's analysis.

5   Bain, *op. cit.*, p. 179 for comment upon the 'industrial relations system'; cf. Hyman and Price, *op. cit.*, pp. 17–21 and passim for Hyman's response; J. Hinton, *The First Shop Stewards' Movement*

(George Allen & Unwin, 1973) for an example in the discipline of labour history.

6   J. Zeitlin, 'Craft Regulations and the Division of Labour: Engineers and Compositors in Britain, 1890–1914' (PhD Warwick, 1981); A. J. Reid, 'The Divisions of Labour in the British Shipbuilding Industry, 1880–1920' (PhD Cambridge, 1980).

7   J. Zeitlin, 'The Emergence of Shop Steward Organisation and Job Control in the British Car Industry', *History Workshop Journal* X (1980); K. McClelland and A. Reid, 'The Shipbuilding Workers, 1840–1914' (1981), in R. Harrison and J. Zeitlin (eds), *Divisions of Labour* (Harvester Press, 1985).

8   Reid, *op. cit.* (1980); Zeitlin, *op. cit.* (1981).

9   Zeitlin, *loc. cit.* (1980).

10   J. Melling, '"Non-Commissioned Officers": British employers and their supervisory workers, 1880–1920', *Social History* V (1980).

11   D. F. Schloss, *Methods of Industrial Remuneration* (Williams and Northgate, 1907), pp. 2–3.

12   M. L. Yates, *Wages and Conditions in British Engineering* (Macdonald and Evans, 1937), p. 3; J. Hinton, *The First Shop Stewards' Movement* (George Allen & Unwin, 1973), p. 24.

13   Ibid., p. 96; M. and J. B. Jeffreys, 'The Wages, Hours and Trade Customs of the skilled engineer in 1861', *Economic History Review* XVII (1947), for a discussion of piecework; K. Burgess, *The Origins of British Industrial Relations* (Croom Helm, 1975), Ch. 1.

14   Engineering, 'Modern Manufacturing Methods', *Engineering*, 6 February 1903, pp. 181–2; also *Engineering* 5 June 1903, pp. 753–4 for comments on standardisation; *Engineering Times*, 'Skilled Labour Scarce', 28 March 1907, p. 359 for GEC; 'The Characteristics of a Foreman', *Engineering* 18 December 1908, pp. 825–6.
C. K. Harley, 'Skilled labour and the choice of technique in Edwardian industry', *Explorations in Economic History* XI (1974); E. H. Lorenz, 'The labour process in British and French shipbuilding industries: Two patterns of development' (unpublished paper Cambridge, 1981); R. C. Floud, 'Change in the productivity of labour in the British machine tool industry, 1856–1900', in D. N. McCloskey (ed.), *Essays on a Mature Economy* (Princeton UP, 1971), pp. 333–4; cf. J. Melling, 'Leading Hands and Industrial Techniques . . .', (1985).

15   K. Williams, *et al.*, *Why Are The British Bad At Manufacturing?* (Routledge & Kegan Paul, 1983) provides a lucid survey; J. McGoldrick, 'Crisis and the Division of Labour: Clydeside Shipbuilding in the Interwar Period', in A. Dickson (ed.), *Capital and Class in Scotland*, (Donald, 1982); Reid, *op. cit.* (1980).

16   R. C. Floud, 'The Adolescence of American engineering competition, 1860–1900', *Economic History Review* XXVII (1974), pp. 60–5; Yates, *op. cit.*, pp. 20–1.

17   Ibid.

18   Ibid., pp. 30–1.

19 A Foreman, *Pattern Making: A Practical Treatise* (Crosby Lock-wood, 1894), pp. 294–8, 302–3.
20 Melling, *loc. cit.* (1980).
21 Ibid; cf. Zeitlin, *loc. cit.* (1983).
22 Melling, *loc. cit.* (1980).
23 W. Knox, '"Down with Lloyd George!": The apprentices strike of 1912', *Journal of Scottish Labour History Society* XIX (1984), pp. 22–36, for Clydeside background.
24 Engineering Employers' Federation (cited hereafter as EEF) Files, F9(1), Letter of Maudslay to Dyer 4 February 1898 for proposal of a benefit scheme endorsed by George Livesey; also J. Melling, 'Employers, industrial welfare and the struggle for workplace control in British industry, 1880–1920', in H. F. Gospel and C. R. Littler (eds), *Management Strategies and Industrial Relations* (Heinemann, 1983), pp. 55–81.
25 'The characteristics of a foreman', *Engineering* 18 December 1908, pp. 825–88.
26 Melling, *loc. cit.* (1980); E. Wigham, *The Power to Manage* (Macmillan, 1973), pp. 63–85; B. Webb, 'The success of professional associations', *New Statesman* IX (27 April 1917), pp. 20, 35–7 and passim; *Foreman Engineer and Draughtsman*, 1 November 1884, pp. 162–4; *Engineering Times* 7 February 1907, p. 164, and 30 May 1907, p. 664.
27 A. Reid, 'Dilution, Trade Unionism and the State in Britain during the First World War', in S. Tolliday and J. Zeitlin (eds), *Shop Floor Bargaining and the State* (CUP, 1985); also I. McLean, *The Legend of Red Clydeside* (Donald, 1982) for a comparable interpretation of craft conservation and sectionalism; cf. J. Melling, 'The "Servile State" Revisited: Employers and State Intervention, 1911–1916' (unpublished paper, 1982).
28 Amalgamated Society of Engineers (ASE), Edinburgh District Committee No. 1 minutes, 29 July 1915–19 August 1915.
29 Melling, 'Servile State Revisited'.
30 Ibid., 8 March 1916 for the controversial case of Bruce Peebles; ibid., 27 February 1916–14 April 1916 for the spread of committees in response to the dilution programme; ibid., 15 May 1917.
31 Hinton, *op. cit.*, pp. 213–54; J. Melling, 'Scottish industrialists and the changing character of class relations in the Clyde region, 1880–1918', in T. Dickson (ed.), *Capital and Class in Scotland* (John Donald, 1982) for a discussion of this point.
32 Wages data from Connells compiled by Keith Burgess, revealing a sharp erosion of differentials in the war years.
33 Anon., 'Wanted: A National Association of Engineering Foremen', *Engineering* 27 July 1917, includes references to the RAF establishments. Anon., 'The hard case of shipbuilding and engineering foremen', *Engineering* 12 October 1917, pp. 390–1.
34 Letter from 'Workshop Foremen' (12 August 1917), in *Engineering*, 17 August 1917.

35  Ibid., p. 182.
36  National Foremen's Association (NFA), Executive Council Minutes, 19–20 January 1918, 16 February 1918; National Amalgamated Society of Foremen, Rules (1918) and Fourth Annual Report (1921), Widnes in TUC Library, HD6661 C4.19. The NASF was a localised organisation based in Cheshire.
37  G. D. H. Cole, 'Non-Manual Trade Unionism', North American Review CCXV (1922), p. 39; G. D. H. Cole, Organised Labour (1923), pp. 99–102.
38  Anon., 'The hard case. . . .', loc. cit.
39  Ibid., 23 March 1918–25 May 1918; cf. 29 June 1918 for Erith Branch objections; ibid., 16 February 1918.
40  Ibid., 27 November 1920, 24 March 1923; Anon., 'National Conference of Foremen Associations', Industrial League and Council Journal (May 1921), pp. 80–1; R. Nuttall, 'Functions and Places of Supervisors in the Industries', at ibid., p. 81.
41  ASE Edinburgh DC minutes, 21 March 1917–18 April 1917, for example of East Scotland.
42  EEF E(1)41, for West Country correspondence 13–30 December 1918; CSA circular letters RD 241 13/3–8. Letters 7 May 1921 and especially 2 December 1921.
43  EEF E(1)50, Letters from Vickers, 7–8 March 1919 and from a demoted foreman, 16 November 1919; ibid., Memorandum of Vickers, 28 September 1920 and correspondence relating to V. A. Coward, 7 December 1920; these revealed large numbers of foremen had been disrated or left the company by 1920, only a substantial minority remaining with the FMBS.
44  Ibid., p. 6; ibid., Local Conference of 21 November 1919, verbatim notes, pp. 14–15.
45  Ibid., pp. 14–15, 20.
46  Ibid.
47  EEF E(1)39, Letter from Liverpool Engineering Employers' Association, 9 September 1918; E(1)48 for Leicester Association Letter, 19 December 1919; G. Schaffer, Light and Liberty, Sixty Years of the Electrical Trades Union (ETU, 1949); Hayes, pp. 9–10, 31; EEF E(16)66 Notes of C. J. Hardy (Chief of Cammell Lairds' Labour Department at Penistone) on interview with Matthews, ETU District Secretary.
48  Ibid., Letter of Ministry of Labour, 5 September 1920; Sheffield Daily Telegraph, 30 August 1920, cuttings in file: ibid., Letters of Sheffield EEA to Federation 23 July 1920.
49  Ibid., Allan Smith to Rowan at Central Conference p. 6; ibid., Notes of C. J. Hardy, pp. 4–5; E(1)66, verbatim notes from Central Conference, 16 September 1920, pp. 10–11.
50  Ibid., Circular from the Secretary of the Federation to local Associations, 6 September 1920, p. 3.
51  Ibid., Report of an interview with the Minister of Labour (T. J. Macnamara), 4–5 September 1920.

52   Ibid., verbatim notes of Central Conference, 16 September 1920,
     p. 9:
     'Smith: If we are to come to an agreement, you and we must do it
     . . . without outside interference.
     Rowan: Still, I would rather like the man who built the bridge to
     explain the construction.
     Smith: If we can cross it without bothering about the construction,
     is it not better?'
53   Ibid., Notes prepared for Sir Allan Smith, pp. 2–3, stated that 29
     Associations claimed union membership was *not* a decisive factor in
     promotion to foremen, as against four Associations which believed it
     to be a vital consideration in the policies of their members.
54   Ibid., Letter from Hardy to Smith, 31 August 1920, enclosing a
     copy of the Pilkington's agreement.
55   Ibid., notes prepared for Smith, p. 1.
56   Ibid., notes of J. McNeil Allan (Managing Director) on strike,
     pp. 1–2; Text of speech of Matthews to Penistone strikers in corre-
     spondence of Sheffield EEA to EEF, 19 July 1920; EEF E(1)50,
     Letters from Vickers, 7–8 March 1919 and from a demoted
     foreman, 16 November 1919.
57   EEF E(16)66, giving relative strength in the marine engineering
     districts.
58   NFA minutes, 7 May 1921, 28 January–26 February 1922 for bitter
     criticism of client societies; Scottish Foremen's Protective Associ-
     ation (SFPA), 'Financial Statements' (December 1918–October
     1919), SRO FS 7/69 for figures which suggest an estimated member-
     ship of perhaps 900–1000 at most.
59   Ibid., Transcript of telephone conversation between Vickers and
     Federation, 13 November 1919, concerning FMBS membership.
60   Ibid., Central Conference of 9 January 1920, verbatim proceedings,
     conclusion.
61   EEF F(11)13, correspondence from the Wigan Association, 15 July
     1926, complaining of the harassment and abuse of foremen queuing
     in labour exchanges: 'As you can imagine this is rather tending to
     undo the work we have tried to carry out in encouraging the Society
     as they are being made to feel very forcibly that by being members
     of the Society they are outcasts.'
62   EEF F(11)3, Letter 19 May 1920 concerning the British Thomson
     Houston foremen; F(1)4 for London Association correspondence 14
     June 1920, and Hawthorn Leslie to Allan Smith, June 1920; ibid.,
     Letter from Thomas Biggart, 16 November 1920.
63   Ibid., Biggart to Federation, 20 December 1920–25 February 1921;
     F(11)6, G. B. Richardson to D. S. Marjoribanks, 9 September 1921.
64   Yates, *op. cit.*, pp. 111–15.
65   Amalgamated Engineering Union (AEU) (formerly ASE), District
     Committee minutes, 1 July 1921, 22 August–14 September 1921,
     for example; ibid., 24 April 1921.

66  AEU DC District Lock-out Committee minutes, 23 February–29 March 1922; cf. 20 April 1922 for the return of some apprentices.
67  Ibid., 13–14 March 1922, 23 February 1922; cf. AEU Glasgow, *Lockout Bulletin*, F331.8812 AMH, for Glasgow situation. I owe the latter reference to Keith Burgess.
68  *The Foreman* (May 1921), p. 13.
69  NFA minutes, 18 May–7 August 1920; EEF F(11)4, correspondence 6 May–4 June 1920 for the views of critics such as Thorneycrofts and Elliots.
70  Ibid., for reference to the Partington dispute; also correspondence from Electrical Power Engineers' Association, National Association of Supervisory Electricians, and the Amalgamated Managers' and Foremen's Association, 11 August 1920, 14 September 1920.
71  *The Foreman* (January 1922), p. 5; ibid. (June 1922), p. 4.
72  *The Foreman* (May 1922), p. 11.
73  NFA minutes, 26 March–29 April 1922; ibid., 29 April 1922 gives details of wage cuts offered foremen in lock-out; and 30 July 1922 for the alleged victimisation of a prominent Association officer.
74  TUC General Council, 'Memorandum on Trade Union Policy towards Foremen, supervisory, technical, Staff . . .', TUC Library TB48, pp. 15–16.
75  Ibid., 15 September 1923; ibid., 2 July–6–7 August 1921.
76  *The Foreman* (May 1922), p. 4 for President F. E. Watts.
77  Yates, *op. cit.*, pp. 5, 9–10; R. Croucher, *Engineers at War 1939–1945* (Merlin, 1982), pp. 3–7.
78  B. Alford, 'British Industries Between The Wars', R. Floud and D. McCloskey (eds), *The Economic History of Britain since 1700: Vol. 2* (CUP, 1981), p. 319.
79  Sir H. Fowler, 'Shop Management', *Engineering*, 20 January 1922, p. 75; T. R. Gourvish, 'Mechanical Engineering', in N. K. Buxton and D. H. Aldcroft (eds.), *British Industry Between The Wars* (Scolar Press, 1979), pp. 144–5.
80  Committee on Industry and Trade (Balfour Committee), *Survey of Metal Industries* (HMSO, 1928), pp. 152–5, 197, 206–11; G. C. Allen, *British Industry* (Longmans Green, 1944), pp. 19–24 and passim; R. Samuel, 'The workshop of the world: steam power and hand technology in mid-Victorian Britain', *History Workshop Journal* III (1979); Reid, *op. cit.* (1980); Zeitlin, *op. cit.* (1981).
81  Yates, *op. cit.*, p. 7 for shipbuilding.
82  Cf. Zeitlin, *loc. cit.* (1980), pp. 119–37. D. Lyddon, in the following issue, offers a compelling critique of this interpretation.
83  Yates, *op. cit.*, pp. 13, 31–2; Croucher, *op. cit.*, pp. 8–10; W. West, 'The importance of the tool-room', *The Foreman* (September 1922), pp. 16–17.
84  M. Miller and R. A. Church, 'Motor manufacturing', in Buxton and Aldcroft (eds.), *op. cit.*, pp. 193–4, 203, 209; *Survey*, *op. cit.*, pp. 226–7, Ibid., pp. 246–9; 256 for comparable motor cycle industry's performance.

85 Croucher, *op. cit.*, p. 6. I am indebted to Steven Tolliday and Steve Jefferys for their helpful criticisms on the interpretation of car manufacturing.
86 Yates, *op. cit.*, pp. 72–3, 80.
87 The case of Dick, Kerr at Leyland is discussed below.
88 Clyde Shipbuilders' Association (CSA), 'Conditions of Labour and Yard Management', SRA TD241,12,1, files of correspondence between west Scotland and North-East coast; cf. McClelland and Reid, *loc. cit.*; E. H. Lorenz and F. Wilkinson, 'Shipbuilding and British Economic Decline: 1880 to 1965' (Cambridge, 1983), offers a persuasive interpretation.
89 SEF minutes of EC, SRNA 7 SEF 1/1–4, as surveyed by R. Barker, reveals the problems of fragmentation in this period; CSA TD 241 12/1, for the Clydeside case.
90 EEF E(1)33, correspondence of 29 December 1914–19 January 1915 for Benjamin Browne at Hawthorn Leslies; ASE DC minutes 10 November–12 March 1919 for experience at Edinburgh and case of Leith charge hands; SEF minutes 19–20 June 1919, 15 July 1919 to 6–7 November 1919, etc.
91 EEF F(1)20, West of England correspondence 17–22 August 1914; E(1)50. Local conference proceedings, 21 November 1919, p. 10, at which an employer notes: 'That was in the Shipyard, but what takes place in the Shipyard never controls what takes place in the Engineering Department, and that principle has never been adopted in the Engineering Department.'
92 EEF E(1)56, Cammell Lairds and local conference, 19 April 1920, pp. 4–5, 9.; ibid., p. 6 for Godsell of the Boilermakers' Society: 'We are one of the pioneer trades and one of the strongest in the country. The Engineers' Society was never organised before the War.'
93 Ibid., pp. 5–7.
94 SEF File on Foremanship, SRNA 1/3645 c.1, memoranda 6 May 1925 for Birkenhead case.
95 Amalgamated Society of Woodworkers (ASW), letters to branches of ASW (previously the Amalgamated Society of Carpenters, Cabinet-makers and Joiners), MRC 78/ASW/3/1/31, letters 25 May–8 June 1923; 24 June 1925 in 3.1.10.
96 'Foremen Boilermakers' file in SRNA 1/3645 a.1.
97 Ibid., Federation J.S.B. memorandum, 9 January 1931; SEF to Bristol Channel Association, 24 April 1931; H. S. Ratcliffe to Federation Secretary 30 September–7 October 1931.
98 Yates, *op. cit.*, p. 7.
99 EEF F(11)9, 12 February 1923; and F(11)19, 29 June 1932 for foremen working with the tools at Greenock.
100 EEF F(10)19, Kincaids and the Boilermakers' Society correspondence, 29 June 1932, etc.; Croucher, *op. cit.*, p. 9.
101 EEF E(1)164, report of a Works Conference of 2 March 1938.
102 River Thames Shiprepairers' Association, minute 11 December 1923 in SEF 1/3645 a.1., for comment of E. J. Hill to E. A. Moir.

103 ASW 3/1/31, letter to Swansea branch 11 June 1923; 3/1/37 for 12 December 1924 to Liverpool; 3/1/21 for 24 June 1925 to Liverpool; for policies on foremen.

104 Ibid., 3/1/37 for 29 January 1925 to Bristol; 3/1/36, letter to Gillingham: 'the E.C. cannot lay down the conditions under which Foremen members will be allowed to remain at work in future disputes.'

105 Ibid., 3/1/43 for 21 May 1926 on Bolton victimisations; 3/1/44 23 July 1926; ibid., 3/1/30, 23 December 1922; 3/1/42, 22 December 1925 for support given to Scottish TUC campaign against subsidised societies, promising to 'do its utmost to defeat the obvious desire of certain sections of employers to promote a third party in industry'; 3/1/49, 1 October 1927; 3/1/38, 25 March–24 June 1925 for developments in the North East.

106 Ibid., 3/1/21 for 1 December 1920 to Cameron at Liverpool; 3/1/46 for 8 December 1926 to Exeter; 3/1/31 for 6 July 1923 to Swansea on fines, etc.

107 EEF A(1)55, Blackburn Aircraft Company at the Clyde Foundry, proceedings of Local Conference 27 January 1939; interview with C. B. Wood, Dumbarton (27 June 1984), pp. 5–6, 8–10, for contemporary conditions at the works and rate-fixing standards.

108 Croucher, op. cit., pp. 39–41.

109 Ibid., pp. 19, 28.

110 A. Exell, 'Morris Motors in the 1930s', History Workshop Journal VI (1978), pp. 52–78; Croucher, op. cit., p. 25.

111 The dispute occur at the Dick Kerr works of the English Electric Company at Preston. On the car industry in this period, see Chapter 9 and other work by Steven Tolliday.

112 Melling, loc. cit. (1980); Knox, loc. cit. (1984).

113 Croucher, op. cit., pp. 46–57; A. McKinlay, 'The 1937 Apprentices' Strike: Challenge from "An unexpected quarter"'. Unpublished paper (Oxford, 1984). I am grateful for the opportunity to read and cite this interesting paper.

114 EEF F(10)22, correspondence 10–15 June 1938; Local conference verbatim report 30 June 1938. The foreman involved, Wesson, departed shortly before his expected retirement date to resolve the dispute; Croucher, op. cit., pp. 31–3, 56–9.

115 NFA minutes, 30 December 1922, 22 March 1924.

116 Ibid., 17 October 1931, 8 February–18 July 1936 for the case of rate-fixers; cf. 27 September 1941 for refusal to admit Metro Vickers rate-fixers and planning engineers, regardless of their claim that 'the Management side and the craft unions could do nothing for them'.

117 Ibid., 6–7 August 1921.

118 Ibid., 26 March 1922, 10 May 1930.

119 Ibid., 30 January–19 March 1932.

120 Ibid., 14 July–15 September 1923; cf. 10 July 1926 when the executive acknowledged that the 'difficult and invidious position in which some of its members have been placed in carrying out the Associ-

ation's neutrality regulations rigidly, under conditions which render them a menace to their livelihood in circumstances which neither their own Association, other unions, or the TUC could obtain for them redress for victimisation'; cf. ibid., 23 July 1927 for the ADC decision to continue affiliation to the TUC.

121  Ibid., 25 November 1922 for EEF relations; and ibid., 26 February 1921, 14 July 1923, 30 January 1926 and 15 August 1931 for the complex and problematic relationship with the railway companies.

122  EEF F(11)5, 10 February 1920 and F(11)11, 5 September 1923 for discussion of ancillary schemes; CSA TD 241 13/7 for copy of letter 20 December 1922 from Biggart of FMBS to SEF on question of ancillary scheme.

123  EEF F(11)7, Management Committee of EEF's discussion of non-union labour question, 27 January 1922 and statement of Marjori-banks, p. 3.

124  NFA minutes, 25–26 January 1919 recommendation to local branches on this point.

125  A. H. Seymour, 'Successful foremanship in modern industry', *Labour Management* XVIII (June 1936), pp. 105–6; F. J. Burns Morton, *The New Foremanship* (Chapman & Hall, 1946), introduced by Beharrell of Dunlops. It is significant that the EEF firmly refused to cooperate with 'outside' investigations of industrial supervision as late as 1943/44.

126  H. R. Northrup, 'The Foremen's Association of America', *Harvard Business Review*, XXIII (1945), pp. 187–9, 198–9; R. H. Keys, 'Union membership and collective bargaining by foremen', *Mechanical Engineering*, LXVI (1944), pp. 251–2; C. P. Larrowe, 'A meteor on the industrial relations horizon: the Foremen's Association of America', *Labor History* II (1961), pp. 262, 271–2, 285–6, 294: 'the most significant difference between the periods of growth and decline of the union has been the presence and absence of protective legislation'; Bain, *op. cit.*, pp. 156–7; T. W. Agar, 'Victory at Dagenham', ASSET II, no. 5 (September 1944), pp. 91–2.

# 8

# The Development of Bargaining Structure: The Case of Electrical Contracting, 1914–39

*Howard F. Gospel*

The structure of collective bargaining is a combination of the levels, units and forms of bargaining and the power relationship between the bargaining parties. As such it is a key phenomenon of any industrial relations system. In Britain in the nineteenth century, collective bargaining, where it existed, had first developed for groups of skilled workers on an *ad hoc* basis, at factory, site or mill level. Very often the level was that of the shop or department or work group. Slowly and unevenly from these beginnings bargaining extended to district level, covering a number of firms in a city or locality. The industrial conflicts of the 1890s led to the establishment of new, more formal, collective-bargaining machinery in a number of industries, including the beginnings of national-level bargaining. These included the 1893 Brooklands Agreement in cotton spinning, the Wages Conciliation Board of the same year in coal mining, the 1895 Terms of Settlement in the footwear industry, and the more famous 1898 Terms of Settlement in engineering. These were followed by similar agreements in building in 1904 and shipbuilding in 1906. Such agreements were mainly procedural in nature and made little provision for substantive matters relating to wages and conditions of employment. Exceptions were the agreements in coal mining and shipbuilding, under which national percentage changes were made to the district base rates which had grown up, though the rates themselves were not uniform between districts and were minimal rather than standard. In cotton weaving what might be considered the first national substantive agreement in Britain were established in 1892, viz. a uniform list of piece prices for plain weaving. In cotton spinning the number of lists was reduced to two, the Oldham and Bolton lists, and from 1906 onwards these were adjusted simultaneously.

However, this centralisation and uniformity in cotton textiles was exceptional and rendered possible by a combination of factors—the geographical concentration of industry, the high level of organisation on both sides, and the relative standardisation of production techniques.

Before 1914 wages and conditions bargaining in Britain, therefore, still took place at workplace and district level, covered only certain classes of labour (usually skilled men), and was largely *ad hoc*. As earlier chapters in this volume have shown, it was during the war and the immediate post-war years that not only was there a considerable extension of the number of industries covered by collective bargaining but also there occurred a growth in more formal systems of bargaining at national level. This chapter examines this process in one industry which, though small, provides an interesting example of the growth of national bargaining. Indeed there evolved in electrical contracting one of the more centralised systems of national multi-employer agreements to emerge during the interwar period. Moreover this was in an industry where on *a priori* grounds such a development might have seemed highly unlikely. Yet the national system which did emerge has proved in the post-Second World War period to be one of the most resilient.

Electrical contracting was one of the new industries of the late nineteenth and early twentieth centuries. Along with the spread of electricity, there had grown an increasing demand for the installation of electrical power and equipment in industrial establishments, public and commercial buildings and private houses. This grew through the First World War and the interwar period, along with the building of the National Grid in the 1920s and 1930s. Though the trade suffered in the depression of the early 1920s, this was only a temporary setback, and overall it fared considerably better than most of the building trade and industry generally.

By many of the criteria used to classify product markets, electrical contracting was a highly competitive industry. It was characterised by a large number of one-man businesses and small firms. It was relatively easy for former workmen to set themselves up in business, and contractors were continually complaining about the growth of 'mushroom' firms and 'carpetbaggers'.[1] This competition was accentuated by the uncertainties of scheduling work in the building industry and by the system of competitive tendering for contracts. The reduction and regulation of this competition and uncertainty was a major objective of the firms in the industry, and to attain this end contractors resorted to various practices. In the first place, from the early twentieth century, their trade association lobbied Parliament to place restrictions on entry into the industry and in particular on competition from direct labour departments of local authorities. Further, contracting firms through their trade association entered into collusive agreements with suppliers of cables, wire and other electrical equipment: they agreed to buy exclusively from the manufacturers' cartels and in return were given preferential discounts and rebates. In this way quality competition could to some extent be controlled and newcomers could be discouraged by exclusion from these arrangements. In addition and perhaps even more important, within their local markets the firms engaged in various forms of collusive tendering, market sharing, and price-fixing.[2]

Electrical installation firms were first established in London and the large provincial towns and markets were at first highly localised. Contractors operated within a radius determined by the maximum reasonable travelling time from their shop. Slowly, however, as a result of the building of the National Grid, better transport and communications, the building of the suburbs, and the erection of factories outside the centres of towns, there was an extension of the boundaries of local product markets. Also in the 1930s some larger firms set up branch offices and began to work outside their original areas. In this way the scope of the market was expanded.

The argument presented in this chapter is that the nature of competition and the extending boundaries of the product market were key factors shaping the collective bargaining system in the industry.

Certain characteristics of the labour force and work organisation in the industry are also pertinent. Approximately half the labour force were skilled journeymen electricians. Overall labour costs represented about 40–50 per cent of total costs[3] and therefore were a crucial factor in competition between firms. Moreover, electrical contracting was a trade where it was difficult for the employer to exercise close or continuous supervision over the work process. The journeyman enjoyed a high degree of independence, working at a distance from the employer's premises on jobs which were all slightly different. In these circumstances, it was difficult for firms to compete with one another through an intensification of the labour process.

The Electrical Trade Union (ETU) which organised the industry had, before the First World War, become reasonably well established in London, Manchester and a number of other large towns. In the immediate pre-war period and during the war, membership increased considerably not only in contracting, but also in engineering and shipbuilding, in maintenance work, and in electricity supply.[4] For the union there was, however, a major difficulty in recruiting and maintaining membership in the electrical contracting industry, characterised as it was by a large number of small firms, a variable workplace and a high turnover of both men and firms. This made formal national recognition by the contracting employers important for the union.

Another problem—for the union leadership at least—was district autonomy. As in other craft organisations district committees had from the beginning been strong in the ETU. Since before the war there had been a struggle in particular between the National Executive and the London District Committee which was particularly independent and militant.[5] As will be described below, this committee was suspended in 1915 and 1932 and for a time was expelled in 1937.[6] Throughout the interwar years there was a steady centralisation of power within the union: in 1924 a centralised banking system was introduced; in 1930 the headquarters were moved from Manchester to London; in 1935 full-time district officials, elected and paid as secretaries of the district committees, were replaced by full-time area officials paid and controlled by the National Executive Council.[7]

On the employers' side, from the turn of the century a national trade association had been established and at local level employers' organisations had existed for consulting on labour matters. In 1916 a national employers' organisation, the National Federated Electrical Association (NFEA) was established in response to growing ETU pressure during the war and the uncoordinated local arbitrations which the employers felt were being used to leapfrog wage increases. In the words of this Association, the employers' organisation was established 'so as to prevent the employers receiving applications for increases from various sources, such as the electricians, the building trades, the engineering trades joint committees, and the trade councils'.[8] The employers saw the need to establish their industry as a distinct bargaining unit and to deal with just one union. Like the ETU, however, the Association had some difficulty organising the industry, but, because of the discounts and other trade advantages it offered, by the late 1930s it had 1661 members (including most of the large and medium firms), and these comprised roughly 65 per cent of the industry's labour force, a density somewhat higher than that of the ETU.[9]

Informal *ad hoc* recognition of the union by some local masters' associations had existed since the turn of the century. But it was immediately before and during the war that formal recognition was established. The breakthrough really came in London in 1914 when after a four-month strike the London employers formally recognised the ETU. Similar recognition agreements were then concluded in other towns and more followed on the establishment of the NFEA and the formal national recognition agreement it concluded in 1916.[10] In 1919 this was further formalised, at the initiative of the employers, by the establishment of a Whitley system, with a National Joint Industrial Council (NJIC), local Joint District Councils (JDCs), and district and national disputes procedures.

The employers were aware of the advantages of recognising the one union and maintaining its authority in the industry. In some areas they were prepared to enter into exclusive arrangements under which they undertook to hire only ETU members, and the union in return agreed that its members would work only for federated employers. The South Wales local working rule, for example, stated that, 'No federated firm shall engage non-union labour, and on the other hand no union member shall engage himself to any non-federated employer.'[11] At national level the employers were not prepared to concede a closed shop but they were ready to support the union, or at least the leadership, in other ways. In particular they felt it necessary to support the leadership against factions in London and Liverpool, especially when these latter took unconstitutional action or threatened to break away from the national agreement. In June 1922, for example, when the ETU's fortunes were at a low ebb and when the employers were discussing the level of wage reductions to be demanded, the chairman of the NFEA Labour Committee stated,

In my view, any attempt to take advantage of the present weakened position of the trade union, although it might be temporarily successful, would only weaken the control of the saner leaders and lead to their being replaced by others of the type we have suffered from in the past.[12]

Thus both the NFEA and the leadership of the ETU, for their respective but overlapping reasons, had an interest in maintaining 'constitutionalism' in the industry.

Two notable London disputes reveal the importance of the national procedure and how it was used by the employers. The first concerns the strike in the spring of 1931 by electricians working on the building of the Ford Motor Co. plant at Dagenham. The men struck in pursuit of a claim to be paid the London rate for the part of the site which was within the London area. The strikers do not appear to have been claiming a supplement to the national rate, and the site was genuinely partly inside and partly outside the 12 miles London radius. Both the NFEA and the ETU declared the strike unconstitutional, though the men got support from the London District Committee. The NFEA for its part declared it was prepared to risk an area-wide strike and to force a lock-out to maintain what it considered 'constitutionalism' in the industry. The dispute was settled after the NFEA had further leant on the ETU and after the executive had in turn put pressure on the men to return to work. A compromise composite rate was conceded which did not undermine the principle of the nationally determined standard rate.[13] The same electricians struck again in the autumn of 1931 over the use of a mate on a particular job and for a further adjustment in the rate. Once again the NFEA and ETU declared the strike unconstitutional. This time the firm concerned, backed by the Association, dismissed all the men on site and engaged 120 replacements.[14] When in the following year the London district committee gave support to a further strike, the ETU executive finally suspended the London Committee.[15]

The second dispute occurred in January 1937 when the London committee, without the consent of the National Executive, called a strike of 100 electricians at the Earls Court Exhibition site over a claim for dirt money. The Association informed the ETU that it was holding the union responsible and threatened a national lock-out. The union executive ordered the men back and declared that it would stand by the procedure. It then expelled the London

Committee. The strike lasted seven weeks and in the end was settled by a compromise with some dirt money being paid for the period during which the conditions on site were agreed to be abnormal.[16]

These two strikes not only show the closeness of the relationship which developed between the national leaders on both sides around the defence of constitutionalism, they also give an indication of the system of wages and conditions which had developed in the industry by the 1930s.

The industry-wide wages and conditions agreement in electrical contracting was a good example of the type of national wage system that was developing in some industries during the interwar years. However, by the late 1930s, in its tightness and discipline, it had become something of an extreme example. It provides an interesting case study of how product and, to a lesser extent, labour market factors could shape an industry's wage-bargaining system.

It is uncertain to what extent firm- or site-level bargaining existed in electrical contracting in the late nineteenth and early twentieth centuries. However by the early years of the twentieth century district rates had begun to emerge, though these appear to have been somewhat informal and unstable.[17] In the years before the war more permanent local masters associations were formed in London, Liverpool and other towns, and formal agreements were concluded. The London Electrical Masters' Association, for example, had been formed in 1913 to counter ETU wage claims and to bring about 'uniformity in the minimum rates of wages and terms of employment'.[18]

To prevent the leapfrogging which wartime conditions and arbitration was causing, in 1917 the newly-formed NFEA approached the Committee on Production for one single arbitration for the whole of the country.[19] In this they were supported by the ETU which wanted to establish its own position as the bargaining agent for the electrical contracting industry and to extend awards to areas where it was not well organised.[20] During the war the Committee on Production made seven awards covering the industry. These were added on to the local pre-war district rates, thereby narrowing percentage differentials between areas. As in many other industries this familiarised the trade with the notion of national bargaining.

The first national wages and conditions agreement was

concluded under the NJIC in January 1919. It consolidated wartime additions into the pre-war basic rates and reduced hours from a spread ranging from 50 to 54 to a uniform 47. Thereafter the NFEA refused to accept local claims and insisted on national settlements. In November 1919, a national Standardised Wages Agreement was concluded which provided the basis for the industry's wage system throughout the rest of the interwar period. It established for journeymen electricians four geographical grades—Grade A covering London; Grade B for Manchester, Liverpool and South Wales; Grade C taking in a number of specified cities and large towns; while Grade D included the remaining smaller towns and other districts. The rate for electricians' mates was set at 75 per cent of that of journeymen, and it was explicitly stated that all rates were to be standard and henceforward only to be altered nationally.[21] In the following year a regrading exercise took place with more towns being added to Grade B. Again it was stated that the rates were to be standard: they were not to be minima or maxima and could only be altered at national level.

Wage reduction in the industry began in spring 1921. In order to regularise that process in the autumn of that year the NFEA persuaded the ETU to accept a cost of living sliding-scale system. With slight adjustments, this indexation system continued throughout the rest of the interwar period. It suited the employers because it gave them a degree of stability and predictability. The union regularly pressed for adjustments—an extension of the period of review during downswings, a shortening during upswings, and other changes in the formula intended to produce more favourable results for them. But overall the ETU also supported a system which offerred them security and stability.

From time to time other modifications of the national system were made. Areas were occasionally upgraded on appeal after being reviewed by the national leaderships on both sides. In the 1930s some large towns such as Birmingham and Bristol had their boundaries redrawn as contractors in these cities started to work further afield. London, Liverpool and Belfast rates were increased in 1929, 1934 and 1936 respectively.[22]

The original Standardised Wages Agreement had equalised wages within local product markets. However the extension of markets through the 1920s and 1930s gradually put pressure on these rates. Thus contractors from A and B areas increasingly found themselves doing work in C and D areas and vice versa. The former felt that they were disadvantaged in competition with the lower-wage firms and pressed for an upward narrowing or even a complete elimination of differentials. In this they were supported by the ETU which not surprisingly favoured a levelling-up of wages. Equally predictably it was opposed by C and D employers. In 1939 at the initiative of the NFEA Council (dominated by the larger employers in Grades A and B) the system was redrawn: a large number of C districts were raised to B and all the differentials were narrowed.[23] However, it took the war and further integration of the national economy to reduce the number of grades to two, one for London and another for the rest of the country. This was achieved in 1946.

In addition to this process of wage equalisation a greater standardisation in conditions and working rules took place over the interwar period. From the pre-war and wartime years there existed a series of working rules covering matters such as hours, overtime and shift arrangements, travel expenses, various overnight allowances and dirt money.[24] From its earliest days the policy of the NFEA was to standardise these local arrangements and to work towards a set of national rules.[25] As early as 1916 it drew up Model Working Rules which were to be applied in areas which did not have agreements and against which all amendments to existing local working rules were to be vetted. This was no mere rubber stamping: before going to the NJIC for ratification, local rules were examined carefully by a committee of the NFEA and those which set undesirable precedents or created anomalies were vetoed. In 1919, for example, an NFEA veto led to a strike by Merseyside electricians and a lock-out by the local federated firms which accepted the NFEA veto rather than defend their own agreement.[26]

Supplementing and superseding these local agreements there was gradually built up a series of national working rules. These covered overtime and shift arrangements, travel time and fares, the proportion of journeymen, mates, apprentices and boys on jobs, and other detailed aspects of working arrangements. These were consolidated in the National Working Rules Agreement of 1939.

The intention of the NFFA was from the beginning to make its national agreements 'thoroughly watertight'[27] and in particular 'to maintain complete control of the standard rate of wages'.[28] To this end NFEA bye-laws forbade member firms negotiating directly with the ETU.[29] Equally the Joint District Councils of the NJIC were not allowed to negotiate wage supplements and their working rules had to be referred to the NJIC.[30] Fortunately for the system both the employers and the union opposed piecework. In fact such an opposition was essential to the standard rate. The NFEA realised this and feared also that piecework would lead to 'quality competition' between firms.[31] The ETU for its part felt that payment by results was inappropriate for skilled men, would reduce stability in earnings, and set workman against workman.[32]

The 1920 Agreement did allow special additions to be paid in the form of merit and long-service money. At first sight these might appear to have posed a threat to the standard rate. However, it was laid down that they were to be individually awarded at the discretion of the employer and were not negotiable with the union. They do not appear to have been extensively used. Equally, local working rules included allowances for dirt money, but this was also closely defined and the evidence would seem to suggest that it was not freely given.

Of course, there were deviations from standard rates and working conditions. A number of cases of payment above the rates occurred in 1919 and 1920 and in the late 1930s, while there were payments below in the early and mid-1930s. When such firms were discovered by the Association, they were either forced to comply or were expelled with the loss of trading discounts and exclusion from local contracting groups this implied.[33] The Dagenham and Earls Court disputes referred to above are further proof that both leaderships were determined to maintain the integrity of the system. A comparison of movements in wage rates and earnings over the interwar period shows that there was more correlation between the two in electrical contracting than in most other industries such as engineering, shipbuilding and building, suggesting that standard rates were for the most part adhered to by federated contracting firms.[34]

The Executive of the ETU did not encourage domestic supplements to the standard rate. They probably felt that many of their members in smaller firms would not be able domestically to secure rates as advantageous as those negotiated nationally. Also, in the context of the struggle with the District Committees, the ETU Executive wanted itself to be seen to be securing increases for its members. At the same time the employers were prepared, in return for the maintenance of the standard rate, to operate the system with some flexibility, for example conceding special increases and upgradings for London, Liverpool and Belfast and forgoing reductions due under the sliding-scale arrangements.

Thus a system was created which appealed to both the employers and the union. The ETU appreciated the value of a national wage-fixing body for keeping up wages in areas where union organisation was weak and defended the national system against London and Liverpool Districts as a threat to its own authority.[35] The employers were aware of the advantage of maintaining the position of the ETU so as 'to reduce the amount of labour which was available at lower than the proper rates'.[36] By putting firms in a position of wage rate equality, the standard rate helped to reduce competition in the local product market by taking one element of costs out of competition. This supported and strengthened their collusive practices. Also in an industry where labour costs represented a high proportion of total costs, there was an extra need to prevent leapfrogging and the upward spiralling of wages. The employers also favoured the automatic sliding-scale since this eliminated unexpectedly large changes in rates and helped them in estimating costs when tendering for long-term contracts. The employers preferred that wages should be changed in a regular and predictable manner 'which would enable them to make contracts without fear of any great alteration in the cost of labour'.[37]

This centralised and comprehensive industrial relations system thus grew out of a certain configuration of market circumstances. Before and during the First World War inter-regional rates and earnings differentials had narrowed in percentage terms. This facilitated a system of industry-wide bargaining which appealed to both parties. As local product and labour markets extended, so the areas of standardisation grew and the wage system became more centralised. However, though encouraged by market circumstances, the bargaining structure was equally the outcome of a particular power balance in which the employers had the initiative during the interwar years. The strong organisation they developed in turn strengthened the authority of the union, and it was on the basis of this interdependence and shared interests that the equilibrium of the system depended. The communist takeover of the union after the Second World War for a time upset this balance. But with the subsequent change in leadership after the ballot-rigging trial there was a further development of this highly formalised system of national standard wages and conditions.

Before the First World War Britain was a country of emerging, but still unstable, district agreements and more informal workplace bargaining. The war and the economic forces it generated superimposed on top of that a system of national bargaining and produced in most British industries a multi-level structure. However, there were great variations between industries. Electrical contracting might be said to be at one end of the spectrum. One might also include here shipping, flour milling, electricity supply where there also developed during the interwar period systems of standard rates and close relationships between employers' organisations and trade unions. At the other end of the spectrum was an industry such as motor cars where, as the case study in this volume shows, unionisation and collective bargaining were extremely weak and fragmented. Some of the firms were covered by the national engineering agreement, but this was itself always skeletal. In effect it was made up of a series of pre-war district minimum rates for certain classes of labour and a national bonus, to which flat rate additions and subtractions were made. Within this framework the actual level of earnings were determined at workplace level by a combination of unilateral management regulation, workplace bargaining, and informal understandings. Thus there was a gap between the national rules and what actually happened at the workplace, a gap which the engineering employers did not try to fill. Between these ends of the spectrum there was a spread from cotton textiles to footwear, building, printing and chemicals, where national bargaining had varying degrees of comprehensiveness and control.

The complexity and unevenness of the structure of bargaining in Britain was revealed after the Second World War. Then the looseness and fragile nature of many of the arrangements was challenged by a changed market situation and the advent of full employment which destabilised bargaining structures which had been put in place in another age.

## Notes

1   See for example, *Electrical Contractors Year Book 1923–24* (hereafter *ECYB*) p. 138, and *Electrical Contractor and Retailer* (hereafter *ECR*), September 1935, p. 686.

2   See Standing Committee on Trusts, *Report on the Electrical Cable Industry*, Cmd. 1332 (1921); Monopolies and Restrictive Practices Commission, *Collective Discrimination*, Cmd. 9504, (1955); Registrar of Restrictive Trading Agreements, *Report 1 July 1969 to 30 June 1972*, Cmnd. 5195, (1972), p. 11.
3   A. G. Bruty, in *ECR*, July 1938.
4   ETU, *The Story of the ETU* (1954), p. 66.
5   G. Schaffer, *Light and Liberty: Sixty Years of the ETU*, (1949), pp. 72–3.
6   ETU, *op. cit.*, pp. 85, 152–3.
7   Ibid., p. 148.
8   *ECYB 1918–19*, p. 45.
9   *ECYB 1937–38*, p. 206; NFEA, vol. V, Pensions for Operatives in the Electrical Installation Industry (n.d.).
10  *ECYB 1918–19*, pp. 61–94.
11  NFEA, I, Council, 18 June 1919; NFEA, I, Council, 27 April 1920; Ministry of Labour, *Report on Collective Agreements*, (1934), p. 408; *ECYB 1939–40*, p. 505.
12  NFEA, I, Council, 21 June 1922.
13  London NFEA Branch, II, Special General Meeting, 23 March 1931; London NFEA Branch, II, Committee, 1 April 1931.
14  London NFEA Branch, II, 2 September 1931.
15  *Electrical Trades Journal*, 5 May 1934, p. 119.
16  NFEA, V, Council, 16 March 1937; G. Schaffer, *op. cit.*, pp. 72–3.
17  ETU, *op. cit.*, pp. 63–4.
18  London Electrical Masters' Association, I, Letter from L. G. Tate to Electrical Contractors, 5 June 1914.
19  *Electrical Contractor*, March 1917, p. 67.
20  NFEA, I, Executive and Finance Committee, 18 January 1917.
21  For copies of all the agreements see *ECYB 1939–40* and *ECYB 1949–50*.
22  NFEA, III, Council, 23 January 1930; NFEA, III, Council, 18 September 1934; NFEA, IV, Council, 30 January 1936.
23  For more details see H. F. Gospel, 'Employers' Organisations: Their Growth and Function in the British System of Industrial Relations in the Period 1918–1939', unpublished PhD (London, 1974), p. 243.
24  See *ECYB 1939–40*, pp. 470–524 for a list of these.
25  NFEA, I, First Meeting of NFEA, 18 April 1916.
26  ETU, *op. cit.*, pp. 93–4; NFEA, I, Council, 26 November 1919.
27  NFEA, I, Council, 27 April 1920.
28  NFEA, IV, Council, 19 March 1935.
29  NFEA, I, Council, 20 May 1921; NFEA, I, Council, 18 October 1921.
30  *ECYB 1939–40*, pp. 388–40.
31  See frequent references in *ECYB* and NFEA, II, Council, 21 October 1925; NFEA, III, Council, 23 January 1932.
32  Schaffer, *op. cit.*, p. 7.
33  See Gospel, *op. cit.*, pp. 272–82.

34  Such an exercise for the interwar years has real limitations and the details are not reproduced here. See however ibid.
35  ETU, *op. cit.*, p. 92.
36  NFEA, III, Council, 21 November 1923.
37  NFEA, V, Council, 16 November 1937.

# 9

# The Failure of Mass Production Unionism in the Motor Industry, 1914–39

*Steven Tolliday*

How you worked was like this. You'd have a stack of metal sheets, just sheets. And you'd slide one in with your two hands, grab it, and put it in the press. Put your foot down. Slap, down, the safety guard would hit you in the chest, push you back out of the way. And then the thing would slide out the other side. There'd be another man the other side stacking up. The edges of the metal were like a razor blade, and all the sheets were sprayed with a very thin oil. When you tried to slide the top sheet off the pile it was so slippery, you could easily let it go, and that could mean being cut anywhere. My brother went straight into the Press Shop when he went to work at Radiators. He hadn't ever done that sort of work before—he was only 18 at the time, and had come to Oxford from South Wales—and I could have cried when I saw him coming home. There were blisters on his hands, all across. The blisters stood right up, where he'd blistered them picking up this metal and putting it in the press. That's what they had to do, one hundred every hour, nearly two a minute. And that's how you'd go, all day, like that.

(Arthur Exell, a worker at Morris Radiators in
Oxford in the 1930s)[1]

Mass production methods entered the motor industry in the interwar years, symbolised, though not dominated, by the moving assembly-line. For most workers, as for Arthur Exell and his brother, the central experience of mass-production work was intense, repetitive physical labour regulated by the clock or by piecework. But production on an unprecedented scale required new technologies, new forms of work organisation and a new labour force. These developments were not, however, matched by any corresponding new forms of union or labour organisation. Before the outbreak of the Second World War, trades unionism remained confined to small groups of skilled workers in the toolrooms and craft shops. Four of the 'Big Six' motor companies—Ford, Morris, Standard and Vauxhall—had practically no union organisation among semi-skilled workers and the other two—Austin and Rootes—had very little. The trades unions had demonstrably failed to establish themselves in the pioneer sector of mass production.

This essay analyses this failure from two points of view. The first part considers the interaction of employers' business strategies with their labour policies, particularly their payment systems and the organisation of work at the point of production, and attempts to identify the main constraints or opportunities that these posed for union organisation. This approach grows out of a growing body of literature which attempts to widen the traditional focus of labour history by attempting to integrate the history of industrial relations with business history in particular.[2] Within this context, the second part of the essay looks at the evolution of the labour force and the response of workers and their union organisations to the challenge that they faced. In particular this takes up the debate on the legacy of the craft tradition in shaping the emergence of mass production unionism.

### Employers, labour and the coming of mass production

In a number of recent articles, Wayne Lewchuk has argued that the spread of mass-production methods based on the model of Henry Ford in America was precluded, or at least seriously delayed, by the political and economic power of labour in Britain in the early part of the twentieth century and that this had profound long-term detrimental consequences for the future of the British motor industry.[3]

Lewchuk's argument rests on the assumption that it was both possible and rational for British manufacturers to imitate Ford's methods and that the size of the British market was adequate to sustain high levels of standardised mass production. In fact, however, the contrasting markets pointed the way towards quite different production strategies. The standardised Ford Model T was predicated on a boundless uniform market based on mid-western farmers needing cheap, tough, easy-to-repair cars for all roads. In 1914, Ford produced 300,000 Model Ts: in 1923, when Model T sales peaked, Ford's US production totalled 1.9 million.[4] In contrast, total UK car production was only 182,000 in 1929, reaching a pre-war peak of 390,000 in 1937. No single firm sold more than 100,000 cars in any year before the war: no single model attained 70,000.[5]

Not only was the market quantitatively smaller, it was also qualitatively different. The work of Maxcy and Silberston and Church and Miller has demonstrated that through the 1920s the UK market was a restricted quasi-luxury one dominated by the well-off who bought family cars of medium size and price. In the late 1920s this market was stagnating and sales almost stood still from 1925 to 1933. It was only the general recovery of middle-class incomes in the 1930s that boosted sales to a new higher plateau in the mid-1930s. A whole new income layer was tapped by small but diverse and well-equipped cars. Competition was by model and design, not primarily price, and the diversity of the market precluded the firms with the leading mass-produced models from exerting or increasing their dominance in the overall car market.[6]

Ford's system in America emerged from very different circumstances. Ford married a technology to a distinctive production and labour strategy in response to the American pattern of demand. Between 1912 and 1914 Ford pioneered a technical solution to the problem of dramatically increasing output and productivity in the absence of an adequate supply of skilled labour. But, as Meyer has shown, he was only able to realise the potential of the technology to the full by adding on a labour strategy to overcome the disabling anarchy and instability of the factory floor. In 1913, Ford experienced a labour turnover of 370 per cent: each day an average of 10 per cent of the labour force was absent: carelessness, ignorance and lack of foresight proliferated breakdowns and undercut the technology. The second phase of Fordism, therefore, was to add on a system of labour discipline based on intense driving supervision and the enforcement of work norms on his raw immigrant labour force, dominated by newly arrived Poles, Germans, Ukrainians and East Europeans. To do this, supervision was jacked up to 1 supervisor for every 15 workers. An army of clerical progress chasers was enlisted, and high wages and the Sociology Department were deployed to stabilise and socialise the workforce. The success of these changes produced a renewed quantum leap in productivity.[7]

Thus in America, Fordism emerged out of a convulsive leap from craft to mass production. Once in place, the task at the Highland

Park factory was to run an insatiable machine-paced technology flat out and enforced work norms, intense supervision and day-rate payment were appropriate organisational forms. But British mass production emerged from a long transition period of intermittently enlarging quantity flow production. The keynote of the market was quality and continuous improvement rather than quantity and price competition: mere internal economies of scale could not guarantee market dominance and profitability depended primarily on bringing forward the right new models in an evolving market. The frontier of mechanisation was, therefore, continuously shifting, tasks were regularly reorganised and even in the most advanced flow systems of the 1920s and early 1930s, the separate operations at each stage still needed time and attention for efficient completion. Firms therefore looked to adaptable payments systems with strong incentive elements to get the most out of their new machines and forms of work organisation.

The more limited levels of output and different goals of production still made possible the adoption of many important elements of Fordist mass production. Even smaller, relatively specialised, firms like Humber or Rover utilised many of these techniques, such as special-purpose machine tools, the moving assembly-line, work rationalisation and the purchase of components from specialised outside suppliers. But these elements could be adopted gradually without launching a full-scale Fordist system. Indeed it would have been counter-productive to pursue the inflexible indivisibilities of American-style Fordism. Many of Europe's leading automobile producers were seduced by the power and technocratic beauty of Ford's factories and sought to imitate them. But the conditions did not exist for them to transplant the integrated system of marketing, production and labour that characterised Ford in America. Ford, themselves, as we shall see, sailed close to disaster as a result of trying to graft their strategy onto British conditions. In France and Italy, Berliet, Citroën and Fiat were 'dazzled by the Ford spectacle' and nearly ruined themselves when their capital-intensive plants designed for single mass products could not cope with the upheavals resulting from demands for more varied and changing models.[8]

The impact of these product and market factors on employers' labour policies can be made clear by a comparison of Ford's British operations with those of Morris Motors, the largest British car producer for much of the interwar period.

Ford established manufacturing operations in Manchester in 1911, bringing in engines and chassis from Detroit and manufacturing their own bodies.[9] At first they encountered considerable problems with the craft unions in the bodymaking departments. In 1911–12, Percival Perry, the Managing Director, reported to Detroit that the Sheet Metal Workers 'have almost broken my heart' with their activities.[10] As a result, in 1912, Detroit sent in one of their leading managers, Charles Sorenson, to bust the unions with a deliberate campaign of sacking unionists and wooing the remaining workers away from the unions with high wages and promises of job security. The result was that, by April 1914, Perry could report to Henry Ford that 'the unionism which has always been cropping up heretofore has been absolutely broken up'.[11] And Sorenson noted on a return visit that even though there was no other employer in Manchester 'who is not obligated in some manner to labor organisations, I can also say that we are the only company in the vicinity who are absolutely free and independent and who are not having controversies any more with their men'.[12]

Until the Manchester plant was closed when Dagenham opened in the early 1930s, Ford maintained this union-free environment there. One senior manager from this period recalled how 'the men were treated like nothing . . . we hired and fired so rapidly that it was hard to keep track of what was going on'.[13] Yet despite this high level of unilateral control over the labour force, Ford were unable successfully to 'Americanise' production at Manchester in the 1920s while their business strategy of transplanting American methods and models from the USA to Britain carried them to the verge of economic disaster.

The period 1919–28 was the 'American era' in Ford of Britain. Detroit aimed to Americanise their British management and introduce a complete imitation of American methods. At times this went to absurd lengths. Until 1923 Henry Ford refused to allow the production of right-hand drive Model Ts for Britain on the grounds that if left-hand drives were good enough for America they were also good enough for Britain. They also slavishly pursued other American practices such as regular price-cutting and the establishment of an exclusive dealership network with similar detrimental results.[14] Crucially, until the late 1920s, Detroit resisted continuing appeals for a new smaller car for the European market to replace the hefty and dated Model T whose sales were utterly collapsing during a period of rapid expansion of car sales in Britain. Between 1913 and 1929 Ford's share of the British market fell from 24 per cent to 4 per cent.[15] By 1926 their senior managers recognised that 'we have been defeated and licked in England'.[16]

Ford pursued the form of American methods without the necessary substance of demand, models or output. The result was a bizarre combination of local management shackled on overall policy by Detroit and improvising locally whenever they could evade Detroit supervision to adapt the functioning of the factory to local conditions. Ford's labour strategy made little sense for their British management. In the 1920s their European policy was characterised by two main features. The first was a vigorous hire-and-fire policy, designed to keep out unions and maintain the pressure for maximum intensity of work from individual workers. This was epitomised by the work of the 'Yougos', a selected team from Detroit who toured the European plants in the mid-1920s sacking any 'surplus' labour they could spot. (Their name derived from their practice of patrolling departments and sacking people on the spot: 'OK, you go, you go and you go!')[17] But this could create serious problems for local management whose needs to adjust production to erratic levels of capacity utilisation, to deal with irregular supplies of parts of sometimes inadequate quality, to cope with frequent interruptions to production, or to solve accumulated problems of detailed engineering, required a more stable and integrated workforce. Local management therefore often sought to keep their workforce together, to stabilise fluctuations in employment when sales fluctuated wildly and even to operate their own informal seniority system for workers.[18] At the same time they saw advantages in seeking a contented labour force through allowing self-help welfare activities in the factory or tolerating working practices such as smoking on the job or teabreaks which scandalised the Detroit inquisitions. Such working practices existed only as long as management tolerated them: when a Detroit team in the winter of 1923 overrode the wishes of local management they were scrapped 'with practically no objection' from the men.[19] Detroit's diagnosis was that the main problem in regard to labour was not the resistance of the workers but the attitudes and practices of management and supervision. They were scathing about the 'bunch of clowns' who managed their British operations and the 'stiff white collars' of supervision who refused to get their hands dirty and drive production.[20] Periodically Detroit might decide to instruct someone 'to go over and fire the whole bunch' as they did in 1924, but the new management that they installed invariably had similar attitudes.[21] In 1928 Ford gave up their campaign to Americanise the management and brought back their pre-war managing director, Percival Perry, with a newly enhanced degree of branch autonomy.

The second leg of Ford's 1920s labour policy was their high-wage policy. In the USA high wages were linked to high output and high effort, but in British conditions of work organisation the link was more tenuous. There was a clear logic to their European policy of paying between 10 and 25 per cent above local rates to make unions unattractive, but at Manchester the high-wage policy was treated as something of a fetish and became quite separate from considerations of high productivity. By 1928 Ford wages were up to three times as high as those in neighbouring factories. Before Perry returned to Manchester, Henry and Edsel Ford had regularly turned down requests from British management to be allowed to cut wages. Perry argued strongly that, 'High wages are a good investment on our part, but only up to the point where we can use high wages as an inducement to greater industry and efficiency, and I am convinced that we have passed that point. . . . Our present rates are past even the limits of philanthropy.'[22] Eventually he got permission to hire new labour at reduced rates though *not* to cut the wages of existing workers. Henry and Edsel's commitment to high wages had become almost a dogma. Here, as in their wider labour and business strategies, their attempts simply to replicate the American 'formula for success' in very different conditions was inappropriate. It was only with Perry's more creative reinterpretation of the formula in the 1930s at Dagenham that Ford's fortunes began to be restored.

The new works at Dagenham was still designed to be a one-tenth scale version of the River Rouge plant in Detroit, but Ford's model policy at last began to address some of the real problems of the UK market. The shift had begun with the model 'A' which Perry brought in in 1928 and which stemmed the decline, but Ford's real salvation was the Model 'Y' whose introduction more or less coincided with the opening of Dagenham in 1932 and which represented Ford's first real small European car. Even with the revival of sales associated with the 'Y' and the later Popular, however, Ford were never able to generate the volume of sales necessary to run Dagenham at more than half its total capacity.[23] They were only able to sustain this volume by slashing their prices, and, as a result, the company went through the 1930s with a more or less permanent cash crisis and a constant drive to cut costs to the bone.

The major implication for labour was the reversal of the high-wage policy of Manchester. In April 1932 wages were cut by 10 per cent, and this precipitated a period of labour unrest culminating in a significant strike and the first stirrings of union activity in the plant.[24] This was, however, quickly crushed. Twenty years after his first union-busting mission to Manchester, Sorenson was again sent in to 'clean house' and again achieved the desired results.[25] The unions were purged from the plant or driven underground, where they remained until the war, despite attempts by the local Trades Council and the TUC to organise Ford's by outside organising campaigns.[26] Through most of the 1930s Dagenham was 'a place of fear', with an extensive anti-union spy system, arbitrary lay-offs and sackings, and speed-ups and driving supervision.[27] In the late 1930s the company introduced rudimentary pensions and paid holidays and began to put up wages again, partly to keep ahead of the unions, but at no time was there any infringement of their 'right to manage'.[28]

It was the British firms of Morris and Austin that devised the most effective business and labour strategies to respond to the growing and shifting market. Unlike Ford, they attached a much higher priority to quality and improvements in their models and looked for continuous productivity improvements in the production process rather than seeking to establish a system with a fixed level of productivity. They avoided excessive capital intensity in order to maintain flexibility both for model improvements and so that they could respond to the seasonal and cyclical fluctuations which continued to mark the industry throughout this period by utilising lay-offs and short-time working. In combination with this they drove labour to intense efforts through tightly controlled piecework systems and took great pains to ensure that they retained a free hand continuously to rationalise the production process.

During the 1920s Morris established a clear lead in British car manufacture. In the early 1920s he annihilated competition by making high-quality, medium-sized cars at low prices. Between 1919 and 1928 the main Cowley plant was exclusively geared to the mass production of a single model, the 11.9 h.p. Cowley. In 1921, Morris made 3000 cars: by 1925 this had risen to 55,000. Morris was fascinated by Ford's methods, and this explosion of output would appear to provide a basis for imitating them. In some of his key business methods, such as his strong preference to buy in components from outside suppliers and concentrate Cowley on assembly rather than manufacturing operations, he drew on lessons from Ford. But within the factory itself he developed his own system, incorporating selected elements of Ford's methods. He had an assembly-line of sorts at Cowley from 1914, with cars rolled along a track by hand to the next workstation: but he did not mechanise it and make it a *moving* assembly line until 1933. At the same time he was willing to experiment with the most advanced forms of mechanisation such as a pioneer transfer machine introduced by Frank Woollard at his Coventry engine factory in 1923: but he quickly abandoned it when it became apparent that the rigidity of the technology was too great for current needs.[29] Instead he focused on continuous incremental improvements in productivity, and as a result, even after the great leap forward of the early 1920s he was able to keep the workforce stable at around 5–6000 but increase output of cars per head from 6 to 11.6 between 1924 and 1934 (against a British average of 6 in 1935).[30]

Morris's methods of labour organisation in the 1920s were explicitly Tayloristic, based on the subdivision of tasks and the timing and measurement of jobs. But Morris did not aim in the 1920s to eliminate handwork or labour inputs that required a significant degree of care and attention. This flowed from the product strategy. While engines and chassis were standardised and changes kept to a minimum, Morris continually made body-styling changes which were greatly facilitated by the continuing use of labour-intensive methods. One consequence was that when visitors from the Dodge Motor Co. in Detroit visited Cowley in the mid-1920s, they found the Cowley machinery 'more complicated' and less based on single-purpose operations than anywhere else in Europe. Morris rationalised and mechanised where possible, but beyond a certain point kept the whole system moving forward

primarily by driving use of a piecework system.[31] Morris himself
provides a clear description of how this worked:

> We were turning out 425 cars per week on line assembling, but we
> wanted 500. We could have got it by putting men on overtime, but we
> do not pay a bonus for any work done on overtime. Instead of taking
> the obvious course, the works manager went over the line and retimed
> all the stages. At several stages he found he could speed-up by putting
> on additional men. Finally he decided to put on four extra men.
> Naturally the men already on the job grumbled. We said: 'All right,
> these men will not take part in the [group] bonus to start.' At the end
> of the fortnight we were getting 500 cars a week. The foremen actually
> came and asked the works manager to put the other men on bonus,
> since they did not think it fair they should be without their share.[32]

Almost complete non-unionism and high pay levels facilitated the
continuing manipulation of the payment system to keep levels of
productivity at high levels, and this situation continued to prevail
through the 1930s even while more of the factory became machine-
paced.

The central role of piecework systems was a key feature of
all the major British car firms in this period even though their
management differed in many ways. Rover's brief and rapidly
abandoned flirtation with the Bedaux system was predicated on
the idea of a leap into the mass production of a single small car
which was equally quickly abandoned.[33] Apart from this, however,
the major manufacturers were unanimous that Fordist systems
of machine pacing and day rates were not applicable to British
conditions. Even those who were once attracted by the Fordist
model were forced to rethink their ideas. For instance, C. R. F.
Engelbach, who was the head of production engineering at Austin
through most of the 1920s acknowledged in 1933 that:

> A change has come over the spirit of our dreams of quick-time floor-
> to-floor production performances, accompanied by the spectacular
> removal at miraculous speeds of chunks of metal to the musical ticking
> of stop-watches. . . . Rapid changes in fashion and ideas have slowed
> up the progress of special single operation machines. Continuous high
> production is too uncertain for special machines to be further developed.
> Designs have to be changeable at short notice . . . [and] at present there
> is probably no market likely to develop sufficiently that will lead to the
> extension of such specialised tool methods.[34]

Instead he, like most other manufacturers, looked to flexibility achieved through the intensive deployment of labour governed by a piecework system. The key to productivity therefore, as he argued elsewhere, was that earnings must be 'calculated literally on a scale which pays in units based on the amount of sweat given off by the workers. Nothing else is real.'[35]

The corollary of this reliance on piecework systems was the need for management to retain a high level of control over rates of pay and mobility of labour. The experience of the 1960s was later to demonstrate how piecework systems could be captured by strong workplace unions and transformed to their advantage.[36] But the British motor firms of the 1930s were uniformly determined to keep unions out of the workplace. As Percy Keene the head of the cost department at Austin noted in 1928: 'We definitely set out to manage as managers and the result is that we have no representation anywhere from the workers' side. No shop stewards, or shop committees, or anyone wanting to interfere with management.'[37]

The employers achieved a high degree of success in implementing these policies. Until the late 1930s the conditions that prevailed in most motor factories were, on the one hand, high wages and a high pace of work; on the other, arbitrary discipline and lack of job security. High proportions of youth labour on low rates who were laid off when they reached full adult rates were common, Standard Motors in Coventry, for example, was known as 'Boys' Town'. Until seasonality of production began to be mitigated in the late 1930s summer lay-offs were the rule and were used as an occasion for 'cleaning house' of undesirable elements. Trades unionists or those whose faces did not fit would simply not be rehired. In addition, short-time working or compulsory overtime were frequent features. In many factories workers would be laid off without pay for the rest of the day, or for several days, with little or no notice. New hirings and the allocation of better jobs were largely at the discretion of powerful works foremen, and away from the small craft preserves there were almost no effective job controls over the manning of machines or the mobility of labour. The first significant changes in this sort of workplace regime did not come about until the very changed conditions of the Second World War.[38]

## Labour and the Trades Unions

The employers had not always enjoyed such a strong hand. Before the First World War, trade unionism had reached significant levels, not only among skilled workers but also among semi-skilled, particularly in the Coventry area. In Britain, unlike the USA, there was a gradual transition from craft to mass production in the motor industry, and this pattern had important implications for the development of union structures. Zeitlin, for instance, has argued that 'patterns of shop steward organisation and control characteristic of craftsmen in the older sectors of the economy [came] to be diffused among workers in the new mass-production industries',[39] while Lyddon has argued against this that shop steward organisation in motors was *sui generis*, 'the institutional expression of what has been called "the spontaneous association of workers on the shopfloor"'.[40] This section looks at the impact of union structures and recruitment strategies on the industry and their role in the belatedness of union growth in the industry and on the forms in which it ultimately began to emerge.

In the first place, it is important to remember that even before the First World War, motor production was not exclusively a craft industry. Particularly in the machine shops there was a certain amount of repetition production, extensive use of jigging and large numbers of single-purpose machine tools. In the aftermath of the 1897 lock-out, motor employers had been able to introduce new machines fairly easily. But they introduced these modern tools not primarily to facilitate *quantity* of output but because it was only with these modern tools that they could achieve the sort of high quality and precision needed for machining engines and related parts. Because of the variations in product and short runs that remained prevalent they needed to use these machines in a versatile way using the skills and adaptability of the workforce.[41]

The problem was not so much the introduction of new machines but resistance by the workforce to the intensification of effort or their refusal to man several machines at once. Faced with the problem of restrictions on output (ca'canny) employers turned to incentive systems. By 1913, 84 per cent of all fitters and turners in Coventry were on piecework, 48 per cent of them on the most sophisticated of these systems, premium bonus.[42] This situation facilitated the rapid rise of semi-skilled workers in Coventry motor firms between 1910–14. As production runs got longer, it was easy for employers to slip from using skilled to semi-skilled workers simply by using the same machine tool in different ways. Coventry had never had the same traditions of craft militancy as other engineering centres and the breakdown of craft preserves proceeded much more smoothly there. By 1914, the skilled engineer was no longer much in evidence on production work, though skilled workers on body production still remained predominant. The period just before the war also saw significant incursions being made into motor firms by the rapidly growing general union, the Workers' Union, recruiting these semi-skilled workers, particularly where the skilled engineering unions were reluctant to take them in. The Workers' Union was able to capitalise on the fact that, unlike labourers, these semi-skilled workers had an array of real skills in machining and assembly departments that gave them increasing bargaining power. At the same time, in a period of wider industrial and political turmoil, they were able to bring a new type of union growth to the industry, rapid recruitment based on support for mass action and the political excitement of the Black Country strikes of 1910 and the rolling wave of strikes in 1913 that brought with them recognition from the Coventry District Engineering Employers' Association (CDEEA).[43]

The Workers' Union had an unprecedented commitment to growth and an unwillingness to accept a subordinate status to the ASE and other craft unions as an automatic assumption. Unlike the Gas Workers or the NAUL, the Workers' Union had no long-standing membership with interests to protect and could, therefore, take risks and go for an all-or-nothing strategy. At the same time, unlike these other general unions, they had not evolved as a 'labourers' union' specifically recruiting jobs which stood in a traditionally hallowed relation of subordination to craftsmen.[44]

One consequence of this was a much more balanced and ambiguous relationship between skilled and semi-skilled unions in Coventry during the war than was the case, for instance, in either Clydeside or Sheffield. Though the local unofficial body, the Coventry Engineering Joint Committee (CEJC) excluded the Workers' Union formally, in practice there was significant cooperation between the ASE and the Workers' Union, most notably in the CEJC's demand for all-grade shop stewards to be elected by all the workers in a particular shop regardless of their union affiliation. The national ASE would not countenance such inroads into their exclusive jurisdiction over their workplace representatives, and in the 1917 Agreement with the Engineering Employers' Federation (EEF) they pushed for and got recognition only of shop stewards representing *single* trades unions.[45]

The major split between skilled and semi-skilled workers in Coventry came only late in the war when the Workers' Union refused to support the ASE's strike against the Reserved Occupations Act—the creation of a legal category that made for highly invidious comparisons between Workers' Union and ASE members working on similar machines, since they might be 'Reserved' and exempted from military service or not, mainly depending on which of the unions they were in. Nevertheless the general pattern was a high degree of cooperation between the unions at workplace level, and by the end of the war, the unofficial movement in Coventry was exerting considerable pressure on the employers' control of the shopfloor.

It was in the years 1914–20, according to Lewchuk, that the power of the unions defeated moves towards Fordism in the British motor industry. He argues that during the war, the EEF 'tried to create the conditions for a Ford-style industrial strategy' and were defeated.[46] The growing strength of the shop stewards' movement convinced the Coventry car manufacturers in particular that a 'Fordist' strategy of direct control of the labour process centred on machine pacing and intense supervision was impractical. Instead, at the end of the war, rather than enter a protracted and possibly unsuccessful struggle to Americanise British shops and labour attitudes, management chose to share control over labour effort norms and factory coordination. In particular, Lewchuk argues, employers fell back on piecework as a substitute for direct managerial control. Labour 'was induced through the cash nexus to work at a pace which management was unable to enforce directly'.[47] These piecework systems 'resulted in a sharing of management authority and a crude form of industrial democracy, since labour was allowed control over the pace of work'.[48] It was left to the ASE, with their continuing demands for day rates, to provide the last impetus towards Fordism. If the EEF had accepted their case, they would have been 'forced along a path similar to the Ford system'.[49] But they rejected it, and, according to Lewchuk, the patterns laid down by the early 1920s structured labour–management relations in the industry until the early 1970s and were a major cause of the long-run decline of the industry.[50]

We have already argued that British management was not pursuing Fordist strategies, and as the rest of this essay makes clear, Lewchuk seriously overstates the power of labour in shaping the industry. By arguing that the technical preconditions for Fordism existed, that management wished to implement them and that day wages and enforced work norms were the missing link, Lewchuk stands the issues on their head. His insistence that Fordist day wage structures are the most complete form of managerial control and that other payment systems represent concessions to labour is abstract and essentially ahistorical. Piecework can be as coercive as day work under appropriate conditions, and either can operate as tight or slack systems. In the conditions of the early twentieth century, management's demands for the extension of piecework were not a defensive position motivated by loss of control in the workshops, but part of a managerial drive going back to before the war to obtain complete control over the terms and conditions under which new techniques and practices should be introduced in the shops. Yet by setting up a simplified model of 'control' of the production process, Lewchuk inverts the picture. The ASE's defence of day wages as part of their attempt to sustain craft controls is seen as partisanship of Fordism and the employers' defence of their 'right to manage' through payment by results systems is seen as 'shared control'.

In any case, the growing power of workplace organisation was very short-lived. By 1918 the tide had already turned against the unions, by 1919 their position was sliding and the years 1920–22 saw something of a rout, culminating in the 1922 lock-out and leaving the union presence confined almost solely to craft shops. The post-war recession hit the Coventry firms which concentrated on quality cars and luxury production particularly hard. The bankruptcy of small firms eliminated along with the firms many pockets of craft unionism. The firms that adapted to the conditions of the 1920s and survived by moving over to small cars and large-scale production to cut prices, such as Morris or Austin, were situated away from the old union seedbeds in Coventry. The most dramatic and direct consequence of the recession was the virtual annihilation of the Workers' Union by unemployment. In 1918 it was the largest union in Coventry. The union had 90,000 members in Coventry and Birmingham in 1920. By 1923 this had fallen to 15,000. They lost 50 per cent of their membership in the single year of 1921 alone, and they lost 90 per cent in the 1920s. Their decimation effectively broke up union organisation among semi-skilled motor workers.[51]

The AEU (formed by a merger between the ASE and other craft engineering unions) was also hit badly by the recession. In addition, however, they compounded their problems by the form their retreat in the face of adversity took—a retreat into craft defensiveness. In 1920 they had 13,115 members in Coventry. By 1925 this figure had fallen to 3035 and their membership remained below this figure until the mid-1930s. Their defeat in the 1922 lock-out was a major contribution to their decline, but the union's own behaviour in the aftermath intensified the impact. They insisted on taking strict disciplinary action, including imposing heavy fines, on those who had returned to work early. Many left rather than pay the fines, and while nationally the AEU lost 30 per cent of its membership between 1920 and 1923, in Coventry they lost 57 per cent.[52]

The AEU effectively lost any real presence in the workplaces at this time and did not begin to regain it for more than twelve years. They lacked information on workplace matters and had no effective control over their remaining members who often pursued local unauthorised deals, including wage cuts, with management. As we shall see, the bargaining environment in the workplaces was not wholly unsuited to union development, but the AEU cut themselves off from the currents of potential growth in the industry. In the first place, though formally an industrial union from 1920, nearly all their branches resisted the recruitment of semi-skilled workers. J. B. Jefferys argues that the growth of the AEU's semi-skilled Sections 5 and 5A after 1927 represents the transformation of the AEU into a true industrial union recruiting mainly semi-skilled workers. But as Claydon has shown, this is misleading. The figures in fact reflect many skilled workers opting to go into the semi-skilled sections because subscriptions were cheaper. Instead, despite the fact that semi-skilled workers were in a large majority in the industry, they remained a minority in the Coventry AEU until 1937.[53]

Perhaps the central weakness of the recruitment strategy of the AEU was the Coventry district committee's insistence on recruiting only those earning the district rate. Yet in the motor industry, while most workers were employed on lower rates than engineers in the northern engineering towns, they were usually getting much higher earnings through piecework and overtime. The Coventry DC were more insistent on the district rate than the National Executive, and it was only under pressure from the latter in 1936, concerned with the threat of recruitment of semi-skilled workers by the TGWU, that the DC agreed to allow a wider framework of recruitment. The DC's main concern was that a broader base in semi-skilled workers might weaken the position of those receiving skilled rates, particularly the toolmakers who dominated the DC. But this concern to protect the rights of the skilled was outdated in a changing industry, and the conservative and hierarchical vision on which it was based appealed almost solely to the rapidly shrinking body of skilled workers, making the AEU in the mid-1930s little more than a toolroom club in many works.[54]

Similar internal weaknesses disabled the National Union of Vehicle Builders (NUVB) from responding to opportunities to organise semi-skilled workers from the late 1920s onwards. The NUVB was an amalgamation of woodworking craft societies and by 1920 they had 23,300 members. The NUVB were not locked out in 1922 and their membership held up much better than that of the AEU or the Workers' Union in the 1920s. For a time they became the largest union in Coventry. They thrived in the 1920s on the demand for bodymaking skills, particularly in the high-class trade and in commercial vehicles, and their relative health gave a new lease of life to their traditional craft forms of organisation, giving them encouragement that they might be able to continue to control entry to their preserves and exclude semi-skilled workers. However, they were squeezed by the collapse of high-class work at the bottom of the depression in 1931–33 and the simultaneous rise of new techniques such as all-steel bodies and cellulose spray painting which eliminated many of their crafts. Like the AEU, they also contributed to their own decline. As unemployment rose they sought to sustain their traditional friendly society role and pay out relatively high levels of unemployment benefits to members. But this could only be sustained by imposing unacceptably high levies on their shrinking number of members in work and this drove many to leave the union. Their Coventry membership fell by 50 per cent between 1931 and 1933.[55]

Thereafter, the NUVB were not able to adjust to the changed

conditions. Theoretically they were open to semi-skilled workers, but, as in the case of the AEU, the branches were resistant to such changes. They still had significant strategic strengths in the industry, notably those arising from the fact that annual model changes were largely in effect annual body changes. But rather than exploit such avenues, they concentrated on traditional but increasingly ineffective forms of craft control. For instance, when firms like Armstrong Siddely or Harper Bean refused to pay NUVB rates in the early 1930s, the NUVB withdrew their members from the firms and instructed their members to 'black' them. They were quickly replaced by non-unionists and the NUVB were excluded from the shops. They refused to attempt to recruit on the basis of workplace struggles—as the TGWU were soon to do effectively—because they feared that any such recruits would prove to be 'birds of passage' and not 'real trades unionists'. During the war there were to be many recriminations against the Coventry officers for this policy which it was then recognised had allowed the TGWU to steal a march on the NUVB and break into its territory.[56]

The TGWU which took over the collapsed remnants of the Workers' Union in 1929 had a more positive and flexible attitude to recruitment. But even so it was partial and slow to develop. Until the mid-1930s, the union's leader, Ernest Bevin, was afraid to overstretch a union that had already expanded at a prodigious rate through amalgamations. He was not ready to devote resources to actively building the union in engineering. However, the union was ideologically committed to being open to all and a certain degree of local autonomy prevailed. Thus, when recruitment was virtually thrust upon them by explosive strikes at Rover in 1930, Lucas in 1932, Standard and Pressed Steel in 1934, they did not reject the potential members as, in several of these cases, the AEU and NUVB did. At Rover, for instance, the NUVB refused to recruit the striking female trimmers and they went instead to the TGWU. However, the women workers recruited in this way were ghettoised in the union and though the TGWU accumulated a substantial women's membership at this time in these firms it remained almost solely a paper membership. Most of the TGWU's membership in the motor industry at this time arose out of such spontaneous struggles by women or other unskilled groups, but the TGWU were not ready to build on these struggles and were often ready to settle disputes over the heads of their newly recruited members. Elsewhere they allowed new members to drift away, or, as at Pressed Steel, where they made a quite exceptional breakthrough into large-scale recruitment, they found themselves in a prolonged battle to control a workplace membership that was ready and willing to take matters into its own hands and pursue higher wages and the closed shop through aggressive local bargaining.[57]

The defeat of the unions in the early 1920s had not been followed by a major attack on wages. Management had won the freedoms it wanted over overtime, the use of boys on men's jobs, output restrictions and mobility of labour. As profits rose and output increased firms were prepared to pay high wages for intense effort through piecework systems. Motor industry wages were everywhere well above average local rates and many semi-skilled workers could hope to earn £5 per week in the late 1930s. The main issues in the workplace, therefore, were insecurity, conditions and the arbitrary fixing of job prices and discipline rather than wage issues *per se*. With management adopting a hostile stance towards any appearance of union organisation so as to preserve its freedom of action, it was hardly surprising that there was often reluctance to join unions even though high earnings were often based on exhausting effort and long hours. The lack of sustained union pressure from the outside meant that only those with some sort of political commitment or motivation tended to stick their necks out to pursue union organisation in the shops.

At the same time, the centre of gravity of the industry shifted away from Coventry before the war towards areas without strong local labour traditions such as Longbridge, Oxford, Luton and Dagenham. There, on the basis of largely 'green' workforces, management was able to move into large-scale production without any restraints from labour. The scale of migration must be emphasised. Dagenham was based on an almost entirely new labour force with a high proportion of Manchester and Scottish workers: in 1936 46.7 per cent of Oxford motor workers were migrants. The pattern was similar in other motor towns. Large numbers of these migrants came in waves from the depressed areas (21.5 per cent of all migrants to Coventry in 1937 were Welsh; 11 per cent of Oxford migrants in 1936 were Welsh). But large numbers were also drawn in from smaller towns or the semi-rural hinterlands of new towns (56.4 per cent of Oxford migrants in 1936 had come from the South-West, London and the South-East).[58] Zeitlin has argued that the largely migrant workforce in the industry posed the possibility of union traditions being imported from outside by workers migrating from traditionally unionised sectors such as mining, steel or shipbuilding. Certainly the prominence of Welsh migrants in the unionisation of Pressed Steel gives credibility to this view, particularly in the light of the fact that 40 per cent of the Oxford Welsh migrants came from a single district, Maesteg, and a striking 70 per cent of these from a single village, Pontycymmer.[59] But it is important to exercise caution on this issue. 'Union traditions' cannot be simply imputed to whole areas. The 'traditions' of Welsh mining communities at this time, for instance, were much shallower than is often supposed: many migrants from Wales in the 1920s and 1930s came from families that had only settled in Wales during the boom years of 1890–1914 and who remained relatively mobile.[60] Moreover many of the migrants were young and lacking in work experience even where they came from families with trade union backgrounds. Moreover, as Waller's recent work on the new Nottinghamshire coalfields of the interwar years shows, union traditions cannot be simply transplanted into radically different social and economic environments: even labour forces drawn from the highly unionised South Yorkshire coalfields could provide a basis for an almost wholly non-union workforce in new towns in Nottinghamshire only 20–30 miles away.[61] Moreover the migrants encompassed a broad spectrum of potentially countervailing 'traditions', including agricultural workers or workers from the South-East. There are plenty of examples of allegations that migrants undercut the position of local labour, and it is clear that young workers, lacking in experience and without any support networks to fall back on, were vulnerable and as likely to be passive as active as a whole. For the time being, the most accurate formulation is probably Claydon's argument that the contribution of migrants 'lay not so much in arousing local workers to action as in providing organisation and leadership once it had begun'.[62]

Conditions in the motor industry presented many problems for union recruitment. The combination of managerial hostility, high earnings and insecurity of employment made it a daunting task. Most of the unions concerned concentrated on defending their existing limited membership by traditional methods, which were often inappropriate or proved counter-productive. The AEU and NUVB focused their demands on issues of workplace control. But these were the areas where employers were most intensely jealous of their hard-won freedom of action, and it was hard for them to defend their existing positions, let alone extend them. When the revival of union activity came in the late 1930s it centred on active piecework bargaining in the shops, accepting the rules of the game but bargaining for a bigger share of the cake. It was when the unions began to show that they could deliver the goods in the workplace that opportunities for rapid development began to open up. Once the TGWU began to make inroads on these lines, inter-union rivalry acted as a powerful spur to other unions to change their approaches.

In each of the unions that we have considered, the sluggishness of union responses was partly due to the fact that their motor membership was on the periphery of their vision. The industry was unionised by unions whose cores were woodworking trades, skilled heavy engineering and docks and transport, and none of them at this time had the organisation of motor workers as a major priority in their broader strategies. But it would be unwise to attribute too much of the failure of unionisation to the forms of craft and general unionism that were on offer and to argue that an industrial union for motor workers could have been a radical and simple trigger for a breakthrough, even if this had been a possibility. In later years the existing unions showed that their craft and general origins were no barriers to creative adaptation in organising the motor industry.

Rather an analysis of the failure to spread unionisation in the emergent mass production motor industry has to be pitched at two levels. On the one hand, the existing unions can be criticised for tactical and strategic failures and for not making better use of opportunities for growth that did exist within their potential frames of reference. Most of the criticisms implied in this essay are at that level. But on the other hand it must be borne in mind that the *mass* unionisation of semi-skilled workers in new industries was a task in a different league from that of routine trades unionism. In the USA the problem was only cracked by a major period of insurgency in the shops backed by sympathetic state legal regulation.[63] In France it emerged out of a period of social and political turmoil.[64] It is probable that something on this scale—the equivalent of the period of the emergence of 'new' unionism between 1889 and 1914—would have been necessary for a dramatic development of mass production unionism. But the wider political context of a National government and a weakened Labour Party and the depth of political stability made this unlikely. Meanwhile, high wages diminished the workplace demand for union organisation and the unions failed to exert sustained pressure from the outside, and union development in the car firms remained in its infancy until the coming of the Second World War.

## Notes

Place of publication is London unless otherwise stated.

1  Arthur Exell, 'Morris Motors in the 1930s', *History Workshop*, no. 6 (Autumn 1978), p. 58.

2  See for example, H. Gospel and C. Littler, *Managerial Strategies and Industrial Relations* (1983); and the earlier A. Friedman, *Industry and Labour: Class struggle at work and monopoly capitalism* (1973).

3  W. Lewchuk, 'Fordism and British motor car employers, 1896–1932', in Gospel and Littler, *Managerial Strategies*. 'The role of the British government in the spread of scientific management and Fordism in the inter-war years' *Journal of Economic History*, vol. XLIV. no. 2 (June 1984). 'The British motor vehicle industry, 1896–1982: the roots of decline', in B. Elbaum and W. Lazonick (eds), *The Decline of the British Economy* (Oxford, 1986); 'The origins of Fordism and alternative strategies: Britain and the US, 1889–1930', Paper presented to the International Conference on the Automobile Industry and its Workers, Coventry, June 1984.

4  A. Nevins with F. E. Hill, *Ford. The times, the man, the company.* (New York, 1954): M. Wilkins and F. E. Hill, *American Business Abroad. Ford on Six Continents* (Detroit, 1964); S. Meyer, *The Five-Dollar Day: Labor management and social control in the Ford Motor Company, 1908–21* (New York, 1981).

5  G. Maxcy and A. Silberston, *The Motor Industry* (1959).

6  R. Church and M. Miller, 'The Big Three: Competition, management and marketing in the British motor industry, 1922–39', in B. Supple (ed.), *Essays in British Business History* (1977); 'Motor Manufacturing', in D. Aldcroft and N. Buxton (eds), *British Industry between the Wars* (1979); Maxcy and Silberston, *Motor Industry*.

7  Meyer, *Five-Dollar Day.*

8  D. Bigazzi, 'Management strategies in the Italian car industry, 1906–45. Fiat and Alfa Romeo'; and S. van de Casteele-Schweitzer, 'Management, labour and industrial relations. France 1914–39', in S. Tolliday and J. Zeitlin (eds), *The Automobile Industry and its Workers. Between Fordism and Flexibility* (Cambridge, 1986). J. P.

Bardou, J.-J. Chanaron, P. Fridenson and J. M. Laux, *The Automobile Revolution. The impact of an industry* (North Carolina, 1982), pp. 91–139.

9  Nevins and Hill, *Ford*, p. 407.

10  P. Perry to Henry Ford, 26 February 1913, Acc. 62, Box 59. Ford Archives, Detroit. I am grateful to the Ford Motor Co. for permission to consult these archives.

11  P. Perry to Henry Ford, 14 April 1914, Acc. 38, Box 52.

12  C. E. Sorenson, Report to Henry Ford, 3 June 1914, Acc. 62, Box 59.

13  H. Mortimore, Sales Manager Ford Ltd, interviewed by Mira Wilkins, 26 August 1960. I am grateful to Prof. Wilkins for allowing me to consult her interview transcripts.

14  R. Church, 'The marketing of automobiles in Britain and the USA before 1939', in A. Okochi and K. Shimokawa (eds), *The Development of Mass Marketing* (Tokyo, 1981).

15  Church and Miller, 'Big Three', pp. 168–73.

16  E. Kanzler, quoted by Nevins and Hill. *Ford*, p. 410.

17  Wilkins and Hill, *American Business abroad*, pp. 155–7.

18  Reports from E. C. Kanzler, T. Gehle and W. Klann on Manchester operations 1923–24, in Select File (Ford Archives); W. S. Carnegie, 'Report on foreign branches' n.d. [1925?], Acc. 157, Box 264.

19  Reports by Gehle and Klann, Winter 1923–24.

20  Klann Reminiscences (Ford Archives), p. 141.

21  Ibid.

22  P. Perry to Edsel Ford 7 August 1928 (Select File).

23  Wilkins and Hill, *American Business Abroad*, pp. 199–310; Church and Miller, 'Big Three', pp. 168–73.

24  Nina Fishman, 'Trades unionism at Dagenham, 1933–45' (unpublished paper).

25  C. E. Sorenson, 'Memorandum', 4 October 1933, Acc. 572, Box 18.

26  Fishman, 'Trades unionism'.

27  Interviews with Ford workers by the author.

28  P. Perry, interviewed by Mira Wilkins, August 1960.

29  On Morris's methods see: R. J. Overy, *William Morris. Viscount Nuffield* (1976); P. W. S. Andrews and E. Brunner, *Life of Lord Nuffield: a study in enterprise and benevolence* (Oxford, 1955); L. P. Jarman and R. I. Barraclough, *The Bullnose Morris* (1965); R. C. Whiting, *The View from Cowley: The impact of industrialisation upon Oxford, 1918–39* (Oxford, 1983), pp. 29–53, 83–7. The best sources for the technical side are: H. K. Thomas, 'Fundamentals of cost reduction', *Proceedings of the Institute of Automobile Engineers*, vol. XVIII (1923–24), pp. 434–40; 'Progressive production', *The Motor*; 2 July 1934, pp. 955–6; A. A. Rowse, 'Thirty cars an hour at Cowley', *Motor Trader*, vol. XL, October 1927.

30  L. Rostas, *Comparative Productivity in British and American Industry* (Cambridge, 1948), p. 173.

31  G. S. Davison, *At the Wheel* (1931), pp. 85–103; W. R. Morris,

'Policies that built the Morris motor business', *Journal of Industrial Economics*, vol. I (1954).

32 W. R. Morris, Interview in *System*, February 1924.

33 S. Tolliday, 'Background paper on the Rover Motor Co.', First report to the ESRC, King's College Research Centre, 1982; 'Militancy and Organisation: Women workers and trades unions in the motor trades in the 1930s', *Oral History*, vol. 11. no. 2 (1983).

34 C. R. F. Engelbach, 'Presidential address', *Proceedings of the Institute of Automobile Engineers*, vol. XXVIII (1933–34), p. 7; see also Engelbach's 'Some notes on reorganising a works to increase production', *Proceedings of the Institute of Automobile Engineers*, vol. XXIX (1924–25), pp. 496–544.

35 C. R. F. Engelbach, Letter to the editor, *Automobile Engineer*, February 1931, p. 42.

36 S. Tolliday, 'High Tide and After: Coventry engineering workers and shopfloor bargaining, 1945–80', in W. Lancaster and A. Mason (eds), *Life and Labour in a 20th century city: the case of Coventry* (Coventry, 1986).

37 P. Keene, 'Production. A dream come true', *Proceedings of the Institute of Production Engineers* (1928), p. 28.

38 For the example of Vauxhall, see: L. T. Holden, 'Think of me simply as the Skipper: Industrial relations at Vauxhall, 1900–50', *Oral History*, vol. 9, no. 2 (1981); and 'A History of Vauxhall Motors to 1950: Industry, development and local impact on the Luton economy', (Open University M.Phil, 1983). On wartime and post-war developments see: S. Tolliday, 'Government, employers and shopfloor organisation in the British motor industry, 1939–69', in S. Tolliday and J. Zeitlin (eds), *Shopfloor Bargaining and the State: Historical and comparative perspectives* (Cambridge, 1985).

39 J. Zeitlin, 'The emergence of shop steward organisation and job control in the British car industry: a review essay', *History Workshop*, no. 10, Autumn 1980.

40 D. Lyddon, 'Workplace organisation in the British car industry', *History Workshop*, no. 15, Spring 1983. See also: J. Zeitlin, 'Workplace militancy: a rejoinder', *History Workshop*, no. 16, Autumn 1983.

41 Cf. W. Lewchuk, 'The economics of technical change: a case study of the British motor industry, 1896–1932' (Cambridge University PhD, 1982); J. Zeitlin, 'Craft regulation and the division of labour: engineers and compositors in Britain, 1880–1914' (Warwick University PhD, 1981); S. Tolliday, 'Management and Labour in Britain, 1896–1939', in Tolliday and Zeitlin, *Automobile Industry*.

42 Lewchuk, *Thesis*.

43 Tolliday, 'Management and Labour in Britain'; Friedman, *Industry and Labour*, pp. 191–4; J. Hinton, *The First Shop Stewards' Movement* (1973), pp. 210–20; R. Hyman, *The Workers' Union* (1971), pp. 160–80; E. Wigham, *The Power to Manage* (1973).

44 Hyman, *Workers' Union*.

45  Ibid., and Hinton, *First Shop Stewards' Movement*, p. 225.
46  Lewchuk, 'Fordism', p. 89.
47  Lewchuk, 'Origins of Fordism', p. 26.
48  Lewchuk, 'Role of British government', p. 360.
49  Lewchuk, 'Fordism', p. 91.
50  Lewchuk, 'British motor vehicle industry', pp. 135–7.
51  Hyman, *Workers' Union*.
52  F. W. Carr, 'Engineering workers and the rise of labour in Coventry, 1914–39' (Warwick University PhD, 1978), pp. 278–80; T. J. Claydon, 'The development of trades unionism among British automobile and aircraft workers, 1914–46' (Kent University PhD, 1981), pp. 71–6.
53  J. B. Jefferys, *The Story of the Engineers* (1946); Claydon, *Thesis*, pp. 355–8.
54  Carr, *Thesis*, pp. 448–55.
55  Tolliday, 'Management and Labour in Britain'; Claydon, *Thesis*, pp. 363–5.
56  Tolliday, 'Management and Labour in Britain'.
57  Tolliday, 'Militancy and organisation'; Whiting, *View from Cowley*, pp. 75–83.
58  On migration to Oxford see: Whiting, *View from Cowley*, pp. 87–107. *A Survey of the Social Services in the Oxford District*, vol. 1 (1938); G. Daniel, 'Some factors affecting the movement of labour', *Oxford Economic Papers* (1940), pp. 165–7; 'Labour migration and age composition', *Sociological Review*, vol. 31 (1939). On Coventry: R. Croucher, 'Communist politics and shop stewards in engineering, 1935–45' (Warwick University PhD, 1977), pp. 190–6; W. Lancaster, 'Who's a real Coventry kid? Migration into 20th century Coventry', in Lancaster and Mason (eds), *Life and Labour*; G. L. Marson, 'Coventry, a study in urban geography' (Liverpool University MA, 1949). On Dagenham: D. R. Littlewood, 'The location of the British car industry, 1880–1940' (Leicester University MA, 1962), pp. 128–50.
59  Zeitlin, 'Rejoinder', p. 133.
60  G. Williams, 'From Grand Slam to Great Slum', *Welsh History Review*, vol. 11, no. 3 (June 1983).
61  R. J. Waller, *The Dukeries Transformed: The social and political development of a 20th century coalfield* (Oxford, 1983).
62  Claydon, *Thesis*, pp. 380–5.
63  On the USA see: H. Harris, 'The snares of liberalism? Politicians, bureaucrats and the shaping of federal labour relations policy in the USA c. 1915–47', in Tolliday and Zeitlin (eds), *Shopfloor Bargaining and the State*.
64  E. Hobsbawm, 'The "New Unionism" in perspective', in *Worlds of Labour* (1984).

# Index